ALTERED STATES

Altered States

*THE UNITED STATES
AND JAPAN SINCE THE
OCCUPATION*

Michael Schaller

New York   Oxford
Oxford University Press
1997

Oxford University Press

Oxford   New York
Athens   Auckland   Bangkok   Bogotá   Bombay
Buenos Aires   Calcutta   Cape Town   Dar es Salaam
Delhi   Florence   Hong Kong   Istanbul   Karachi
Kuala Lumpur   Madras   Madrid   Melbourne
Mexico City   Nairobi   Paris   Singapore
Taipei   Tokyo   Toronto   Warsaw

and associated companies in
Berlin   Ibadan

Copyright © 1997 by Oxford University Press, Inc.

Published by Oxford University Press, Inc.
198 Madison Avenue, New York, NY 10016

Oxford is a registered trademark of Oxford University Press

Library of Congress Cataloging-in-Publication Data
Schaller, Michael, 1947–
Altered states: the United States and Japan
since the occupation / Michael Schaller.
p. cm.
Includes bibliographical references and index.
ISBN 0-19-506916-1
1. United States—Foreign relations—Japan.
2. Japan—Foreign relations—United States.
3. United States—Foreign relations—1945–1989.
4. United States—Foreign relations—1989–
I. Title.
E183.8.J3S28 1997   327.73052—dc21   97–8995

1 3 5 7 9 8 6 4 2

Printed in the United States of America
on acid free paper.

This book is dedicated to Sue and to our children,
Nick, Gabe, and Daniel

CONTENTS

ALTERED STATES

Alexander Portnoy, the narcissistic narrator of Philip Roth's 1969 novel, *Portnoy's Complaint*, reveled in telling the story of Miltie, stationed with American forces in Japan. "Mamma," Miltie tells his mother excitedly in a phone call from Yokohama, "I have good news. I found a wonderful Japanese girl and we were married today. As soon as I get my discharge, I want to bring her home, Mamma, for you to meet each other." "So," Mamma replies, "bring her home." "Wonderful," shouts Miltie, "But Mamma, in such a little apartment, where will Ming Toy and I sleep?" "Where?", says mother, "Why in the bed. Where else would you sleep with your bride?" "But then where will you sleep, if we sleep in the bed? Are you sure there's room? Miltie, darling, please," says the mother, "everything is fine, don't you worry, there will be all the room you want: as soon as I hang up, I'm killing myself." To a considerable degree, this exchange mirrored the ambivalence many Americans felt toward Japan since the Occupation.

Since the United States restored Japan's sovereignty in 1952, relations between the two nations have evolved in mostly unforeseen ways. For more than a decade after the signing of the San Francisco peace treaty, American policymakers worried that Japan's feeble economy required massive foreign assistance to prevent Tokyo from reaching an accommodation with China or the Soviet Union. The underlying concern, as John Foster Dulles, peace treaty negotiator and, later, secretary of state, often remarked, was that "unless Japan worked for us . . . it will work for the other side." Unfortunately, Dulles believed, Japanese products had "little future . . . in the United States" since they were just "cheap imitations of our own goods." Survival as a member of the free world required that

Japan limit trade with China and develop markets in "underdeveloped areas such as Southeast Asia" under American protection. Much of what follows examines how this nexus of beliefs—some accurate, some distorted—fostered cooperation between the United States and Japan while leading to conflict with China, Korea, and Vietnam.

Throughout the 1950s and 1960s, the United States urged Japan to play a more forceful role in the cold war, such as expanding its armed forces and assisting American military efforts in Korea and Vietnam. Yet, the more Washington pushed, the more determined to resist these demands Tokyo remained. The ruling Liberal Democrats as well as their Socialist opponents stressed the constitutional prohibition on armed forces, their fear of revived militarism, Japan's economic weakness, and the danger of being dragged into conflict with China or the Soviet Union as reasons for going slow. Despite divisions over domestic priorities, the Liberal Democrats and Socialists forged a tacit alliance to resist American pressure.

As Yoshida Shigeru, Japan's pivotal postwar prime minister, put it in the early 1950s, rearmament would come some day "naturally if our livelihood recovers." It was best to "let the Americans handle [our security] until then." Yoshida considered it Japan's "god-given luck that the constitution bans arms." He noted the irony that the American-inspired document provided him "adequate cover" to deflect Washington's demands. Yoshida dismissed politicians who wanted to amend the constitution as "oafs." During the past half-century, nearly all Yoshida's successors shunned an activist foreign policy in favor of economic nationalism and commercial expansion made possible by the cold war.

Takeshita Noboru, a conservative power broker who served as prime minister in 1988–89, remarked that throughout the cold war the "Liberal Democrats had used the possibility of criticism by the Socialists to avoid unpleasant demands by the United States, such as taking a more active role internationally." In that sense, "there was a sort of burden sharing between" the rival parties that Takeshita characterized as "cunning diplomacy." And so it was.

By the early 1970s, the economic pendulum had swung so far in the other direction that American political and business leaders considered Japan's export-driven economy a threat to U.S. security. A member of the Nixon cabinet complained in 1971 that "the Japanese are still fighting the war," with the "immediate intention . . . to try to dominate the Pacific and then perhaps the world." Uncertainty over how to respond to Japan's trade onslaught, along with a desire to enlist Chinese power to contain the Soviet Union and end the war in Vietnam, prompted President Richard Nixon's journey to the People's Republic in 1972. In a remarkably nimble reversal of twenty years of cold war rhetoric, Nixon told Mao Zedong that the United States–Japan Security Treaty protected China from both Soviet and Japanese threats.

After 1985, America's simultaneous unease with and dependence on Japan increased dramatically. As the perceived threat from the Soviet

Union abated, Japan took on many of the trappings of the former "evil empire." Theodore White, a leading journalist who covered Asia, accused Japan of carrying out "one of history's most brilliant commercial offensives" calibrated to "dismantle American industry." Japan's ministry of finance "provided the launching pad from which MITI (Ministry of International Trade and Industry) directed the guided missles of the trade offensive." American corporate executives seeking government aid blamed many of their woes on predatory Japanese competition. A prominent business lobbyist urged Congress to plow tens of millions of dollars into cold fusion research—the high technology equivalent of snake oil—on the grounds that MITI was secretly "working on the plan" to control this revolutionary technology and to dominate the world.

Even as the U.S. economy reeled under the impact of annual trade deficits with Japan topping $50 billion, Americans recognized the critical role played by Tokyo in buying billions of dollars worth of bonds issued by the U.S. Treasury. Without these loans, neither the huge federal budget deficit generated by "Reaganomics" nor the standard of living enjoyed by Americans could have been sustained. Political and financial leaders in both nations felt uncomfortable with this relationship, but neither side envisioned an acceptable alternative.

This economic transformation, as important as détente with the Soviet Union, the opening to China, the exit from Vietnam, and the end of the cold war, would have startled the politicians and diplomats active when Japan regained its sovereignty. Then, stripped of its colonies and military power, hovering on the fringe of Communist-dominated Asia, and producing few marketable exports, Japan seemed an unlikely candidate for recovery, no less evolution into an economic superpower.

Until 1965, Japan ran a chronic trade deficit with the United States, prompting Presidents Dwight D. Eisenhower and John F. Kennedy to do all they could to boost Japan's exports to America. Since 1965, every presidential administration has wrestled with the seemingly intractable problem of how to limit Japan's growing trade surplus with the United States. Despite these strains, as well as disagreements over military spending and policies toward China and the Vietnam War, the Pacific alliance forged in the aftermath of World War II proved remarkably durable.

In the early 1990s, the belief that Japan had changed from ward to usurper found expression in opinion surveys in which a majority of Americans labeled Japan a greater threat to national security than the Soviet Union. Following the dissolution of the Soviet empire in December 1991, presidential hopeful Paul Tsongas (lifting a line from Japan scholar Chalmers Johnson) quipped that for America "the good news is that the cold war is over. The bad news is that Germany and Japan won."

In fact, during the Occupation period and beyond, the United States pursued a coherent strategy in East Asia designed to deny Japan's industrial potential to the Communist powers. This motive underlay efforts to contain China, block Communist influence in Southeast Asia, and promote

Japanese trade expansion. To a remarkable degree, the United States achieved its goal, although not precisely under the circumstances it originally envisioned.

The wars in Korea and Vietnam, for example, involved huge costs for the United States and produced unimagined consequences. Military spending in both conflicts spurred Japanese economic growth and forged links between Japan, the United States, and Southeast Asia. The Vietnam War, fought to shield Japan and Southeast Asia from a Chinese threat, resulted ultimately in renewed American cooperation with China designed, in part, to counter Japan's growing power. In the case of Japanese-American relations, the law of unintended consequences operated regularly. By the same token, nations, like individuals, must be careful what they wish for since sometimes they get it.

This narrative examines Japanese-American relations in detail from the Occupation through the mid-1970s. Documentation becomes sparse beyond that. The Epilogue traces developments through the end of the cold war in the 1990s. The account focuses more intensely on American rather than Japanese motivation. By using Japanese memoir, press, and secondary sources—little primary documentation is available—I have tried to provide insights into both sides of the altered relationship. Japanese names are rendered in the traditional style, surname followed by given name.

Many friends and colleagues have encouraged this project. Robert Schulzinger and Chalmers Johnson were especially conscientious readers and critics of the entire manuscript. Nick Cullather and Ernest Young read part of the manuscript and made helpful suggestions. Leonard Dinnerstein was always available to test ideas on. The National Endowment for the Humanities, the University of Arizona's Social and Behavioral Sciences Research Institute and its Udall Center, the Lyndon B. Johnson Foundation, and the Dwight D. Eisenhower Foundation all funded portions of my research. Robert Wampler of the National Security Archive helped unearth many important documents. Nancy Lane, my editor at Oxford University Press, encouraged this project from its inception. I am gateful to these individuals and organizations.

1 *JAPAN: FROM ENEMY TO ALLY,*

1945–50

*I*N the spring of 1946, as Japanese diplo-
mat Yoshida Shigeru formed his first postwar cabinet, he remarked to a
friend that "history provides examples of winning by diplomacy after losing in war." As ambassador to London during the 1930s, Yoshida viewed
with alarm Japan's aggression in Asia. The ruin later visited on his country
seemed proof of the folly sewn by reckless militarism. In 1945, Yoshida
joined those urging the emperor to negotiate an end to the war before a
Soviet invasion or leftist revolution. Although this led to his arrest by the
military police, it paid a handsome dividend when the Americans
exempted him from the postwar purge.

Japan's postwar achievements, many of which can be credited to
Yoshida, seemed proof of his aphorism. Between 1945 and 1950, Japan
experienced what Occupation Commander General Douglas MacArthur
called a "controlled revolution," the partial uprooting of political, economic, and social structures that had contributed to repression at home
and aggression abroad. In retrospect, it is clear that many Occupation
reforms changed less than their American sponsors hoped and that important aspects of the pre-1945 power structure continued to operate in the
new Japan. During the two years after the end of the Pacific War, Japan seldom commanded attention among America's leading officials. Europe
dominated foreign policy concerns, followed by the Near East and China,
where General George C. Marshall tried, in vain, to mediate a civil war.
Japan glowed dimly in the foreign policy firmament.

Testy relations between Douglas MacArthur and the Truman administration further complicated matters. Despite public praise lavished on the
general by civilian and military leaders during the Second World War,

many of these individuals privately disparaged him. Texas Democrat Tom Connally, who chaired the Senate Foreign Relations Committee, voiced a common concern in the summer of 1945 when he told Truman it would be a "big mistake" to appoint "Dugout Doug as Allied Commander in Chief" in Japan. MacArthur, he predicted, would use the post to "run against [Truman] in 1948."

Secretary of the Interior Harold Ickes also questioned the appointment, but believed that public pressure made it "inevitable" that "MacArthur should be cast for this role." Ickes imagined that the "man on horseback" would behave in Japan as he had in the Pacific, taking "every advantage of this dramatic situation to get himself spread all over the papers." Truman agreed, although he told Ickes that it was not really fair to "blame on him the appointment of MacArthur" as Occupation commander. Domestic politics ensured that he "couldn't do anything else." The root of the problem, Ickes thought, lay with Roosevelt, who made a "mistake in taking MacArthur away from the Philippines" in 1942. He should have been left "to clean up his own mess"—or the Japanese allowed to solve "the MacArthur problem." To keep the general out of Tokyo now would make a "martyr out of him and a candidate for president." He would, Truman lamented, "be a candidate anyway."[1]

Americans arriving in Japan in August 1945 found a land of ruined cities, idle factories, and homeless refugees. One and one-half million soldiers had died, along with nearly a half million civilian victims of air raids. In a letter home, one GI described the eerie sensation of approaching Tokyo. Instead of seeing a great city, the closer in he drove, the more "everything seemed completely flat with destruction." The defeated nation had to feed and shelter not only current residents but seven million Japanese soldiers and civilians returning from China and Southeast Asia.[2]

In a mark of despair, the ultranationalist East Asia League admonished its members to obey the Americans and "align themselves with world Jewry, which had now proved its invincibility by triumphing over Hitler." Six days after surrender, the Japanese government, fearful that "sexstarved" American Occupation troops would behave as Japanese forces often had abroad by raping every woman or girl in sight, recruited thousands of "comfort women" to slake the passions of foreign soldiers in official brothels. The prostitutes and war widows pressed into service were told that their mission "was to be a sexual dike to protect the chastity of Japanese women" and prevent pollution of the race.[3]

As Supreme Commander for the Allied Powers, or SCAP—an acronym applied to himself as well as headquarters—MacArthur represented the victorious allies. A token number of allied troops served alongside the American garrison. To soothe British, Soviet, and Chinese irritation over being ignored, Washington created two Occupation oversight committees: the Far Eastern Commission and the Allied Council for Japan. Neither had the slightest influence on policy anytime during the next six years.

After accepting Japan's formal surrender aboard the battles[...] *souri* in Tokyo Bay on September 2, MacArthur set up his General [...] quarters (GHQ) in the Dai Ichi Insurance Building, one of the few m[...] structures left standing in central Tokyo. SCAP consisted of a dozen or s[...] sections, corresponding to the Japanese cabinet and American army orga- nization. Among the most important groups were an intelligence section that monitored both Japan and southern Korea, Government Section that oversaw political reform, and Economic and Scientific Section with broad economic policy authority. The respective heads of these sections, Generals Charles Willoughby, Courtney Whitney, and William Marquat, were mem- bers of the so-called Bataan gang, a circle of acolytes whose loyalty to MacArthur extended back to prewar Manila. At high tide in 1948, just over 3,000 Americans and a handful of foreign nationals served in SCAP. It relied heavily on the Japanese government for information and policy implementation.

As Occupation commander, MacArthur cut a figure at once ubiquitous and aloof. Labor expert Theodore Cohen recalled his surprise after arriving in Tokyo at how the local press seldom printed the name of any American other than MacArthur. SCAP censors discouraged Japanese newspapers from describing the actions of President Truman or his administration. "As far as the Japanese people were concerned," Cohen observed, a single indi- vidual had "displaced the United States Government." [4]

During nearly six years in Tokyo, MacArthur followed a strict routine. Driven from his home in the former American ambassador's residence each morning at 10:30, he worked for several hours at the Dai Ichi Building before returning home for lunch and a nap. He repeated the journey each afternoon. MacArthur usually communicated with Japanese officials in writing and met few in person. Before the outbreak of the Korean War in June 1950, he left Tokyo only twice, to attend independence ceremonies in Manila and Seoul.

Neither then nor in retirement did he reveal many inner feelings about Japan. Once, in a casual remark to an aide in Tokyo he described the Japan- ese as a "brooding" people whose country had "an ominous quality" that put him on edge. He told an Australian colleague in 1948 that "as a matter of general principle," he advised dealing with Orientals by first "spitting in their eye." He compared the Japanese to "second-grade students" capable of absorbing advanced concepts only at a remedial pace. In 1951, MacArthur told a congressional inquiry that "measured by the standards of modern civilization," the Japanese "would be like a boy of twelve as compared with our development of forty-five years." [5]

The Reform Period, 1945–47

The initial reform agenda represented a compromise between planners who believed a progressive Japanese government had been "highjacked"

ıg the 1930s and those who insisted that deeply flawed
ı economic structures in Japan led to dictatorship and
group argued that Japan had "stumbled" into war, the
's misdeeds "rooted" in its institutions.[6]

ıdled the "stumble" and "root" debate, calling for a
the existing "feudal" order while backing moderate
E. Wood, a conservative ally and head of the prewar
group America First, questioned SCAP's advocacy of "socialis-
uc reforms," MacArthur defended his program as an effort to purge a
"decadent past" and "clear the way for the ultimate development in Japan
of a healthy economy based upon free, competitive private enterprise."

The general's grandiloquent rhetoric confounded Americans across the
political spectrum. MacArthur, who sought the Republican presidential
nomination in both 1944 and 1948, considered Japan a political stage on
which to demonstrate his executive ability. Yet, after observing the Occupation commander up close, Theodore Cohen concluded that he had only a
"primitive" notion of economic issues. Raised in the West, MacArthur had
little "urban and no industrial experience that might have prepared him
for the great American and European social conflicts after World War I."

Although a fierce opponent of the New Deal, MacArthur recalled nineteenth-century populist rhetoric about selfish bankers and predatory corporations. Perry Miller, a historian of Puritan thought, recognized this sensibility while serving as a visiting scholar in occupied Japan. MacArthur
wanted to transform Japan into a "new Middle West—not of course the
Middle West as it is, or in fact ever was, but as it perpetually dreams of
being."[7]

The "controlled revolution" began in earnest in October 1945 when
SCAP issued a civil liberties directive releasing political prisoners, legaliz-
ing all political parties, and assuring protection of the rights of assembly
and speech. The cabinet of Prime Minister Higashikuni Naruhiko (formed
shortly after surrender) resigned in protest, warning that the gates to Communist revolution had been thrown open.

Early in 1946, the SCAP government section startled the Japanese government when it produced a new constitution and threatened to submit it
to a popular vote unless it was quickly accepted by the Diet. The document, which had to be translated into Japanese, stripped the emperor of
temporal authority, enhanced the Diet's power, extended voting rights,
and declared the legal equality of women. Article IX, to Washington's later
regret, forbade creation of armed forces or the right of the state to conduct
war.

In addition to the verdicts returned against top wartime leaders at the
Tokyo war crimes trials, SCAP neutered the influence of many senior
politicians through a purge in 1946. At the insistence of MacArthur and
officials in Washington, however, the emperor was declared an opponent
of militarism and aggression and thereby exempt from indictment for war
crimes. Political moderates and most ordinary Japanese favored cleansing

the landscape of militarists and ultranationalists. But the purge proved extremely selective. About twenty young American military officers were assigned the task of investigating 2.5 million cases. The burden fell on Japanese bureaucrats who easily shaded evidence. Ultimately, about 200,000 Japanese, over 80 percent from military and police ranks, lost their political rights. Relatively few politicians and fewer bureaucrats or business leaders fell victim to the purge. Among those who did, most had their rights restored before or just after the Occupation ended.

In rapid fashion, SCAP redressed the chronic problem of farm tenancy. MacArthur endorsed a plan "to tear down the large feudalistic land holdings in order that those who till the soil will have the opportunity to reap the full benefit from their toil." Advocates of reform claimed that it would expand food production, democratize the rural economy, and prevent the type of peasant revolts sweeping China and Southeast Asia.

In addition to tenants, many Japanese academics and bureaucrats recognized the exploitive nature of the rural economy. During the war, the military government had struck a blow against landlords by limiting their right to collect rent and purchasing rice directly from cultivators. By the time the Occupation ended, nearly a third of Japan's land had changed hands. Land reform created a class of small farmers loyal to the conservative politicians who initially opposed the law. In 1950, China's deposed leader, Jiang Jieshi (Chiang Kai-shek) paid eloquent tribute to the reform when he wrote to MacArthur from Taiwan that if he "could have done in China what you did in Japan, I would still be there today."

Reform touched nearly every major institution during the first three years of Occupation. SCAP reorganized the national police, remodeled public education along Western lines, voided repressive labor codes, and seemed pleased that by 1947 nearly half the urban workforce joined trade unions.[8]

Despite these important reforms, many powerful structures resisted change. Prewar career bureaucrats remained in charge of most ministries, hardly touched by the purge or new constitution. MacArthur's concern with free elections obscured the fact that, because of their prewar roots and financial links to big business, conservative parties continued to dominate the Diet.[9]

Continuity, as much as change, characterized Japanese politics after 1945. Unlike what occurred in Germany, the Japanese government and bureaucracy—except for a small number of purged individuals—remained in place, subject to supervision and direction by American authorities. In the first postwar election of April 1946, two conservative parties—the Progressives and the Liberals—won a majority of Diet seats. The conservatives supported the emperor system, favored the prevailing economic structure, and urged limits on the power of organized labor. Personalities, instead of ideologies, accounted for most of the differences between the main groups. The political weight of rural districts gave the conservatives a built-in electoral advantage.

Even with the rapid growth of labor unions, parties on the left faced serious impediments under the new system. After decades of police repression, the Socialists and Communists had little experience in contesting open elections. Campaign finances were meager and factional squabbles pervasive. Until 1950, the Japan Communist Party was more reformist than revolutionary. The Socialists often took a more radical Marxist line toward industry and favored strict, unarmed neutrality in the cold war.

Yoshida's conservative coalition cabinet held power for a year. By June 1947, the Socialists won enough Diet seats to organize a short-lived minority Socialist cabinet under Katayama Tetsu. This coalition collapsed early in 1948 and Yoshida soon returned as prime minister, a position he retained until December 1954. With some short lapses, protégés of the so-called Yoshida school dominated Japanese politics until 1993.

Initial American interest in dissolving Japan's large, interlocking industrial and banking conglomerates—the *zaibatsu*, or money clique—remained unfulfilled. In 1945, the State and War Departments instructed MacArthur to promote a wider "distribution of income and ownership of the means of production and trade" by pursuing a vigorous anti-monopoly program. When SCAP hesitated to attack the *zaibatsu*, the State and Justice Departments dispatched a "Special Mission on Japanese Combines," led by economist Corwin Edwards, and a Reparations Mission under oilman Edwin Pauley. In 1945–46, both groups proposed comprehensive reparations and anti-monopoly programs. But neither President Truman nor his advisers took much interest in the issue and the programs faltered. The impasse over economic policy contributed to falling production, rising unemployment, soaring inflation, and a large trade deficit. Merely to prevent economic collapse and starvation, the United States provided annual assistance of $400 million through the army's Government and Relief in Occupied Areas program (GARIOA).

Rethinking the Occupation

When the Truman administration finally turned its attention toward Japan during 1947, it did so under dramatically altered circumstances. The deterioration of relations with the Soviet Union and the failure of the West European, German, and Japanese economies to recover frightened American policymakers. Navy Secretary James Forrestal brought Undersecretary of State Dean Acheson, Secretary of War Robert Patterson, Agriculture Secretary Clinton Anderson, former ambassador to Moscow Averell Harriman, and former president Herbert Hoover together to discuss how to "have a run for our side in the competition with the Soviet Union." Containing the Soviets, Forrestal insisted, required putting "Japan, Germany and the other affiliates of the Axis . . . back to work." All agreed that European recovery and security required the revival of German industry. Everything said about Germany, Forrestal stressed, "applied with equal force to Japan."

The group concluded that MacArthur's disdain for civil authority and his political ambition were "wrecking" the Japanese economy and risked a "complete economic collapse." Someone had to be placed in Tokyo who would follow orders. Unless Truman agreed to send a "super diplomat" to Tokyo to "break the grip of General MacArthur," Acheson warned, the situation would deteriorate. [10]

Yet Truman hesitated to intervene. He had recently appointed George C. Marshall to replace James F. Byrnes as secretary of state. The War and Navy Departments remained bitterly divided over budgets and declined to challenge MacArthur. Meanwhile, economic decline in Western Europe and Japan accelerated, posing greater peril to American security than Soviet military power.

The loss of colonies and colonial rebellions in Southeast Asia, the legacy of wartime hatred and physical destruction, and the division of Europe—all inhibited recovery. Also, the spectacular economic growth of the United States during the war magnified the troubles of Europe and Japan, since in their weakened condition they could hardly compete in world commerce with the American colossus. The resulting trade imbalance, the so-called dollar gap between the world's need for American food, raw materials, and manufactured goods and the inadequate hard currency available for their purchase, threatened to paralyze world trade. Unless their production and export earnings were restored, Europe and Japan would soon run out of dollars and raw materials. Caught between threats of social disorder and Communist power, America's key partners might seek an accommodation with the Soviet Union.

This prospect convinced planners such as Dean Acheson, James Forrestal, George Kennan, and Army Undersecretary William H. Draper that Washington had to promote industrial recovery in Europe and Japan. By providing capital and raw materials, the United States could stimulate production and exports vital to the stability of these areas and, in the long run, to the United States. Planners hoped that after initial American aid, the Europeans and Japanese could use some of their scarce dollars to purchase raw materials from developing nations and sell manufactured goods to them. The growth of regional markets would create efficiencies of scale, promote stability in developing countries, and blunt Communist influence globally.

Secretary of State George C. Marshall encouraged Acheson and Kennan to develop proposals along these lines. Joined by James Forrestal, named head of the new Defense Department late in 1947, and other civilian and military specialists, they contributed to the evolving containment program. At its inception, containment focused on recovery in Europe and Japan in order to deny control of their industrial capacity to the Kremlin. Eventually, the planners believed, the Soviet Union would respond to this policy by altering its behavior in ways favorable to the West.

Although MacArthur had no principled objection to this policy change, he bitterly resented efforts to interfere with SCAP. Any suggestion that Japan required a special recovery program implied that he had not done

enough. Even worse, a new recovery program would extend the Occupation beyond early 1948—when he hoped to leave Tokyo in triumphant
pursuit of the presidency. MacArthur maintained that in accomplishing
Japan's disarmament and democratization, he had fulfilled the essential
goals of the Occupation. Economic problems could be resolved after the
Americans left. He dismissed the Soviet threat to a neutral Japan and
insisted that a "simple article" in a peace treaty providing for UN protection would assure Tokyo's security.

President Truman struck a dramatically different tone in his March 12,
1947, message to Congress concerning the crisis in Greece, occasioned by
British withdrawal of support from the conservative regime fighting a civil
war. In what became known as the Truman Doctrine, the president blamed
Moscow and its agents for threatening not only Greece and Turkey, but free
governments everywhere. He asked Congress to assist Greece and Turkey
as a down payment on a far wider aid program.

Truman's appeal prompted MacArthur to lash out at the administration's policy at a press conference on March 17. He boasted that the "spiritual revolution" he had presided over insulated Japan from internal or external threats and eliminated the need for an expensive recovery program.[11]

These assertions contrasted with the belief of nearly all policymakers
in Washington that an early end to the Occupation would cause economic
collapse and, quite possibly, Communist incursions. In a speech delivered
on May 8, Dean Acheson revealed a new approach to foreign policy. The
dollar gap and the grim economic situation abroad, the undersecretary
asserted, stemmed from the "grim fact of life" that the "greatest workshops
of Europe and Asia, Germany and Japan" remained idle. World stability
required rebuilding the "two workshops" on which the "ultimate recovery
of the two continents so largely depends." American forces would stay in
Germany and Japan until their economies revived.[12]

In July 1947, without consulting Washington, MacArthur unveiled his
own recovery package. Since 1946, he had blocked a proposal (formally
known as FEC 230) to dismantle the Japanese industrial combines or
zaibatsu. Now, just as Washington resolved to make industrial recovery a
priority, MacArthur ordered the Diet to pass a bill dissolving the combines
and decentralizing industry.

George Kennan warned cabinet members that out of ignorance or
duplicity, MacArthur had opened Japan to Communist influence. The
"socialization" attack on big business, Kennan predicted, would cause "economic disaster, inflation . . . near anarchy which would be precisely what
the communists want." He portrayed the attack on the zaibatsu as a
"vicious" scheme to destroy the major barrier to Soviet penetration in Asia.
William H. Draper complained that SCAP had turned Japan into an economic "morgue." Army Secretary Kenneth Royall charged that MacArthur's
plan resembled "socialism . . . if not near communism." The survival of the
free world, James Forrestal told Truman, required giving priority to rebuilding Germany and Japan, "the two countries we have just destroyed."[13]

As the general's critics suspected, his support for *zaibatsu* dissolution reflected his political ambitions. MacArthur had encouraged supporters to enter his name in several midwestern presidential primaries. The earliest vote took place in Wisconsin, home of the general's father and where he himself lived briefly. To enhance his native son status, MacArthur's campaign relied on Phillip LaFollette, scion of the influential Wisconsin political dynasty renowned for its anti-monopoly crusade.

While MacArthur ignored formal requests to delay Diet action on the *zaibatsu* bill, the Army Department received news from Tokyo that confirmed the link between the deconcentration program and presidential politics. A Japanese informant reported that when the Diet almost adjourned without passing an anti-monopoly bill, an aide to MacArthur told Prime Minister Katayama that the law must "be passed so as not to embarrass" the general who "expected to be nominated for president." MacArthur allegedly told the Japanese that he did not care about strict enforcement of the law, but insisted that there be "no sign of dissension in Tokyo." If the Japanese caused him problems, it would "prejudice the future of Japan when the Supreme Commander became president."[14]

A bitter war of words erupted between Washington and SCAP at the end of 1947. Army and State Department officials leaked unflattering accounts of the Occupation to members of Congress and journalists who then accused MacArthur of promoting reforms "far to the left of anything tolerated in America" and of embracing the "lethal weapons" of socialism. The general retorted that the deconcentration program targeted only fifty-six families and that his reforms would prevent a "bloodbath of revolutionary violence."

Ignoring MacArthur, diplomats and military planners proposed sweeping changes in Occupation policy that they euphemistically called a "switch in emphasis." But Truman, so unsure of his prospects that he contemplated asking Dwight D. Eisenhower to run in his place, hesitated to act before the primary elections.[15]

The general's presidential boomlet burst on April 6, 1948. Wisconsin Republicans, divided by local issues, were influenced by Senator Joseph McCarthy's tirades against MacArthur. The "great general," the senator declared, was "ready for retirement." Although he claimed to be a Wisconsin native, "neither his first nor his second marriage, nor his divorce took place in Wisconsin" and "neither wife ever resided in Wisconsin." Swayed by this logic, most Republicans voted for Minnesotan Harold Stassen. This poor showing in his "native" state torpedoed the general's candidacy. After another defeat in Nebraska, MacArthur abandoned his second quest for the GOP nomination. Although he remained as Occupation commander in Tokyo for three more years, he had lost the charisma that allowed him to defy Washington with impunity.

Kennan's Policy Planning Staff had for some time considered ways of halting or reversing many Occupation reforms. The "radically changed world situation," the Planning Staff reported, required that Japan be made "internally stable," more "amenable to American leadership," and "industrially revived" in order to assure the stability of "non-communist Asia." To prevent left-wing influence or Soviet penetration, America should "crank-up" the Japanese economy and bind Tokyo to the West through a defense pact.

Russia's conduct, the planners asserted, precluded a neutral Japan. Instead, "Hirohito's islands" should be made a "buffer state" against the Soviet Union. Although Kennan and his staff doubted Stalin would attack Japan, Kennan feared that Communist control over Manchuria, China, and Korea would provide a "lever for Soviet political pressure" unless Japan obtained "vital raw materials and markets elsewhere," particularly in Southeast Asia. Japan's survival as an ally and the denial of its industrial base to the Soviets required action "to prime the Japanese economic pump."[16]

Kennan and Army Undersecretary William H. Draper observed the situation firsthand during a March 1948 visit to Tokyo. In a hectoring monologue aimed at Kennan, MacArthur defended his actions and denounced the idea of linking Japan to a regional containment program. The business purge, he insisted, affected only "elderly incompetents" similar to "the most effete New York club men." He denied that the anti-*zaibatsu* program resembled socialism, but accused the State Department of coddling leftists. As an "international official," the general argued, he was free to defy Washington.

MacArthur's geopolitical nostrums and blathering about planting the "seeds of Christianity" among a "billion of these Oriental peoples on the shores of the Pacific" repelled Kennan. The "degree of internal intrigue" in the general's headquarters, the diplomat wrote to a colleague, resembled "nothing more than the latter days of the court of the Empress Catherine II, or possibly the final stages of the regime of Belisarius in Italy." The "fragile psychic quality" exuded by MacArthur's entourage echoed the mood in Stalin's Kremlin. SCAP's social engineering, Kennan feared, would wreck Japan or be rejected as an alien creed after the Americans left, leaving Communism to fill the void.[17]

During his brief time in Japan, Kennan began to redraft the Occupation agenda. As he saw things, MacArthur had sewn the seeds of disaster by crippling industry and purging business leaders. It was vital to revive, not dissolve, industrial combines, clamp down on, not promote, labor unions, and bolster conservative, not leftist, political forces. Nothing should be permitted that "operated against the stability of Japanese society" or recovery.

At the same time as Kennan reached these conclusions, Army Undersecretary William Draper escorted a business delegation to Japan led by Chemical Bank chairman Percy H. Johnston. After meeting with *zaibatsu* representatives, the group issued its own critique of SCAP's "radical" economic policies and told journalists they favored curtailing reparations and the assault on the *zaibatsu* while providing substantial assistance to Japanese industry. The "bad times were over," Draper reportedly told the Japanese.[18]

On April 26, Draper released the findings of the Johnston committee. They recommended suspending reparations and attacks on industry while curbing labor unions. In place of industrial reform, the report urged promoting production and boosting exports, even at the cost of reducing living standards.[19]

These proposals for a new Occupation agenda were formalized in a document submitted by the Policy Planning Staff to the National Security Council during the summer of 1948 and approved as NSC 13/2 by President Truman in October. It proclaimed economic recovery as the "prime objective" in Japan. Reparations were halted and restrictions on most industry lifted. SCAP and the Japanese government were to preferentially allocate raw materials and credit to firms that produced for export. Congress helped by passing the Economic Recovery in Occupied Areas (EROA) bill and cotton credits, offering substantial amounts of capital and raw materials.

To gut the deconcentration law, the army sent a special review board to Tokyo. The board exempted all banks from scrutiny and overturned or softened all but a handful of the 325 dissolution orders already issued against the *zaibatsu*. By 1949, the board declared the anti-monopoly program a success and terminated it.

Following his election triumph in November 1948, Truman committed his full authority to the so-called reverse course. On December 10, he issued an economic directive that consolidated the themes of NSC 13/2, the Johnston report, and related calls for cranking up industry. He named a special emissary, Detroit banker Joseph Dodge, to oversee SCAP and implement the program.[20]

Before going to Tokyo in February 1949, Dodge established ties with a private lobbying group that had been among MacArthur's most trenchant critics. The previous year *Newsweek* editor Harry Kern, the magazine's Tokyo correspondent Compton Packenham, business lawyer James Lee Kauffman, and former State Department Japan specialist Eugene Dooman had founded the American Council on Japan (ACJ). Its members included some two dozen journalists, lawyers, retired diplomats, and military officers who acted as a liaison between Japanese business and political leaders—including many purgees—and officials such as William Draper and George Kennan.

Dodge distributed a report from the ACJ to his staff that denounced SCAP as a "bureaucratic, inefficient, dictatorial, vindictive, and at times corrupt" organization. It accused MacArthur and his staff of destroying the "very individuals and classes" who supported the United States in the cold war while giving Communists free rein.[21]

The so-called economic czar imposed budget and industrial policies that breathed new life into the *zaibatsu*, curbed inflation, drove down worker's living standards, limited the rights of unions to bargain and strike, and aimed to restore Japan as an industrial exporter. After his political reversal, MacArthur accepted Dodge's economic initiatives as well as moves by Yoshida that curbed union power and promoted big business.

During 1949 and early 1950, Dodge held to a rigorous program of neo-classic economic policy designed to rationalize an inflation-driven economy operating at little more than two-thirds of its prewar level. He envisioned Japan as a high-volume, low-cost exporter of consumer goods primarily to Asian markets. To reduce what he considered frivolous spending, he ordered major reductions in the public welfare budget, curtailment of business loans, and the firing of 250,000 government workers. These actions decreased domestic consumption and shunted bank credit, foreign currency, and raw materials to large enterprises engaged in export production.

In April 1949, Dodge and a now compliant SCAP encouraged the Japanese government to organize a Ministry of International Trade and Industry (MITI). Modeled on the wartime Munitions Ministry and staffed by many of that agency's veteran bureaucrats, MITI provided "administrative guidance" to banks and corporations. It directed the flow of domestic credit, foreign currency, imported raw materials, and foreign technology to favored companies that produced primarily for the export market and sold goods for hard currency. Japan's government-guided, export-driven economy, later described as a "capitalist development state" or, less charitably, "Japan, Inc.," was nurtured by American directives.[22]

Dodge considered industrial recovery, export promotion, and containment of Communism as related goals. A stable Japan, he argued, would serve as a key "border area in the world-wide clash between communism and democracy." Ideologically tied to the West and commercially linked to Asia, Japan would deflect "totalitarian pressures" and counter the Communist "pan-Asiatic movement." Through Japan, the United States could apply "tremendous influence over our relations with all of the Orient." In the future, Dodge told a congressional committee early in 1950, Japan could be "used as a springboard for America, and a country supplying the material goods required for American aid to the Far East."[23]

The Sinews of Containment: Japan, China, and Southeast Asia

The commitment to Japanese recovery raised the question of where, outside the United States, it could find affordable raw materials and an export market. Sustained growth, American planners believed, required revived Asian trade so that Japan could import raw materials from nondollar areas that constituted her natural export markets. As one State Department official observed, aside from its reliance on force, there was much economic merit in Japan's "plan for a Greater East Asia."[24]

Just as China, Manchuria, and Korea had formed the pivot of Japan's prewar Asian trade, Southeast Asia appeared the most promising area for future commerce. Army Undersecretary William Draper noted this in pressing his staff to prepare an "economic aid program, similar to the Marshall Plan, for the Far East." Ralph Reid, an adviser to Draper and Joseph Dodge, proposed linking Japan's economy to "strong, independent governments [in Asia], friendly towards the United States and opposed to Communism in order to provide a bulwark against Soviet encroachment, to assure the U.S. sources of strategic raw materials, and to deny to the Soviet Union the manpower potential of the Far East."[25]

During 1949, Reid and Joseph Dodge cooperated with SCAP's Economic and Scientific Section to implement a "Program for a Self-Supporting Japanese Economy." Known as the "Blue Book" because of its binder, it postulated a five-year program of American aid to boost production and help Japan develop "key markets and indispensable sources of raw materials . . . in the natural market areas in Asia."

Reid and Assistant Army Secretary Tracy Voorhees saw the Asian "Marshall Plan" as a way of integrating Southeast Asia and Japan. But first the United States had to suppress nationalist rebellions and Communist encroachment. With multicolor charts depicting Japan as the locus of a regional economy, they proposed to "create democratic governments, restore viable economies, and check Soviet expansion." The program could "advance the dignity of man," and keep "vital raw materials" out of Communist control.[26]

Although a Marshall Plan for Asia never went beyond the planning stage, the Communist advance in China and the upsurge of rebellion in Indochina, Malaya, and the Dutch East Indies focused greater attention on the importance of Southeast Asia. As with Germany and Japan, Kennan's Policy Planning Staff (PPS) took the lead in calling for a new approach to the region. John P. Davies, a member of the PPS staff, circulated a memorandum in December 1948 that shaped the American government's thinking about the link between Japan and Southeast Asia. American interests, he argued, required

> creating an apparatus which will enable us to employ our and Japan's economy as an instrument of political warfare with respect to Communist Asia; acquiring necessary raw materials for U.S. strategic and economic requirements; developing economic stability and interdependence among the Western Pacific islands (including Japan) Malaya, and Siam; encouraging a flow of raw materials from Southeast Asia to the [Western European] ERP countries.[27]

When Dean Acheson replaced George Marshall as secretary of state early in 1949, he brought to the job a deep interest in Southeast Asia. He hoped to refocus the attention of Congress away from the debacle in China where, he argued, America could do nothing until the "brick, dust and smoke clears away." If China was lost, protecting Japan's industrial base and Southeast Asia's mineral wealth required "drawing the line" against Communist encroachment. Acheson asked the PPS to formulate a regional policy along the lines sketched by Davies.

The PPS accused the Kremlin of launching a "coordinated offensive" against Southeast Asia. By denying the region's mineral wealth to Europe and Japan, the Soviets hoped to divide the globe on a "north–south axis" and strangle the industrialized nations. Because of this, Southeast Asia formed a "vital segment on the line of containment."

To frustrate the Kremlin, Washington had to ease out the European colonial powers and work "through a screen of anti-communist Asiatics" to ensure, "however long it takes" the triumph of genuine nationalism "over Red Imperialism." The United States should "vigorously develop the economic interdependence between [Southeast Asia] as a supplier of raw materials, and Japan, Western Europe and India as suppliers of finished goods." Stability, Acheson's aides concluded in April 1949, would allow Southeast Asia to fulfill its "major function as a source of raw materials and a market for Japan and Western Europe."[28]

The establishment of the People's Republic of China on October 1, 1949, made this question urgent. Few policymakers in the Truman administration believed the "loss" of China directly threatened American security. But many worried that the Communist victory would undermine Japan, whose industry had long drawn raw materials from northeast Asia. As George Kennan observed at a State Department conference assessing the impact of the Chinese revolution, "You have" the "terrific problem" of how the "Japanese are going to get along unless they again re-open some sort of empire to the South." Philip Taylor, a SCAP veteran, noted that with China passing into the Communist orbit, "We have got to get Japan back into, I am afraid, the old Co-Prosperity Sphere."

To assure future cooperation, Kennan recommended keeping Japan on a short tether. A prosperous yet dependent ally would best serve American interests. This required imposing controls "foolproof enough and cleverly enough exercised . . . to have power over what Japan imports in the way of oil and other things." Economic controls would give Washington "veto power over what she does."[29]

Most civilian policymakers agreed that Japan's industrial potential made it both a critical American asset and Soviet target in Asia. If Japan were "added to the Communist bloc," Dean Acheson told British Ambassador Oliver Franks in December 1949, "the Soviets would acquire skilled manpower and industrial potential capable of significantly altering the balance of world power."[30]

Much of the debate within the Truman administration about China and Southeast Asia reflected concern over Japan. Would American "moderation" toward Beijing hasten a break between Mao and Stalin or would it be seen as appeasement and encourage Communist expansion? Given Japan's need for trade outlets, would regulated commerce with China speed Japanese recovery or simply hand the communists a means for blackmailing Tokyo? Where, besides China, could Japan find affordable raw materials?

Articles by journalists Joseph and Stewart Alsop highlighted the consequences for Japan if Southeast Asia, like China, was "lost." Reporting from the region in August 1949, Stewart wrote that following their victory in China the Soviets planned to build a Communist Co-Prosperity Sphere. Since China and Southeast Asia "comprise Japan's whole natural trading area," economic "pressure alone could be enough ultimately to bring Japan into the Soviet sphere." With "Japan's industrial potential added to the natural riches and huge population of Southeast Asia and China," the Soviets could achieve "a vast upset in the world power balance."[31]

After another trip through the region early in 1950, Stewart Alsop described the Kremlin's effort to "organize another infinitely vaster Asiatic Co-Prosperity Sphere." Citing a bowling analogy (which preceded the domino theory), Alsop wrote:

> The head pin was China. It is down already. The two pins in the second row are Burma and Indo-china. If they go, the three pins in the third row, Siam, Malaya and Indonesia, are pretty sure to topple in their turn. And if all the rest of Asia goes, the resulting psychological, political and economic magnetism will almost certainly drag down the four pins of the fourth row, India, Pakistan, Japan and the Philippines.

Alsop mentioned an interview with Japanese Communist leader Nozaka Sanzo as proof of this plan. Nozaka, he said, outlined a great crescent of Soviet power stretching from Siberia to New Guinea. With a "broad, cheerful grin," he told Alsop that "it won't be long" before this "immense new Russian empire" absorbed Japan.[32]

With some misgivings, President Truman supported the recommendations of Dean Acheson that the United States adopt a nonconfrontational approach to the Chinese Communist regime. Refuting Republican critics in Congress and the Joint Chiefs of Staff who advocated further aid to the Nationalists on Taiwan or intervention in China, Acheson insisted that, by avoiding provocations, the United States would allow the "full force of nationalism" in China eventually to turn against the Kremlin. As China's Communist leaders grew frustrated with Soviet interference and inadequate aid, they would seek "amicable relations with the world community." This outcome, Acheson admitted, might take years, but made more sense than aiding the Nationalists or fighting the Communists.

These signs of American flexibility toward the People's Republic of China had major consequences for Japan. Chinese Communist leaders, despite their disapproval of American Occupation policy, remained eager to revive trade with Japan. China's industrial infrastructure, especially in the northeast, relied heavily on Japanese equipment. For Japan, Manchurian coking coal, soybeans, and other primary products were staples of industrial development. Japan's defeat and China's civil war had blocked trade, but both sides saw value in restoring commercial ties. American economists estimated that two-way Sino-Japanese trade might total $50 million in 1950 and at least five times that by 1953.

Trade with Japan would allow China to earn foreign exchange, acquire new technology, and avoid total dependence on the Soviet Union. Communist officials, who shunned contact with the few American diplomats still in Beijing, spoke with Consul General O. Edmund Clubb early in 1949 about resuming Sino-Japanese trade.[33]

The strong antipathy toward Communism among Japan's business and governing elite did not blunt their interest in trade. Soon after he recognized the likelihood of Mao's victory, Prime Minister Yoshida stated that he anticipated "without any anxiety the possibility of a total [seizure] of China by the communists." He hoped that restoration of central government in China would restrain the Soviet Union, restore trade opportunities, and give Japan some additional leverage with America. Whether China was "red or green," the prime minister asserted, it was a "natural market, and it has become necessary for Japan to think about markets." In 1949, Trade Minister Inagaki Heitaro predicted that Japan might eventually conduct as much as a third of its foreign trade with China. Yoshida and his business allies, American analysts realized, were more than ready to "gamble on their own skills in pursuing an independent" policy toward the new China.[34]

Although state, army, and SCAP officials recognized that Sino-Japanese trade could hasten recovery and reduce American aid costs, they foresaw political complications. Most hoped to maintain influence over Japan by tethering it to American-controlled sources of critical imports. Access to Chinese raw materials might alter "Japan's political and strategic orientation." By promising preferential trade access or threatening to withdraw favors already granted, Chinese leaders might pull Tokyo "into the Communist bloc." For example, if Japan's steel industry relied on Chinese coking coal, what would prevent Beijing from abruptly cutting off supplies to force a "serious economic crisis" for political purposes? By the same token, Japan might simply drift toward neutralism to avoid offending China.

The Department of State advocated a two-track policy, permitting Japan limited trade with China as a "breathing space before the development of better trade conditions for Japan in Southeast Asia." Meanwhile, development aid to Southeast Asia should serve the "dual purpose" of advancing American influence by "providing insurance not only for Japan's future economic independence" but also for the degree of economic stability required for "political independence throughout the Far East."[35]

In March 1949, President Truman approved a China trade policy reflecting Acheson's view that a total embargo would hurt American allies and drive China closer to the Soviet Union, the opposite of what Washington desired. Regulated trade could be of "significant importance" in hastening Japanese recovery. Acheson admitted that dependence on China "would provide the communists with potentially powerful leverage over Japan after the United States Occupation and financial support had been withdrawn." He persuaded Truman to accept this "calculated risk" so long as "every effort" was made "to develop alternative resources," particularly "in such areas as southern Asia where a need exists for Japanese exports."[36]

In executive testimony before the Senate Foreign Relations Committee in January 1950, Acheson expanded on this theme. China, he predicted, would eventually fall out with its Soviet patron. In the interim, the United States should shift its "real center of interest" to the countries bordering

China on a "crescent or semicircle which goes around . . . Japan at one end and India at the other." Undertaking either military action or economic warfare against China, as Republican critics and some inside the administration demanded, would devastate Japan, which "lived on foreign trade." Prohibiting Japan's trade with China before finding an alternative would do little to injure the Communists but would make Tokyo a "pensioner of the United States."[37]

Acheson proposed using funds from the recently approved Mutual Defense Assistance Program (MDAP), from $100 million left unspent in the 1948 China Aid Act, and from other sources in "such a way that we can get double benefits from them . . . in the Far East." By solving the "great question" of Japan's economic needs, he told the senators, Asia could be saved from Communism. An economically desperate Japan, he warned, might resume aggression, turn toward the Soviets, or "ask for bids back and forth between the two sides." Because Southeast Asia could potentially supply so many of Japan's needs, Acheson testified later, the United States should concentrate on this region rather than China. For Stalin, he quipped, controlling "China without Indochina and Siam and Malaya," was "like getting to third base and not getting to score." Undersecretary of the Army Tracy Voorhees echoed the theme of linking aid to Japan and Southeast Asia. "Continuing or even maintaining Japan's economic recovery," he informed the National Security Council, depended on "keeping communism out of Southeast Asia, promoting economic recovery there" and developing the countries there "as principal trading partners for Japan."[38]

During the first half of 1950, the Truman administration dispatched several economic missions to Japan and Southeast Asia. The Army and Agriculture Departments sent a joint delegation led by Deputy Undersecretary of the Army Robert West and Stanley Andrews of the Office of Foreign Agricultural Relations. R. Allen Griffin, of the European Cooperation Administration, led a team of State, Defense, Treasury, and ECA representatives on a mission to lay the basis for "expanded trade between the [Southeast Asian] countries and Japan." They were especially eager to promote exchanges of Southeast Asian raw materials for Japanese manufactured goods.[39]

Army Undersecretary Voorhees proposed rebuilding Japan's armament industry as a source of export earnings. In one stroke, this would enhance Japan's heavy industry, assure an export market in Southeast Asia, and restrain Communist insurgencies. Southeast Asian customers could pay with raw materials, offering Japan an alternative to Chinese supplies. This typified proposals from State, Defense, and Treasury for financing regional trade.[40]

American involvement in Indochina increased dramatically during the six-month run-up to the Korean War. In February 1950, the Soviet Union and China recognized Ho Chi Minh's Vietminh movement as the government of Vietnam. Washington quickly swallowed its misgivings about the Bao Dai regime and recognized the French puppet state of Vietnam. Over the next three months, State and Defense planners urged economic and military aid for Indochina and Truman ordered that it be expedited as a "matter of priority."[41]

Diplomatic Gridlock

Japan's diplomatic prospects remained as unsettled as its economic outlook. With the State and Defense Departments deadlocked over the terms of a peace treaty, the Occupation dragged on. During 1949, Secretary of State Acheson and most civilian planners cautioned Truman that growing uneasiness and restiveness among the Japanese tired of American control might make them "easy prey to Commie ideologies." The Joint Chiefs of Staff countered that in light of the "debacle" in China and the "developing chaos on the Asiatic mainland," the United States could not risk leaving Japan.

Most diplomats dismissed the likelihood of a Soviet assault on Japan and believed that a centralized police force, a leased naval base or two, and continued economic aid would assure its security. MacArthur, who initially resisted retaining any bases in Japan (as opposed to Okinawa and the Philippines) came to favor maintaining a "tripwire" American presence to deter aggression.

The Joint Chiefs had other ideas. Although China and the Soviet Union posed little military threat to Japan, the Joint Chiefs considered American air, naval, and land bases in Japan as vital "staging areas from which to project military power to the Asiatic mainland and to USSR islands adjacent thereto." Since any peace treaty would diminish their freedom of action, the Joint Chiefs hoped to prolong the Occupation.[42]

During the final days of 1949, a State Department working group circulated a draft treaty whose main provisions limited Japan to control of the four major and specified minor islands, granted America trusteeship over the former Pacific mandated islands as well as the Ryukyus, and required preservation of representative government after the Occupation. A bilateral security pact would permit a small contingent of American forces to remain in Japan indefinitely. After five years, Japan would be free to rearm.[43]

The Joint Chiefs denounced the proposal as premature and urged Truman not to act until the Japanese rearmed and granted the United States permanent bases on their territory. Communist advances in Asia, they argued, made "continuation of our dominant position in Japan of paramount importance to U.S. security." Defense Secretary Louis Johnson joined the Joint Chiefs in declaring that

> unsettled political and military conditions and uncertain military action on the Asian continental areas near Japan . . . the highly unstable political and military situation in Taiwan and Southeast Asia . . . and the fact that a

treaty consistent with the terms of the armistice by which Japan surren-
dered could not at this time assure the denial of Japan's ultimate exploitation by the USSR or assure her orientation toward the western powers
made it important to postpone a peace settlement.[44]

Truman's reluctance to resolve the dispute between State and Defense
left Japan policy adrift. Early in 1950, Acheson tried to appease the Joint
Cheifs and Defense Secretary Johnson by endorsing limited Japanese rearmament and resumption of military production. Like MacArthur, he
would insist that Tokyo accept the basing of modest American forces for an
indefinite period after a treaty came into effect. The secretary of state even
proposed linking an end of the Occupation to a "Pacific collective security
arrangement" that included Japan, the Philippines, Australia, and New
Zealand.

Failure to move forward, Acheson warned Truman, would encourage
the Soviet Union to "concentrate its attention on China and Southeast
Asia," creating a puppet empire to blackmail Japan. But Acheson's warning did not sway the president. Right through June 1950, Defense officials
refused even to concede that most Japanese wanted the Occupation to end.
"The only propaganda for a peace treaty," they told Acheson in April,
"came out of the Department of State." To prevent any changes in Japan
that might inhibit "offensive operations against the Soviets in the event of
war," military planners promoted a scheme to allow Tokyo greater home
rule while leaving Occupation forces in place.[45]

In February 1950, China and the Soviet Union signed a friendship pact
pledging, among other things, to counter "aggressive action on the part of
Japan or any other state which should unite with Japan, directly or indirectly, in acts of aggression." Few in Washington considered the possibility
that Moscow and Beijing really feared a revival of Japanese militarism.
Instead, they interpreted the Communist pact as an attempt to intimidate
Japan and drive out the Americans. The Sino-Soviet alliance undermined
those predicting an early split between Moscow and Beijing and was used
to justify prolonging the Occupation.

That same month, Senator Joseph McCarthy, a Wisconsin Republican,
leveled his first public attacks on an allegedly subversive clique within the
State Department responsible for the "loss" of China and appeasement of
Communism in Asia. To defend his flanks, Acheson reassigned his friend
and frequent conservative target, the assistant secretary for Far Eastern
Affairs, W. Walton Butterworth, as ambassador to Sweden. He named
Undersecretary of State Dean Rusk, who enjoyed good relations with Congress and the Pentagon, as his principal adviser on Asia. In a further effort
to soothe congressional critics, Acheson recruited Republican foreign policy spokesman John Foster Dulles as his adviser on Japan.

Compared to Acheson, Rusk and Dulles advocated more vigorous support for Taiwan. Acheson had appointed them in part to convince the
Defense Department to compromise over Japan. Dulles agreed on the need

to end the Occupation quickly. He favored resolving security questions through a bilateral defense treaty and a Pacific pact. Unless the United States induced Tokyo to align itself freely with the West, Dulles argued, Japan would prove a useless ally irrespective of how many military bases the Pentagon extracted.[46]

Dulles's appointment coincided with a Japanese initiative to harness American interest in recovery and cold war cooperation into a peace settlement. Yoshida Shigeru, like most Japanese, longed for the early restoration of sovereignty. However, bureaucratic infighting among American policymakers delayed a settlement. Unresolved questions about Soviet participation in a peace conference, rearmament, and whether to establish permanent American bases in Japan proved especially contentious.

As strongly as most American planners hoped to anchor Japan to the anti-Communist West, most Japanese aspired to at least nominal neutrality in the cold war and concentration on economic recovery. This required that Japan avoid large-scale rearmament, reach a peace settlement that included China and the Soviet Union, and prevent or minimize the presence of American bases on its territory. Although a fervent anti-Communist, Yoshida largely shared these sentiments. To the fury of the Joint Chiefs of Staff, so did Occupation Commander General Douglas MacArthur.

By April 1950, however, Yoshida recognized that the Truman administration, Congress, and the American military establishment saw matters differently. Although the prime minister and his fellow conservatives did not fear external Communist aggression, they worried a great deal about alienating their patron and losing the economic assistance only the United States could provide.

A year before, Chinese Communist leader Mao Zedong coined a phrase in his effort to woo Soviet support while maintaining some freedom of action. China, he declared, would "lean to one side" in the cold war. Like Mao, Yoshida hoped to hasten an end to the Occupation and promote recovery by leaning toward the United States. Prudence, however, dictated that Japan not embrace its patron too closely. In 1947, Japanese leaders broached the idea of leasing bases in Okinawa and the Bonin Islands to the United States in return for a peace settlement. But the Joint Chiefs demanded military facilities within Japan and State Department planners considered it too early to end the Occupation.

In April 1950, Yoshida attempted to break the deadlock. He told American diplomat Cloyce Huston that despite the public's support for "neutralism," he recognized the value of American protection even if it meant providing bases on the home islands. Although rightists and leftists would accuse him of bowing to Washington, the prime minister "humorously" recalled his patron's humble origin. Just as a weak America eventually dominated Great Britain, he quipped, "If Japan becomes a colony of the United States, it will also eventually become the stronger." He offered to accept "whatever practical arrangement the United States might consider necessary" to end the Occupation.[47]

Since MacArthur forbade Yoshida to negotiate directly with Washington on security matters, he had to bypass SCAP. Yoshida used the ruse of sending three delegates (personal aide Shirasu Jiro, Finance Minister Ikeda Hayato, and Miyazawa Kiichi, an aide to Ikeda) to Washington ostensibly to discuss economic issues with Joseph Dodge. Although it was the most important Japanese mission to visit Washington since 1941, Occupation rules limiting yen-dollar exchange made it difficult for the men to scrape together enough dollars for the trip. Sympathetic SCAP personnel helped by listing the group as an "education mission" entitled to discounted hotel rooms ($7 a night for a double) in Washington.[48] In the United States, Ikeda conveyed Yoshida's proposal:

> The Japanese government herein formally expresses its desire to conclude a peace treaty with the United States as early as possible. In the case of such a peace treaty being concluded, the Japanese government thinks it will be necessary to station American forces in Japan in order to preserve the security of Japan and the Asian area. If it is difficult for the United States to make such a request, the Japanese government itself is prepared to make the offer.

By allowing foreign bases on its soil, Ikeda noted, Japan would incur Soviet and Chinese wrath. Consequently, he and Yoshida anguished at rumors that Washington considered "writing off" such areas as Taiwan, South Korea, and Indochina. All, they argued, must be defended as Japan's outlying security zone.

An assertion of American resolve would solve several problems. Within Japan itself, the deteriorating economy had boosted the Communist Party in the 1949 Diet election. Early in 1950, the Soviet Union and China formally recognized Ho Chi Minh's insurgent movement battling French forces in Vietnam. The South Korea regime faced challenges from the hostile communist North and a bloc of southern legislators opposed to the autocratic rule of President Syngman Rhee. The Communist victory in China magnified these events and led Japanese conservatives to question whether the United States would "draw the line" in Asia as it had in Europe.

Ikeda tweaked American anxiety by predicting that Moscow might tempt Japan by offering Tokyo a generous "peace treaty in advance of the United States." If the Soviets offered to "return Sakhalin and the Kuriles" (islands seized in 1945) and if the Americans refused to relinquish control of Okinawa, it could drive Japanese opinion far to the left. He urged Washington to preempt the Soviets by submitting a quick and generous settlement. The Japanese were "desperately looking for firm ground." They needed to know "just what and when and where the United States would stand firm [in Asia], and particularly with respect to Japan."[49]

Yoshida hoped to ease Japan back into the world community without incurring the costs of rearmament or alienating the United States. In exchange for the grant of bases, Japan would secure protection and access to the world's largest market. American diplomats appreciated Yoshida's "official" recognition of the need to choose sides in the cold war and believed he asked only fair market value for Japan's cooperation.[50]

Assistant Secretary of State Dean Rusk promptly incorporated the Yoshida/Ikeda message into an appeal to Dean Acheson and Harry Truman that the United States vigorously defend Taiwan, South Korea, and Indochina—all former parts of Japan's empire—against Communist encroachment. Given the "active public discussion in Japan" about the value of an alliance with the United States, Rusk argued in May 1950, Washington must show the Japanese "just what and when and where the United States would stand firm."[51]

Rusk, like Dulles and Dodge, believed the Japanese would accept something close to the State Department draft treaty as "the best they can get under the circumstances and as quickly as possible." A Japanese government White Paper issued on June 1 revealed a willingness to conclude a "separate" peace treaty with the United States even if Moscow and Beijing refused to sign.[52]

During May and June, Dulles and Rusk floated a package deal by treaty opponents. They hinted that if Jiang Jieshi were deposed on Taiwan—perhaps by an American-supported coup—the State Department might then agree to defend the island. This, along with increased military aid to Indochina, Rusk and Dulles speculated, might move Secretary of Defense Johnson and the Joint Chiefs to support a Japanese settlement. Boldly "draw[ing] the line" around China would reassure those engaged in an "active public discussion in Japan" about "who will win in the Struggle of the Pacific."[53]

From Tokyo, MacArthur waded into the debate. Since losing influence over Japan policy in 1948, the general had sided with Republican critics of Truman and Acheson's decision against defending Taiwan. He warned that Communist control of the island (an "unsinkable aircraft carrier and submarine tender") would jeopardize the entire Pacific defense perimeter. Attempting to pressure Acheson to defend Taiwan, MacArthur warned that if the Chinese Communists took the island, he could no longer advocate the "urgent need" to end the Japanese Occupation.[54]

In mid-June, the State and Defense Departments dispatched rival fact-finding missions to Tokyo. Dulles led one delegation while Secretary of Defense Louis Johnson and Joint Chiefs of Staff chairman General Omar Bradley headed the other. The latter carried a checklist of reasons for *not* ending the Occupation regardless of concessions made by treaty advocates. For example, since Pentagon analysts concluded that the Soviets would respect a neutral Japan, Bradley and Johnson labeled neutralism a primary danger. Neutrality would lead to a natural accommodation between Japan and China. In case of war, it would render impossible utilizing Japan as an "active ally" in efforts to "end Russian domination of Manchuria and China" and roll back Communist influence in Asia. The Defense position opposed any treaty until Japan fully rearmed "or until the world situation radically changes," two conditions unlikely to occur soon.[55]

Dulles and his staff (John Allison, Maxwell Hamilton, John Howard, and Robert Feary) worried far more about Japan's political and economic viability than its value as a military platform. In their minds, making Japan an "example" to Asians of the material rewards that flowed from cooperation with the West far outweighed the value of securing additional airfields. The principal threat stemmed from the fact that Japan's "natural sources of raw material" and markets lay in the "communized parts of Asia." Even though Dulles and his aides saw potential value in a limited "counteroffensive" against China and North Korea, they considered it more important to concentrate American energy on developing "outside of the communized area adequate sources of raw materials and markets for Japanese industry." Necessity justified allowing Japan limited trade with China, but securing Southeast Asia was vital lest "dependence on Communist-controlled areas . . . expose Japan to successful Communist-blackmail at a subsequent date."

As he flew toward Tokyo, Dulles pondered the danger he saw in the military's plan to push Japanese rearmament and use Japan "as a major *offensive* air base." "Overmilitarization," as he called it, slighted the long-term interests of both Japan and America. If, on the other hand, the United States showed a determination to "stand fast" in Korea, Taiwan, and Southeast Asia, where real military threats existed, Washington could protect Japan with merely a "*defensive* guarantee, stiffened by a skeleton U.S. force" and limited Japanese rearmament.[56]

The split between the American delegations became public when both reached Japan on June 17. At an impromptu briefing, Louis Johnson denounced the "State Department crowd" in terms one diplomat called "shocking." Declaring that Japan could only be trusted so long as American forces remained in control, Johnson dismissed Dulles as an "impractical man who approached the world's problems with a religious, moral and pacifistic attitude."[57]

After more than a year of sniping from the periphery, MacArthur savored the role of mediator between the competing delegations. He met separately with each group, listened to their arguments, and proposed a deal giving both group partial satisfaction. He urged linking an end to the Occupation of Japan with a commitment to defend Taiwan. Like Dulles, he believed the two issues overlapped since maintaining an anti-Communist outpost on the contested island would deflect Chinese wrath away from Japan and Southeast Asia and reassure Japanese conservatives that the United States would protect its allies.[58]

Johnson and Bradley disputed MacArthur's contention that if Truman agreed to defend Taiwan, it would not be necessary to retain substantial American forces in Japan or compel Japanese rearmament. Dulles, however, agreed with the general's outlook. He also followed MacArthur's advice that he consult with a "large cross section of Japanese leaders, foreign diplomats, businessmen and others with views about the treaty." Not surprisingly, most of these contacts endorsed MacArthur's proposals.

During his final days in Tokyo (after fighting began in Korea), Dulles received a private message purportedly from the emperor transmitted through

Newsweek reporter Compton Packenham. The journalist had grown up in Japan and boasted of his ties to many purged politicians. Packenham's boss, *Newsweek* foreign editor Harry Kern, had organized the American Council on Japan. The emperor urged Dulles to consult "older people, the majority of whom have been purged" because of "their alleged former militaristic outlook" but who, in light of the Korean crisis, might provide "valuable advice and assistance to the Americans." During this and later visits, Kern and Packenham arranged meetings between Dulles and Japan's old guard.[59]

When Dulles urged Yoshida to placate the American military by rebuilding a small army—in the 100,000 man range—the prime minister retorted that the new constitution as well as public opinion made this impossible. Diplomat William Sebald complained that the "puckish" Yoshida spoke in "parables" and refused to "talk sense." But Yoshida encouraged Dulles to confer with MacArthur, indicating he would be guided by the general's advice. MacArthur, with whom Yoshida claimed to have a "secret understanding," told Dulles that instead of raising an army, Japan should make its security contribution to the free world by rebuilding its munitions industry to assist the "reconstruction of American armaments."

Speaking with Bradley and Johnson, MacArthur expanded Yoshida's offer of base rights. In exchange for granting American forces virtually "unrestricted" base rights throughout Japan, Washington should offer Tokyo a peace treaty and pay $300 million per year in new aid to balance Japan's trade deficit. MacArthur also proposed diluting the concept of Japan's "neutrality," possibly by creating a small self-defense force.

Although these concessions appeared to meet the demands of the Joint Chiefs, Bradley and Johnson refused to budge and left Tokyo determined to block a settlement. Dulles, who complained that Yoshida would not publicly commit to rearmament but wanted "protection from the United States, preferably from long range," departed a few days later still supporting a peace treaty.[60]

On June 25, 1950 (June 24, Washington time), North Korean troops crossed the 38th parallel into South Korea. This assault served as a catalyst that transformed U.S. policy throughout East Asia. Within a few days, President Truman sent troops to Korea, ordered the Seventh Fleet to protect Taiwan, and expanded military and economic assistance to French Indochina and the Philippines. The resources mobilized by the United States and the militarization of its Asia policy dramatically affected Japan. Within fifteen months, the United States agreed to end the Occupation while massive defense procurements lifted Japanese industry from its postwar torpor. The war in Korea set the stage for Japan's economic "miracle."

Less than five years after unconditionally defeating Japan, the United States had not only committed substantial resources to its recovery, but began bidding for Tokyo's loyalty by defending parts of the former Co-Prosperity Sphere against the Red peril. As Yoshida predicted, skillful diplomacy and playing the part of a "good loser" could be the next best thing to outright victory.

2 *THE KOREAN WAR*

AND THE PEACE WITH

JAPAN, 1950–52

WASHINGTON interpreted the North Korean attack of June 25, 1950, on the Republic of Korea as ultimately directed against Japan. As Dulles commented during the first months of fighting, the "communist offensive in Korea was probably aimed at getting control over Japan, for had Korea been conquered Japan would have fallen without an open struggle." The Korean attack made it "more important, rather than less important" to conclude a treaty. The "very fact" that Communist aggression in Korea sought to "check positive and constructive action" in Japan proved the "importance to take such action." Finally, Dulles warned, if progress toward a peace treaty stalled "because of total preoccupation with the Korean war . . . we may lose in Japan more than we can gain in Korea."[1]

When President Truman sent the Seventh Fleet to protect Taiwan, boosted aid to Indochina, and committed American troops to the Korean peninsula, Japan received a critical economic stimulus and emerged as the locus of the American defense strategy in Asia. State and Defense officials recognized that the Korean War would result in American forces playing an expanded role in and around Japan. MacArthur's June 23 proposal for "unrestricted" base rights became the reference point for security plans. The trick, as Dulles saw it, was to get the military establishment to endorse "in a form as inoffensive as possible to the Japanese," an arrangement giving the United States "broad power . . . to place military forces wherever in Japan the United States may determine to be desirable."

Dulles assured Secretary of Defense Louis Johnson that the United States should have "the right to maintain in Japan as much force as we wanted, anywhere we wanted for as long as we wanted." This, Johnson

[31]

and the Joint Chiefs noted happily, provided a basis to "get together and go places." On September 7, Acheson and Johnson agreed that once the "situation in Korea" had been resolved favorably, a settlement with Japan negotiated by the State Department should take effect. An accompanying bilateral security pact would give American forces virtually unrestricted rights in Japan. The United States would not be obliged to defend or retain its forces in Japan, but could intervene to suppress riots or civil disorder if the Japanese government so requested. This memorandum, approved by the National Security Council the next day as NSC 60/1, endorsed Japan's "right to self-defense." On July 8, MacArthur had already taken the first step toward rearmament by ordering Yoshida to create a 75,000-man National Police Reserve.[2]

Among American officials, only George Kennan—now the largely ceremonial "counselor" in the State Department—questioned the wisdom of integrating a rearmed Japan into a military alliance. Disputing the prevailing view that the United States must roll back Communist influence by unifying all Korea and rearming Japan, Kennan urged Acheson to approach Moscow with a secret offer. Put simply, Washington should "consent to the neutralization and demilitarization of Japan (except for strong internal police forces)" if "the Russians would agree to a termination of the Korean War." This advice, as well as his warning that MacArthur would cause the administration untold grief, was ignored.[3]

Dulles deeply resented Kennan's meddling and did little more than inform friends and adversaries of American intentions in Japan. Foreign input, he made clear, would be confined to signing an American-drafted peace treaty. Even friendly states such as Great Britain, Australia, the Philippines, and New Zealand resented the lack of consultation and the absence of military and economic controls on Tokyo envisioned in the American plan.

When the British complained that renewed Japanese dumping of cheap goods would threaten their position in Southeast Asia, the State Department responded with words familiar to American business leaders in subsequent decades. The British should "face the realities of the situation and be prepared to meet Japanese competition if Japan is to be kept oriented toward the West and free from Communist pressures."

As a courtesy to a wartime ally, Dulles met several times with Soviet UN Ambassador Jacob Malik. He dismissed Moscow's contention that member states of the moribund Far Eastern Commission should draft a peace settlement. Since this would never happen, Dulles argued that the Soviets "would lose nothing" but might win some goodwill (such as favorable consideration of Moscow's claim to some of the Kurile Islands seized from Japan in 1945) by "adhering to the type of treaty" Washington proposed.[4]

When Dulles broached his plan to Australian Foreign Minister Sir Percy Spender, diplomat John Allison recalled that Spender's face became so red it seemed he "would burst a blood vessel." Bitterly recounting

Japan's aggression, the Australian questioned why Dulles would "propose a treaty with no restrictions on the remilitarization of Japan." Along with New Zealand and the Philippines, Australia wanted "firm guarantees" that the United States would offer them protection "against Japanese aggression."[5]

Dulles favored the idea of a multilateral Pacific defense alliance, but insisted that nothing slow progress toward a settlement with Japan. Even after November 1950, when Chinese troops inflicted a humiliating defeat on American forces in North Korea, Dulles persisted. Unless Washington moved quickly, he argued, Japan would respond to events in Korea either by stiffening its peace terms or sliding toward neutrality. Already, security provisions he could previously have extracted from Japan "merely by suggesting them" now had "to be negotiated for and obtained as fully as possible." Truman agreed and on January 10 elevated Dulles to the rank of ambassador with full power to negotiate treaties with Japan, the Philippines, Australia, and New Zealand.[6]

In Japan, the Treaty Bureau advising the prime minister recommended pursuing a settlement with all wartime adversaries, including China and the Soviet Union, and remaining unarmed. While appealing in principal, Yoshida recognized this as unrealistic. In January 1951, he approved a plan to negotiate a settlement with the United States that restored sovereignty, contained few political or economic restrictions, and sanctioned the right of self-defense.

Yoshida predicted that a security pact posed more difficulties than a peace treaty. Years later, the prime minister's daughter explained that her father considered the security treaty with Washington a necessary, if transitional, evil. "It was the only thing that could be done at the time," she remarked, "yet he always knew that it was a very unnatural position for us to be in."

In October 1950, presumably as a bargaining ploy, Yoshida revived the old idea of leasing military bases on the Bonin and Ryukyu Islands, rather than in Japan proper. Although the prime minister knew this was unacceptable, he may have raised the idea only to give in and then bargain for slower rearmament.[7]

Before Dulles returned to Tokyo at the end of January, *Newsweek* editor Harry Kern offered him some insights into Japanese thinking. The "protestations about the disarmament clauses of their constitution and their desire for perpetual peace" voiced by Yoshida were "made largely for bargaining purposes," Kern insisted. He worried, however, that the Japanese might "overstate their case" and somehow convince Dulles to allow them "disarmed neutrality." Kern saw "no harm in letting them have the fun of doing a little bargaining," so long as Dulles knew when to crack the whip.

Kern also reported that *Newsweek's* correspondent in Tokyo, Compton Packenham, planned to follow up on "the suggestion conveyed . . . last summer from the Emperor" to bring Dulles together with Japanese businessmen and veteran politicians. Kern even undertook some lobbying, telling Dulles that James L. Kauffman, fellow member of the American Council on Japan and a lawyer representing Japanese firms, had a message from the Tokyo Shibaura Electric Company, the "General Electric of Japan." The company had "great interest in obtaining contracts from the United States for the production of electrical equipment useful in our war effort," Kern reported. Other Japanese wanted to speak to Dulles about making "use of some of their intelligence agents who formerly operated in China."[8]

Kern's advice found further expression in a feature run by *Newsweek* before Dulles's departure for Japan. The magazine's cover pictured a smiling, elegantly dressed Yoshida Shigeru standing in scholarly repose beside a bouquet of chrysanthemums. Titled "Late Enemy into Latest Ally?," the article stressed the importance of assuring that in the coming "world showdown," Japan "cast its lot with the West, not the Communist East."

The special report, probably written with Dulles's assistance, outlined the likely terms of the peace and security treaties. It praised Japan's industrial prowess, the bravery and social cohesion of its people, and concluded that these traits made the former enemy the "most formidable nation in the Far East." Two dramatic maps summarized what the magazine called the key outstanding issues. One showed how American air and naval forces operating from this "northern anchor" could dominate much of China and Siberia. The second, superimposed on an outline of the Co-Prosperity Sphere, described Japan's critical need to "look to Southeast Asia" as a replacement for the coal, iron, soybeans, and other raw materials formerly imported from China. Because this new trade would develop slowly, Japan would remain dependent on American markets for some time. Also, *Newsweek* advised, the threat of Communism "nearly everywhere . . . in Southeast Asia" required "something like a American-Japanese Alliance" to defend that region.[9]

Dulles made conciliatory remarks on his arrival in Tokyo on January 25. "We look upon Japan as a party to be consulted," he declared, not as a vanquished nation to be "dictated to by the victors." In private, he told his aides that the "principal question" to be answered was "do we get the right to station as many troops as we want where we want and for as long as we want or do we not?" The entourage (including Robert Feary and John Allison from State and Assistant Secretary of the Army Earl Johnson, General Carter Magruder, and Colonel Stanton Babcock from Defense) spent the next two and one-half weeks pressing for an answer.[10]

During a discussion with Yoshida on January 29, Dulles learned that American military reversals in Korea had, as he feared, stiffened the prime minister's spine. Yoshida spoke of canceling Occupation reforms that had liberalized family and business laws and stressed Japan's need for additional American capital. Dulles found the prime minister's remarks about Japan's "long-standing necessity" for trade with China ("war is war" but "trade is trade") along with his opinion that Japanese businessmen could serve as a "fifth column for democracy against the communists" especially vexing.

Yoshida seemed to be "throwing out bargaining hints," Dulles complained, but refused to discuss "broad principles." The approach struck him as "inane, naive and unrealistic." Since America's allies demanded tighter economic controls on Japan, he told Yoshida not to press for concessions. Dulles wanted to know what kind of military contribution (he now thought in terms of a 300,000-man army) Japan could make to "the free world." Yoshida infuriated Dulles by insisting that the threat of "underground" militarism, economic weakness, and public opposition made any "precipitate rearmament" inadvisable. (To make sure the American took this seriously, Yoshida secretly encouraged anti-rearmament demonstrations during Dulles's visit.) Put off by this refusal to make "at least a token contribution" to collective security, Dulles left the meeting muttering about Yoshida's "puff ball" performance.[11]

Yoshida turned to MacArthur for help. Knowing that the general opposed large-scale rearmament, he would tell Dulles that since Japan faced no credible invasion threat, it had no need for major ground forces. Instead, Washington should utilize Japan's "capacity for military production" and trained manpower on behalf of the "free world." Dulles promptly received from SCAP and Japanese sources a list of idle defense plants ready to start production.

On January 31, Dulles and Yoshida reached partial agreement on several matters. Japan and the United States would cooperate as "equal partners" by allowing American forces remaining in Japan to defend it against attack. As its contribution to collective security, Japan would begin gradual rearmament. Technical details would be worked out at the staff level.[12]

Subsequent discussions revealed contrasting priorities. The Americans saw a peace treaty as a worthy goal, but considered a security pact the foundation of future relations. It must provide extensive base facilities, commit Japan to establishing at least a small army, and take effect as soon as the Occupation ended. Japan could not meet these obligations simply by expanding its police force or boosting military production. Until Yoshida accepted his position, Dulles declined to discuss the terms of the peace treaty.

Unlike the Americans, most Japanese considered the restoration of national sovereignty a primary objective. To obtain it, they would swallow the bitter pill of a military pact, preferably one that made reference to the United Nations and had limited duration. Ideally, it would commit the United States to defend Japan without requiring extensive bases or large numbers of American soldiers. Nearly all Japanese opposed raising a large army or making the armed forces available for service abroad. Despite his warnings about latent militarism, Yoshida did not object to the principle of rearmament so much as its pace and direction. He insisted that economic recovery come first and that Japan's troops not become American surrogates charged with policing Asia.[13]

To placate Dulles, the prime minister delivered an unsigned memorandum to the American delegation on February 3 in which he pledged to create a 50,000-man army separate from the National Police Reserve after the peace treaty took effect. This new force would coordinate its planning with U.S. authorities; its modest size and flexible timetable made it unsuitable for early foreign deployment—say, in Korea.[14]

Dulles accepted this proposal as a token of good faith and shortly after receiving it presented the Japanese with a six-page draft of a peace treaty imposing few controls and demanding no reparations. It specified Japan's right to self-defense and stipulated that the Ryukyu and Bonin Islands be placed under American control in a sort of trusteeship. Yoshida described the terms as "magnanimous and fair."[15]

On February 6, Dulles handed the Japanese a reworked draft that called for a simple collective defense agreement that relegated all contentious details concerning bases and the status of American forces to an administrative agreement to be negotiated later and subject to approval by the Japanese cabinet rather than the Diet. In effect, the Diet would vote on the less controversial peace and security pacts before learning the details of the more intrusive administrative agreement.[16]

Although Dulles ignored Yoshida's request to use the treaty discussions as a cover for overturning liberal reforms, he nodded in that direction. On February 6, he conferred with several veteran politicians hosted by *Newsweek*'s Compton Packenham. The group included prominent purgees such as Hatoyama Ichiro and Admiral Nomura Kichisaburo, Japan's representative in Washington at the time of the Pearl Harbor attack. Dulles's mere presence at this gathering signaled a changed attitude toward members of the old regime.

Negotiations culminated on February 9 when Yoshida and Dulles initialed five documents. These included a provisional description of the peace treaty, a draft collective self-defense agreement, a draft agreement permitting U.S./UN forces to utilize Japanese facilities in support of Korean operations, a draft status of forces agreement, and an agreement regarding services and facilities that Japan would provide to American forces.

The two parties decided that Yoshida would "request" the United States to maintain "land, air and sea forces in and about Japan" for use anywhere in the Far East. These forces were not required to defend Japan, could be withdrawn at any time, or used to suppress internal disturbances. Without setting specific targets, Japan pledged to assume "increasing responsibility for the defense of its homeland against direct and indirect aggression." The security treaty could be terminated only by mutual consent. Yoshida later claimed that Dulles informally agreed that rearmament would depend on the pace of economic recovery and future aid.[17]

On February 11, Dulles flew to Manila and then to New Zealand and Australia. America's three closest Pacific allies voiced misgivings over the proposed settlement. In addition to military controls, Filipinos insisted that Japan pay war damages and reparations. Dulles suggested then and in later talks that Japan might agree to process raw materials from the Philippines at no charge in lieu of reparations. If this formula were applied generally, Dulles hoped it "might help to reopen a channel for trade with the Philippines, Malaya, Burma and other reparations claimant countries," thereby helping Japanese industry. This trade could initiate the regional flow of raw materials and result "in an overall advantage to Japan." To allay Filipino security fears, Dulles supported a Washington–Manila bilateral defense pact.[18]

The ambassador's reception in Canberra and Wellington resembled the one he encountered in Manila. To officials in New Zealand and Australia, Dulles admitted, "Russia looks a long way off" while "resentment, fear and hatred of Japan was a daily reality." He proposed to counter their anxiety over future Japanese aggression with the expedient of another defense pact. Although the subsequent ANZUS treaty pledged the United States to consult and cooperate in case of attack, neither it nor the Philippine pact included automatic defense guarantees like those contained in NATO.[19]

The treaty momentum continued even after President Truman dismissed General MacArthur from his Korean and Japanese commands on April 11, 1951. Truman had considered relieving the general as early as the previous August when he had publicly called for attacks on the Chinese mainland. MacArthur's criticism of administration strategy grew increasingly shrill after Chinese forces entered the Korean conflict in November 1950. Like Truman, the Joint Chiefs gradually lost faith in the general's leadership, judgment, and motives. In March 1951, as the battle line stabilized, MacArthur sabotaged a peace initiative toward China. By April, the president and the Joint Chiefs feared he might provoke an expanded conflict with China to justify use of the atomic weapons they intended to transfer to the Pacific in order to deter Chinese or Soviet escalation of the war.

The command crisis became a partisan issue on April 5 when Republican Congressman Joseph Martin of Massachusetts released a letter from MacArthur critical of administration efforts to limit the scope of the war. Declaring there was "no substitute for victory," the general tacitly endorsed Martin's charge that Truman's limited war strategy made him responsible for the "murder" of thousands of American soldiers. This incident provided a pretext for Truman to dismiss "the Big General in the Far East." Six days later, on April 11, the president named General Matthew Ridgway commander in both Korea and Japan.[20]

Although MacArthur intimated that his "removal was [part of] a plot in Washington" to "hand over" Taiwan to "Red China," followed by the Philippines and Japan, the dismissal had less impact in Tokyo than Americans feared. Japanese leaders realized that since 1948 MacArthur had played a much diminished role in setting Occupation policy. Finance Ministry official Miyazawa Kiichi reassured Ralph Reid, an assistant to Joseph Dodge, that "MacArthur's discharge did not really shake Japanese minds," since they did not expect it to "bring about nor is [it] a result of, any change in U.S. diplomatic policy." Many Japanese felt "sorry for MacArthur," but they "recognized that the peace treaty business is in the secure hand of Mr.

Dulles." Miyazawa predicted that the general's recall would cause more of a "showdown" in Washington than in Tokyo. "MacArthur," he observed sharply, "landed in the Philippines in 1944, Japan in 1945, and now is about to land in the United States! How do you like it?"[21]

The change in Occupation commanders accelerated the conservative drift in Japanese domestic politics. On April 9, Yoshida had sought MacArthur's "advice" on modifying eleven laws and nine executive orders issued since 1945. When the prime minister met Ridgway on April 18, he claimed (contrary to fact) that MacArthur had consented "in principle" to amend reforms "at variance with the actual needs of the country." Yoshida proposed to centralize police forces, weaken safeguards for accused criminals, revise the education system, relax anti-monopoly laws, reestablish men as legal heads of households, and institute primogeniture for inheritance of small farms and businesses.[22]

Although the State Department blocked most of these changes, Ridgway showed his lack of attachment to early Occupation reforms and his concern about ensuring cooperation from the Japanese government. In May 1951, he allowed Yoshida to appoint an advisory committee to reexamine all laws enacted since August 1945. This Ordinance Review Committee proposed changes to reform statutes, many of which were implemented after the Occupation ended. In 1952, the Diet also passed an Anti-Subversive Activities Act modeled closely on U.S. legislation. Ridgway relaxed purge orders that barred career politicians and military officers from public life. During 1951–52, nearly 200,000 former officers were de-purged. Prominent conservative politicians, including Hatoyama Ichiro, Ishibashi Tanzan, and Kishi Nobusuke had their political rights restored. These rivals of Yoshida reentered politics and eventually succeeded him in office. Curtailment of the purge permitted many lesser-known politicians to resume their careers. In the first post-Occupation Diet election held in October 1952, 42 percent of those seated in the lower house had been purgees.[23]

In the wake of MacArthur's recall, Truman and Acheson sent Dulles back to Tokyo "to reassure Japanese leaders of our intentions." Before accepting Truman's request, he cleared the mission with Republican leaders. Senators Taft, Smith, Wiley, and Milliken told Dulles he should serve as Truman's emissary only if he could guarantee that the Chinese Communist government would not be a party to the peace settlement with Japan or be permitted to take control of Taiwan. Former Republican presidential candidate Thomas Dewey told Dulles he "was the only person who could perhaps salvage the situation in Japan." After securing his right flank, Dulles agreed to "help salvage something" so long as he was not set up as the "fall guy" in a Democratic plan to "appease the communist aggressors or abandon the Asiatic off-shore island chain."[24]

In Tokyo, the American envoy reassured Yoshida that "U.S. policies toward Japan have firm bipartisan support and are unchanged." He listed points in the treaty draft that elicited opposition. The British wanted to mandate the return of Taiwan to China. The Philippines and some other nations demanded reparations from Japan and military controls. The Pentagon insisted on a more explicit right for American forces in Japan to fight in Korea. Dulles and Yoshida agreed to minor modifications, but the basic outline reached the previous February held. With Yoshida on board, Dulles set about calming America's restive allies.[25]

Convincing the British to drop their demand that China participate in the peace settlement presented a major hurdle. Dulles courted London by making small changes concerning the payment of war damages and restricting Japan's prewar rights to sell textiles in the Congo basin. Without specifying a final amount, Dulles committed Japan to negotiate reparations payments with claimants after the treaty came into effect. He flattered Prime Minister Clement Attlee by asking Britain to co-host the peace conference. But he would neither invite China to a peace conference nor surrender Taiwan.

He argued that since Chinese views were merely a "parrot-like echo of what the Soviet Union has said," the United States could "look after the interests of Communist China a lot better than Mao Tse-tung can." America had been China's friend "for a hundred and fifty years" while Mao was "nothing but a puppet." Whether or not Dulles believed this, he sensed that with Chinese troops fighting Americans in Korea, any opening to Beijing would risk catastrophe when the Japanese treaty came before the Senate.[26]

In June, while Dulles visited London for talks with Foreign Minister Herbert Morrison, he again vetoed a proposal to reconsider Taiwan's status as part of the Japanese peace treaty. Rather than fight over Chinese representation, Dulles proposed that neither Chinese regime, Communist or Nationalist, be invited to the peace conference. Instead, Japan would be allowed to sign a separate peace agreement with either Taipei or Beijing after signing the multilateral treaty. But, as Dulles admitted, "the formula proposed as regards China would almost inevitably lead Japan to align herself with United States policy" and cut a deal with Taiwan.[27]

The Joint Chiefs of Staff, after sitting on the draft defense treaty and administrative agreement for nearly six months, raised last minute objections. Since neither Japan nor the United States were required to defend the other, the Joint Chiefs wanted the pact to be known as a "security treaty" instead of a collective self-defense treaty. To remove restraints on operations against China or the Soviet Union, the Joint Chiefs altered the so-called Far Eastern clause to state that American forces in Japan "may be utilized to contribute to the maintenance of international peace and security in the Far East and to the security of Japan against armed attack from without." This allowed U.S. forces to do pretty much as they pleased.[28]

On August 22, two weeks before the scheduled opening of the San Francisco conference, the Joint Chiefs submitted additional objections to the administrative agreement. To limit the reach of Japan's legal system, the Joint Chiefs were determined to retain legal jurisdiction over American troops accused of crimes against Japanese off base or while off duty. Dulles and his aides condemned this as a throwback to the nineteenth-century "unequal treaties" and possibly a ruse to prolong the Occupation. The time had come, Dulles argued, for the Pentagon to stop regarding the Japanese as "defeated enemies and as orientals having qualities inferior to those of occidentals." Like the China question, the administrative agreement became an obstacle for Dulles to overcome.[29]

In mid-August 1951, the United States published the text of the draft treaty and joined Great Britain in inviting over fifty nations to attend a September 4 "signing conference" in San Francisco. India and Burma, angered by the exclusion of China and a rule forbidding amendment of the text, refused to attend. Dulles and Acheson were startled when the Soviet Union, Poland, and Czechoslovakia accepted. Determined to bar any disruption of the proceedings once the conference began, Secretary of State Acheson, in his capacity as conference president, overruled Soviet proposals to invite China or open the treaty for amendment. Acheson even exercised veto rights over Yoshida's speech. After deciding that the draft the prime minister intended to deliver called unwanted attention to several controversial issues, Acheson had an aide (William Sebald) rewrite the address.[30]

On September 8, Japan and forty-eight other nations signed the treaty essentially as presented. The Soviet Union and its two allies refused. The treaty ended the Occupation, restored sovereignty, and pledged Japan to negotiate reparations agreements with claimants. Tokyo's "residual sovereignty" over the Ryukyu Islands was confirmed, but it had to surrender administrative control to these and several other small islands to the United States. The treaty affirmed Japan's right of collective self-defense.

In a private ceremony that same day, Acheson, Dulles, two U.S. senators, and Yoshida Shigeru signed a security treaty along with a subsidiary agreement that authorized U.S. forces to use bases in Japan for Korean operations. A few days before, the United States reached defense pacts with the Philippines, Australia, and New Zealand. These agreements (supplemented by the SEATO treaty and pacts with Taiwan and Korea) formed the core of the American military presence in the Asia-Pacific region for a quarter-century.

Despite these achievements, Dulles faced additional obstacles, many placed in his path by the Pentagon, before completing the administrative agreement and gaining Senate ratification. Only half in jest, he told Truman and Acheson that "getting the [American] colonels out of their Japanese villas" would be the most impressive military victory over Japan since the Pearl Harbor attack. He feared the Defense Department would continue to raise objections to the treaties in order to "bargain for position" and get their way with the contested clauses of the administrative agreement. Dulles believed that the Japanese were prepared to accept many "burdensome and irksome conditions," but should not be forced to provide "extraterritorial privileges" to American forces. A Pentagon victory might well rouse the Japanese to eventually throw off their alliance with the

United States. "Treating the Japanese as inferiors" would convince Asians of the truth behind the Communist claim that Americans "find it congenitally impossible to deal with Orientals on a basis of respect and equality."[31]

Truman weakly pressed the Defense Department to moderate its position, but the military fought tenaciously. Assistant Secretary of State Dean Rusk, assigned the task of preparing a mutually acceptable text, spent three months sparring with Pentagon officials. In February 1951, he carried a draft to Tokyo where he spent an additional month negotiating with the Japanese. The document approved on February 28 gave the United States wide leeway in selecting several hundred post-Occupation facilities and bases. If the Japanese hesitated to grant leases on existing bases, American rights would be extended automatically. The United States retained jurisdiction over American personnel charged with criminal offenses against Japanese, although it promised to waive this right in special cases. The status of forces agreement was much less equal than those governing forces stationed in NATO countries. Japanese negotiators finally dug in their heels against demands that in time of crisis their security forces be placed under "combined command." They agreed merely to "consult."[32]

Even as Dulles and Rusk overcame objections from the Pentagon and the Japanese, the China issue flared up. Most Japanese resented American pressure to deal exclusively with Taiwan. As staunch an anti-Communist as Yoshida suggested that Japan should have some relationship, especially economic, with the People's Republic. Responding to questions in the Diet during October 1951 when the peace and security treaties came up for ratification, he declared that Japan eventually hoped to "conclude a peace treaty with China and the Soviet Union" and would "wait and watch" the course of events. Even if formal relations with China were delayed, Yoshida told a special committee of the upper house, he favored "opening trade relations with that country and of establishing a commercial office in Shanghai." He hoped such hints of flexibility would ease opposition and mobilize popular support behind the treaties.

As its defenders later admitted, the peace treaty served as a sweetener for the less equitable security treaty. The security treaty, in turn, screened criticism of the still more controversial administrative agreement that Yoshida planned to ratify by executive agreement. In the Diet, the Communists and Socialists opposed both treaties for failing to include China and the Soviet Union and sanctioning a military alliance with the United States. Within the conservative coalition, Yoshida's Liberals fell in line behind the prime minister. Democratic Party members supported the treaties with misgivings. "Pan-Asianists" among the Democrats preferred closer relations with China than the Americans sanctioned. They also favored a more independent military force and a security policy less subordinate to the United States.

Major Japanese business organizations endorsed both treaties, in large part because they saw them as prerequisites to trade, aid, and military orders. Public opinion polls revealed that while a majority of Japanese favored ratifying the peace treaty, many preferred making peace with all former enemies. About 43 percent approved of the security treaty, but nearly as many opposed its unequal terms and base provisions. In October 1951, nearly all conservative Diet members voted in favor of the two treaties while most Socialists were against them. The peace treaty passed 307 to 47 and the security pact won by a margin of 289 to 71.[33]

Although Yoshida's hint of flexibility on China muted some domestic criticism and pleased Great Britain (its Parliament approved the peace treaty on November 26), Taiwan's friends in the U.S. Senate became suspicious. In September, California Republican William Knowland and fifty-six colleagues sent Truman a letter declaring that they "would consider the recognition of Communist China by Japan or the negotiation of a bilateral treaty with the Communist regime to be adverse to the best interest of the people of both Japan and the United States."[34]

Dulles feared a Senate revolt if Yoshida made any gesture toward China. He also questioned Acheson's resolve. Before the Korean War, the secretary of state favored allowing Japan to trade with China. Dulles may have blamed Acheson for Britain's refusal to join the United States in pressing Japan to sign a treaty with Taiwan. During the San Francisco conference Senator H. Alexander Smith told Dulles he believed that Acheson had purposely "left the door open for the Japs to recognize and make a treaty with Communist China and not the Nationalists." Smith described Dulles as so "disturbed" by this prospect that they jointly warned Yoshida against pursuing any loopholes.[35]

Mindful of the Senate defeat of the Versailles Treaty that he had helped to negotiate as a young man, Dulles returned to Tokyo in December 1951. He brought along Alabama Democrat John Sparkman and Republican H. Alexander Smith of New Jersey, both members of the Senate Committee on Foreign Relations. Dulles told General Ridgway, British diplomat Sir Esler Dening, and Yoshida that Japan must adopt a China policy "generally compatible" with the United States policy of defending the "offshore island chain" stretching from Japan to the Philippines. Since Taiwan constituted a key element in this strategy, Japan must conclude a treaty with the Nationalist regime. As a concession to Yoshida's fear of being dragged into China's civil war, Dulles suggested that he need only recognize Nationalist authority in territory actually controlled by the Republic of China—in other words, Taiwan not the Chinese mainland.

The Americans accused the British of encouraging Yoshida's China heresy. They singled out diplomat Sir Esler Dening for trying to blunt "Japanese competition in the trade of Southeast Asia" by turning Tokyo toward "the Chinese mainland and the Soviet Union to the north." Yoshida told Senator Smith that the British encouraged Sino-Japanese trade so Tokyo "would not interfere . . . in Southeast Asia." Smith urged Dulles "to speak to [Yoshida] very plainly, pointing out that the United States was more powerful than Great Britain and could help Japan more in her economy and security."

Although Yoshida relented, he complained that Anglo-American conflict placed Japan in an awkward position. If he met Washington's demand to deal with Taiwan, the British might retaliate against Japanese exports to Southeast Asia. Japan, he argued, needed to trade with both China and Southeast Asia.[36]

To settle matters, Dulles, Sparkman, and Smith handed Yoshida a letter for his signature. Addressed to Dulles, it declared that the Japanese government "is prepared as soon as legally possible" to conclude a treaty with the Republic of China (Taiwan). The treaty would apply to territories "now or hereafter under the actual control" of the Republic of China. It stated that Japan had "no intention to conclude a bilateral treaty with the Communist regime of China." Without this "minimum" declaration, the Americans added, "it would probably be impossible to obtain ratification of the Treaty."

Yoshida signed, but asked that "his" letter not be released until after the January visit to Washington of Prime Minister Winston Churchill and Foreign Secretary Anthony Eden. He hoped the British could be persuaded to alter their position or that the United States would agree to "take the blame so that Japan would not be subject to counteraction on the part of the British." Yoshida requested economic aid and, to Dulles's discomfort, argued that Japanese businessmen could play a role in the "counterinfiltration of Communist China."[37]

The new Conservative Party cabinet led by Prime Minister Winston Churchill and Foreign Secretary Sir Anthony Eden pursued a China policy close to that of its Labor predecessor. British Ambassador Sir Oliver Franks, followed by Churchill and Eden, charged that making an agreement with Taiwan the price for Senate ratification of the peace treaty deprived Japan of freedom to set its own foreign policy and violated Dulles's June 1951 pledge to allow Tokyo to chose which Chinese regime it would deal with. Dulles retorted that his earlier agreement with the Labor government did not "prevent Japan independently acting in its own interest" and that Yoshida's decision to negotiate with Taiwan was his own. It was simply "inconceivable" that "Japan should pursue foreign policies which cut across those of the United States."[38]

Tired of quibbling, Acheson told Churchill and Eden that Washington had to prevent "the great shift in the world power situation" that would result "if Japan with its military virtues and industrial capacity went over to the Communist side." Although the British saw few risks and much advantage in promoting Sino-Japanese trade, Acheson considered Japan vulnerable because it lacked strong ideological ties to the West and could be tempted to align itself with the Communist bloc for purely economic reasons. Joint Chiefs of Staff chairman Bradley echoed this fear, telling his colleagues how difficult it would be "to prevent the suicide of neutralism" among Japanese. Acheson informed the British he would not relent.[39]

On January 16, 1952, immediately after Eden's departure from Washington, but before he informed the cabinet of America's intent, Dulles and Acheson instructed the Japanese government to release the "Yoshida letter."

The British Foreign Office complained of being "completely taken aback" by the disclosure. Dulles made an effort to soothe Churchill's anger by apologizing for the hasty release of the letter and expressed "sorrow" that "in the last day or two there has developed some misunderstanding between our governments with reference to Japan's China policy." Eden condemned Dulles's assertion as "thoroughly dishonest." Exasperated British diplomats still urged Eden to promote commercial links between Tokyo and Beijing. They hoped this might "reduce the need for the Japanese to resort to dumping tactics on the markets of Southeast Asia so as to maintain their essential exports."[40]

On January 19, 1952, three days after the release of Yoshida's pledge, the State Department sent the peace and security treaties to the Senate. In both public and executive testimony to the Foreign Relations Committee, Dulles and Acheson emphasized that the United States required a friendly Japan as much as Japan needed American support. "Soviet leaders," Dulles declared, "did not disguise the fact that they seek above all, to be able to exploit the industrial capabilities of Japan and Germany." If the Kremlin controlled these countries, "the stage would be set for a climactic struggle of doubtful outcome." The peace and security treaties with Japan, along with the ANZUS and Philippine defense pacts, would blunt Soviet penetration of the Pacific.

This argument carried the day, as Republicans joined the Democrats in support of the treaties. Except for William Jenner, a conservative Republican from Indiana who wanted to impose added restrictions on Japan, senators found little to criticize in either pact. On March 20, the Senate approved the peace treaty by a vote of 66–10, and the security pact by a margin of 58–9.[41]

To pressure Tokyo to reach an accord with Taiwan, agree to a fisheries deal, and sign the administrative agreement, Truman held in abeyance the effective date of the treaty. With some American arm-twisting, Japan and Taiwan agreed to treaty terms on April 28, 1952, just hours before the multilateral peace treaty came into effect. SCAP ceased to exist, but 200,000 American troops remained in place. When General Ridgway departed in May, General Mark Clark assumed command of American forces in the Far East.

Republican charges of Democratic failure in Asia affected the selection of the first ambassador to Japan. Dulles declined Truman's offer to send him to Tokyo. "There was no point in being at the end of a transmission line," he explained, "if the power house itself was not functioning." Acheson then tapped Robert Murphy, an aide to General Dwight Eisenhower in North Africa during World War II and currently ambassador to Belgium. As a European specialist, Murphy admitted he had "never even set eyes on the Pacific Ocean." Like many of his colleagues, he guessed he was chosen primarily *because* he was an "ignoramus about the Orient." Acheson "wryly remarked" to Murphy that given Senator Joseph McCarthy's attacks on Asian specialists, the Senate "would probably confirm me speedily because I never had occasion to express an opinion about Far Eastern issues."[42]

Murphy spent eleven months in Tokyo, complaining much of the time about the subversive activities of the Soviet mission (he resented their free distribution of Marxist literature) and Japanese politicians who seemed "determined to avoid the issue" of rearmament. He publicly scolded the Japanese for their desire to resume trade with China. "I can hardly comprehend," the ambassador told the Tokyo Chamber of Commerce and Industry, "why Japanese business seeks to trade with continental China, a trade which would serve only to strengthen the fighting potential of communism. Would it not be a far better policy to cooperate in the effort to check communist aggression?" In Murphy's opinion, it was fortunate that Yoshida was in "no position to resist most things the Americans really wanted . . . and knew when to yield." Eisenhower's election as president in November 1952 and his appointment of John Foster Dulles as secretary of state cut short Murphy's tenure. Dulles selected his close associate and Japan specialist John Allison as ambassador, a gesture appreciated in Tokyo.[43]

Rearming Japan

American participation in the Korean War coincided with the decision to rearm Japan. As Occupation forces were deployed to the peninsula, MacArthur and the military chiefs in Washington decided that Japanese troops should partly fill the void. On July 8, 1950, MacArthur ordered Yoshida to create a National Police Reserve (NPR) of 75,000 men and expand the existing Maritime Safety Force (MSF), a coast guard, from 8,000 to 10,000 men.

The NPR was organized and maintained separately from the existing police and placed under the direct control of the prime minister. Filling the ranks proved simple. However, MacArthur's refusal to employ former Imperial Army officers created a leadership gap. When General Ridgway replaced MacArthur in April 1951, he relaxed this prohibition. To maintain the fiction of the NPR's status, SCAP put an Annex of the Civil Affairs Section in charge of its training. Major General William Shepard explained the drill to American officers, including Colonel Frank Kowalski, who supervised Japanese recruits. Kowalski would be the

> only one in the camp who will know that you are organizing an infantry battalion. Others, of course, will suspect it. But only you will know. As far as the Japanese are concerned, and that applies to all Japanese, the governor, the police and the NPR [recruits themselves]—you are organizing a police reserve. The Constitution of Japan prohibits an army. You will not call the men soldiers and you will not call the officers by any military ranks. The men are policemen and the officers will be superintendents. If you ever see a tank, it isn't a tank, it's a special vehicle. You can call a truck a truck.[44]

During 1952, the United States unilaterally devised plans to expand the police reserve to a 300,000-man force of ten ground divisions with air and naval capability. A military this large could defend Japan, free American troops for other missions, and be useful in joint operations. In lobbying Congress for funds, General Ridgway argued that for "each dollar expended" the United States could "purchase more security through the creation of Japanese forces than can be purchased by similar expenditures in any other nation in the world, including the United States."

During the summer of 1952, the army issued the "policemen" rifles, machine guns, mortars, bazookas, flame throwers, artillery, and tanks. The navy supplied the maritime force with eighteen patrol frigates and fifty landing craft. The Bureau of the Budget estimated that by the end of 1952 the value of the equipment and training provided Japan exceeded $1 billion.[45]

Yoshida deflected American pressure to rearm more extensively and deploy Japanese forces in Asia. During the remainder of his term, the prime minister did just enough to avoid a break with Washington on military issues. Although Yoshida raised NPR force levels to 110,000 in 1951, this represented only a third of what Washington demanded. Shortly before the Occupation ended, Yoshida called for transforming the police reserve into "something along the lines of a Self-Defense Force." Japanese ground forces were located in thirty-seven bases mostly near urban centers of domestic Communist strength and organized into four army divisions. In Kowalski's words, it possessed "great potential for future development."[46]

During the Korean War, Japanese military personnel assisted American forces. Minesweepers of the Maritime Safety Force helped clear harbors along the Korean coast. The U.S./UN command secretly employed Japanese shipping and railroad experts with past service on the Korean peninsula. Without them, Ambassador Murphy asserted, "allied forces would have had difficulty remaining in Korea."[47]

The Japanese public tolerated but had little enthusiasm for rearmament. (The Supreme Court refused to decide whether the NPR violated the constitution.) After visiting Japan at the end of 1951, *Newsweek* editor Harry Kern complained to Dulles that except for a "tiny minority," Japanese "feared the comeback of the military caste" more than communism and regarded the NPR as "American mercenaries."[48]

On December 6, 1951, the tenth anniversary of Japan's attack on the United States, the Japanese press described a boom in base construction throughout the archipelago. Without irony, the *Nippon Times* reported that new air, ground, and naval facilities for American and NPR forces would make Japan "Pearl Harbor proof" against a surprise Communist attack.

Like most of his compatriots, Yoshida accepted rearmament, foreign bases, and constraints on ties to China as the price Japan must pay for ending the Occupation and gaining economic assistance. Over the next decades, as Japan rebuilt its economic and social foundations, and as the United States expanded its presence in Asia, the two nations continually recalculated the fee charged and the value received in this transaction.

3 *UNITED STATES–JAPAN*

ECONOMIC COOPERATION,

1950–53

ON appropriate occasions, Japanese compose short poems called *haiku* that express a single overwhelming emotion in seventeen syllables. In April 1952, just before the Occupation ended, the *Nihon Yukan* newspaper ran a *haiku* as an editorial: "Cherry trees have blossomed out; we will be independent soon. Why don't we feel as happy as we should?" It seemed clear, an American diplomat remarked of the poem, that "anxiety over Japan's economic survival" restrained celebrations over regaining sovereignty. Having lost the war and an empire, 85,000,000 Japanese were confined to an island area unable to produce "enough food or industrial raw materials to supply the[ir] minimum needs."[1]

As of June 1950, despite two years of American assistance, Japanese industry lacked needed capital and export markets. The austerity program initiated by Joseph Dodge during 1949 curbed inflation and halted deficit spending, yet it also triggered a severe recession. By June, unemployment reached 500,000—twice the level of the year before. Share prices fell sharply on Tokyo's stock exchange and small business failures increased dramatically. The index of industrial production had risen to over 80 percent of its prewar level, but a credit crunch limited investment in plants and equipment. More ominously, Japan exported less than half the amount of textiles and manufactured goods it had before the war.[2]

The Toyota Motor Sales Company typified heavy industry. The company was squeezed between declining sales, unions resisting layoffs, and a credit crunch that prevented acquisition of badly needed technology. In June 1950, Toyota produced barely 300 trucks. President Kamiya Shotaro flew to the United States hoping to induce the Ford Motor Company to invest in Toyota. He arrived on June 24, just as the news broke of the Korean attack.

At first, the fighting appeared to doom Toyota's prospects since the Defense Department discouraged Ford from diverting resources by sending a management team to Japan. Despondent, Kamiya left Detroit with a sense of failure. The next month, however, Toyota received a military order for 1,000 trucks. Within a year it had sold 5,000 vehicles to U.S. forces and boosted monthly production to over 2,000 units. Workers' annual wages doubled and the company paid its first dividend since 1945.

Years later, Kamiya described these orders as "Toyota's salvation." The company used profits from military sales and technology transfers to modernize its operations, reduce the power of organized labor, and begin passenger car production. Kamiya's happiness over Toyota's good fortune was tempered only slightly by a "sense of guilt that I was rejoicing over another country's war."

Many companies had reason to celebrate. As Jeeps and other vehicles used in Korea needed repair, they were often brought to Higashi Nippon Heavy Industries (later part of Mitsubishi Heavy Industries) near Tokyo. More than a hundred U.S. military and civilian technicians, using the latest imported machinery, supervised the Japanese workforce. Miyahara Toshio, production manager and later a director of Mitsubishi Motors Corporation, recalled that "everyone in the plant, from the foreman down, was given a chance to learn a mechanized, integrated process."

Benefits from military procurement spread beyond heavy industry. Shortly after fighting began in Korea, the U.S. Army Procurement Officer in Yokohama called in officials of firms that made bags for holding rice. "We need all the gunny sacks you have," he told them, "and we need them urgently for making combat sandbags. It doesn't even matter if they're used. Name your price and we'll pay for it." These companies eventually sold 200 million sacks to the U.S. Army at twice the usual price. This enabled the Nippon Matai Company to expand its force of sewing machine operators from 30 to 150. By adding new equipment and diversifying production, it eventually employed over 1,000 people.[3]

War orders benefited the textile, construction, automotive, metal, communications, and chemical industries. At the peak of the Korean conflict, nearly 3,000 Japanese firms held war-related contracts while many others arranged with U.S. companies and the Defense Department to acquire new technology. During the first year of the Korean War, procurements totaled some $329 million, about 40 percent of the value of Japan's total exports in 1950. During 1952, procurement and other forms of military spending reached $800 million. The index of industrial production finally surpassed the pre-World War II level in October 1950, rose to 131 percent in May 1951, and kept climbing. By 1954, Japan earned over $3 billion in defense expenditures, initiating a two-decade period of 10 percent annual growth in the GNP.

The outbreak of fighting in Korea breathed life into the dormant Japanese economy and stock market. Small wonder that when Prime Minister Yoshida learned of the North Korean attack he reportedly exclaimed,

"It's the Grace of Heaven," or that Bank of Japan governor Ichimada Naoto called the procurement orders "divine aid." Speaking in the Diet early in 1951, Yoshida asserted that the "Korean War provided more stimulus for Japanese economic resurgence than did all the occupation efforts." Ambassador Robert Murphy described the war as a "godsend" that enabled Japan to rebuild at "maximum speed." The procurement boom, he remarked, "transformed" Japan into "one huge supply depot, without which the Korean War could not have been fought."[4]

The initial effort to promote Japanese export production presumed that China, Southeast Asia, and, to a lesser degree, the United States, would furnish the raw materials and consumer markets Japan required. Because of anticipated resistance from American manufacturers, and concerns about product quality, American economic planners doubted that Japan could substantially increase exports to the United States. China's entry into the Korean War and the resulting American-led embargo of trade with Beijing left Tokyo dependent on U.S. military orders, American consumers, and the promise of Southeast Asian development.

During the Korean War, American and Japanese officials initiated some of the regional economic projects proposed before June 1950 but never funded. The U.S.–Japan Economic Cooperation program begun in May 1951 linked the procurement of military items in Japan with efforts to boost Japanese trade with Southeast Asia. This was designed to deflect Japanese trade from China while reducing the need for direct American aid to Tokyo.[5]

When Joseph Dodge returned to Tokyo in October 1950 after an absence of several months, the tight money policy he had instituted the previous year to balance the budget and rationalize industry had been rendered obsolete by the boom in war orders. He told business leaders in Yokohama that Japan had begun "receiving the benefit of a substantial and unexpected windfall of foreign exchange from direct procurement for the war in Korea." But, he cautioned, the orders would only be temporary (China had not yet entered the conflict) so they should not squander the windfall on consumption. Instead, dollar earnings should be invested in "essential capital improvements" for export expansion. He warned against any impulse to "ease up on the drive for industrial improvement, efficiency . . . and rationalization."

Dodge pressed both government and industry to apply procurement profits to "achieve the long sought goal of economic self-support which is a fundamental requirement of political independence." Along these lines, he authorized the Japanese to use nearly 90 billion yen from U.S.-controlled counterpart funds (yen deposited in return for American aid) to upgrade transportation, power, shipping, and communications. This aid also provided credits for the purchase of critical foreign technology and for the Export-Import Bank of Japan, which promoted foreign sales.[6]

John Foster Dulles also saw Japan's economic stability as essential to the peace and security treaties. In October 1950, he told a group of current and former policymakers that unless Japan was "assured a satisfactory livelihood . . . without placing [it] in a position of dependence upon the Communist-dominated mainland of Asia," the "peace treaty will be a failure." In January 1951, he told congressional leaders that the "economic stability of Japan" was the key to its security. Because of Japan's "precarious economic situation," he alerted the legislators, they might have to appropriate substantial aid after the Occupation ended.

Dulles worried greatly about how Japan could cope with "the loss of the normal trading areas of China and Manchuria and the threatened loss of Southeast Asia with its ricebowl and other raw materials." Keeping Japan on the "side of the free world," Dulles told Charles Wilson, director of the Office of Defense Mobilization, depended on making sure "its industry can keep running and that it will receive sufficient quantities of the necessary raw materials." Without access to vital commodities, "it would be futile to expect the Japanese to keep away from Communism."[7]

During his February 1951 treaty negotiations in Tokyo, Dulles discussed economic issues with General William Marquat, head of SCAP's Economic and Scientific Section (ESS). Among influential Americans, Dulles asserted, the "principal problem" in Asia was "How is Japan going to get along economically?" Would the United States have to carry Japan's trade deficits for an "indefinite period" or be compelled to "admit large quantities of Japanese goods to the United States?" With China off-limits, Dulles and Marquat feared the consequences should "any one or all" of Japan's other "Asiatic markets pass out of the picture." Unless Japan "worked for us," they concluded—in an epigraph that captured American concern for the whole cold war—it "will work for the other side."

Both men doubted that Japan could expect to sell many consumer products in the United States. For the short run, Japan's only real option was to "utilize unused industrial capacity . . . for the support of the United States mobilization effort." If a country did not make "what the world wants, which today means war materials," Marquat opined, "it cannot get by." Yet, a modest investment might put enough idle plants to work to raise Japan's index of industrial production from the current 116 percent (of the pre-World War II level) to 200 percent.[8]

The ESS staff argued the case further in a detailed study, *Japan's Industrial Potential*, issued in three sections starting in February 1951. With sufficient raw materials, technology, tools, and financing, it contended, Japanese plants could easily supply military items to the United States and Southeast Asian nations. Military orders would also promote "psychological" adjustment to cold war doctrines and ensure that idle industry did not become a "means of ingress of subversive influence."[9]

Marquat's appeals found favor in the Pentagon. In March 1951, Secretary of Defense George C. Marshall instructed the armed services and the Munitions Board to make greater use of Japan for the "acquisition of supplies and equipment for use of U.S. forces, particularly in the Pacific area and in support of proposed U.S. military assistance programs in Southeast

Asia." Marshall directed that industrial mobilization planning address post-Korea military requirements by placing what he called "educational orders in Japanese industry."[10]

In April, Marquat conferred in Washington with officials from several agencies. He admitted that the main reason Japan continued to experience a trade imbalance was the "preclusion of normal trade relations with China and Manchuria occasioned largely by the political influence of the United States." American restrictions denied Japan "those sources of cheap non-dollar primary raw materials" it would otherwise obtain from China. For now, American influence in Tokyo and the Korean War boom persuaded the Japanese to follow Washington's lead. But when the Occupation and Korean War wound down, Marquat cautioned, the United States must have plans ready for Japan to participate in Western rearmament programs on a normal commercial basis. If not, pressure would build in Tokyo to "resume trade with Communist China which could well be attended by strong movements of local dissonant elements to achieve political reorientation with the communist orbit." Without new export options, China would become an irresistible temptation.[11]

On May 17, 1951, about the same time as Marquat visited Washington, President Truman approved NSC 48/5, a wide-ranging review of American objectives and courses of action in Asia. The Truman administration concluded that the Soviet Union planned to gain control of East and Southeast Asia, and Japan, "primarily through . . . exploitation of the resources of communist China." To prevent this, the United States would need to apply countervailing military, political, economic, and psychological power to depose the Chinese government or force a change in its policies. Washington must assist Japan to become "economically self-supporting and to produce goods and services important to the United States and to the economic stability of the non-communist area of Asia." Japan was expected to develop "appropriate military forces" and begin "the production of low cost military material in volume for use in Japan and in other non-communist countries of Asia." This confirmed the ideas broached by Marquat and Dulles.[12]

On his return to Tokyo on May 10, Marquat spoke confidently of Washington's support for long-term "United States–Japan economic cooperation." After he conferred with General Ridgway, SCAP announced a "program for future United States-Japanese economic cooperation, including the use of Japan's industry to help build democratic might against the threat of Communist aggression." It promised the "fullest economic cooperation and assistance, including United States government and private credits."

Although vague on long-range commitments and aid levels, the program promised "many orders on an individual basis starting soon." American officials agreed that Japan's industrial potential should be used "to a maximum extent to increase production of raw materials and also the industrial potentiality of Southeastern Asia." Japan would be encouraged to "supply Southeast Asia and other areas with capital and consumer goods not now available from normal sources in countries engaged in war production." American aid missions would promote the "development of programs linked to the overall United States-Japanese economic cooperation program."[13]

Charles Wilson, head of the Office of Defense Mobilization, followed this lead in July by organizing an interdepartmental committee on Far East mobilization to seek means to "exploit the unused industrial capacity of Japan in the defense program of the free world." Wilson maintained that if "one-third to one-half" of Japan's idle industry was fully utilized, it could export "90 percent of the materials" that U.S. aid programs earmarked for Southeast Asia. This would ease strains on the American economy and assure that "economic prosperity will come to the Pacific area." The Economic Cooperation Administration (ECA), which supervised nonmilitary aid in Southeast Asia, established a Tokyo field office to encourage the "fullest utilization of the industrial capacity of Japan in the operation of the American aid program in Asia."[14]

At the committee's initial meeting on August 1, chairman William Y. Elliott called for coordinated solutions to the "financial, material, shipping and other problems of Japan and Southeast Asia." He stressed the links between the problem of "economic recovery and political defense in the Pacific." Members discussed whether to emphasize "securing critical supplies from the area or strengthening Japan." General Carter B. Magruder asserted that since Japan would become America's key Pacific ally, efforts should focus on linking Japan's "economy insofar as possible to the U.S. economy." This meant boosting Japan's defense production. Yet American defense contractors objected to Defense Department purchases from Japan of anything not urgently needed in Korea.

As an alternative, ECA representative R. Allen Griffin suggested placing orders in Japan for civilian equipment needed in Southeast Asia. Since this might elicit "unfavorable reaction in Southeast Asia" where anti-Japanese sentiment persisted, State Department delegate Emmerson Ross recommended using Japan as a supplier not only of consumer goods but mining and other industrial equipment that Southeast Asian nations required for their own "broad development programs." With luck, Ross predicted, this might open a way "for Japan to . . . replace its Chinese markets."

In order to lower American aid costs, the committee recommended "developing Japan as an alternative source of certain critical items of equipment and supply" needed in Korea and by American allies. It endorsed the "mobilization of the complementary economic strength of Japan and Southeast Asia in order to strengthen the political situation in the entire area."[15]

During the summer of 1951, SCAP's Kenneth Morrow led a joint American-Japanese mission to Southeast Asia to "investigate prospects for increasing the flow of raw materials to Japan." It sought opportunities for "Japan to supply machinery, heavy equipment, consumer goods, and technical aid" in exchange for commodities. British diplomats in Tokyo reported that the mission hoped to acquire raw materials for industries "which would contribute to rearmament" and to the production of goods vital for the "maintenance of U.S. garrison troops and facilities." In public, however, the Americans were "anxious not to overemphasize the rearmament procurement side of these plans" as it "could easily be misinterpreted as a U.S. conspiracy to revive Japanese leadership of a Greater East-Asia Co-Prosperity Sphere with the added drive of U.S. backing."[16]

During the final half of 1951, the cooperation program led to procurement orders totaling $241 million, a big increase over the $141 million spent in Japan during the first six months of the year. By the end of the year, the Defense Department began placing orders in Japan for ammunition to be used by the National Police Reserve. During 1952, the Munitions Board began buying military items in Japan destined for areas outside Korea.

Ridgway, Marquat, and Morrow hoped to maintain a remnant of the ESS staff in Tokyo after the Occupation ended. Without it, they feared, the Pentagon might use Japan like a department store, servicing Korean orders but slighting long-term industrial mobilization.[17]

The giant shadow cast by China's intervention in Korea affected all of Japan's economic prospects. In December 1950, SCAP suspended Japan's small but growing trade with China. During 1951, a UN resolution imposing a trade embargo on China and North Korea as well as the Battle Act, passed by Congress to prohibit aid to any country violating U.S. export controls, resulted in wider trade restrictions. United States authorities formulated a list of 400 items that Japan could not sell to China, a more stringent ban than applied to Western sales to the Soviet Union. Shortly before the Occupation ended, SCAP transferred enforcement power to the Japanese government. In the summer of 1952, Japan joined the American-sponsored Coordinating Committee for Export to Communist Areas (COCOM) and subsequently took a seat on COCOM's China Committee (CHINCOM).

In addition to these control measures, in September 1952, the United States pressed Japan to sign a secret bilateral agreement that imposed limits on Japanese exports to China that went beyond even the COCOM/CHINCOM restrictions. Only the United States, South Korea, and Taiwan—which prohibited all trade with China—imposed tighter restrictions. These measures shrank Japan's 1952 trade with China to a mere .04 percent of total exports and .7 percent of imports—a dramatic change from 1941 when Japan drew 17 percent of its imports from China and sold it 27 percent of its exports. In 1941, Japan obtained 50 percent of its coal, 25 percent of its iron ore, and 75 percent of its soybean imports from China. Analyzing these numbers, a CIA study of May 1952 predicted that unless a substitute for China could be found quickly, Japan would be "tempted to seize opportunities for closer economic and political relations with the [communist] Bloc.[18]

In the final weeks of the Occupation, Dodge and Marquat worked with their Japanese counterparts to formulate plans for continued economic cooperation while Yoshida requested a large development loan as a sort of "going-away present." This, Dodge believed, reflected "psychological and political rather than . . . any immediate financial need." Like Dulles, Dodge sympathized with the fact that Japan, 7,000 miles distant from its patron, found itself surrounded by unfriendly or enemy nations and seemingly had "no place to turn for assistance but the United States." Yoshida wanted the aid to compensate for "some domestically unpalatable economic and political decisions," such as committing a "substantial part of [Japan's] budget for increasing domestic security forces and [making] a treaty with [the] China Nationalists." There was "public resistance to the first and public repercussions from the latter."

Dodge worried that Yoshida conceived of economic cooperation as a program in which "the United States will plan and blueprint the needs of Japan and then fit the economy of the United States into those needs— instead of the reverse." To avoid this, he called for implementing mechanisms that linked the "expansion of Japan's industrial potential" to "the enlargement of her security forces." Dodge summarized his views in the following way.

> There will be a substantial reliance on Japan in the posttreaty period for
> a. Production of goods and services important to the U.S. and the economic stability of non-Communist Asia
> b. Cooperation with the United States in the development of the raw material resources of Asia
> c. Production of low cost military material in volume for use in Japan and non-Communist Asia
> d. Development of Japan's appropriate military forces as a defensive shield and to permit the redeployment of United States forces[19]

Suto Hideo, Director General of Japan's Economic Stabilization Board, responded to Dodge on February 12, 1952. He proposed utilizing idle factories by "promoting and tightening" Japan's "economic cooperation with the United States, Southeast Asian countries and other democratic countries in order to contribute to their defense production and economic development" while assuring "imports necessary for Japan," raising living standards, and "strengthening progressively her self-defense power." Japan would contribute to the "rearmament plan of the United States [by] supplying military goods and strategic materials, by repairing and establishing defense industries with the technical and financial assistance from the United States" and thereby assuring increased dollar earnings. Japanese officials remained wary of selling military equipment to countries other than the United States, but were eager to cooperate "more actively with the economic development of Southeast Asia" to speed that region's development and "increase the imports of goods and materials from this area."

In terms of military procurement, Japan desired long-term contracts to build and repair vehicles and aircraft, expand petrochemical production, construct ships, manufacture uniforms and other textiles for American troops, boost steel and aluminum production, and increase electrical generation. Tokyo would assist Southeast Asia "mainly with technical skills and surplus machinery production capacity" and by providing fertilizer. By having the Mutual Security Program purchase goods and services in Japan bound for Southeast Asia, Japan could earn vital dollars.[20]

Marquat and Dodge appreciated these ideas, but objected to Yoshida's reluctance to link American assistance to expansion of Japan's armed forces. As Marquat told Dodge, under the prime minister's concept of economic cooperation, "Japan doesn't have to do anything—it's all up to Uncle Sam." Nevertheless, by the time SCAP went out of business in April 1952, nearly 3,000 Japanese firms held military contracts and about 42 percent of Japan's exports went to the Asia and Pacific region, twice the level of 1935.[21]

The security treaty's administrative agreement, signed in February 1952, also promoted economic cooperation. It established a "Joint United States–Japan Committee" on security and a joint economic council composed of embassy staff and Japanese to direct industrial mobilization plans. The economic council included a "procurement coordination subcommittee" with a staff of eleven Americans, including several SCAP/ESS veterans, financed by Mutual Security Act funds.[22]

Japan's business community responded enthusiastically to the procurement program. In April 1951, the four largest business confederations declared that "above all else, organized business wanted the full mobilization of Japan's industrial power under a joint United States–Japan mutual defense program, which would provide the necessary financial resources."[23]

Following the San Francisco peace conference, business groups established councils to work with government agencies in planning for post-Occupation economic cooperation with the United States. The councils advocated procurement contracts that encouraged broad economic growth, rather than production of military end items. The powerful Federation of Economic Organizations (Keidanren) urged SCAP to return confiscated munitions facilities to their former owners. During SCAP's final days of authority, Ridgway responded by transferring to the Japanese government control of 1,000 confiscated munitions plants and permitting Japan to resume production of aircraft and weapons.

When the peace treaty came into effect, the Federation of Economic Organizations established an Economic Cooperation Council whose subcommittees dealt with general policy, Asian development, and defense production. A prominent industrialist led each group, with Kiyoshi Goko, head of Mitsubishi Heavy Industries, in charge of the defense subcommittee. Big business worked closely with government organs, such as the Ministry of International Trade and Industry (MITI) and the Supreme Economic Cooperation Conference, to shape procurement policies. The Diet assisted large enterprises engaged in military production by relaxing the deconcentration laws during the summer of 1952.

Yoshida and MITI returned 859 of the 1,000 munitions plants released by SCAP to their former owners. The Japanese government confirmed its commitment to military mobilization in September 1952 by designating the weapons industry as a "national policy industry." This allowed MITI to select firms to participate in arms production and offer them subsidies, tax breaks, access to hard currency, and other privileges.[24]

Apart from the infusion of American technology and capital, procurement orders hastened the introduction to Japan of American management techniques—then considered the most progressive in the world. Even before the Korean War, SCAP invited business consultants to visit Japan. Several, like statistical quality control expert W. Edwards Deming, made useful suggestions on how to improve quality and increase efficiency. But, without assured export markets, Japanese industry lacked the money and incentives to carry out many of these recommendations. With Korean War orders for motor vehicles, munitions, and electronic equipment, they had both the motive and the capital to implement techniques that assured improved productivity, quality, and efficiency. Japanese managers recognized that, without such changes, they would be unable to hold onto export markets after the Korean War ended.

During 1950–51, Occupation authorities recruited consultants to teach such concepts as statistical quality control, continuous improvement in manufacturing, and worker training projects. Deming's particular interest in quality control found an avid audience when Japanese companies were required to produce advanced military equipment to exacting standards.

Numerous individuals and groups contributed to the managerial revolution. Among the most important was Training Within Industries, Inc. (TWI), a consulting group that specialized in innovative training techniques in the use of new equipment and technologies. TWI techniques evolved during the Second World War to speed production and innovation within American munitions plants. During the Korean War, the army and air force expanded a TWI pilot program in Japan to enhance the training of managers, supervisors, and skilled workers in such methods as quality control, continuous improvement, use of new machinery, and workers' quality circles. The consultants stressed recruitment of Japanese "trainers," who, by 1953, had introduced one million fellow managers and workers to the program. In the following decades, graduates of the TWI course assumed key positions in such companies as Mitsubishi, Toyota, and Hitachi.[25]

Strategic planning in Washington paralleled the economic cooperation program. In February 1952, as negotiators completed the administrative agreement implementing the security pact, Acting Secretary of State James Webb and Secretary of Defense Robert Lovett urged the president to approve an interim post-Occupation policy. Japan's security was "of such vital strategic importance to the United States position in the Far East" that "the United States cannot permit hostile forces to gain control of any part of the territory of Japan." They urged Truman to authorize American forces to defend Japan even though the security treaty did not require this. Lovett and Webb also called for greater efforts "to promote Japan's economic development, political stability, and military contribution to the collective security of non-communist nations in Asia." This required "building up its industrial and agricultural resources" and "developing and maintaining a strong trading position, particularly with Southeast Asia." Truman approved these recommendations in February 1952.[26]

State Department specialists continued to worry about Japan's "shallow economy" whose expansion remained so dependent on military procurement. Although all forms of American military spending brought Japan $700 to 800 million per year from 1951 through 1953, the economic outlook remained murky, even though humming factories had replaced idle plants. When calculated as exports, procurements boosted Japan's foreign sales to $1.5 billion by the end of 1951. But the war boom had not spilled over into civilian exports. Japan still had to import expensive raw materials, especially from the United States. Discounting procurements, Japan's trade deficit ranged from $600 million to $1 billion between 1951 and 1953. Two-thirds of the deficit resulted from imports from the United States.

William Sebald, the senior American diplomat in Tokyo, questioned the wisdom of linking Japan's growth so closely to military orders and trade expansion with Southeast Asia. He doubted that sales to Southeast Asia would earn enough hard currency to meet Japan's growing food and raw material requirements. Although procurement orders earned dollars, they made Japan subject to the "political inconsistencies of Congressional appropriations and the economic cycles of American business." Imposing even indirect political dependency and economic controls, Sebald predicted, would undermine the "psychological and political support" required for Japan to voluntarily ally herself with the "free world." They would also "provide ammunition" for Japanese favoring "neutrality in the East–West conflict" and for Communist attacks on the United States as "imperialistic." Uncertain that a Japan severed from China could become economically viable or politically stable, Sebald urged his colleagues to take a "more realistic look at the question of Japan's trade with Communist China and come up with a solution" that allowed the importation of raw materials in exchange for nonstrategic consumer goods—"i.e., hard goods in exchange for soft."[27]

Sebald recognized that the Korean War boom masked a host of problems. For example, Japan's exports to Southeast Asia earned a sizeable sterling surplus, but these reserves could not be converted to dollars, nor could the sterling bloc countries of Southeast Asia provide the commodities most needed by Japan. Efforts to boost trade elsewhere in Southeast Asia confronted legacies of wartime hatred, unresolved reparations claims, and regional instability.

While imports of American products into Japan surged to $700 million in 1951, civilian exports to the United States reached only $184 million, with military procurements masking the deficit. Meanwhile, European and American business interests frustrated Japanese plans to expand exports of items such as tuna, textiles, and sewing machines by implementing special quotas.[28]

State Department trade specialists considered Japan's long-run economic outlook as "seriously weak and vulnerable." They viewed with special concern the "strength of the natural economic affinity between Japan and Northern Asia," an attraction that was "probably greater and more fundamental than we like to recognize." Southeast Asia might partially compensate for trade with China, but the region's chronic underdevelopment and lack of purchasing power made it a potential, not a current, prospect.

Many State Department planners concluded that Western governments should lower tariffs and accept more Japanese goods despite opposition from domestic producers. Even this would probably fall short of meeting Japan's needs. Washington would have to take "extraordinary measures," such as a special "system of Japanese trade controls . . . tailored to the economic relations between Japan and the [Chinese] mainland." A limited opening to China appeared the only way to "keep Japan completely on our side." Such trade might become "a lever of some utility in our efforts to bring changes within Communist China."[29]

State Department analysts criticized the refusal by Defense and Commerce Department officials to recognize the difference between strategic and nonstrategic sales to China, even though they made the distinction in exports to the Soviet Union. When Japan joined COCOM, the multilateral agency regulating sales to Communist countries, it would discover that Washington permitted NATO allies to sell to the Soviets many items Japan was forbidden to sell to China, and that these exceptions were made in order "to subsidize certain aspects of the European economy."[30]

Acting Secretary of the Army Karl R. Bendetsen saw only one solution to the dilemma. Southeast Asia could not help Japan in the short run and, he argued, a program "which relies to any substantial degree upon the protracted competitive introduction of Japanese products to the American market" would also fail. Japanese solvency, Bendetsen insisted, required not "artificial substitutes," but access to Northeast Asia. For Japan's sake, he called for action to remove the "political cancer" of Communism that made "China unacceptable as a trading partner of the free world."[31]

British diplomats, having recovered from their initial frustration in dealing with Dulles, accepted the need for a flexible Japan policy. High Commissioner in Singapore Malcolm MacDonald and ambassador to Tokyo Sir Esler Dening agreed that Japan's value in containing Communism in Southeast Asia outweighed Tokyo's economic threat. Like some of their American counterparts, they believed that if Japan were allowed to resume limited trade with China, that could help moderate Communist behavior.[32]

Soon after the Occupation ended, MacDonald, Dening, and foreign office specialists adopted an even more flexible view. Although MacDonald cautioned that "the Japanese have not changed their national character" and remained "by nature dictatorial authoritarians whether of the Right or Left," it was still vital to "support and maintain" Yoshida and "men of his way of thought in office." Japan's "threat," MacDonald argued, lay less in dominating Southeast Asia than in making common cause with China, something that might be brought about by economic desperation.

Although he sympathized with Washington's desire to retain bases in Japan, MacDonald, like other British diplomats, criticized American actions in Japan as "classic examples of doing the wholly right thing in the completely wrong way." MacDonald hoped to tutor the Americans to act "more subtle" with Asians. A colleague observed that there were only "two ways of dealing with the Japanese, either through friendship or hitting them with a big stick." Since the Americans possessed a big stick and were committed to Japanese recovery, Britain had no choice but to follow that lead if it hoped to "keep Japan out of the Communist camp."

Given U.S. determination to restrict Sino-Japanese trade, MacDonald and Dening believed that London must "do everything that we can" to make up for this loss by expanding Japanese trade in Southeast Asia. Although this would injure British interests, there was some political advantage in getting cheap consumer goods into the hands of Southeast Asians. London, like Washington, would have to balance the risk of using Japan to contain Communism with the danger of Japan's desire to "dominate economically if not politically [much] of the Far East." Japanese Foreign Minister Okazaki, MacDonald added, made the point that promoting trade with Southeast Asia would encourage Japan to "make an effective stand against any further advance of communism beyond China."[33]

In August 1952, the National Security Council assembled the disparate views of trade and security policy for President Truman's review and approval. The NSC recommended that Truman formally commit the United States to defend Japan, retain control of the Ryukyus, and promote economic growth. To prevent Japan from seeking an "accommodation" with China, the United States must enhance "Japan's ability to satisfy its economic needs through relations with the free world." In the "long run Japan's access to raw materials and markets for her exports" would make or break its cooperation with the United States and containment policy in Asia.

The NSC opposed a complete embargo on exports to China, but favored stringent "export controls" on Japan's trade with China. This required the United States to provide Japan with alternative trade outlets both in the West and Southeast Asia. Finally, to encourage its participation in the "defense of the free nations of the Pacific area," the NSC wanted Japan to "develop a balanced ten-division ground force" as well as air and naval strength.[34]

The Secretary of Defense and Joints Chiefs endorsed this approach, but raised a warning flag. Since Japan's ability to rearm and its willingness to follow America's lead depended so heavily on securing access to what the Joint Chiefs of Staff called "her historic markets and the sources of food and raw materials in Southeast Asia," U.S. "objectives with respect to

Southeast Asia and United States objectives with respect to Japan" appeared "almost inseparable." The "loss of Southeast Asia to the Western World," would "almost inevitably force Japan into an . . . accommodation with the Communist-controlled areas in Asia."[35]

The perilous French position in Indochina had led the NSC (as well as the Joint Chiefs of Staff) to warn that the "loss of any of the countries of Southeast Asia to communist control" would have "critical psychological, political, and economic consequences" regionally as well as globally. In an early iteration of the "domino theory" later popularized by President Eisenhower, the NSC predicted that the "loss of a single country would probably lead to relatively swift submission to or an alignment with communism by the remaining countries" of the region. Projecting ahead, the NSC warned that in "all probability," Communist control of Southeast Asian resources would "make it extremely difficult to prevent Japan's eventual accommodation to communism" and would even jeopardize the Middle East and Western Europe.

Indirect Chinese aid to the Vietminh guerrillas, rather than invasion, seemed to pose the greatest threat to French survival in Indochina. A Vietminh victory in Tonkin (northern Vietnam) would cause defeatism in Paris and a likely decision to abandon Indochina, thereby delivering all Southeast Asia to Communist control. To avert this catastrophe, the NSC proposed warning China against expanded intervention in Vietnam, boosting military aid to French and local anti-Communist forces, and initiating covert operations against the Vietminh. If France pulled out of Indochina or China intervened, American air and naval forces might be committed to combat or used to blockade China. Unfortunately, the NSC observed, the American public remained largely indifferent to this struggle and it called for a propaganda campaign to "make clear to the American people the importance of Southeast Asia to the security of the United States so that they may be prepared for any" course of action.[36]

It fell to John Foster Dulles, nearing the end of his service to the Truman administration and anticipating higher office in the event of a Republican victory in the November 1952 election, to carry forth word of this policy. Addressing the prestigious French National Political Science Institute on May 5, he described the wars in Korea and Indochina as common efforts to contain Chinese expansion. Although some Americans "misinterpreted" the Indochina war as "an effort by a colonial power to maintain its rule," Dulles praised the French for dispelling this myth by granting partial autonomy to the so-called Associated States of Vietnam, Laos, and Cambodia. He recalled his own effort to enhance their stature by inviting them to attend the 1951 peace conference on Japan. Americans now recognized that in Indochina an "alien despotism" fought "in the name of liberation, to impose a servitude, which would be a step toward further conquest."

But the most emphatic reason Dulles offered for holding the line against Communism had little to do with extending freedom or preserving French glory. "Indochina," he declared, "is the key to Southeast Asia, upon the resources of which Japan is largely dependent." Its "loss to Communism would gravely endanger other areas and it is thus a matter of general concern."[37]

As the key to continuity between the Truman and Eisenhower eras, Dulles played the single most important role in setting policy toward Japan, China, and Vietnam during the 1950s. Containing China and defending Southeast Asia, he made clear, were facets of a Japan-centered strategy. Should France waver in its commitment to Indochina, the United States stood ready to pick up the cudgels in defense of the anchor of containment in Asia.

4 IN THE SHADOW OF THE OCCUPATION: JAPAN AND THE UNITED STATES, 1952–55

THE Occupation ended in April 1952, but Japan remained a client state for many years after. The presence of 200,000 American troops on hundreds of bases as well as foreign control over Okinawa and other outlying islands left Japan less than fully independent. Japan's diplomacy, security, and trade remained tethered to priorities set by Washington. Subordination, however, did not require passivity. During the long twilight of the Yoshida era, political and business leaders managed to steer many American initiatives in directions favorable to Japan. While Washington promoted rearmament, the isolation of China, and containment in Southeast Asia, Japan sought to expand trade with China, penetrate Southeast Asia commercially, and utilize military assistance for economic development. For Yoshida and his successors, Japan's drive to increase exports was not only a formula for prosperity but a kind of proxy nationalism and foreign policy strategy.

In Japan after 1952, neither the foreign office nor Self-Defense Forces played as important a role as the Ministry of Finance, MITI, or big business. During the cold war, America's high level of defense spending and promotion of liberal trade allowed the "banks and the economic bureaucracy," in the view of Japanese economists, to "function as a general staff behind the battlefield in this second 'total war' [of] high economic growth."[1]

Japan's leaders considered defense procurements and increased exports to the United States essential to growth. Although the Liberal Democrats were intensely divided along factional lines, and the Socialists and Communists denounced each other as well as the Conservatives, nearly all parties tacitly agreed on the need to insulate Japan from direct participation in the cold war and to promote economic growth.

American and Japanese officials recognized the connection between rearmament and policies toward China and Southeast Asia. But although the United States wanted a rearmed Japan to share the burden of containment in Asia, most Japanese placed a higher priority on economic growth than on defense. From Tokyo's perspective, restraining Communism and securing markets could best be achieved through trade with China and fostering Southeast Asian economic development.

The issues of rearmament, China, and Southeast Asia dominated bilateral relations through the 1950s and beyond. To hold the alliance together, each side compromised some core values. For the United States, maintaining military bases in a stable Japan and isolating China outweighed the value of pressing Japan to rearm. For the Japanese, the need to assure procurements and access to American consumers proved more important than scrupulously observing the "no war" clause of the constitution or establishing diplomatic ties with China. In a recurring ritual, Americans criticized Japanese foot-dragging on rearmament while Japanese grumbled about American nuclear testing in the Pacific, restrictions on the China trade, and inequalities in the security treaty. Yet each side profited enough from the bargain to continue it. The relationship forged in the post-Occupation years proved remarkably durable.

The Japanese Political Context

In the October 1952 election to the Diet, the first after the Occupation ended, 42 percent of the winning candidates—mostly members of the Liberal and Democratic parties—were former purgees. Many of these new Diet members looked to fellow ex-purgees Hatoyama Ichiro and Shigemitsu Mamoru, rather than Yoshida Shigeru, as natural leaders. The left- and right-wing Socialists and other opposition parties retained about one-third of Diet seats. Yoshida continued to lead a ruling coalition, but his grip had loosened.

The prime minister's position grew more tenuous following an outburst in February 1953 when he called a Socialist legislator a "damn fool" for questioning several bills that weakened Occupation reforms. Anti-Yoshida Conservatives joined the Socialists to pass a Diet resolution censuring him and forcing new elections. The Diet elected in April 1953 contained even more of Yoshida's conservative opponents while the two Socialist parties retained their one-third bloc. Factionalism within the Liberal and Democratic parties allowed Yoshida to cling to power until December 1954, but his rivals dominated the Diet.

The divisions within both the Conservative and Socialist parties had an important influence on the rearmament debate. Yoshida insisted that Article IX of the constitution required a cautious program. Conservatives such as Hatoyama and Shigemitsu acknowledged the constitutional problem, but proposed to solve it by an amendment authorizing the creation of armed forces. Reliance on the Americans and the security treaty, they complained, placed Japan in a subordinate position that prevented it from dealing more realistically with China, Southeast Asia, and the Soviet Union. By amending the constitution, Japan could assume responsibility for its own defense and compel Washington to renegotiate the terms of the security pact. These so-called revisionists linked constitutional change to rearmament, nationalism, and a more independent foreign policy.

Yoshida and the Socialists formed a de facto bloc against constitutional revision and what it implied. The prime minister highly valued the "cover" for limited rearmament provided by Article IX. The security treaty, whatever its indignities, offered protection at bargain rates. The Socialists, for their part, opposed even limited rearmament and feared that constitutional change would revive militarism and domestic oppression. Yoshida's Liberal Party supporters and the Socialists tacitly agreed to blunt the revisionist agenda.

These divisions presented American policymakers with a dilemma. Yoshida's stalling often frustrated Washington, but he was far preferable to the Socialists and their vision of neutrality. Some aspects of the revisionist agenda, including constitutional change and rearmament, appealed to Dulles and other senior members of the Eisenhower administration. At the same time, Americans reacted warily to the revisionists' call for an independent military and normal relations with Moscow and Beijing. As a result, the Eisenhower administration hesitated to encourage Yoshida's conservative critics. They urged, instead, organization of a single conservative party committed to the alliance with America, favoring rearmament, and implacably opposed to the Socialists.

Rearmament

Throughout the 1950s, the American military and diplomatic establishment rued the fact that their only ally in East Asia capable of mounting a strong military challenge to the Communist bloc remained a cheerleader rather than a player on the field of the cold war. Yoshida's stance frustrated American officials concerned with security planning who complained about 200,000 troops tied down in Japan and the lack of Japanese forces available to counter Communist challenges elsewhere in Asia.

In 1951, Congress passed the Mutual Security Assistance Act (MSA) to coordinate the numerous military aid programs that had blossomed during the Korean War. MSA provided money and weapons for allies willing to bolster their own defenses. But Yoshida did not jump at this ring and in January 1952 capped the Self-Defense Force at 110,000 men, a third the size that Washington called for.

The issue arose again in September 1952 when Ikeda Hayato, Yoshida's confidante, conferred in Mexico City with Treasury Secretary John W. Snyder and Joseph Dodge. The Americans suggested that if Japan agreed to an interim expansion of its security force to 180,000 men, and pledged eventual growth to 325,000, Congress would provide $300 million to defray the costs. But Yoshida remained defiant and American pressure flagged with the election of a new president and the delays caused by the transition of power.[2]

The change in administrations, along with Eisenhower's determination to end the Korean War quickly, affected Japan more in style than substance. Unlike China and Korea, Japan had not been the subject of partisan squabbles or public recrimination. Dulles, who served both Truman and Eisenhower, personified the continuity of policy.

Eisenhower and his aides hoped that market forces ("trade, not aid," as they put it) would stimulate economic growth and contribute to stability among allies. They also planned to reduce defense costs by substituting the threat of massive nuclear retaliation, the so-called New Look, for the commitment of American troops to regional conflicts. But Pentagon planners insisted that any reduction of forces in Japan be offset by an expansion of the Japanese military. The MSA program was considered a sweetener to make this acceptable in Tokyo.

Dulles considered Japan's participation in the MSA program a natural extension of the peace and security treaties. In December 1952, as secretary of state designate, he told this to Shirasu Jiro, then visiting the United States as Yoshida's personal representative. The Japanese envoy explained Yoshida's reluctance to expand the military "without first re-educating the people" who believed in the constitution's military prohibition. Shirasu warned that ignoring popular sentiment risked "political upheaval," a Socialist sweep on a "neutrality platform."

Dulles dismissed this argument, insisting that "self-respect" alone should convince Tokyo to "bear some responsibility and a fair share of the common burden of defense of the free world." In May 1953, before consulting the Japanese government, the secretary of state informed members of Congress that he expected Japan to accept MSA support and create a ten-division, 350,000-man security force.[3]

At least some of Yoshida's reluctance to embrace MSA reflected his belief that with the fighting continuing in Korea, Japan could easily rely on the United States to carry the procurement burden and not be concerned with its own rearmament. Currently, Japanese defense suppliers made large profits and maintained full employment at the expense of the American taxpayer. A business consensus for domestic rearmament would come only with peace in Korea and a slackening in procurement orders.[4]

As armistice negotiations in Korea made progress in 1953 (agreement came in July), Japanese industry feared a precipitous decline in military orders. Although shipping, fishing, and textile companies hoped to make up losses by resuming their traditional trade with China, heavy manufacturers as well as chemical and financial interests considered participation in the American defense program their preferred option.

In July, the powerful Federation of Economic Organizations, Keidanren, endorsed a "properly planned" procurement program funded by

MSA. It advocated the transfer of high-technology and general economic assistance to industry in addition to orders for strictly military production. Keidanren's defense production subcommittee (led by Kiyoshi Goko, former head of Mitsubishi Heavy Industries) broke ranks with Yoshida and endorsed the proposal for a 300,000-man ground force along with naval and air contingents.[5]

Foreign Minister Okazaki confided to John Allison, the new American ambassador, that while the business sector favored MSA, the public and the prime minister feared "any participation in an American security program would mean Japanese forces would be sent abroad to fight America's battles." Allison defended MSA as a voluntary association to enhance Japan's self-defense capacity and "thus permit our troops to begin to leave." Yoshida proved more receptive to negotiations following a visit to Tokyo on May 30 by Senator Everett Dirksen. The Illinois Republican, stressed the connection between MSA and America's economic "goodwill."[6]

During June, after further consultation with Allison, both the prime minister and foreign minister announced their willingness to consider joining MSA, although Okazaki stressed the "economic" rather than "military" aspects of participation. At the end of the month, Tokyo and Washington exchanged notes clarifying their positions. Any aid extended, the State Department affirmed, would be primarily to assist Japan to "safeguard its internal security" and fulfill its inherent right of individual and collective self-defense. The promotion of economic stability would be an "essential element for consideration in the development of Japan's self-defense capacities." Nothing in a MSA agreement required Japan to "use its security forces except in self-defense."[7]

Talks on Japanese participation in the security program began in mid-July and quickly ran into trouble. Pentagon representatives, Allison complained, barely concealed their desire to "make Japan into a forward bastion of American strategic strength, with Americans calling the tune and the Japanese meekly accepting their secondary role." This included plans for a 1,500-man military advisory (MAAG) group and appointment of an American coordinator of the Japanese defense industry. Japanese negotiators, in contrast, were interested in MSA aid to industry, but reluctant to discuss the expansion of military forces.

Dulles raised Japanese hackles by issuing a statement on July 10 to the effect that MSA would permit the rapid tripling in size of Japan's security forces to over 300,000. This infuriated Yoshida who had told the Diet he had weighed the possibility of a 40,000-man increase. Allison prevailed on Dulles to announce that the ten-division force was merely a long-term goal. But his ambiguous clarification blurred the distinction.[8]

Tension surrounding the MSA talks increased with the news that Dulles intended to visit South Korea early in August to discuss a bilateral security pact. Yoshida, like many Japanese officials of his generation, disliked Koreans in general and despised South Korean president Syngman

Rhee. Dulles' failure to make a courtesy stop in Tokyo en route to Seoul, Ambassador Allison feared, would enrage Yoshida and impede progress.

Although Dulles ultimately agreed to visit Tokyo, just before leaving Washington he told journalists that he was exploring the prospects not only of a defense pact with Seoul, but also a "mutual security pact covering Japan, Korea and Nationalist China." This assertion was guaranteed to enrage Yoshida, confuse the Diet, and terrify the public. Allison thought it might scuttle Japanese participation in MSA. To calm the storm, a spokesman for the Eisenhower administration denied any intention of forcing Japan to join a regional military pact. The United States then announced it would return to Japan the Amami Oshima Islands located at the northern end of the Ryukyu chain. Although Dulles and Defense officials wanted to dangle the islands as bait during MSA talks, Eisenhower thought it "silly" to play coy with the tiny islands and risk "the loss of our main objective . . . Japan's friendship and loyalty over the long run." He "stated emphatically that to him it was a 'must' to return these islands to Japan."

Although this offer smoothed Dulles's reception in Tokyo, on returning to Washington he squandered the small reservoir of goodwill by telling journalists of his "dissatisfaction with the passive attitude of the Japanese government toward the defense of Asia." The Pentagon made matters worse by announcing a plan to redeploy up to four army divisions from Korea to Japan following an armistice—even though the Japanese government wanted to reduce the size of American forces. All this convinced Allison that Dulles badly misunderstood Japan and wrongly believed that tough talk would encourage rearmament.[9]

Just before a second round of MSA talks resumed in October, Yoshida and his chief conservative rivals, Shigemitsu and Hatoyama, agreed on a defense agenda with the aim of securing American aid. (They also proposed laws to limit strikes in key industries, enhance police power, restore veterans pensions, relax anti-monopoly rules, and reduce the power of the leftist Japan Teachers Union.) Yoshida and Shigemitsu endorsed plans for moderate rearmament and proposed legislation to transform the security force into a "self-defense force" that encouraged and would "keep step with the gradual reduction of U.S. security forces."[10]

Ambassador Allison and Foreign Minister Okazaki unraveled another problem that infuriated the Japanese—the virtual extraterritorial immunity from prosecution granted American military personnel for crimes committed in Japan. On September 27, they signed a revised protocol on criminal jurisdiction that placed American forces under Japanese legal jurisdiction just like U.S. forces in NATO countries. Allison received a private assurance that "in actual practice Japan would . . . exercise its right of jurisdiction in very few cases."[11]

Yoshida sent four close aides to Washington to negotiate a final MSA agreement. They included former finance minister Ikeda Hayato, Miyazawa Kiichi, Aichi Kiichi, and Suzuki Gengo, all with backgrounds in finance

rather than national security. They were instructed to make as few concessions as possible. As Yoshida put it to Miyazawa, Japan could "never pull
off the so-called rearmament for the time being, nor is there any interest in
it among the people." Rearmament would come some day "naturally if our
livelihood recovers." At the risk of sounding "selfish," Yoshida preferred to
"let the Americans handle [our security] until then." He considered it "our
god-given luck that the constitution bans arms. If the Americans complain,
the constitution gives us adequate cover. The politicians who want to
amend it are oafs."

The Japanese brought many nonmilitary issues to the MSA talks,
including proposals to ease trade restrictions with China, requests that
Washington help Tokyo improve its relations with Southeast Asia, and provide increased economic assistance. The chief American delegate, Assistant
Secretary of State for Far Eastern Affairs Walter Robertson, whom an aid
described as "an extraordinarily affable but virulently anti-Mao Virginia
banker," disputed all these points.[12]

President Eisenhower, who played little direct role in the MSA negotiations, expressed hope "that the Japanese will . . . pick up some of the load
and establish their own security organization." He complained about the
American-imposed constitution, but believed the time had come for the
Japanese "to become responsible for their own internal defense, even though
to avoid frightening our other friends in the Pacific, we must always provide
the naval and air strength required in that region by the free world."[13]

When serious talks began on October 5, Ikeda announced that "there
were certain special circumstances that made increased defense outlays
difficult for Japan." Assistant Secretary of State Roberston and Joint Chiefs
Chairman Admiral Arthur Radford disregarded this plea. They insisted
that Japan faced a Soviet-Chinese military threat and must raise a ten-division army of some 325,000 men along with modest naval and air power.
Washington would supply the hardware, some money to procure military
end items in Japan, and allow Tokyo additional time to repay its debt of $2
billion left over from the Occupation. The Americans handed the Japanese
detailed proposals and awaited a reply.

Ikeda's response of October 13 sidestepped American demands. Most
Japanese, he suggested, were more anxious for the United States to "relax
the restrictions on the Red China trade" than sponsor large-scale rearmament. They wanted MSA aid to promote industrial development and
enhance Japanese trade opportunities in Southeast Asia. If this were done,
Japan would expand troop strength to 180,000 over three years and gradually develop modest naval and air forces.

The Americans considered this response totally "inadequate" and
demanded that Japan meet the 180,000 goal in one year and the 350,000-
man force in two or three more years. If Tokyo agreed, the United States
could increase military procurement by $100 million, grant Japan $50 million in agricultural commodities, and support a cotton credit and International Bank loan to build power plants.

Throughout the talks, Ikeda explained that Japan's constitution barred creation of other than purely defensive forces. Even an enlarged military would not be allowed to serve outside Japan. As Ikeda put it to Robertson, there was "no way except to proceed with an incremental plan, the minimum necessary." After a final, inconclusive session on October 30, the Japanese government characterized the discussions as a useful exercise that "deepened mutual understanding."

The two sides released a statement about the "profitable," "informal" exchange of views that laid the "groundwork for further cooperation" in Japan's effort to enhance its self-defense capacity. The only assistance mentioned was a $50-million grant of agricultural commodities (for sale in Japan with yen proceeds used for financing defense production), a $40 million International Bank loan, and a $60-million credit from the Export-Import Bank.[14]

Once back in Tokyo, Ikeda told Allison that he and Yoshida hoped to sign an MSA agreement that provided a maximum of economic aid and required a minimum of military expansion. Aware of the depth of opposition to rearmament, Allison privately sympathized with this approach and considered Dulles and Robertson wrong for seeing the Japanese as nothing more than footdraggers. This view of Japan, however, was reinforced by Vice President Richard Nixon's visit to Tokyo in November 1953.

The vice president arrived in the midst of a two-month Asian tour. As the first "state guest" since 1945, the Japanese were both honored by his presence and irked by his behavior. Nixon's advance team made elaborate arrangements for crowds of schoolchildren to line the route of his motorcade. They prepared photo ops to show him shaking hands with "ordinary people," most of whom, Allison reported, were quite uncomfortable when the foreigner pumped their hands before the cameras.

Nixon carried letters from Eisenhower to Yoshida and the emperor that warned of the threat to Japan posed by the Soviet bloc and implored Tokyo to hasten rearmament. The vice president told the Japan-American Society:

> Now if disarmament was right in 1946, why is it wrong in 1953? And if it was right in 1946 and wrong in 1953, why doesn't the United States admit for once that it made a mistake? And I am going to do something that I think perhaps ought to be done by people in public life. I'm going to admit right here that the United States did make a mistake in 1946.

This depiction of a central Occupation reform and constitutional provision as a "mistake" embarrassed Yoshida—who hid behind Article IX—and heartened his conservative rivals.

In discussions with Yoshida, Nixon warned of Red infiltration, the danger of neutralism, and the need to limit trade with China. According to Japanese journalists, Yoshida found the vice president so upsetting he suffered severe nosebleeds in Nixon's company. Worse still, the vice president met with Shigemitsu, who promptly declared the similarity between their basic views.[15]

MSA negotiations resumed in December 1953 when Robertson and Radford visited Tokyo, and continued through March 1954. The Defense Department still insisted that MSA aid be overseen by nearly 1,500 American officers and that American funds would be tied to rearmament. Yoshida's stiff resistance to a rapid force buildup resulted in an agreement in March 1954 along the lines Ikeda had proposed the previous October. Japan pledged to develop modest air and naval forces but capped ground strength at 180,000.

The prime minister secured modest economic assistance while limiting Japan's military obligations. In the agreement that became effective on July 1, Tokyo received an initial gift of military equipment valued at $150 million, $100 million in procurement orders, a grant of agricultural commodities, and a promise of technical aid to the Japanese defense industry.

The preamble to the MSA agreement stressed Washington's expectation that Japan would "increasingly assume responsibility for its own defense." But it also affirmed Japan's demand that, in planning the defense program, "economic stability will be an essential element for consideration" and that Japan would "only contribute to the extent permitted by its general economic conditions and capacities."

Foreign Minister Okazaki, on signing the agreement on March 8, 1953, explained that carrying out the duties and responsibilities of the agreement depended on the "conditions that exist in, and the separate interests of, the two countries." Japan's obligations would be "completely fulfilled by her carrying out the commitments already undertaken" in the existing security treaty. "There are no new and separate military duties," he made clear, nor would any question arise concerning "overseas service and so on for Japan's internal security forces." Despite nearly unanimous criticism of MSA from the Japanese press, intellectuals, and left-wing parties, the American embassy reported, "forces far more weighty"—namely, the bureaucratic, financial, and industrial circles—assured speedy Diet approval of the pact.[16]

Despite Yoshida's hope, the MSA agreement failed to bolster his political base. Following the July 1953 armistice in Korea, military procurement orders declined and the 1953 trade deficit (not including procurements) swelled to $1 billion. Even with MSA, American defense spending in Japan for 1954 totaled about $600 million, well below the 1951–53 average of $750 million. The trade deficit caused a serious erosion in Japanese currency reserves and forced Yoshida to implement an austerity budget.

Attacked by opponents on both the left and right, Yoshida and his aides issued thinly veiled warnings to Washington that, in light of the recent (May 1954) Vietminh victory at Dien Bien Phu, Japan might become more flexible in dealing with the Communist bloc unless it received more American assistance. In August, Ikeda told Ambassador Allison that when Yoshida visited Washington in the fall, it was "indispensable" for the prime minister "to bring back real presents from the United States." He did not care whether opponents called him a "puppet of somebody," so long as he was the "puppet of [a] benevolent somebody." These pleas and threats, however, elicited little response. Dulles believed Yoshida had lost too much influence among the bureaucracy, big business, and fellow conservatives to warrant new aid commitments.[17]

By September 1954 the budget crisis led Yoshida to reduce by 10 percent Tokyo's contribution to the military buildup. Coming so soon after making the commitment, this cut so angered John Allison that he fired off messages to Washington that condemned Japan as neither an ally nor partner "but a nation which for the time being is forced by circumstances to cooperate with the United States but which intends while doing so, to wring out of this relationship every possible advantage at the minimal cost." Despite its modern veneer, he sneered, the Japanese possessed "no abstract sense of right or wrong—their guide to conduct is situational and specific rather than general and ideal."[18]

Defense officials expressed even greater displeasure. General Carter B. Magruder, chief of staff of the Far Eastern Command in Tokyo, accused Japan of caring more about placating the Soviet Union than resisting communism. Magruder charged that Yoshida's scheme to make "Japan rich before we make her militarily strong would only weaken the moral fiber of her people" and postpone rearmament indefinitely. Unless Japan mustered the will to rearm, he considered it a "waste of money" to extend further aid.

Magruder proposed a last-ditch effort to "kindle . . . a more aggressive spirit." Washington might "actively seek the replacement of the present Japanese government," reduce aid to force Japan to defend its interests, or urge "Japan to seek a position of leadership in Northeast Asia." To foster a more militant outlook, he proposed that the United States indicate it "would view favorably the re-establishment of the Japanese Empire under a moderate Japanese Government."[19]

After Allison blew off steam, he decided that for the time being the goals of political stability and economic recovery "should be given absolute and urgent priority in our programs." Unfortunately, Japan held "no basic convictions for or against the free world or communism" and Tokyo pursued any course that would "advance Japanese interests." The task for the United States was to convince Japanese leaders that "they need us at least as much if not more than we need them." Tokyo had to realize that temporary setbacks in Southeast Asia did not alter the basic fact that "ours is the winning side."[20]

The Ashes of Death

Even while Washington grumbled over Japan's laggard defense effort, a deadly cloud stoked new popular resentment against the nascent alliance. On March 1, 1954, the United States exploded its first thermonuclear (hydrogen) bomb at Bikini Atoll in the Pacific. Undetected by spotter planes, a 100-ton Japanese fishing boat, the *Fukuryu Maru*, or *Lucky Dragon* # 5, trawled for tuna in the waters near the Marshall Islands, about eighty-five miles downwind from Bikini and just outside the previously announced danger zone. The unexpectedly powerful 15-megaton blast along with a shift in wind direction dispersed radioactive debris beyond the security cordon, requiring emergency evacuation of American test personnel as well as 200 Marshall Islanders. Unknown to American officials, contaminated ashes and rain fell on the crew and cargo of the *Lucky Dragon*. Alarmed by what had happened, the captain headed back to Japan.[21]

Up to this point, American nuclear tests in the Pacific had not become a source of conflict with Japan. Even if Tokyo had raised objections to atmospheric detonations, the United States was so determined to speed development of the H-bomb that it would surely have brushed aside complaints. Although Japan relied heavily on ocean fishing, the Yoshida government could not afford to raise American hackles by questioning the safety of nuclear testing in the Pacific.

The captain of the *Lucky Dragon* did not report the incident until after his vessel returned to Japan on March 14 and he had consulted with the ship's owner. By then, several crew members showed symptoms of radiation illness and entered a Tokyo hospital. News of their exposure quickly leaked out to the press, which reported that the ship and crew had been "dusted by the ashes of death."[22]

The U.S. Atomic Energy Commission (AEC) was so concerned with maintaining secrecy about the hydrogen bomb's technical characteristics that its behavior transformed a human tragedy into a crisis in the Pacific alliance. Although AEC chairman Louis Strauss assured Eisenhower that his agency could handle any problem, it made a bad situation worse. Strauss initially believed the *Lucky Dragon* "was a Red spy outfit," commanded by a Soviet agent who intentionally exposed his crew and catch of fish to radiation to embarrass the United States and ferret out nuclear secrets. Furious at this alleged setup by "Russian espionage," Strauss opposed revealing data to Japanese medical personnel on the chemical composition of the radioactive ash since it might disclose details of the bomb's construction.

Secretary of State Dulles issued a bland statement of regret and instructed Ambassador Allison to press the Japanese government to place the *Lucky Dragon* under de facto control of the U.S. Navy. The AEC dispatched two medical scientists to Japan, with their primary intent to limit public disclosure and monitor the effects of radiation poisoning, not to treat the ailing crewmen.

AEC foot-dragging and presidential uncertainty delayed action on Allison's proposal that he soothe Japanese feelings by making a tentative apology and promising compensation if the United States was proved to be at fault. After a week passed with no apology, Diet members expressed outrage. The situation grew worse when tuna from several other boats were found to be slightly radioactive. This caused a brief panic and the dumping of suspect fish.[23]

Nasty disagreements between Japanese and American medical personnel over treatment of the crew kept the incident in public view. The physician caring for the injured men, Dr. Tsuzuki Masao, harbored a grudge against Americans since Occupation officials confiscated his research notes on the effects of radiation in Hiroshima and Nagasaki—and then published the information without crediting him. Furious over the effort of the AEC to muscle in on his new case, he charged that some of the fishermen would die because of "irresponsible" American behavior. The standoff intensified when the AEC maintained silence on the composition of the radioactive ash and Japanese doctors refused to turn over the injured men for treatment by Americans. Diet members, the press, and the Japanese public accused Washington of showing indifference toward human life and called Yoshida an American toady for not doing more to help the crew. Several American congressmen responded by accusing Japan of using fishing boats for spying and exaggerating the injuries suffered. By the end of March, leaders in both countries realized they faced a crisis.[24]

When Dulles pressed the AEC to be more forthcoming with the Japanese, Strauss responded that critics of his agency "grossly exaggerated" the problem. On March 30, Eisenhower finally weighed in, ordering that Strauss explain publicly how atmospheric conditions, not indifference or secrecy, caused contamination of the *Lucky Dragon*. But Strauss only made matters worse by again questioning the severity of the crew's illness and noting that the Marshall Islanders downwind from the test appeared healthy. Adding insult to injury, the AEC chairman gratuitously boasted that the hydrogen bomb had the power to "take out . . . any city."[25]

From Tokyo, Allison informed Washington of the "ominous" implications of the problem. The *Lucky Dragon* incident coincided with the deterioration of Yoshida's grip on power, the French defeat at Dien Bien Phu and subsequent Geneva Conference, and the mounting opposition by leftists and neutralists to rearmament in association with what they now called "war-loving America." The ambassador thought the only way to staunch the mounting hysteria in Japan was by cooperating more closely with local officials, providing better medical assistance, monitoring the tuna industry, and offering immediate compensation for damages.

These sensible proposals came too late. Under attack for its initial refusal to protest the Pacific nuclear tests or make the *Lucky Dragon* a cause célèbre, the Yoshida cabinet now feared appearing too eager to reach a settlement with the United States. To hold the prime minister's feet to the fire, the Diet passed a resolution demanding the suspension of nuclear tests in the Pacific. Public discontent swelled after the American medical specialists sent to Tokyo became angry with local arrangements and left in a huff. About the same time, the American image received another blow when the U.S. Navy barred a Japanese research vessel from surveying the sea near the Marshall Islands.

Responding to popular outrage, the Japanese government demanded that Washington give compensation to the *Lucky Dragon* crew and their families, pick up medical costs, and pay damages to the tuna industry. The United States offered only token compensation to injured crew members without admitting liability. At the end of May, Allison was authorized to propose a $150,000 settlement, far short of the $7.5 million demanded by Tokyo.[26]

Allison then returned to Washington to discuss both the *Lucky Dragon* incident and a visit to the United States by Yoshida. The ambassador told the president, vice president, and secretary of state the importance of resolving the *Lucky Dragon* affair before it further damaged the alliance. Given the anxiety in Washington regarding Japan's economic uncertainty and political restiveness, its pleas for expanded trade with China, and mounting troubles in Indochina, Eisenhower and Dulles agreed to authorize a $1 million payment to make the problem go away.[27]

By then, however, Japanese domestic politics and popular sentiment limited Yoshida's room to maneuver. Crew member Kuboyama Aikichi died on September 23. At the autopsy, Dr. Tsuzuki again charged that American callousness had killed his patient. Although Allison expressed personal regrets to the widow and offered a one-million yen ($2764) consolation payment, Foreign Minister Okazaki declared that more than money was required to resolve the crisis. Okazaki appealed to Washington to move the site of future nuclear explosions, provide advance notice of tests, and offer "sufficient compensation" to the fishing industry.[28]

These demands stiffened American resistance. Allison and Dulles objected less to the money Yoshida demanded than to his inability to control the bureaucracy or public opinion. By October 1954, they guessed he would soon be out of office and decided to delay a settlement until a successor was chosen. When Foreign Minister Okazaki came to Washington in October to discuss Yoshida's impending visit, and warned that payment of less than $2 million might "end the Yoshida government," his threat carried no weight. Dulles put him off by saying that Congress must approve a large settlement and this risked "bad reactions" among the public.[29]

On December 29, shortly after Yoshida's resignation, Dulles approved $2 million in compensation (paid from MSA funds) to settle claims arising from the *Lucky Dragon* affair. The new prime minister, Hatoyama Ichiro, and foreign minister, Shigemitsu Mamoru, portrayed it as evidence of Washington's support for their leadership. Eisenhower and Dulles welcomed resolution of the dispute as an inexpensive way to curtail antinuclear and anti-alliance sentiment within Japan.[30]

The nuclear tests at Bikini also provided a backdrop for *Godzilla: King of the Monsters*, the first of over twenty Japanese so-called creature features. Produced quickly and released a few months after the *Lucky Dragon* affair, the original Godzilla (or Goijira, in Japanese) was hatched by South Pacific nuclear tests and rose from the ocean's depths to rampage across Japan. Director Honda Inoshiro and producer Tanaka Tomoyuki, who considered the film a social critique, employed the monster genre as an acceptable way to question U.S. nuclear testing in the Pacific, a subject forbidden during the Occupation and discouraged afterward. Although a generation of American youth screamed in wonder as the fire-breathing dragon destroyed population centers, among Japanese who survived the Pacific War Godzilla's wrath recalled the destruction of Tokyo, Hiroshima, and Nagasaki. To Washington's dismay, the fallout incident and film kindled a growing antinuclear movement.[31]

The End of the Yoshida Era

On September 26, 1954, three days after the death of the *Lucky Dragon* crewman, a politically wounded Yoshida left Japan for a two-month tour of Europe and North America. In the United States from November 2 to 13, he conferred with Eisenhower and Dulles and made several speeches. Having outlived his usefulness as the "puppet of a benevolent somebody," Yoshida received courtesy but no patronage.

The prime minister relied on MITI Minister Aichi Kiichi to conduct discussions with the Americans. Aichi requested additional military procurements, help in expanding trade with Southeast Asia, the relaxation of export restrictions to China, and assistance in obtaining GATT membership for Japan. Yoshida received indulgent smiles from Eisenhower and Dulles when he spoke of boosting Japanese immigration to Latin America and paroling war criminals.

To the discomfort of his hosts, Aichi expressed doubts about the new American-sponsored Southeast Asian Treaty Organization (SEATO) and military involvement in Indochina. The "test of strength in fighting communism" in Southeast Asia, he asserted, "lies as much if not more so, in the political and economic fields as in the military." The region's chronic underdevelopment, lack of capital, and unresolved reparations claims posed more daunting barriers to Japanese trade expansion than Communist aggression.

In a public talk, Yoshida warned that if China's economic progress "outstrips her neighbors," the "gravitational pull will be too much to resist and Southeast Asia will fall to the Communists without a struggle." From a "political point of view," his aides informed the Americans, if the "greater part of Southeast Asia should be placed under the Communist sphere of influence, Japan will find it impossible to stand out of it alone."[32]

Yoshida issued a final plea for the United States to increase economic assistance to Asia tenfold. A $4 billion Asian Marshall Plan, he and Aichi asserted, would boost production of raw materials in Southeast Asia and allow the region to buy more Japanese goods. Regional prosperity would help contain China.

Yoshida and Aichi tried, in vain, to get Dulles to alter America's economic offensive against China. They drafted a "joint declaration" in which

Eisenhower and Yoshida announced that free world security would "better be served by a properly regulated intercourse between the peoples of Japan and China than by the interposition of an impenetrable wall designed to cut off all relationship." Instead of trying to maintain an impossible vacuum around China, Washington and Tokyo would attempt to channel the "inevitable forces leading to a greater understanding between China and Japan into a road open to friendship and trade." Dulles promptly vetoed this proposal and remained noncommittal about expanding aid to Southeast Asia and Japan.[33]

On November 10, a bland communiqué appeared in the name of Eisenhower and Yoshida. It stressed their desire to cooperate with the "free nations of Asia" and acknowledged that Japan's prosperity had importance to "the entire free world." The United States would help promote Japan's exports, provide additional surplus food under more flexible terms, and assist regional development. Eisenhower expressed regret for the Bikini incident, but included an offer to promote in Japan the "peaceful uses of atomic energy."[34]

Yoshida's failure to win additional economic or political support in Washington sealed his political fate. By the end of November his support within the Liberal Party disappeared. The three top contenders to succeed him—Kishi Nobusuke, Hatoyama Ichiro, and Shigemitsu Mamoru—were all former purgees. Kishi, wartime head of the munitions ministry, had spent three years in Sugamo Prison under investigation for war crimes. Nevertheless, Ambassador Allison threw his support behind Kishi who, as we will see, became an American favorite after his release from prison. Kishi advocated merging the main conservative groups into a unified party (achieved in 1955) and inspired confidence by telling embassy staff that "for the next twenty-five years it would be in Japan's best interests to cooperate closely with the United States."[35]

Yoshida received a no-confidence vote in the Diet on December 6, 1954, and resigned the following day. The conservative coalition disappointed Washington by selecting Hatoyama, rather than Kishi, as prime minister. Although Hatoyama's past support for rearmament had pleased Washington, his interest in forging closer ties with the Soviet Union and China spelled trouble.

Robert Murphy, former ambassador to Tokyo and now deputy undersecretary of state, articulated American concerns in a speech entitled "America, Japan and the Future of the Pacific." Murphy described "three main objectives" of the Communists in the Pacific. They sought control of Chinese manpower, Japanese industry, and Southeast Asian resources. The first objective had been obtained and China now "threatened Southeast Asia as the best path to Japan." Unless China were contained, Tokyo's trade with the United States expanded, and Southeast Asian resources protected, Murphy warned, he saw little hope of "keeping Japan out of China's maw." This outlook proved a driving force in Japanese-American relations during the 1950s—and beyond.[36]

5 CHINA AND JAPAN,

1952–60

*I*N July 1953, as the Korean armistice took hold, the Japanese Diet unanimously passed a resolution favoring increased trade with the People's Republic of China. Conservative and Socialist politicians joined business and labor groups to demand that Washington release Tokyo from special restrictions that forbade Japan from selling to China many products that Europeans sold freely. With the "exception of the problems arising from the presence in Japan of United States Armed Forces," embassy counselor Frank Waring reported, "no other single issue affects Japanese-United States relations so adversely." In their desperate search for increased trade, Japanese saw neither "justice or reason" in demanding greater restraints on them "than from other allies."

In August, Bank of Japan Governor Ichimada Hisato told John Foster Dulles that although sales to China would probably remain limited even if trade controls were relaxed, the "problem had become a political issue of first magnitude." The China trade question assumed symbolic overtones of sovereignty with the result that the partial embargo contributed to a "growing spirit of anti-Americanism" that threatened all aspects of the alliance.[1]

Western and Japanese trade with the Soviet bloc was regulated by the Coordinating Committee of the Paris-based Consultative Group (COCOM) established at the behest of the United States in 1949. During the Korean War, COCOM created a special China Committee (CHINCOM) to control exports to the People's Republic. Japanese resentment focused on restrictions covering 400 items that the United States pressured Japan to include in a secret bilateral accord of September 1952. Relaxing these rules, Waring estimated, would yield additional Japanese sales to China of only $25 to

$50 million per year. Since NATO countries were allowed to sell many of the Japan-embargoed items directly to Beijing—and others indirectly via the Soviet Union—permitting additional Japanese exports would not enhance China's industrial or war potential.

Some Japanese anticipated a revival of the brisk trade that prevailed during the 1930s when China, by some estimates, absorbed as much as 20 percent of Japan's exports and supplied 12 percent of its raw materials. But COCOM/CHINCOM controls, coupled with China's limited financial resources and economic nationalism, made this unlikely. As Waring pointed out, the insult of unequal treatment angered the Japanese at least as much as the injury of lost trade. Alluding to the cataclysm of 1941, Waring warned that the "volatile and emotional Japanese," if "thwarted in achieving a legitimate objective" were "capable of turning quickly to extremes." Denied equal treatment, they might break with the United States on more important security matters. It seemed foolish to alienate Japan in order to "uphold a policy involving" a few million dollars "in sales of non-strategic goods." With Ambassador Allison's blessing, Waring recommended that the same rules governing trade with China be applied to Tokyo as to the European allies.

Japan's desire to expand trade with China became a focal point of tension with the United States during the 1950s and divided President Eisenhower from many of his advisers. British and Japanese pressure eventually forced the United States to modify the entire system of trade controls with the Soviet bloc. This meant scrapping both the special restrictions on Sino-Japanese trade and the so-called China differential, the prohibition on selling China products approved for export to the Soviet Union.

The Truman administration initially favored regulated trade between China and Japan. Ideally, it would speed Japanese recovery, ease America's aid burden, and possibly draw China away from the Soviet orbit. Following China's entry into the Korean War, however, Washington pressed its allies to cease most trade with Beijing. After the Korean armistice, Great Britain and Japan were especially anxious to expand trade with China by applying the same rules that governed exports to the Soviet Union. The United States, however, insisted on retaining the so-called China differential as well as the even more restrictive controls on Sino-Japanese trade.

The Eisenhower administration considered trade a critical component of the "wedge strategy" designed to fracture the Sino-Soviet alliance. The wedge, however, had both "hard" and "soft" components. Officials such as Secretary of State John Foster Dulles, Assistant Secretary of State Walter Robertson, Treasury Secretary George Humphrey, Joint Chiefs of Staff Chairman Admiral Arthur Radford, and Joseph Dodge (who now chaired the Council on Foreign Economic Policy) held that stringent export controls would make China completely reliant on a Soviet patron unable to meet its economic needs. Forced to its knees—and senses— China would break with the Soviet Union and return to the Western fold.

Proponents of a "soft" wedge, most notably President Dwight D. Eisenhower, considered it "hopeless to imagine that we could break China away from the Soviets and from Communism short of some great cataclysm." Flexibility, not hostility, he believed, held out a better chance to induce Beijing to cast off the Soviet embrace. "History," the president remarked in 1954, indicated that "revolutions rarely arose in societies that were completely ground down by poverty and hunger." But when "they got a taste of better things of life [the issue at hand involved the sale of surplus butter!] their discontent with their lot flamed into revolt."

Eisenhower also stressed the need to accommodate allies such as Great Britain and Japan. If "all trade between the free world and the Soviet bloc is completely cut off," he wondered "how much will the United States then do to help those free world countries which depend on trade, such as Japan?" Was the United States prepared to subsidize Tokyo or to risk its economic collapse? A total embargo on China "simply slammed the door in Japan's face."

In his first months in office, Eisenhower argued that trade "could be a weapon on our side." Allowing Japan to export "harmless manufactured goods" would "serve the dual purpose of relieving Communist China's dependence on the USSR and Japan's dependence on our own Treasury." Throughout his presidency, despite two confrontations with China in the Taiwan Strait, he remained a persistent, if behind-the-scene, advocate of flexible trade toward the People's Republic of China (PRC). Demonstrating a grasp of economics that often surpassed that of his expert advisers, Eisenhower consistently maintained that access to Chinese markets "was indispensable to the livelihood of Japan."[2]

Both Japanese conservatives and leftists favored greater contact with China despite American multilateral trade controls and the anathema Washington pronounced on diplomatic relations between the two countries. Even Yoshida, who pledged not to recognize the PRC, insisted that, for trade, it did not matter whether China was "red or green." By separating politics and economics, a policy known as *seikei bunri*, the Japanese government managed to observe the prohibition on official contact with China without sacrificing all commercial advantage. It also provided Yoshida and his successors some cover from accusations that by slavishly following American policy they undermined Japan's interests. The Socialists went along with this policy that allowed opposition members of the Diet and leftist intellectuals to serve as intermediaries in cultural and commercial exchanges between China and Japan. Performing such quasi-governmental functions increased their legitimacy and coincided with their goal of weaning Japan away from its cold war alliance with the United States.

Between 1952 and 1958, Japan concluded four "private sector" commercial agreements with China using intellectuals, business organizations, labor unions, and Diet members as negotiators. Private groups such as the China-Japan Trade Promotion Association, Dietman's League for the Promotion of Japan-China Trade, Japan-China Friendship Association, Japan Association for the Promotion of International Trade, and the Japan-China Importers and Exporters Association arranged trade, tourism, and cultural exchanges.

The first agreement, arranged by three Diet members in Beijing on June 1, 1952, proposed the barter of goods worth $84 million. China would exchange coal, soybeans, iron ore, rice, and bristles for Japanese iron, steel, textile machinery, and insecticides. Since many of these Japanese goods were on the U.S. embargo list, the agreement had more symbolic than commercial value.[3]

After the Korean armistice, Chinese Premier Zhou Enlai told a prominent Japanese intellectual visiting Beijing that the two countries should expand cultural and commercial contact even in the absence of diplomatic ties. Zhou followed this by hosting a delegation from the nonpartisan Dietmen's League for Promotion of China Trade. In October 1953, Diet members and industrialists signed a second trade agreement with China that contained a Chinese request for the barter of forbidden goods and a mutual pledge to discuss the exchange of permanent trade representatives. The pact's quasi-official tone piqued Washington's concern. Japanese officials assured American diplomats that the agreement would not increase trade much but would help counter Socialist complaints.[4]

Triangular Trade Diplomacy: Washington, London, and Tokyo

In public, the Eisenhower administration showed few signs of flexibility toward China or Sino-Japanese trade. In a nod to hardliners, Eisenhower announced in his inaugural speech that the Seventh Fleet would no longer block Taiwan from attacking the Chinese mainland. Washington also delivered jet fighters to the Nationalist air force. But the "unleashing of Chiang Kai-shek," as the press called it, had little practical effect. In private, Eisenhower and Dulles criticized Truman's earlier decision to send modern weapons to Taiwan and ordered aides to "hold up deliveries" until a "commitment had been obtained" from Taiwan to "play ball" and not use these weapons "recklessly and in a fashion to embarrass" Washington. Dulles appointed the vehemently anti-Communist Walter Robertson as Assistant Secretary of State for Far Eastern Affairs, but allowed him little influence over policy.[5]

The first comprehensive review of China policy undertaken by Eisenhower's National Security Council (NSC) called for maintaining "hard wedge" pressure on the PRC to speed its defection from Moscow or compel the replacement of its Communist leadership. At the same time, the NSC suggested the need to provide China with an "avenue of escape" should its leaders alter their "pro-Soviet, anti-U.S. orientation." Eisenhower and his advisers soon realized that Tokyo had as much need for an "avenue of escape" as Beijing did.[6]

During the first two years of the Eisenhower administration, presidential advisers expressed ambivalence about Japan's need for a China market. Speaking at an NSC meeting on March 31, 1953, Dulles noted that Japan "was living to a considerable extent off United States expenditures for the prosecution of the Korean War." When the fighting ceased, Japan would require an infusion of economic assistance, the "amount . . . depend[ing] on American trade policies" toward China and Southeast Asia. The Director of Mutual Security, Harold Stassen, agreed. Continued military procurements could "accomplish wonders" in developing Japan's "great potentiality," he asserted, but locating markets for its civilian exports required an "Asia wide approach to foreign trade."[7]

Cabinet and NSC discussions about Japan focused on the economic dilemma posed by Communist control of China. "Was it even thinkable," Treasury Secretary Humphrey asked in April 1953, "that Japan could have a viable economy if . . . confined to the home islands? [W]ere we not simply kidding ourselves?" Dulles responded that current levels of assistance might sustain Japan for "perhaps five years," but after that no policy that "separated Japan from the Asiatic mainland would be practical."

Eisenhower came at the question differently, suggesting that "there was no future for Japan unless access were provided for it to the markets and raw materials of Manchuria and North China." Even "over the short haul," he believed, "a certain amount of Japanese trade with Communist China should be permitted in place of the complete embargo and blockade which now existed." Dulles still hoped for a "revival of Japanese trade with the various free nations of Asia as at least a temporary substitute" for China.

Robert Cutler, the president's assistant for national security, wondered if the administration should simply "adopt a policy which would look to the restoration of Japan's lost colonial empire." Eisenhower agreed only that the United States should help to "open up new trade possibilities for Japan." Worried that he meant China, Treasury Secretary Humphrey warned that "we could not hope to keep Japan as a loyal ally of the West if it became dependent economically on Communist China." Trade provided "the Chinese Communists with a terrible club to hold over Japan."[8]

On the eve of the Korean armistice, Dulles described Japan's economic prospect as "desperate." He predicted a decline in military procurements, making it nearly impossible for the Japanese to solve "their terrible trade deficit." Although Dulles urged boosting Tokyo's trade with Southeast Asia, he recognized that "continued hostility toward Japan" in that area presented "an obstacle" only time and reparations could overcome.

Eisenhower wondered why his civilian advisers did not agree to help Japan by liberalizing trade with the Communist bloc and why the Pentagon opposed relinquishing control over several islands seized from Japan in 1945. After all, "retention of Japan and of its potential strength" was far more vital to "our own security interests" than possession of some rocks.[9]

The president responded to the decline in procurements, the surging trade deficit, and the Diet resolution on China by telling Dulles on August 10,

1953, that he considered it "indispensable" to encourage nonstrategic trade between Japan and China. However, when the State Department drafted less restrictive rules, the Defense and Commerce Departments objected to their undercutting the objective of isolating China. Hesitant to impose his will on a divided bureaucracy, Eisenhower settled for immediate removal of twenty items from the forbidden list and promised Tokyo that his administration would review the remaining restrictions.[10]

During the vice president's autumn trip through Asia, Nixon echoed Eisenhower's position. Despite the administration's tough anti-China rhetoric, he told Britain's High Commissioner in Singapore Malcolm Mac-Donald, if Beijing "became more reasonable about the Korean political talks, we should then seek to help them further." Eisenhower, Nixon explained, was "keen on this idea" to "improve trade with China" as a reward for moderation.[11]

The president admonished the NSC that the "only sensible course of action" on trade with Communist nations was to "apply the criterion of the net gain. What do we get out of this policy in terms of what we put in?" He considered trade a "powerful weapon" to "weaken the Sino-Soviet alliance," adding "facetiously" that he would even "send jet aircraft to the Chinese Communists if it could be shown to our net advantage." In any case, "we could not afford to forget about Japan and its need for economic viability."[12]

While Washington avoided a decision about easing export controls, Prime Minister Winston Churchill announced on February 25, 1954, that he would press for a general relaxation of COCOM controls on sales to the Soviet Union. When Pentagon, Commerce, CIA, and State Department spokesmen warned that this would provide China with increased access, via Moscow, to forbidden goods, Eisenhower asked them "How could we rationally insist that neither we nor our allies . . . sell any of these materials to the Soviets" when the United States produced "a vast agricultural surplus" and could not absorb additional exports from Europe and Japan? Sales to the Communist nations stirred such "emotion and prejudice," he complained, that otherwise intelligent people lost sight of "what we are going to do to [help] our allies over the long term." Their loyalty would erode quickly if the United States tried to "stifle the trade of the free world."[13]

"Trade," Churchill wrote to Eisenhower on March 24, "means contacts and probably involves a good deal of friendly infiltration which I think would be to our advantage from every point of view, including the military." The "arrival of Germany and Japan in the world market," he added, "make it necessary that we should open our trade in every possible direction." Eisenhower replied that while Britain's position went "a bit further than seems wise or necessary," he predicted that when "we pass from the general to the concrete we shall be able to reach agreement." In fact, with American consent, in July 1954 COCOM expanded the list of items approved for sale to the Soviet Union.[14]

Although this action did not eliminate the China differential, Eisenhower partially appeased Tokyo. In April 1954, he released Japan from the higher level of trade restrictions stipulated in the 1952 bilateral agreement. The State Department notified Tokyo that so long as it did so gradually and quietly, Japan could begin sales to China of most of the 400 items it alone was forbidden to export. This left in place the China differential, but it at least applied the same standard to European and Japanese trade with China.[15]

These token changes reduced some of the resentment felt by the Japanese but neither resolved the larger China trade issue nor bolstered Japan's sagging economy. Speaking to legislative leaders on June 21, 1954, Eisenhower chided key groups in Congress that seemed set on "no trade with Red China," "no [U.S. participation in] war in Southeast Asia," and "no further liberalization of trade" with Japan. If "we didn't do a little of some of these things," he warned, "we would lose Japan." Then the "U.S. would be out of the Pacific and it would become a communist lake."[16]

The recent Vietminh victory at Dien Bien Phu and the ongoing talks at the Geneva Conference over the fate of Southeast Asia (discussed later) underscored the president's warning. In a speech to the National Editorial Association on June 22, Eisenhower declared it had become "absolutely mandatory to us" to prevent the loss of Japan's industrial war-making potential. Stressing the challenge of supporting eighty-five million people in an area the size of California, he observed:

> Japan cannot live, and Japan cannot remain in the free world unless something is done to allow her to make a living. Now if we will not give her any money, if we will not trade with her, if we will not allow her to trade with the Reds, if we will not try to defend in any way the Southeast Asian area where she has a partial trade opportunity, what is to happen to Japan? It is going to the Communists.

None of these initiatives alone, he admitted, would save Japan, and "any one of them pursued to an extreme would ruin us." But American self-interest demanded that all be pursued.[17]

During 1954, the trade debate grew more intense as the British pressed to loosen further export control. Eisenhower often seemed the only member of his administration who sympathized with allied demands. On July 2, he opened an NSC discussion by saying he "might just as well sit back and listen to what the members of the Council had to say on . . . East–West trade because, as the members of the Council well knew, he thought they were all wrong on the subject."

Most of Eisenhower's advisers opposed the British initiative. Secretary of Commerce Weeks, Defense Secretary Wilson, and Treasury Secretary Humphrey warned that relaxation of trade with the Soviet Union would prompt Japan to demand "trade in strategic items with Communist China." Eisenhower asked that Weeks "answer me this question: What *are* we going to do about Japan? If you forbid them to trade with Communist

China and if you will not admit their products to the United States, or if you do not find some other way out for them, they will slip into communism." Before the president went further, Dulles persuaded him to postpone any action on East–West trade until after the conclusion of the Geneva conference.[18]

On August 6, the president and his cabinet discussed Japan's economic plight and what Dulles called "communist efforts to win over Japan by economic proposals." Japan had gone to war once to secure markets and raw materials and unless assured of both might not remain "on our side," Dulles warned. Since he was certain American consumers would shun Japanese goods as merely "cheap imitations of our own," Dulles described Southeast Asian markets as vital to Japanese progress. For the moment, he urged lowering tariffs to give Japan a temporary niche in the American market.

Eisenhower thought Dulles had inadvertently proved the "absolute fallacy" of saying "there should be *no* East-West trade." Exchanges of Japanese consumer goods for Chinese coal and iron ore, for example, should be encouraged. When Commerce officials suggested making Japan's exports more price competitive in the West by forcing down wages, Eisenhower snapped that this would only make Japan "ripe for communism." Closing trade options or driving down living standards would push Japan "beyond the point of no return." The United States must either "hold Japan for the free world or we must go to war to keep it in the free world."[19]

The transition of power in Tokyo, from Yoshida to Hatoyama in December 1954 highlighted these deliberations. CIA director Allen Dulles characterized the new prime minister as generally pro-American. However, he had made a deal with the Socialists to hold elections in February 1955 and Dulles speculated (correctly) that the left would gain enough seats to block constitutional reform and rearmament. Hatoyama also intended to pursue offers by the Soviet Union and China to improve trade and perhaps diplomatic relations. Even the usually pro-American foreign minister in the new government, Shigemitsu Mamoru, adopted a position that troubled Washington. Although Japan had no "concrete plans for regularizing Japanese relations with the Communist bloc," Shigemitsu explained, it did not "want to block off Red China in a watertight compartment." This prompted a flurry of warnings to Tokyo concerning the danger of flirting with Beijing.

Eisenhower told his colleagues that Shigemitsu's remarks made his case for trade flexibility. Did anyone in the CIA, he asked, possess the competence to assess the "net effect on China of encouraging Japan to export a variety of consumer goods for use in North China and Manchuria?" Was it not likely that freer trade would "result in an infiltration of democratic ideas" into China? Even if the "political temper" within America forced him to retain a complete embargo on China, why should this "also apply to Japan" whose "traditional trade with China" was a "vital necessity?" Trade could be a diplomat's "greatest weapon" and the State Department needed to "make use of such weapons."[20]

Early in 1955, the Dietmen's League, with nearly half of all Diet members in its ranks, joined the Japan Association for the Promotion of International Trade, composed of over forty leading industrialists, to invite a Chinese trade delegation to negotiate a new trade pact in Tokyo. When Dulles and Allison complained that this invitation verged on recognition, the trade issue moved from the margin to the center of Japan–U.S. relations.

Prime Minister Hatoyama, already on thin ice with Washington because of his effort to improve ties with the Soviet Union, presided over an unstable coalition of conservative parties and factions. Several of his coalition rivals saw a tilt toward Beijing or Washington as a way to improve their own political standing. Foreign Minister Shigemitsu, for example, hoped to assure American backing for a bid to replace Hatoyama by insisting that Japan could not afford to cross Washington on this issue. MITI head and political hopeful Ishibashi Tanzan argued with equal vigor that Tokyo had every right to host a Chinese trade delegation and must expand its commercial outlets.

Hatoyama compromised by permitting the PRC delegation to visit Japan but distanced his government from its activities. To placate Washington, he restricted travel of the Chinese within Japan and, with an assist from the American embassy, pressured larger firms that exported products to the United States or produced goods for the American military to avoid contact with the delegation.[21]

After five weeks in Japan, the two sides concluded the third private-sector trade pact on May 4, 1955. Once again, China insisted on the barter of its raw materials for embargoed Japanese manufactured goods, effectively limiting commerce. But in a departure from the earlier agreements, it went beyond barter by providing for financial transactions to be handled by the central banks of the two countries, creating a joint arbitration system for contractual disputes, and calling for reciprocal trade fairs. The provision that most upset Washington called for Japan and China to post permanent trade representatives in each other's capital.

Hatoyama initially approved this proposal but backpedaled when Shigemitsu warned that official approval of an exchange of representatives would gravely injure Japan's ties with the United States. The prime minister permitted an aide to tell the Dietmen's League to inform the Chinese delegation that he expressed informal, rather than official, "support and cooperation" for this arrangement. Hatoyama informed the Diet on May 15 that he "might consider" the mutual posting of consular representatives if it did not involve diplomatic recognition of the PRC. After this, Allison, Dulles, and other American officials routinely cautioned the Japanese that diplomatic dealings with Beijing might provoke pro-Taiwan, anti-PRC elements in Congress to undercut Eisenhower's economic support for Japan. Although the exchange of trade representatives was deferred, Sino-Japanese trade reached $151 million in 1956, or 2 percent of Japan's total two-way trade.[22]

Disputes with Great Britain and Japan over controls on exports to the Communist bloc in general, and over the China differential in particular, vexed American policymakers for the next several years. British prime ministers Churchill, Anthony Eden, and Harold Macmillan, in succession, demanded that the United States loosen East–West trade controls. In the face of growing German and Japanese competition, British industry sought added commercial outlets in Eastern Europe and China. London believed the China differential impeded its own and Hong Kong's trade with China while forcing Japan to dump cheap goods in Southeast Asian markets, which hurt British exports.

Although Eisenhower agreed with this view, he found few allies in his cabinet or Congress—most of whom chastised Britain and Japan or sought to place the blame for trade restrictions solely on Moscow and Beijing. The president thought this was unlikely to impress foreigners who heard rabid anti-Chinese "speeches by Senator Knowland and other members of Congress" and believed they "represented the Administration's policy."

Eisenhower's reluctance to impose his will on policy showed in his acceptance on April 9, 1955, of an NSC paper on Japan. The NSC predicted "serious friction" between Japan and the United States as Tokyo pursued "closer relations with the Communist bloc." Although Washington did not oppose the establishment of diplomatic relations between Japan and the Soviet Union, it viewed Japanese recognition of China and unrestricted trade as likely to make Japan "dependent upon Communist areas for essential and raw material supplies and export markets." Dulles tried to soften the impact of this position by telling Foreign Minister Shigemitsu in August 1955 that American studies suggested that China would not buy much from Japan even if export controls were eliminated. "Revision of the export list" might be "inevitable," but the "time had not come yet."[23]

On December 1955, the British decided the time had indeed come for revision. London informed Washington it would unilaterally eliminate the China differential unless the Consultative Group moved quickly to do so.[24] Admiral Radford predicted that if the United States went along with this demand, "we would be finished in the Far East" and Japan would pass "under the control of Communist China." But most of Eisenhower's advisers agreed with Dulles who now recognized that the only hope of preserving a vestige of multilateral controls lay in "agree[ing] to something like the British suggestion." Japan had put nearly as much pressure on the United States to "reduce the CHINCOM list," Dulles noted. By now, the argument that trade controls gave the United States "negotiating value" over China "had just about reached the zero point." Dulles told Eisenhower he "simply could not hold the dike any longer; his thumb was not big enough." Dubbing his secretary of state the "Chief Salvage Official," Eisenhower instructed Dulles to work out a deal with the British and Japanese to gradually place trade with China on the same basis as with the Soviet Union.[25]

In advance of his January 31, 1956, meeting with Prime Minister Eden, the president sparred with his critics. Some, like Radford, warned that relaxing trade barriers would weaken the morale of anti-Communist Asians and push them toward an "accommodation with Beijing." Joseph Dodge predicted that trade liberalization would bolster the Soviet "economic offensive" against the free world and undermine national security. Eisenhower retorted that if Washington tried to "dam up international trade," the dam would eventually burst and "overwhelm" America. The president thought the whole debate could be solved in a "one page memorandum" that showed "what this system of trade controls was actually costing the United States and its allies." Moreover, Eisenhower stressed, "he was not afraid of Communist China—not in this decade at least."[26]

Eisenhower and Eden got on better than either anticipated. The prime minister backed away from his threat to abandon multilateral trade controls. "All I am trying to do," he explained, "is to get those [Soviet and Chinese] control lists nearer together" and "get the matter moving." Eisenhower accepted this and added that if "we did not let Japan trade with Communist China . . . we would be in for serious trouble." He supported decontrol primarily "to favor Japan." The president thought it might actually help "Indochina, Burma and the other countries of Southeast Asia . . . if they were able to sell to Communist China various raw materials" now embargoed.

Turning to Dulles, Eisenhower declared, "This is what I want you to do; get in everyone, get in the Defense Department and the others, and see what we can do to back away from" the China differential. It seemed foolish to maintain "that we made a flat decision in 1952 that cannot be altered in any detail." As a sop to his domestic opponents, Eisenhower persuaded Eden to defer final action by announcing a review of the control procedure while they turned the problem over to "experts." After "the technicians" spoke, the two leaders would act.[27]

Eisenhower's promise to Eden proved hard to implement. In the aftermath of the summit, the Committee on Foreign Economic Policy (CFEP) as well as the Treasury, Commerce, and Defense Departments all defended keeping part of the China differential in place.[28] Eisenhower complained about supposedly "loyal and reliable" officials who actually "frustrate the policies of their superiors." Trade controls were symptoms of the "hysteria" generated by the "McCarthy problem," the president argued. The best solution would be for the United States to remove "all of its existing trade barriers." Congress he hoped, would face up to this as McCarthy's power waned. In any case, Washington must "do everything that it could . . . to encourage Japanese trade with [its] neighbors, including communist China."

After nearly four years of resisting Eisenhower, Dulles finally decided he was right. In April 1956, Dulles declared it "ridiculous" for the United States to sit on a "vast pile of economic ammunition" (such as surplus agricultural products) that could be used to "raise hell with the Soviets" by offering it to the Communist bloc.[29]

Before Eisenhower could parlay Dulles's support into a new trade policy, Congress intervened. In February 1956, the Senate Permanent Investigations Subcommittee, chaired by Arkansas Democrat John L. McClellan (and including Senators Joseph McCarthy, Henry Jackson, Stuart Symington, Karl E. Mundt, and George H. Bender) opened hearings on what they called the "very disturbing" pattern of East–West trade. Joseph Dodge warned that while the 1954 decision to relax trade with the Soviet Union had angered many senators, extending the changes to China would cause an explosion. In April, a majority of McClellan's committee complained that some recipients of American aid were guilty of "building up Russian war potential." Eisenhower and Dulles worried that Democrats would seize on the accusation and cause "much more trouble than the right-wing Republicans" in threatening passage of the 1957 MSA bill.[30]

When British ambassador Sir Roger Makins protested the delay in implementing Eisenhower's promise to Eden, Dulles admitted the "U.S. had been rather remiss in handling this matter expeditiously." But the "entire question was charged with dynamite insofar as Congress was concerned." Senator Knowland and Congressman Vorys had served notice that tinkering with China trade controls might "jeopardize the passage of the entire Mutual Security legislation this year." Admitting he did not "quite know how to deal with this matter," Dulles suggested that "instead of handling the COCOM review in the glare of the spotlight," it be done "quietly," perhaps without a formal change. He even offered to look the other way if Britain expanded sales to China.[31]

While he dealt with British demands, Japan remained much on Eisenhower's mind. Unless it were allowed to export more to China, Japan might soon have to "pass a tin cup around San Francisco." But the president would or could not forge a consensus within the administration in favor of trade liberalization. Fearful that Congress would label him as "going soft on Communist China," Eisenhower shied away from supporting formal revision of the CHINCOM rules. Instead, he would "continue to wink at the exception our allies make to this list."[32]

By the middle of 1956, both London and Tokyo lost patience with Washington. Britain renewed its threat to unilaterally violate the China differential while Japan demanded the elimination of 100 items from the CHINCOM embargo list. In September, Ambassador Shima bluntly informed the State Department that although Tokyo did not wish to be the first to violate CHINCOM rules, it insisted on a radical change within a few months. Whether this occurred through multilateral agreement or unilateral action, Japan "would expect to receive the same benefits" as the British.

By the "end of the year, if not sooner," the State Department informed Eisenhower, the United States would be unable "to preserve any CHINCOM differential at all" and might also be forced to relax overall trade controls. Despite his tacit support for the demise of trade controls, Eisenhower declined to act. In effect, he let matters drift until after the upcoming presidential election when he anticipated winning a renewed mandate.[33]

Eisenhower found an ally in Clarence B. Randall, an executive from Inland Steel whom he named to head the CFEP in July 1956, following the resignation of Joseph Dodge. Randall shared the president's belief that expanded commerce would both cement the Western alliance and induce positive changes in the Communist bloc. His appointment also encouraged others to speak more openly. CIA director Allen Dulles, for example, now revealed his support for dropping the China differential. NSC staffer William Jackson confided to Randall that the president not only favored "a liberalization of the [China] differential" but said privately that "if I had my way, we ourselves would arm Red China" by giving them "arms off the lower end of the stockpile." Randall interpreted this remark to mean that "a China, independent of Russia, and prepared to resist Russia, might be a very strong force for peace in the world."[34]

As soon as the president won reelection, Randall visited Tokyo. Before departing, he met with Walter Robertson and "for thirty minutes . . . heard fanaticism." The State Department's senior officer for Asia spoke vehemently against "reducing the China differential." Robertson's "will to resist" the Chinese Communists, Randall observed, "lights the same fanatical zeal in his eyes that must shine from theirs." Undeterred, Randall resolved "to go all out in trying to liberalize the China control problem." Japan "particularly need[ed] encouragement rather than inhibitions on trading with China." With American industry already clamoring for limits on Japanese textile sales and other exports, he feared Tokyo was being "left on a pretty precarious basis for filling her role as our principal ally in the Pacific."[35]

Randall's contacts in Japan fortified his determination. Embassy counselor Frank Waring described Tokyo's phenomenal success in doubling two-way foreign trade (from $1.2 to $2.5 billion) in three years, mostly with the United States and non-Communist Asia. Japan bought American goods valued at $780 million and sold Americans products valued at $459. Nevertheless, across the political spectrum, the Japanese deeply resented U.S.-imposed restrictions on trade with China. The problem had assumed political as well as economic significance. The Japanese were furious that the Europeans were free to sell products to China via the Soviet Union that they were forbidden to export to Beijing. Although Randall and Waring saw this as an insult more to Japan's pride than its pocketbook, they recognized the depth of Japanese resentment.[36]

In December 1956, Prime Minister-elect Ishibashi Tanzan, a strong advocate of expanding commercial and political contacts with China, complained directly to Assistant Secretary of State Walter Robertson. The chief danger to Japan, Ishibashi told a skeptical Robertson, came from its weak economy, not a Communist military threat. Calls in the United States for restricting Japanese textile exports (see the following chapter), combined with restrictions on trade with China, led even conservatives to conclude that Washington was "placing the squeeze" on Japan.[37]

On returning to Washington, Randall rejected a CFEP task-force recommendation, drawn up in his absence, to tighten multilateral controls. The president, he insisted, wanted the China differential "reduced, or even perhaps eliminated." He set his staff to work on a new proposal and, on February 5, 1957, the CFEP voted to "effectuate a substantial liberalization of the multilateral controls over trade with Communist China." Both he and the president "intended to reduce the differential on China."[38]

The National Security Council took up the CFEP proposal (now dubbed NSC 5704) on March 6, 1957. Randall argued that "substantial liberalization" of the rules governing trade with China was required to alleviate extreme "tension between the United States and its European allies," to assuage Japan's "bitter resentment of the extra controls" it labored under, and to effect the "general policy" of the Eisenhower administration to "reduce barriers all around the world." The president startled the NSC by declaring that "it seemed to him rather foolish" to put "obstacles in the way of our own U.S. trade with Communist China" at the same time as Washington proposed to lower the barriers faced by others. But, fearful of a congressional backlash, he did not press for dropping the American embargo on China. Eisenhower decided to accept the CFEP/NSC decision to reduce CHINCOM controls because of the "problems posed for our allies."[39]

This new approach, administration spokesmen informed Senator McClellan and other key members of Congress, did "not reflect a desire by the Executive branch to be soft toward China." The United States would maintain a strict embargo on exports and oppose diplomatic ties with Beijing. But if Washington hoped to preserve any trade controls, it must accommodate allies, such as Japan, which was the "best customer for our agricultural surpluses."[40]

Acting Secretary of State Christian Herter and deputy undersecretary for economic affairs Douglas Dillon found legislators receptive to this appeal. Following talks with the congressional leadership on April 10, Herter characterized their reaction as "strikingly similar in that they seemed to feel that in view of the situation faced by the United States," the call for lowering controls seemed as good an answer as could be found. Senator Theodore Green, Democrat of Rhode Island, declared that when confronted by a "choice of evils," the administration made the right decision. Senators Lyndon Johnson and William Knowland "agreed that this new change in policy is right." Even Senator McClellan "accepted it." On April 11, 1957, Eisenhower directed the NSC to implement the new policy.[41]

Unfortunately, the decision to drop nearly half of the 300 items barred exclusively for export to China came too late. In Tokyo, recently elected Prime Minister Kishi Nobusuke informed the new American ambassador, Douglas MacArthur II, that while his government "flatly rejected" domestic pressure to open diplomatic ties with China, he could not support retention of any version of the China differential. Kishi sympathized with the "U.S. rationale" but "the Japanese public did not, and therein lies the gap between the two countries," he explained.[42]

When the China Committee (CHINCOM) met in Paris on May 7, the United States proposed modifying, not eliminating, the China differential.

France, Britain, and Japan insisted on immediate abolition of all special controls, throwing CHINCOM into a deadlock. Unless Washington agreed to "radical modification" of its position by the May 17 CHINCOM meeting, the British government announced, it would act unilaterally.[43]

Prime Minister Kishi dispelled a lingering hope that Tokyo would stand by Washington. The "domestic political" consequences were too dire, he informed MacArthur on May 16. The "virtually unanimous view of Japanese people in all walks of life including socialists, conservatives, business, industry and labor" was that the China differential had to go.[44]

Dulles informed Eisenhower that he faced a "critical" choice on trade controls. From the "standpoint of congressional relations," Dulles thought it "would be better for us to let the British, Japanese, etc., 'go it alone'" rather than accede to any action perceived as a "policy of lessening opposition to the Chinese Communists." On the other hand, he worried that "to split with the British, Japanese and most of the other trading countries on this issue" might provoke them to move even closer to China, thereby provoking "greater anti-foreign sentiment in the Congress."

Eisenhower decided to abolish most special controls on China in return for a CHINCOM agreement to maintain a token China differential. At Dulles's urging, Eisenhower sent British Prime Minister Harold Macmillan a letter to this effect. But the president also "indicated [to Dulles] his feeling that basically Communist China and Soviet Russia should be treated alike." It hardly mattered since at the CHINCOM meetings of May 17 and 21 no other member nation supported the American position.[45]

Macmillan informed Eisenhower of his regret that "this China business has become almost as much an obsession with us as it appears to be with your congress." But he stuck "to the line shared by that large number of countries . . . who want to bring the Russian and Chinese lists together." The time had come to "get this difference settled rather than let it go on and poison our relations." As before, Eisenhower undermined the "official" American position by informing Macmillan that "as an individual" he agreed "with you that there is very little profit in the matter either for your country or for any other." Because so many Americans believed relaxing trade controls was a "terrific psychological blunder," he might be "compelled, in the final result, to differ sharply" with Macmillan in his official capacity. However, he all but assured the British leader that they shared a distaste for special controls on China.[46]

On May 29, Macmillan announced that Britain would no longer observe the China differential. Outraged members of the Defense Department urged the president to impose sanctions on London. But Clarence Randall blamed the outcome on the "complete bankruptcy of the policy advocated by Walter Robertson and Admiral Radford." If, early on, Washington had proposed reasonable terms, the allies might have accepted a small differential. But the hardliners' determination to maintain strict controls had "been defeated by their own conduct."[47]

Although the British action infuriated some members of the administration, Eisenhower responded calmly and virtually encouraged the Japanese to follow suit. In a June 4 meeting with Tokyo's new ambassador to Washington, Asakai Koichiro, the president raised the China question and said he expected other allies to follow London's lead. The Japanese, Eisenhower added, had to "trade for their very survival" and could hardly act otherwise. He had "more or less inherited the position of the embargo on the Red Chinese" but personally believed that "it was wise to trade as much as possible with practically all nations."[48]

At a press conference the following day, Eisenhower mentioned the "very great division of opinion" on whether free trade with the Communist bloc actually hurt the West or could be used as a "very great instrument of government policy." The president spoke of Japan's great need—in light of the trade restrictions it faced "all around the world"—to export consumer goods and light machinery to China. He saw no danger of Japan being "communized" by this contact. "I am personally of the school," he added, "that believes that trade, in the long run, cannot be stopped . . . I don't see as much advantage in maintaining the [China] differential as some people do."[49]

When Prime Minister Kishi visited Washington in mid-June, China trade (along with discussions of aid to Southeast Asia, the status of Okinawa, and the future of the security treaty) dominated his discussions with Eisenhower and Dulles. History, proximity, and economic necessity, Kishi argued, led most Japanese to favor increased trade with China, and he hoped the president would endorse their doing so. Eisenhower assured him that he "understood completely Japan's need for trade with Red China."[50]

Still less enthusiastic than his boss, Dulles balked at Kishi's proposed wording for a joint communiqué that encouraged Japanese efforts to boost trade with all "neighboring countries." Why, Dulles asked ingenuously, did Japan want to "expand trade with Communist China. Was some miraculous virtue to be obtained in that way?" Eisenhower might "tolerate" British and Japanese commerce with China, but he [Dulles] "oppose[d] it as evil." After cutting and trimming, they settled on bland wording that offended no one.

As anticipated, in July 1957, Tokyo announced it would no longer observe the China differential. Administration officials merely expressed hope that trade be kept to modest proportions. This encouraged Clarence Randall to explore the possibility of the United States ending its own embargo on trade with China. But his proposal went nowhere when nearly all cabinet members opposed the initiative, citing domestic political reasons. Eisenhower, who clearly sympathized with Randall, explained "with a smile" that "national security affairs occasionally had to give way when domestic politics raised its ugly head."[51]

The administration revisited this issue early in 1958, when the Europeans and Japanese pressed for further reductions in the trade controls now applied equally to China and the Soviet Union. Anxious to avoid another bruising fight with the allies, Dulles "expressed great doubt" that Soviet or Chinese military potential "was appreciably affected by Western controls." Eliminating the China differential, he now admitted, had few negative consequences.

Eisenhower crowed that in five years of debate "this was the first time that a voice had been raised in support of his position." While aides chuckled, he described the pleasure he took in the fact that Dulles finally joined him in condemning what "he considered damned silly practices." Without further discussion, the NSC endorsed a plan to meet at least "mid-way" allied trade demands.[52]

Ironically, the fruits of Japan's trade victory slipped away at the very moment Washington removed its political impediments. In 1956, Sino-Japanese trade reached $151 million. Even the staunchly anti-Communist Kishi, who became prime minister early in 1957, hoped to expand commerce with Beijing. He informed American visitors that although they could "not fully understand," trade with China had an importance to Japan that went beyond its dollar value. At the same time, he reassured Washington that Japan would not unilaterally establish diplomatic ties with the PRC.[53]

Kishi's continued effort to separate trade and politics played poorly in Beijing. After a brief period of domestic liberalization, Mao Zedong pushed the Chinese Communist Party in more radical directions. During 1957–58, so-called rightists were purged from party ranks and Mao initiated a shock program called the "Great Leap Forward" to speed agricultural and industrial production. Kishi also provoked Chinese ire during a May 1957 tour of Southeast Asia and Taiwan. Standing beside Jiang Jieshi, Kishi endorsed the Nationalist's plan for "recovery of freedom on the mainland."

Despite this challenge, in August 1957, Chinese negotiators entered into discussions with the Japanese for a fourth private trade agreement. Beijing renewed its demand to station trade representatives in Tokyo, an act just short of diplomatic recognition. Foreign Minister Fujiyama Aiichiro explained to concerned Americans that accepting a Chinese presence would allow the Japanese government to undercut the intermediary role played by Socialists and assure central control over contacts with China. Neither Ambassador Douglas MacArthur nor Dulles, who warned of "bad political consequences," were impressed by this argument.[54]

During trade talks in Beijing in the fall of 1957 and spring of 1958, Japanese negotiators followed government guidelines as de facto official representatives. They were willing to allow a small Chinese trade delegation to reside in Tokyo but not a large group enjoying quasi-diplomatic status. The Chinese also demanded the right to fly their national flag in Japan, exemption from the requirement that foreigners submit to fingerprinting, and official endorsement of the trade pact. Japanese negotiators exceeded their instructions by incorporating these terms into the agreement signed on March 5, 1958, an action strongly criticized by Washington and the Chinese Nationalist government.[55]

Buffeted by protests from the United States, Taiwan, and many fellow conservatives, Kishi declined to endorse the pact or permit the official display of the PRC flag by Chinese representatives. China responded by refusing to implement the trade agreement until Japan observed all its provisions. It denounced Kishi for trying to recreate the Co-Prosperity Sphere by relying on U.S. military power. Tension peaked on May 2 when a Japanese rightist tore down a Chinese flag displayed at a Nagasaki trade exhibition. Beijing used Kishi's refusal to prosecute the culprit as a pretext to suspend virtually all trade and cultural exchanges with Japan.

China may have intended the suspension of trade, fishing privileges in its coastal waters, and cultural exchanges to either force Kishi to back down or damage conservative chances in the Diet election at the end of May. If so, the tactic failed and the conservatives retained a large margin in the Diet. After this setback, Beijing demanded that Tokyo reject efforts to create "two Chinas." A few months later, China began shelling Nationalist-held islands off the southern coast, precipitating the second Taiwan Strait crisis. Despite the enthusiasm among Japanese business and political leaders for trade with China, they had no intention of endangering their primary economic and political relationship with the United States. Sino-Japanese contacts lay dormant until 1960.[56]

Even before this standoff, Kishi and some Japanese business groups voiced alarm over the "economic threat posed by the growing industrial strength" of China and fear that Beijing would overwhelm "the economies of Southeast Asia." During 1958, American and Japanese observers reported that China had begun "an attempt to displace Japan in the consumer markets of South and Southeast Asia" as part of a Communist plan to "isolate and soften up this Free World ally." Although Japanese sales of consumer goods to Southeast Asia still exceeded those of China, Beijing had made significant inroads since 1954 in categories such as cotton textiles, pottery, light machinery, glass, bricks, and tiles.[57]

American economists attributed China's success to a policy of selling products below the cost of production and providing cheap credit. Beijing also utilized overseas Chinese merchants to appeal to ethnic Chinese consumers in Southeast Asia. Clearly worried about the political implications of this trade, State Department analysts considered the export drive part of China's "ceaseless warfare against the Free World."

Unlike China, which grew its own cotton and relied on a command economy for production and distribution, Japan had to import raw cotton and sell textiles under real market conditions. To help Tokyo meet China's challenge, American officials recommended expanding subsidy programs that allowed Japan to buy surplus cotton below the price charged to American mills. This would enable Japanese manufacturers to reduce their export price and compete more effectively in Southeast Asia. Unfortunately, it also raised howls of protests among American textile producers who complained that it gave Japan an unfair price advantage.[58]

China's suspension of trade with Japan, like its export drive in Southeast Asia, dashed hopes in both Tokyo and Washington that Sino-Japanese trade could either solve Japan's economic problems or help fracture the Sino-Soviet alliance. Hardliners in Washington expressed relief that these developments mooted any chance that China might use enhanced trade to influence Japan. Moderates, however, saw a cloud around this silver lining. Gloat as the hardliners might, the fact remained that Japan required additional trade outlets to sustain export-driven growth. If China did not play this role, Southeast Asia and the United States became more critical. But underdevelopment, Chinese competition, and political instability made Southeast Asia an insecure market. Calls for trade protection in the United States threatened Japan's export drive just as its consumer goods found a mass market. These factors presented the Eisenhower administration with new dilemmas as it struggled to ensure Japan's economic stability.

6 SOUTHEAST ASIAN DOMINOS AND JAPANESE-AMERICAN TRADE, 1953–60

THE belief that a Communist advance in Southeast Asia represented a dagger thrust at Japan arose before the Korean War and gained credence during the 1950s. Beginning during the Truman administration and continuing under Eisenhower, officials invoked this specter as a virtual mantra, justifying the deepening American commitment to Vietnam.

Like its predecessor, the Eisenhower administration perceived Southeast Asia's strategic value largely in terms of Japanese economic stability. During his first week in office, Secretary of State John Foster Dulles delivered a radio and television address that stressed this linkage. The "Soviet Russians," he explained,

> are making a drive to get Japan, not only through what they are doing in the northern areas of the islands and in Korea but also through what they are doing in Indochina. If they could get this peninsula of Indochina, Siam, Burma, Malaya, they would have what is called the rice bowl of Asia.

The bloodletting in Indochina, he added, posed a double threat, since it limited France's ability to contribute to a "European Army" designed to contain the Soviet threat in the West.[1] Other officials raised similar alarms. At a Pentagon conference held the day after Dulles's broadcast, Joint Chiefs of Staff Chairman General Omar Bradley, Mutual Security Program Director Harold Stassen, and several aides held a discussion on Indochina. Bradley predicted French defeat would "lead to the loss of all Southeast Asia." That, Dulles warned, "would lead to the loss of Japan." With "China being Commie" another setback for the West might not cause the loss of Japan "immediately," but "from there on out the Japs would be thinking on how to get on the other side." Even if France gave up the fight, the conferees agreed, the United States must try to sustain a non-Communist enclave in Vietnam.[2]

American civilian and military planners alike perceived Southeast Asia as a critical link in a strategy that secured the entire Pacific island defense chain. If Japan was the jewel in the crown of Asian containment, Southeast Asia constituted the setting in which the diamond rested. Sustained Japanese recovery, Americans believed, required a shift away from dependence on imported U.S. raw materials and exports to the American market. The United States–Japan Economic Cooperation Plan of 1951 was predicated on high levels of military procurement in the short-term and long-term integration between the economies of Japan and Southeast Asia.

The administration's plan for a self-sufficient Japan, as Dulles frequently explained, envisioned increased trade with Southeast Asia. If that region fell under Communist control, Japan would face two unacceptable options—increasing trade with China or exporting more to the United States. The Joint Chiefs joined State Department officials in concluding on July 10, 1953, that the "loss of Southeast Asia" would "result in such economic and political pressures upon Japan as to make it extremely difficult to prevent Japan's accommodation to Communism." This breach of the Pacific offshore island chain would "seriously jeopardize fundamental U.S. security interests in the Far East."[3]

Vietminh victories in Indochina during 1953 eroded French resolve and increased American anxiety. The Joint Chiefs encouraged the French to lure Communist guerrillas into a set battle by placing a large garrison at Dien Bien Phu, a valley in northern Vietnam. To the horror of both Washington and Paris, the Vietminh, with Chinese logistic assistance, surrounded the outpost early in 1954, immobilized its airfield, and laid siege to the defenders. By March, their fate hung by a thread.[4]

At the same time as Communist guerrillas seemed poised for a breakthrough in Indochina, the Japanese economy experienced a severe recession because of the decline in military procurements that followed the Korean armistice. Fear of military and economic reversals in Asia dominated the outlook of American policymakers as they anticipated the convening, in May, of an international conference in Geneva to discuss the fate of Indochina.

The Joint Chiefs tried to stiffen administration resolve by stressing the danger that defeat in Indochina posed to Japan. Any compromise (such as a cease-fire in place, creation of a coalition government, partition, or nationwide elections) reached at Geneva, the Joint Chiefs reported, would be "generally regarded by Asian peoples" as a "communist victory." Unless the Vietminh were defeated, "all Southeast Asia would be lost." Japan, the "keystone of United States policy in the Far East," would then be forced by "economic and political pressure" to reach an "accommodation with the Communist bloc." By capturing Southeast Asian resources and Japanese industry, China would "ultimately control the entire Western and Southwestern Pacific region and would threaten South Asia and the Middle East."[5]

Ambassador John Allison delivered similar warnings. He predicted that Communist negotiators at Geneva might bait a trap by settling for less at the conference table than they won in battle. The resulting "relaxation of tension" would have a "disastrous effect" on the "emotional Japanese people" who would be beguiled into neutralism or intimidated into an accommodation with the Communist bloc. In place of a diplomatic solution, Allison urged escalating the military effort in Southeast Asia. This would leave Japan "no choice but to abandon its hopes for normalization of relations with China and the Soviet Union."[6]

Dulles warned the cabinet on March 27 that a Red victory in Indochina would "cut our defense line in half." Washington had better take risks "now rather than waiting for several years." Two days later he told journalists that the strategic resources and location of Southeast Asia made it of "transcendent importance" to the containment of China and the security of both Europe and Japan. Even Eisenhower, who hoped to avoid "getting ground forces tied up in Indochina," felt compelled to act. Early in 1954, he sent military trainers to Vietnam. "My God," he told a senator, we "must not lose Asia. We've got to look the thing right in the face."[7]

By April, as the Vietminh tightened their grip around Dien Bien Phu, Eisenhower and Dulles tried to rally Congress and the NATO allies behind intervention in Vietnam. Dulles spoke cryptically of "united action" to protect Southeast Asia. The president also perceived significant stakes in the region, but hesitated to commit ground forces to another Korea-style war. In contrast, Admiral Arthur Radford, chairman of the Joint Chiefs and the most bellicose of Eisenhower's top advisers, proposed conventional or even atomic air strikes against the Vietminh.

Eisenhower and Dulles opposed intervention solely to save Dien Bien Phu or salvage "French prestige." Angered equally by their poor military performance and refusal to grant Vietnam greater autonomy, the president condemned the French as "impossible." He and Dulles considered multilateral intervention vital to assure survival of a non-Communist regime in at least part of Vietnam.[8]

The French government wanted the Americans to save their men at Dien Bien Phu, but refused to alter their colonial policy as Washington demanded. The British, certain that Dien Bien Phu and, probably, all Vietnam were lost, called for negotiating a compromise at Geneva. Congressional leaders voiced little enthusiasm for any form of intervention. "What," asked Senator John Stennis, Democrat of Mississippi, "is meant by `united action' and what is the necessity or the case for it?" When Dulles pressed a group of bipartisan congressional leaders to endorse a show of force in Indochina, all declined unless he first guaranteed that American allies would commit substantial military force to the venture.[9]

In appeals to the governments of Britain, France, and New Zealand, Eisenhower and Dulles warned that the loss of Vietnam would doom all

Southeast Asia, undermine Japan, and breach the offshore island containment barrier. In an emotional letter sent to Churchill on April 4, the president predicted that a Communist victory would place "economic pressures on Japan which would be deprived of non-Communist markets and sources of food and raw materials." Under such conditions, Tokyo could not "be prevented from reaching an accommodation with the communist world which would combine the manpower and natural resources of Asia with the industrial potential of Japan." He likened the risk of inaction to the failure of the democracies to "halt Hirohito, Mussolini and Hitler by not acting in unity and in time."[10]

Despite this appeal, Eisenhower discouraged loose talk of unilateral intervention. Just hours after writing to Churchill, the president told Dulles and Radford that he would intervene at Dien Bien Phu only if Britain, Australia, and New Zealand committed forces, France continued fighting and guaranteed Vietnam's independence, and Congress authorized the dispatch of forces. France promptly rejected American demands. Britain, Churchill observed, had let India go without a fight, so he could hardly rally his people to defend the French empire. With Congress opposed to unilateral intervention, united action came to nothing.[11]

Some have speculated that Eisenhower set the threshold for intervention high to assure that the conditions would not be met. He could appear tough, but avoid entrapment. Yet he worked hard to arouse, not diminish, public concern over Vietnam. For example, at a press conference on April 7, Eisenhower described the rich mineral resources of Southeast Asia that the West "simply can't afford" to lose. Defeat in Indochina, he explained with great emotion, would cause all of Southeast Asia to "go over very quickly," like a "row of dominoes." Japan would gravitate "toward the Communist area in order to live." The "consequences of the loss" of Southeast Asia were "incalculable to the free world."[12]

Vietminh fighters overran Dien Bien Phu on May 7, 1954, as the Indochina phase of the Geneva conference began. Dulles had already pondered ways of salvaging Vietnam, through partition or by organizing an anti-Communist coalition to defend Southeast Asia. He attended the Geneva meeting briefly, but returned to Washington before the conference took up Indochina. Diplomats Walter Bedell Smith and U. Alexis Johnson remained as "observers."[13]

As the delegates at Geneva deliberated, Eisenhower and Dulles mulled their options. For a time they still hoped the Western allies might regain the military initiative and convince the French to hold on. But defeat at Dien Bien Phu brought a new premier to power in Paris, Pierre Mendes-France, who pledged to negotiate a withdrawal promptly or resign. This convinced the British to press harder for a compromise settlement. Churchill informed Eisenhower that Mendes-France intended to "clear out [of Indochina] on the best terms available. If that is so, I think he is right." Churchill hoped a Southeast Asian alliance, similar to NATO, could "establish a firm front against Communism in the Pacific area."[14]

Although Eisenhower and Dulles favored a regional pact (they created SEATO in September), during the summer of 1954 they focused on salvaging Vietnam and shielding Japan from the fallout of Dien Bien Phu. Speaking to legislative leaders on June 21, Eisenhower chided members of Congress who reflexively opposed allowing Japan to "trade with Red China," who shied away from "war in Southeast Asia," and who blocked "further liberalization of trade" with Japan. If "we didn't do a little of some of these things," he warned, "we would lose Japan." Then "the U.S. would be out of the Pacific and it would become a communist lake."[15]

The next day, reviewing with Dulles the text of a speech to newspaper editors, Eisenhower restated his belief that Southeast Asian resources were vital to keep Japan "in our orbit." It was "absolutely mandatory" to ensure that Japan's war-making potential did not fall under Communist control. Yet the burden of supporting eighty-five million people in an area the size of California appeared almost unsolvable. Japan "cannot live, and Japan cannot remain in the free world unless something is done to allow her to make a living," the president told the National Editorial Association. If "we will not give her any money, if we will not trade with her, if we will not allow her to trade with the Reds, if we will not try to defend in any way the Southeast Asian area where she has a partial trade opportunity, what is to happen to Japan? It is going to the Communists." No single approach, he admitted, would save Japan, and "any one of them pursued to an extreme would ruin us." Still, Japan could only be protected by an active policy.[16]

The Geneva accords signed on July 21 proved a mixed blessing. Pressed by the Soviet Union and China to compromise, the Vietminh accepted a cease-fire and temporary division of Vietnam at the 17th parallel. Cambodia and Laos were split off as independent states. Elections for a unified government were scheduled for 1956. The United States "took note" of but did not sign the agreements.

Privately, Dulles described the Communist demands as "relatively moderate in terms of their actual capabilities." In fact, the administration considered partition, along with the emergence of a new political leader in the south, Ngo Dinh Diem, as improving the odds for the survival of a non-Communist South Vietnam. Dulles reportedly agreed to "go along" with partition in return for an Anglo-French promise to "support the American effort to form promptly . . . a Southeast Asia Treaty Organization." Even so, the president and secretary of state voiced mounting anxiety about the impact on Japan of events in Southeast Asia.[17]

Conservative politicians in Japan, such as Liberal Party Secretary General Ikeda Hayato, called attention to events in Indochina. On August 10, he reportedly told party leaders that the American "roll-back policy" in Indochina had failed and that China had seized the initiative in Asia. Consequently, Japan should reduce its dependence on the United States and adopt a more flexible "foreign and economic policy." Ikeda suggested "drastic revision" of current trade practices—code for expanding sales to China.[18]

If Japan's elite lost faith in American credibility, Dulles told the cabinet in August 1954, Chinese and Soviet strategists would employ economic blandishments to lure Tokyo into their camp. Japanese products had "little future . . . in the United States" since they were just "cheap imitations of our own goods." Japan's only solution was to develop markets in the "underdeveloped areas such as Southeast Asia."

Eisenhower adopted an eclectic and less doctrinaire approach. Believing that "no single action would solve the Japanese economic problem," he favored allowing Tokyo "closely watched" trade with China. For the moment, this appeared the best way to avoid an economic decline that would make Japan "ripe for communism."[19]

Following the Geneva settlement, Eisenhower and Dulles agreed that the United States should organize a loosely knit security treaty to discourage Chinese expansion in Southeast Asia. But they acknowledged that subversion, "furthered by economic weakness and social distress," presented the greatest danger to Japan. The Japanese government had already "given some indication of an intention to draw back from its pro-Western orientation until it could appraise the effect of the loss of parts of Indochina" on its trade. "Unless we had confidence that [Tokyo's] future political orientation would be toward the West," Dulles added, it did not make sense to enhance Japan's military potential.

Yet, Dulles admitted, Japan remained the "soul of the situation in the Far East" and if it were not allied to the United States, America's position in Asia would "become untenable." As for Vietnam, he and the president agreed that Washington should buy time for anti-Communist forces in the south by doing everything possible "to avoid having any [all-Vietnam] elections" since the Communists would almost certainly win at the polls.[20]

In September 1954, Dulles convened a foreign ministers' meeting in the Philippines to create the Southeast Asia Treaty Organization (SEATO). This Western-dominated alliance included only two local members, the Philippines and Thailand. By separate protocol, SEATO extended coverage to Vietnam, Laos, and Cambodia. Although this jerry-rigged alliance contained few of the guarantees of the NATO pact, Dulles feared inaction would convey a belief that "we seem [about] to abandon the entire area without a struggle."[21]

The administration recognized that containment in Asia required economic growth as well as protection against aggression. Eisenhower endorsed the principal of regional aid, but urged that "Far Eastern nations should get together themselves and form an economic grouping" before turning to the United States.

During August 1954, the staffs of the State Department and Foreign Operations Administration discussed an Asian Development Fund as large as $10 billion over ten years. Harold Stassen, director of the Foreign Operations Administration (the renamed Mutual Security Agency) favored a "major effort to line up sound economic policies to back up the Southeast Asia military arrangements, the economic arrangement to run from Japan to India." Specifically, he spoke of making Japan the arsenal of Free Asia, supplying weapons for Southeast Asian countries with capital provided through mutual security aid. Dulles agreed that unless the United States "countered the Communist [economic] program . . . the effort to hold back Communism in Asia would be in vain."[22]

In September, after the SEATO negotiations, Dulles visited Tokyo. Yoshida, Foreign Minister Okasaki, and Liberal Party Secretary General Ikeda persuaded him that "economic matters were of considerable concern to the Japanese" that "we may have to lower our sights on Japanese rearmament." It made no sense, Dulles remarked to colleagues, to lose "the vital political sympathy of Japan in our effort to get the desired military levels." When Japan's trade deficit surpassed $1 billion, Dulles concluded that "export markets in Southeast Asia" were essential for economic improvement. Japan should not expect to find a "big U.S. market," he told Yoshida, because it did "not make the things we want."

Dulles repeated this point in November 1954, admonishing Yoshida that "trade with Southeast Asia [was] probably a better prospect for Japan than trade with the United States." He displayed a "brightly patterned flannel shirt made in Japan of cheap material exactly copying a better quality cloth made in the United States." It would, he predicted, never appeal to Americans. (John Allison recalled this conversation with a different twist. He described Dulles "suddenly pulling out of his briefcase . . . a cheap Japanese sport shirt." This, he shouted, "is what you people are doing to us . . . competing with us. You can't do this after all we've done!")

Dulles recognized some of the structural barriers to trade with Southeast Asia (underdevelopment, capital shortage, and lack of purchasing power) as well as continued mistrust of Japan. Also, as one aide noted, some American assistance efforts undercut regional integration. For example, PL 480 aid, which gave Japan low-cost food from American surplus stocks, indirectly "blocked the development of new Japanese markets in Southeast Asia" based on the purchase of local rice in exchange for manufactured goods.

Dulles urged Yoshida to turn the reparations issue to Japan's advantage in Southeast Asia. By offering settlements to Burma, Indonesia, the Philippines, and other claimants, Japan could promote goodwill among wartime victims. The cost, Dulles predicted, would pay for itself through expanded trade.[23]

To placate the Philippines, the 1951 peace treaty allowed signatories to claim reparations. Starting in 1954 and over the next twenty years, Japan paid out $1 billion in direct reparations and $500 million in economic and technical aid to Burma, Indonesia, the Philippines, South Vietnam, Cambodia, Laos, Singapore, Micronesia, and South Korea. Burma, Indonesia, and the Philippines received the largest settlements. Payment ranged from providing consumer goods to the construction of roads, mines, and power grids by Japanese firms.

Japanese economic planners shared many of the American assumptions about Southeast Asia, although with considerably more ambivalence about short-term results. A government study of May 20, 1953, described the prewar "triangular patterns of trade in which Southeast Asian countries had a favorable balance of trade with the United States, which had a favorable balance with Europe and Japan, both of which in turn had a favorable balance with Southeast Asian countries." This pattern fell apart after 1945 in part because of slow economic recovery in Southeast Asia and because synthetics "such as nylon and synthetic rubber contributed to a decline of [Southeast Asian] exports, with the result that they have now a trade deficit with the United States." Japan, the study urged, should make a greater effort to restore regional trade.[24]

Yoshida's doubts about Southeast Asia's commercial value increased after he traveled through the region during 1954. "You have to trade with rich men," he remarked on his return, "you can't trade with beggars." He made a similar point more delicately during his November 1954 visit to Washington when he urged the Eisenhower administration to fund a $4 billion "Marshall Plan for Asia." This, along with loans to Japan and assistance in paying reparations, were necessary to spur Asian recovery, he argued.[25]

The Eisenhower administration shared many of Yoshida's concerns, but moved cautiously. During a news conference on November 9, 1954, Dulles responded to the prime minister's appeal for regional aid by saying that while the administration favored the principle, the United States could help only "within limits that are practical and workable." Preconditions such as industrial infrastructure, skilled workers, plants suitable for rehabilitation, and so on, that made the Marshall Plan so successful in Europe did not exist in most of Asia. In Southeast Asia, "you're starting, so to speak, from scratch." Dulles told Yoshida that an Asian Marshall Plan required "careful prior planning" before the United States put "huge sums of money into the area."[26]

By the time Yoshida left office a month later, Eisenhower and Dulles worried about mounting congressional reluctance to assist Japan. Although Republicans supported the concept of "trade" over "aid" as the foundation of foreign economic policy, Eisenhower complained that many in Congress opposed allowing Japan to expand trade with its major current market (the United States) or its major potential market (China). When the administration proposed to lower American tariffs, "Congress respond[ed] by trying to raise" duties. By discouraging exports both to China and the United States, Americans "slam [ed] the door in Japan's face." This, the president warned, might prompt Japan to "go Communist" and "really build up" Soviet bloc "war potential."[27]

By the end of 1954, anxiety over Japan's deteriorating economy prompted Dulles to empathize with Tokyo's reluctance to rearm. "Japan was a desperately poor country," he told the NSC, and its military expenditures should not be compared to those of the United States. Until its economy was on a "sounder base," Washington should not press "too hard" for rearmament.[28]

The public learned something about this policy debate in newspaper columns written by Joseph Alsop. Early in 1955, while traveling through Southeast Asia and Japan, Alsop wrote a series of reports berating Eisenhower and Dulles for lacking the courage of their convictions about the domino theory. In one account evocatively titled "Tokyo Depends on Saigon," he predicted that unless the United States assured Japan's access to Southeast Asian resources, Communism would sweep over all Asia.

Although both Dulles and Eisenhower had stressed the economic basis of the "domino theory," Alsop complained they found it "politically expedient" to "duck the grim challenge of Dien Bien Phu." Yet the need for cheap, accessible raw materials and markets still held "life and death significance" for Japan. Unless the United States bolstered the fledgling Diem regime in Vietnam and promoted Japan's penetration of Southeast Asia, neutralism would sweep Japan and force the closure of American bases. This would usher in the "great Pacific nightmare": "Japan's industrial potential . . . automatically . . . available to Communist China." Asia, Alsop concluded, was a "seamless web" that, "if torn anywhere," would "unravel everywhere. And it is tearing now."[29]

In talks with journalists and congressional leaders, Eisenhower endorsed a small economic development fund for Asia amounting to millions, not billions, of dollars. A State Department working group under Herbert Hoover, Jr., drafted plans for this fund and the president included a $200-million proposal for fiscal 1956 in his April 1955 budget request to Congress. The Fund for Asian Economic Development (FAED) would dispense money on small projects over several years. This proposal reflected a consensus among American diplomats that Japan would not remain in the American orbit unless it could import inexpensive raw materials from Southeast Asia and export more to the region. This, in turn, required boosting rates of growth throughout Southeast Asia.[30]

In July 1955, Congress included an Asian development fund in the Mutual Security Act. However, the actual 1956 appropriation totaled only $100 million. Disagreements within the administration about what projects to fund resulted in expenditures of less than $5 million during the next year. Japanese officials concluded that the United States thought it could develop Asia on a shoestring.[31]

Nevertheless, even this small American aid program elicited excitement in Japan. In October 1955, Undersecretary of State Herbert Hoover, Jr., met in Tokyo with Foreign Minister Shigemitsu Mamoru, Finance Minister Ichimada Hisato, Minister of International Trade and Industry Ishibashi Tanzan, Minister for Economic Planning Takasaki Tatsunosuke, and Democratic Party leader Kishi Nobusuke. Although they were political rivals, all endorsed the economic aid commitment to Southeast Asia and urged more. Since Washington discouraged expanded trade with China, Ichimada explained, the "economic development of Southeast Asia . . . was of vital importance to the economic future of Japan." He urged creation of a regional development agency, financed by the United States and jointly managed by American and Japanese experts, to spur growth. Takasaki suggested that a combination of American aid and Japanese reparations payments "could help overcome the widespread feeling in Southeast Asia that Japan was undertaking an economic invasion."

MITI Minister Ishibashi cited military production as an example of how American capital could achieve several goals simultaneously. Financing the expansion of the Japanese defense industry and purchasing weapons from it for use by Southeast Asian nations would encourage both Japanese rearmament and regional trade and security. Hoover listened politely to these suggestions, but noted that until Tokyo devoted more of its own resources to defense spending, Congress was unlikely to approve additional funding.[32]

In May 1956, the administration sent Admiral Felix B. Stump, the Navy's Pacific commander, to tell the Senate Foreign Relations Committee that, without additional economic assistance, most of Southeast Asia's vital raw material surplus would "be lost to the free world in a relatively short time." Japan desperately needed the region's rice, rubber, oil, and tin to keep its people fed and employed, Stump testified. Japan "must be able to sell her manufactured products to pay for her imports" and Southeast Asia, "when stabilized," was the "natural outlet for Japan's cheap manufactured exports which are not welcome in the industrialized countries of the world." Explaining that Japan must trade to eat, the Admiral warned that "starving people will listen to any alternative solution, including communism."

The committee prodded Stump to explain the connection between halting Communism in Southeast Asia and stabilizing Japan. Senators who usually clashed over foreign policy, such as Mike Mansfield, H. Alexander Smith, and Alexander Wiley, agreed that without Southeast Asian markets and resources Japan must either "deal with Communist China" or dump goods on America. One senator predicted that any reduction of aid to Southeast Asia would impel China to take over. The Chinese could then "choke" off trade and "with a gun at Japan's breast" say "now you either come our way or you starve, that's all there is to it, economically and otherwise."[33]

Despite this nominal consensus, congressional opposition to foreign aid frustrated administration efforts to spur Asian development. In 1957, Eisenhower proposed allocating an additional $100 million to the Asia fund and establishing similar programs for the Middle East and Africa. Instead, Congress rolled all development aid into a small package. Increasing concern with Soviet activities in the Middle East and Latin America placed Asian development schemes toward the rear of the assistance queue.[34]

American officials continued to discuss regional development programs during 1956 and 1957. Planners in the State Department and the Committee on Foreign Economic Policy were attracted to the idea of applying Japan's repayment of its $2-billion GARIOA debt from the Occupation period to finance projects in Southeast Asia. However, aside from the difficulty of agreeing on a repayment formula (it took until 1961 to reach a $500-million settlement), American diplomats recognized the political risk of making Southeast Asia a dumping ground for Japanese goods and supplier of raw materials to Tokyo. As Ben Thibodeaux, an economic adviser in the Tokyo embassy, observed, any program that relegated Southeast Asia to "the role of hewers of wood and carriers of water for Japan" would probably "turn out to be a dismal failure."[35]

In February 1957, when Kishi Nobusuke became prime minister, he resumed a dialogue with American officials concerning Southeast Asia. He told an American delegation studying the Mutual Security Program that aid should be used to spur Japanese defense production to meet internal needs as well as those of friendly Southeast Asian nations. Washington should also match Japanese reparations payments to Southeast Asia by providing development loans.[36]

The new ambassador in Tokyo, Douglas MacArthur II, encouraged speculation that Washington would cooperate with Japan on regional development. Talking with Kishi's ally, Kono Ichiro, MacArthur stressed that while Japan's immediate prospects in Southeast Asia were limited, it was "necessary to get started without delay in developing the resources . . . so that in time, when they will be even more needed by Japan, Southeast Asia will be a valuable market and source of raw materials." Nothing, the ambassador stressed, was "wrong with the principle and the overall objective of the Greater East Asia Co-Prosperity Sphere, just as there was nothing wrong with the idea of European unification." Washington only opposed "the methods which Hitler and the Japanese militarists employed."[37]

Kishi followed up on these ideas in a meeting he held with MacArthur in April. The prime minister noted that European and American resistance to Japanese exports left Tokyo with only two alternative outlets, China and Southeast Asia. Although Japan preferred to steer its trade toward Southeast Asia, the region lacked the capital and technical expertise to develop its vast resources, while its consumers remained too poor to purchase many manufactured goods. In an early version of what he later called the "Kishi Plan," the prime minister proposed that Japan supply the "know-how" and the United States the money "so that Japan's technological and industrial capabilities may be fully utilized to accelerate the economic development of Southeast Asia."[38]

Kishi toured Southeast Asia and the southwest Pacific during May 1957. Although greeted by angry protests in Australia and the Philippines, he won plaudits from Washington by concluding a $150-million reparations agreement with South Vietnam and endorsing the Chinese Nationalists' call to return to the mainland. Kishi then set off to the United States.

Eisenhower and Dulles embraced the new prime minister. The president played golf with him, arranged for Kishi to address both houses of Congress, and encouraged a wide-ranging discussion. Kishi appealed for the release of imprisoned war criminals, requested the return of Okinawa and the Bonin Islands, and argued for trade expansion. Japan, he insisted, must trade more with China until the potential of Southeast Asia was realized. The region's poverty encouraged Communist infiltration that only economic development could effectively contain. Japanese exporters, Kishi explained, hoped to "build a basis for economic prosperity in Southeast Asia" but lacked the capital to develop the needed infrastructure. He envisioned three regional aid funds for long-term development, medium-term credit, and short-term currency exchange loans. The United States would supply the capital and Japan would contribute technical assistance and personnel.

Eisenhower assured Kishi that he understood "Japan's need for markets," but there were "problems" with the United States "absorbing more goods." Because of this, he accepted "completely Japan's need for trade with Red China" and its request for funds to speed Southeast Asian development. However, both Eisenhower and Dulles noted the limited availability of funds and stressed that "any plan for economic aid to Southeast Asia must be supportable, realistic, and practical."[39]

Two months later, Kishi's newly appointed foreign minister, Fujiyama Aiichiro, followed up on these conversations. He asked Dulles if the United States would bankroll a development program. The "idea of Japan–Southeast Asia cooperation is absolutely fine," Dulles replied, but he refused to commit any new funds to the venture. Dulles urged Fujiyama to develop specific plans for Washington to consider on a case-by-case basis. When told that the Japanese "already had two or three concrete programs in mind," Dulles said "this was fine" but time was short and other questions had to be resolved. The next month Dulles fended off another emissary, Economic Planning Minister Kono Ichiro, by saying that Washington could not appropriate funds for projects in Southeast Asia because, if it did, everyone else would want the same thing.[40]

The pattern repeated itself during the rest of the 1950s. American officials encouraged Japanese trade with Southeast Asia; Japanese officials requested American aid for regional development; and Washington rejected most suggestions brought forward. Following China's May 1958 suspension of trade with Japan, Tokyo became especially anxious to boost trade with Southeast Asia.

To overcome American resistance to providing new dollars to Southeast Asian development, Foreign Minister Fujiyama proposed utilizing GARIOA debt repayment as part of a regional aid plan. For example, Tokyo could allocate yen for trade projects in Southeast Asia and Washington would deduct this sum from the money Japan owed to the United States. Despite its early interest, Washington ultimately rejected linking GARIOA repayment and regional aid.[41]

Opportunities and Limits of the American Market

With China relegated to a minor role in Japanese recovery and Southeast Asia mostly a future option, Eisenhower and some of his aides hoped that liberalized trade with the West could provide an interim solution. They succeeded in arranging Japan's entry into the General Agreements on Tariffs and Trade (GATT) in August 1955. However, half of the thirty-three GATT members, including the European and British Commonwealth states, invoked escape clauses and imposed high tariffs against Japanese textile and manufactured goods until the early 1960s. This left the United States as the one industrial nation willing to absorb higher levels of Japanese exports.

Eisenhower's economic program for Japan relied on both aid and trade. In 1955, American military expenditures in Japan declined from the 1954 level of about $700 million to $550 million. Despite the gradual reduction of American military personnel in Japan, special dollar income continued to flow into Japan from a variety of sources. Among these was a technical assistance program that from 1955 to 1961 spent $22 million sending American industrial managers to organize "productivity teams" in Japanese factories. It also sponsored meetings between Japanese and American labor union officials, recruited Japanese students to study at American universities, and financed travel to Japan by Southeast Asian business, political, and cultural figures.

Between 1954 and 1961, the value of surplus American food sold in Japan for yen totaled about $255 million. The Mutual Security Program procured equipment in Japan or supplied end-use products valued at $886 million during these same years. Spending by American military personnel in Japan also provided a substantial source of dollar income. Between 1953 and 1962, the Foreign Operations Administration (FOA) and its successor, the International Cooperation Administration (ICA), purchased Japanese products valued at about $775 million for delivery to Korea, Vietnam, Taiwan, Cambodia, and India.

While the Japanese feared a steep decline in military procurement after the Korean armistice, purchases continued at a high level. Between 1952 and 1962, it totaled some $6 billion, averaging over $500 million per year. Procurement earnings did not drop below $400 million until 1962, only to increase with the escalation of the war in Vietnam. In addition to procurement and aid funds, about $1 billion in private American capital flowed into Japan during the 1950s. These sources provided enough dollars to balance Tokyo's trade deficit with America and permit Japan to purchase goods and make investments of about $1 billion in third world countries.[42]

To the relief of many—and to the distress of others—trade between Japan and the United States surged after 1955. That year Japan exported goods worth $449 million to the United States. By 1960, helped by tariff reductions from entry into GATT, exports more than doubled, to almost $1.1 billion. Japanese imports of American goods and raw materials increased from $772 million to $1.54 billion. This trade expansion contributed to Japan's accelerating growth, with its GNP rising at least 12 percent in 1958, 1959, and 1960.

Japanese exports of cotton textiles, women's blouses, pottery, and consumer electronics, including transistor radios, made especially dramatic gains. During 1955 alone, for example, Japan's share of the so-called dollar blouse market in the United States rose from 3 percent to 28 percent. Although imports from Japan amounted to less than 2 percent of the total American textile market, domestic textile and apparel manufacturers demanded protection, charging that Japan's low wage rates (averaging 29 cents per hour, as compared to $2.29 for American textile workers), access to subsidized surplus American cotton (sold to foreign mills for up to 25 percent less than domestic prices), and predatory export promotion schemes represented a form of unfair trade. *Textile World*, a trade journal, complained that the Eisenhower administration compensated for the loss of China to Communism by "giving part of the United States textile market to Japan to oil the hinge" of the containment barrier around China. It charged that policymakers in Washington treated domestic manufacturers like a "sacrificial goat." Senator Johnson of South Carolina predicted that textile workers would recall the day GATT's reduced tariffs on Japanese goods came into effect as a disaster as great as the attack on Pearl Harbor.

Accepting the claim of industry lobbyists that imports were primarily responsible for problems in the textile sector, in December 1955, sixty-three senators supported various bills imposing quotas on cotton textiles. State legislatures in South Carolina and Alabama passed laws in 1956 requiring retail stores selling imports to post notices stating "Japanese textiles sold here." Other states considered enacting restrictive legislation.[43]

Not surprisingly, Japanese officials saw the issue differently. In April 1955 (shortly before Japan's admission to GATT), President Ishikawa of the Federation of Economic Organizations sent Eisenhower a letter complaining that tariff barriers in the United States and Europe prompted business leaders to demand more trade with China and the Soviet Union. To avert this, he urged the Western powers to liberalize trade rules. The next year, responding to the restrictive state legislation, MITI Minister Ishibashi Tanzan called on COCOM to reduce trade restrictions on China so Japan could find needed outlets. In December 1956, a foreign ministry spokesman warned a visiting congressional delegation that restrictions on Sino-Japanese trade, coupled with calls for American quotas, played "into the hands of the vocal minority of the anti-American segment of our people."[44]

When Japan complained that South Carolina's action violated both GATT rules and bilateral United States–Japan trade agreements, Dulles appealed to the governor of South Carolina to repeal the law. (He hesitated to take the issue to the Supreme Court, since the administration opposed expanding federal jurisdiction over civil rights on the grounds that states had broad power to regulate commerce and personal services within their boundaries.) Containing Asian Communism, he stressed, required an economically powerful Japan, and this, in turn, dictated "a high level of foreign trade." Aside from the broad question of national security, Dulles pointed out Japan's importance as a customer. In 1955, Japanese firms imported 647,000 bales of American raw cotton, or 26 percent of total cotton exports. The secretary of state contended that Tokyo had unilaterally begun to restrain certain textile exports. Local retaliation would only impede cooperation.[45]

During 1956 federal agencies such as the CFEP studied complaints by the textile industry, including charges that subsidized American raw cotton exports combined with low wages paid to Japanese textile workers made it impossible for American producers to compete. The CFEP concluded that Japanese imports accounted for only a small part of the industry's problems. Cotton textile and clothing producers suffered more from excess capacity, outdated equipment, competition from synthetic fibers, new production in developing countries, and a host of other factors than from Japanese trading practices. The agency recommended reducing price supports to eliminate the differential between the cost of subsidized raw cotton exports to Japan and the price paid by American mills. In place of quotas, the CFEP urged an informal system of "voluntary export restraint" (VER) by Japanese manufacturers to limit export surges in specific categories of textiles and clothing.[46]

In June 1956, the Senate narrowly rejected amendments to the Mutual Security Act designed to impose quotas on imported cotton textiles. To avoid a quota debate just before the 1956 election, Japan agreed in September to discuss voluntary restraints on textile and clothing exports for 1957 and beyond. The Japanese ambassador informed Dulles that Tokyo would do so "based on the condition that all feasible steps will be taken by the U.S. Government to solve the problem of discriminatory state textile legislation and to prevent further restrictive action with regard to the importation of Japanese textiles into the United States."[47]

MITI minister and prime minister-elect Ishibashi Tanzan warned Assistant Secretary of State Walter S. Robertson in December 1956 that proposed restrictions on Japanese textile exports to the United State, combined with CHINCOM controls on exports to China, could have "catastrophic" effects. Even pro-American Japanese feared that by imposing these trade limits, the United States was "placing the squeeze on Japan."[48]

The two sides agreed in January 1957 on a system of "voluntary export restraint" administered by the Japanese government and textile trade associations. Japan pledged not to engage in "disorderly marketing" by concentrating excessively on any particular product but, instead, to diversify textile exports. The five-year deal initially allowed Japan to export 235 million square yards of cotton textiles and apparel to the United States and permitted annual adjustments in particular cloth and clothing categories in response to market conditions.

Eisenhower expressed "delight" at the agreement. He and members of the cabinet believed the deal persuaded trade associations and members of

Congress to drop demands for formal quotas. Not only had the accord solved a sticky domestic problem, Dulles explained, but if Congress had imposed quotas, "the Japanese would almost assuredly have begun to develop closer relations with Communist China." Ambassador-designate to Tokyo, Douglas MacArthur II, agreed. Although the Japanese economy had done remarkably well since 1955, he told Clarence Randall, "serious long-term problems" lay ahead. The United States might become reluctant to absorb ever higher levels of imports, so Japan faced the "compelling necessity to find export outlets" in Southeast Asia. Without that new market, it would fall prey to "the temptation to look to Red China."[49]

Textiles represented one of the few areas in which the United States supported "creative" financing of regional trade. In part to compensate Japanese government and industry for the voluntary restraints, Dulles supported a plan to selectively use foreign aid funds to subsidize Japanese sales to Southeast Asia. In August 1958, he endorsed a plan to allow Japanese mills to acquire surplus America cotton at below-market prices if the cloth produced was sold in Southeast Asia. This would help Japan counter a Chinese trade offensive in the region, make up for lost sales to the United States, and promote links between Japan and its neighbors.[50]

Between 1958 and 1960, lobbyists for many American industries called for imposing various forms of trade restrictions on Japan (even though low-cost textile producers such as Hong Kong and Taiwan were increasing exports to the United States more quickly than Tokyo was) and nearly convinced the Senate to amend the Mutual Security Act to limit offshore procurements and restrict imports. To forestall formal quotas, the administration negotiated with Japan to accept voluntary export restraints on nearly a third of all products it sold to the United States, including plywood, sewing machines, stainless steel flatware, toys, and tunafish.

The Japanese preferred VERs to formal quotas, while the Eisenhower administration considered them a method to assure Japan's access to the American market without provoking a protectionist backlash. As one State Department official noted, it was of "prime political necessity" to appear to "offer the Japanese an opportunity to expand their exports to the United States." Textile exports were a "symbol for most Japanese of our overall intentions toward their country" and created the "essential psychological underpinning of the United States–Japan alliance." When domestic cotton manufacturers resisted Japanese proposals to adjust upward the VER in 1959, American diplomats complained that shortsighted manufacturers threatened the anchor of containment in East Asia for the sake of "a few million yards of textiles."[51]

Through all this, Eisenhower articulately defended his foreign economic policy, particularly its dual emphasis on trade and aid. In a speech at Gettysburg College in April 1959—which Japanese Foreign Minister Fujiyama praised effusively for its understanding and sympathy—he stressed the link between American security, the Japanese economy, and the survival of South Vietnam. The Diem regime, he explained, faced an implacable military threat from the Communist North. To resist subversion, Vietnam required higher levels of trade and economic assistance. A Communist victory in Vietnam, the president warned, "would set in motion a crumbling process" that endangered not only Southeast Asia but also the "struggle to preserve liberty" among all emerging nations.

Eisenhower then discussed the interdependence between Vietnam and Japan, the "essential counterweight to Communist strength in Asia." Since "Japan must export to live," but had lost much of its Asian market, Tokyo risked "becom[ing] dependent as a last resort upon the Communist empire." Only increased trade with the West and Southeast Asia could prevent this "incalculable" danger.

The challenges in Japan and Southeast Asia, Eisenhower concluded, were parts of a single problem. Japan required raw materials and markets; Southeast Asia needed manufactured goods. So "by strengthening Vietnam . . . and Southeast Asia" the United States ensured the stability of Japan and safety of the entire free world. Because this relationship required time to evolve, the United States must remain a trade outlet for Japan.

Eisenhower urged Americans not to confuse this policy with charity. Japan used its export earnings to buy more from the United States than any country except Canada. If Japan sold more, it would also buy more. Any attempt to stifle trade, "would risk the free world stake in the whole Pacific."[52]

From the mid-1950s on, economic planners in Washington recognized that a stable alliance with Japan depended on sustained economic growth. This, in turn, required access to Southeast Asian and American markets. Protectionism in the United States or Communist expansion in Southeast Asia might drive a wedge between the allies and push Japan toward China. At the same time, Japan's search for wider trade options, along with rekindled Nationalist sentiment, encouraged movement away from the American orbit.[53] Efforts by Yoshida's three immediate successors from 1955 to 1960 to expand trade with China, make peace with the Soviet Union, and revise the security pact increased these tensions. Sustaining the Japanese-American alliance under changing circumstances required nimble diplomacy during the latter half of the 1950s.

7 *JAPANESE-AMERICAN*

POLITICAL RELATIONS,

1954–58

IN the five years following Yoshida's resignation, economic and security ties with the United States remained Japan's magnetic north. At the same time, Tokyo's more nationalistically inclined leaders struck out in directions that occasionally unnerved Washington. Aside from questions over China and Southeast Asia, disputes over the pace of rearmament, the terms of the security treaty, and Japan's efforts to improve ties with its Communist neighbors aroused American fears of ideological adultery.

In 1954–55, the Japanese economy began an era of sustained economic growth that surpassed 10 percent annually for the next fifteen years. By 1971, real wages had tripled as compared to 1953. At the time, of course, no one predicted the pace and duration of this expansion. Through 1960, discontent at being tethered to an unequal security treaty surged almost as dramatically as Japanese exports to the United States. Yoshida's successors initiated tentative steps toward a more balanced foreign policy without jeopardizing the benefits of the existing alliance. They discovered that even modest initiatives to improve relations with the Communist bloc elicited rebukes from Washington.

The Eisenhower administration barely tolerated Tokyo's effort to reach a peace settlement with Moscow, discouraged most moves toward Beijing, and balked at revising the security treaty. Only after 1958, when Prime Minister Kishi Nobusuke ended Japan's modest dalliance with the Communist bloc, did Eisenhower and Dulles agree to renegotiate the military pact. To their dismay, the revised security treaty aroused strident opposition within Japan that threatened the foundation of the Pacific alliance.

On December 10, 1954, the new prime minister, Hatoyama Ichiro responded to Soviet calls for improved relations by declaring that "Japan desired, without prejudice to her cooperation with the Free World, to normalize relations with the Soviet Union and China on terms mutually acceptable." This, like Tokyo's plea that Washington ease trade controls with Communist bloc nations, sounded to American ears suspiciously like creeping neutralism.

As noted earlier, American diplomats took every opportunity to caution Japanese officials about the risk of association with Communist powers, especially China. The fact that Washington had diplomatic ties with Moscow, Dulles admitted, "preclude[d] a strong effort to persuade Japan from establishing relations with the U.S.S.R." But Dulles drew the line on forging diplomatic ties to China. Stung by American criticism, Hatoyama focused on the safer option of improving relations with Moscow.[1]

Japanese-Soviet Diplomacy

As of 1955, Japan remained in a technical state of war with the Soviet Union. After refusing to sign the San Francisco treaty, Moscow vetoed Japan's membership in the United Nations, continued to hold several thousand Japanese soldiers captured in the last days of World War II, and retained four small islands just north of Hokkaido seized in August 1945. Hatoyama strove for almost two years to resolve these issues, in the face of internal rifts, Soviet stubbornness, and American suspicion.

The head of the Soviet mission in Tokyo responded to Hatoyama's appeal for reconciliation by calling on the prime minister in January 1955 to arrange negotiations. However, Foreign Minister Shigemitsu, one of Hatoyama's chief rivals, shared little of his enthusiasm for rapprochement with Moscow. Shigemitsu had staked his reputation on promises to revise the security treaty with the United States. He delayed responding positively to the Russian's invitation for a month. Negotiations between Japan and the Soviet Union finally began in June 1955 in London.

Although reluctant to criticize Japan publicly, Dulles worried about its initiatives. He especially resented Shigemitsu's effort to get Washington to accept some immediate changes in the security treaty at the same time Japan was negotiating with the Soviet Union. Dulles suspected that the foreign minister planned to use the possibility of American treaty revision as leverage to extract better terms from the Soviets while brandishing the threat of dealing with the Soviets as an incentive to obtain benefits from the United States. As a result, in April 1955, when Shigemitsu asked to visit Washington just in advance of meeting with the Soviets, Dulles refused to see him.

The status of the so-called northern territories, four small islands north of Hokkaido seized by Soviet forces in August 1945, proved the most contentious issue dividing Tokyo and Moscow. The Yalta accords of February 1945 as well as the 1951 San Francisco peace treaty compelled Japan to surrender South Sakhalin, the Kurile Islands, and other territories seized or acquired by Japan before 1937. However, neither document specified whether the northern territories (the Habomais, Shikotan, Etorofu, Kunashiri) were actually part of the sparsely populated Kuriles. Moreover, Washington insisted that the 1951 peace treaty with Japan superseded the Yalta accords of 1945. (At San Francisco, Yoshida argued that the four disputed islands were not part of the Kuriles and should be returned to Japan. However, during Diet discussion of the peace treaty in 1951, Japanese officials conceded that two of the disputed islands, Etorofu and Kunashiri, were part of the Kuriles.) By refusing to sign the San Francisco peace treaty, American legal experts contended, the Soviets had forfeited their claim to all the Kuriles.

By questioning Moscow's claim to the Kuriles, as well as to the northern territories, Washington hoped to stir discord between Japan and the Soviet Union. In fact, as early as 1947, George Kennan and members of his Policy Planning Staff had discussed the advantages of provoking a territorial dispute. With luck, they remarked, conflict over the northern territories might embitter Soviet-Japanese relations for years. A half century later, the issue still divided Russia and Japan.[2]

Aside from the territorial question, factions within Japan's governing coalition disagreed sharply over whether and how to approach Moscow. The complex negotiations then underway to merge the Liberals and Democrats into a single conservative party (achieved in November 1955) along with disagreements between the foreign ministry and prime minister complicated the process. For example, Foreign Minister Shigemitsu harbored deep resentment toward the Soviets who had pressed for classifying him a war criminal during the Occupation. At the same time, the Japanese public and a Diet majority seemed willing to accept a peace settlement with Moscow that returned only the Habomais and Shikotan. Shigemitsu went through the motions of negotiating with Moscow, but expected that Soviet refusal to surrender any territory would halt progress. This, presumably, would embarrass Hatoyama and place a premium on his own effort to revise the security treaty.

The Eisenhower administration took no official position on the negotiations, but revealed its discomfort by expressing legalistic objections to efforts to resolve the status of the disputed islands. Washington also protested recent as well as past incidents in which the Soviets had shot down two American air force planes that had overflown the Habomais. The United States asserted that since the Soviet Union had no clear title to the islands, it had no right to forcibly defend their airspace.

The first such attack had occurred in October 1952, at the end of the Truman administration. The Eisenhower administration said little about the incident until September 1954. At an NSC meeting, the president fumed over the "damndest stupidity" of the Truman admininstration for having "just given away the Kuriles" with no regard to their value in both defending Japan or containing the Soviets. Dulles and UN Ambassador Henry Cabot Lodge then prepared a legal brief to present to the UN Security

Council that asserted Japan's claim to the Habomais and Shikotan and, by extension, the right of American aircraft to fly over the islands. When the Soviets downed a second plane on November 7, 1954, Dulles issued an official protest, but confided to Eisenhower that "I do not know anything we can do to get the Russians out short of war."[3] These protests boxed in both Tokyo and Moscow, since it would be awkward for a Japanese politician to adopt a less nationalistic position than Washington or for a Soviet leader to return territory in the face of an American challenge.

In April 1955, after informally broaching the idea to Ambassador Allison, Foreign Minister Shigemitsu informed the Japanese press that he intended to visit Washington to discuss the Soviet initiative as well as the possibility of revising the security treaty. Both Allison and Dulles resented this gambit, sensing that the foreign minister had played the Moscow "card" to push the Americans into a hasty rewriting of the defense pact. Dulles tartly spurned Shigemitsu's request for a meeting.[4]

The Eisenhower administration worried about both Japanese assertiveness and hints of Soviet flexibility. Intelligence analysts predicted that in contrast to past practice, the post-Stalin Soviet leadership would show tactical flexibility toward Japan. The prospect of Soviet-Japanese détente troubled the Eisenhower administration. Secretary of State Dulles complained that despite American "proddings which approached the brutal," Japanese leaders refused to assume the military and political responsibilities in East Asia that Washington considered appropriate. If Japanese-Soviet rapprochement further diminished Tokyo's willingness to shoulder military burdens, it would constitute "a grave loss of advantage to the United States."

Under the terms of a new security treaty, Dulles predicted, the United States would have "to forgo its *right* to maintain forces and bases in Japan" and consult Japan about the kinds of weapons stationed on its soil and the missions American forces could mount from its bases. As the Socialists gained strength in the Diet (a trend not halted until 1958), Dulles even questioned the wisdom of pressing Japan to rearm. It made "no sense to do so if you ended up . . . putting arms in the hands of people who are going to shoot in the wrong direction."

If the Soviets returned any of the Kurile Islands, Dulles feared, "the United States would at once experience heavy Japanese pressure for the return of the Ryukyu Islands," including the key base of Okinawa. He speculated that Moscow might give back the so-called northern territories "precisely in order to increase tension between the United States and Japan." If the Soviets pulled back in the Kuriles, Dulles lamented, "it is certain that we would be forced out of the Ryukyus." To avoid this, he persuaded Eisenhower to discourage the Japanese from compromising with the Soviets and rejected Shigemitsu's call to renegotiate the security treaty.[5]

To complicate reconciliation between Tokyo and Moscow, the State Department repudiated its earlier contention that neither the wartime Yalta accords and Potsdam Declaration nor the San Francisco treaty provided a legal basis for the Soviet claim to Sakhalin and the Kuriles. American diplomats explained that while Washington still supported Japan's claim to the Habomai and Shikotan Islands, "it would be legally difficult for the United States to support a Japanese claim to all or part of the Kuriles." They suggested that Japan accept continued Soviet occupation of the Kuriles so long as Moscow acknowledged Japan's "residual sovereignty," in a "manner comparable to the residual sovereignty Japan obtains over the [American occupied] Ryukyus." With luck, this would torpedo a settlement or result in only a nominal return of territory—blunting Japanese pressure to return Okinawa.[6]

Japanese and Soviet negotiations began in London during June 1955. In August, chief Soviet delegate, Jakov Malik, startled his Japanese counterpart, Matsumoto Shunichi, by proposing to return the Habomais and Shikotan, two of the four disputed islands, as part of a comprehensive peace treaty. This astounded Shigemitsu and foreign ministry bureaucrats (mainly Yoshida's disciples) who had counted on Soviet inflexibility to produce a stalemate that would undermine Prime Minister Hatoyama. Moscow's unexpected flexibility threatened the foreign minister's strategy. To stall for time, he kept the Soviet offer secret from Hatoyama.

Suspicious of Shigemitsu, Hatoyama sent a cabinet ally, Agriculture Minister Kono Ichiro, as his personal envoy to London. Through his ministry and business connections, Kono had ties to the fishing industry. Since Japanese boats required Soviet permission to operate in the coastal waters of the Bering Sea, Kono favored a deal with Moscow. On August 11, Soviet negotiators told him of the offer to return the two islands and Kono notified Hatoyama.

During the next several weeks, the Hatoyama faction tried to conclude an agreement while Shigemitsu's representatives worked to scuttle it. The prime minister favored a compromise that involved the return of two of the disputed islands. The foreign minister demanded not only the return of all four, but also Soviet agreement to submit their claim to south Sakhalin and the Kuriles to an international conference.[7]

The competing Japanese factions also tried to enlist the American government. Dulles had previously rebuffed Shigemitsu's effort to meet with him but now agreed to see him in Washington at the end of August. American diplomats reported that the foreign minister's trip was "primarily [an] internal political move" to improve his "personal chances" of ousting Hatoyama. Lacking a strong Diet faction, Shigemitsu hoped to gain favor at home by extracting a prize from Tokyo's patron. He would offer to confine a deal with the Soviets to a "technical" treaty ending the state of war if Dulles agreed to renegotiate the security treaty. As Allison waspishly reported, Shigemitsu worked to advance Japan's national interest "except where his personal ambitions conflict."

To rein in his foreign minister, Hatoyama added two Shigemitsu rivals—Agriculture Minister Kono and Democratic Party Secretary General Kishi Nobusuke—to the Washington-bound delegation. He reportedly hoped that the contending "individuals and cliques" would keep an "eye on each other" to "prevent rivals from monopolizing any political gains" in Washington. Kishi, who made no secret of his desire to eventually succeed Hatoyama, offered to assist State Department officials in "get[ting] to know the thinking of Japan's present leader [Hatoyama] and future leader," himself.[8]

Dulles informed his staff that he would resist making concessions on the security treaty. Any revisions would require the United States to do more for Japan while diminishing the nearly total freedom of action enjoyed by American forces. Dulles also doubted that the Hatoyama government was strong enough "that we wished, in forthcoming negotiations, to give it a political livelihood." Since Hatoyama would probably lose power shortly, Dulles saw no "point in using up our ammunition only to face a later government which would raise the ante."[9]

In joint and individual meetings with Shigemitsu, Kishi, and Kono, Dulles's resolve never wavered. He characterized recent Soviet and Chinese overtures to Tokyo as cynical lures to beguile the weak. Japan, he told his visitors, lacked the "unity, cohesion, and capacity" to justify a revised, more equal security arrangement with the United States. When the conservative factions unified, revised the constitution, and got serious about rearmament, the United States would "do something to help." Dulles showed no embarrassment in lecturing Shigemitsu—who signed the September 2, 1945, surrender in Tokyo Bay—about the need to scuttle the prohibition on armaments and expand Japan's military.

As a group, the delegates agreed on several points. All urged release of war criminals still in custody, return of the Ryukyus, increased military procurement, and greater use of the new Asian development fund to promote regional trade. But Shigemitsu implied that these were secondary concerns. Without quick revision of the security treaty, he warned, leftists would sweep to power on an anti-American platform.

In private asides, the other delegates undermined Shigemitsu. According to Kishi, Japan faced severe economic, not security, problems. Economic growth would do wonders to undermine the Socialists, assure tranquility, and improve alliance relations. But growth required that the United States lower barriers to Japanese exports and increase procurement orders. Appealing to Dulles's concerns about Southeast Asian security and Japanese rearmament, Kishi suggested merging economic and security aid. If Washington paid the bill, Japanese industry could "provide military equipment for countries in Southeast Asia."[10]

In response to Shigemitsu's appeal for immediate revision of the security treaty, Dulles declared that Washington would not accept limits on the freedom of action of American forces in Japan so long as the Japanese constitution barred Japan's own military from operating abroad. Searching for wiggle room, the foreign minister implied that Article IX could be interpreted as permitting the dispatch of Self Defense Forces to the Western Pacific to meet military threats directed at Japan.[11] But when he and Dulles issued a joint communiqué hinting at that, reaction among the Japanese press and Diet members proved so negative that Shigemitsu quickly disavowed this interpretation. His failure to win concessions in Washington contrasted sharply with the success of West German Chancellor Konrad Adenauer who, in a September trip to Moscow, restored German-Soviet diplomatic ties without agreeing to either a territorial settlement or a formal peace treaty on Soviet terms.

Dulles assured Eisenhower that his talks with the Japanese had gone "really well." He had stanched pressure to amend the security pact and had opened a personal channel to Kono and Kishi, two rising stars on the conservative horizon. Dulles had encouraged the "right-wing parties to consolidate and not tear each other apart and seek popularity by joining in the 'American go home' theme." He predicted the conservatives would soon "consolidate on a platform of cooperation with the United States."[12]

In fact, Japanese domestic politics proved less malleable than Dulles anticipated. In October 1955, the left and right Socialist factions merged (they split again in 1959). Adopting a more nationalistic stance than many conservatives, the Japan Socialist Party (JSP) demanded Soviet return of *all* disputed islands, including the Kuriles and southern Sakhalin.

In November, the main conservative groups merged to form the Liberal Democratic Party (LDP), a move celebrated by American diplomats. The party destined to govern Japan for nearly four decades was less a cohesive political organization than an amalgam of interest groups and personalities unified by opposition to the Socialists, financed by big business, and committed to the alliance with the United States. Party barons riven by personal feuds and loyalties divided along multiple fault lines on the questions of constitutional revision, the Soviet treaty, China policy, and revising the security treaty.

At any given time after 1955, the party leadership consisted of eight or more factions, each linked to an individual and his followers in the Diet. Liberal Democratic rules specified that every two years LDP Diet members and a small number of party officials from the prefectures were to elect a party president. Given LDP control of parliament, he became prime minister. Japanese voters had no direct input into the process; individual LDP Diet members had only slightly more influence. In theory, each Diet member cast a single, secret ballot. In practice, faction leaders bargained among themselves to select a party president and generally controlled the votes of their members.

As part of the process, the party leader/prime minister (Hatoyama was chosen as the first LDP president in 1956) appointed a cabinet of faction leaders or their designees. This limited a prime minister's authority and led most to avoid contentious issues. Both by default and by tradition, the permanent bureaucracy exercised a large measure of control over domestic and foreign policies, further insulating the government from voter input. The Japanese citizen, one scholar remarked, viewed political parties as "the bauble of the Dietman, not an integral party of the democratic system in which he must participate fully."[13]

This distribution of political power, often called the "1955 System," confirmed a conservative monopoly of national power and marginalized the Socialists and other opposition groups. However, the ability of opposition parties to hold onto about one-third of the seats in the Diet effectively blocked attempts to amend the "no war" clause of the constitution or repudiate some of the Occupation's liberal legacies. In fact, some elements within the LDP (such as the Yoshida faction) tacitly cooperated with the Socialists to blunt pressure from Washington to rearm.

Liberal Democratic elder Takeshita Noboru, who served as prime minister in 1988–89, explained this tactic. In describing the LDP–Socialist coalition government that ruled briefly in 1995, Takeshita compared it to the tacit cooperation of the mid-1950s. Throughout the cold war, he explained, the Liberal Democrats had used the possibility of criticism by the Socialists to deflect demands by the United States to speed rearmament or play a more active role internationally. "In that sense there was a sort of burden sharing between us," Takeshita observed, an arrangement he described as "cunning diplomacy."[14]

During the fall of 1955, as the new Japanese political structure took form, the Eisenhower administration sent mixed signals to Tokyo. For example, Dulles instructed Allison to inform Shigemitsu that although he would not oppose a Japanese-Soviet deal that repatriated prisoners and returned only the Habomais and Shikotan, he insisted that Japan do "nothing implying recognition [of] Soviet sovereignty over the Kuriles and South Sakhalin" and reject efforts to restrict American naval movements in the Sea of Japan. But, as Dulles surely realized, Moscow would reject any question of its claim to the Kuriles and Sakhalin.[15]

The twists of Japanese politics, as well as American pressure, further complicated the London talks. To counter the Socialists' call for the return of all occupied territory, the LDP platform reversed Hatoyama's earlier compromise position on the northern territories and demanded return of all four disputed islands. At the end of 1955, Japanese negotiators rejected Moscow's offer of the two islands and negotiations stalemated.[16]

Although discussions resumed a few months later, they made little progress. The United States soon raised new objections. During a brief visit to Tokyo in March 1956, Dulles warned the Japanese to be wary of Soviet motives. The time had come, he declared, "for Japan to think again of being and acting like a Great Power, and not accepting . . . insults from the Soviets."[17]

Two days after Dulles offered this advice, the Soviets broke off the London talks. A day later, on March 21, Moscow announced restrictions it intended to impose on Japanese fishing boats along the Siberian Coast during the coming season. Hatoyama responded by sending Agriculture Minister Kono to Moscow. When asked by journalists if he hoped to resolve the fishing dispute, Kono declared, "Who in hell would go all the way to

Moscow to fiddle around with fish? I'm going to reopen the Japanese-Soviet rapprochement talks."

At a meeting with Premier Nicolai Bulganin, Kono agreed to Soviet demands to merge the fishing and political issues. On May 14, they reached an interim agreement to restore fishing rights as soon as either a full peace treaty or diplomatic relations was realized. If, as appeared likely, negotiators could not settle on a comprehensive treaty that included a settlement of the northern territories and Kurile claims, Bulganin proposed a limited settlement like that struck between the Soviet Union and West Germany the previous September. Under this formula, Moscow would release 1,200 Japanese POWs, support Japan's entry into the United Nations, and exchange diplomatic representatives with Tokyo.

Kono flew to Washington to discuss the Soviet offer. Although Dulles did not explicitly condemn these terms, his top aides complained that any settlement with Moscow, while bad enough on its own, would also "spur . . . those [Japanese] who wish to go on and normalize relations with Communist China." Dulles and Eisenhower had recently read two opinion studies concluding that most ordinary Japanese believed that "Communist China" was a contradiction in terms and that Japan's top diplomats believed that "Peiping can be split from Moscow by peaceful means." A second report asserted that "it is abundantly clear that the majority of Japanese believe that American military bases are a bad thing for Japan; and they would like to see American forces withdrawn."

These findings suggested that if the Soviets withdrew from even two of the disputed northern territories, the United States would come under tremendous pressure to surrender its bases in Okinawa or even in Japan. To prevent this, Dulles instructed his aides to send "private transmissions" to Japanese leaders warning of retribution should they do anything to undermine the security treaty or move toward recognition of China.[18]

Domestic political reversals made it more difficult for Hatoyama to salvage a compromise. In May 1956, a Diet coalition of Socialists and the Yoshida faction within the LDP defeated a bill to create small, single member electoral districts in place of the large, multimember districts that currently existed. The change would reduce the influence of small parties and solidify the hold of the revisionist LDP Diet majority at the expense of the minor parties, the Yoshida faction, and Socialists. Hatoyama's failure to change the voting system assured that the Socialists and the Yoshida faction would retain their one-third representation in the Diet and their ability to block constitutional revision. Diet elections held in July 1956 confirmed this.

Following this setback, on July 30, Hatoyama dispatched Foreign Minister Shigemitsu to Moscow to resume negotiations. The Soviets again proposed a comprehensive treaty premised on the return of only the Habomais and Shikotan, Japan's recognition of Soviet title to the Kuriles and South Sakhalin, and restriction of U.S. naval access to the Sea of Japan. To Hatoyama's surprise, Shigemitsu reversed his previous opposition to this formula and publicly urged acceptance. It became the turn of Hatoyama and other cabinet members to reverse their stands. The prime minister demanded that Shigemitsu secure better terms (including the return of all four islands) and consult with Dulles, then in London attending a conference on the Suez crisis, before agreeing to anything.[19]

The secretary of state bitterly resented Shigemitsu's effort to win his approval for this deal. Dulles bluntly told him that Article 26 of the San Francisco peace treaty stipulated that "if Japan gave better terms to Russia, we could demand the same terms for ourselves. That would mean that if Japan recognized that the Soviet Union was entitled to full sovereignty over the Kuriles we would assume that we were equally entitled to full sovereignty over the Ryukyus." In its dealings with Japan, Dulles added, "the United States has been soft where the Soviet Union has been tough. Perhaps the United States should likewise get tough." Spurning Shigemitsu's effort to find some basis for compromise, Dulles declared that "if the Soviet Union were to take all the Kuriles, the United States might remain forever in Okinawa, and no Japanese government could survive."

Although this dressing down left Shigemitsu "worried and distraught," Dulles told his staff he was determined to resist the Soviet claim to the Kuriles and their effort to draw the United States into an international conference on territorial adjustment. The Soviets, he explained, looked for a wedge to split the United States from its allies. If Washington and Tokyo compromised on any territorial issue, this would inevitably open up "disagreeable questions" about the status of Okinawa or Taiwan. However, in response to his staff's concern about the dubious legal basis for objecting to Japan's surrender of the Kuriles, Dulles declared at a news conference on August 28 that he merely "pointed out" the terms of Article 26 but had not decided how the United States would respond to any particular territorial adjustment.[20]

On September 7, after considering how to encourage Japanese resistance to Soviet demands, Dulles issued a formal statement on territorial claims. Neither the Yalta accords nor San Francisco treaty, he insisted, conferred ownership of the Kuriles on the Soviet Union or empowered Japan to transfer title. Dulles also asserted that Etorofu and Kunashiri, as well as Shikotan and the Habomais, were historically part of Japan proper, not the Kuriles, and could not be validly claimed by Moscow. In discussing these points with Ambassador Tani Masayuki, Dulles urged Japan to resist Soviet pressure and also to "think in terms of hardening their position with respect to Communist China."[21]

American demands made it nearly impossible for Japan to reach a comprehensive settlement with Moscow. It would constitute an act of direct defiance for Tokyo to trade its acceptance of Soviet claims to the Kuriles for return of only part of the northern territories. Nevertheless, in October, the LDP leadership decided to send Hatoyama to Moscow in hope of recovering at least two islands.

By then, however, the Soviets had altered their proposal. They offered to return the Habomais and Shikotan—and nothing else—but only if Japan agreed to a comprehensive peace treaty. Since Hatoyama could not accept Moscow's terms, the two sides settled for a minimal agreement. In a joint declaration issued on October 19, 1956 the Soviet Union and Japan announced an interim settlement terminating their state of war, exchanging ambassadors, returning POWs, restoring fishing rights, and endorsing Japan's admission to the United Nations.

The United States scarcely commented on the agreement other than to note its disappointment at Moscow's rejection of Japan's "just claim to sovereignty over Etorofu and Kunashiri, the two southernmost Kurile islands." (This after Dulles had denied they were part of the Kuriles!) In fact, the Eisenhower administration must have heaved a collective sigh of relief at having contained Japan's rapprochement with the Soviet Union. Dulles had blocked Hatoyama's attempt to forge a more independent foreign policy and preserved the security treaty.[22]

Despite this achievement, Ambassador Allison detected storm signals ahead. Shortly before the Moscow–Tokyo agreement, he and his staff warned Dulles that Japan was "on the verge of slowly slipping away from us." As Japan grew strong enough to reclaim a place of leadership in Asia, it chafed under an unequal relationship in which America continued to treat it as an occupied enemy state. It was especially important, Allison argued, for Washington to encourage "genuine consultation" on security matters, recognize Japan's special interest in China, actively support expanded trade with Southeast Asia, keep open America's market, and change policy toward the Ryukyus and Bonin Islands. Only a "fresh start" would reassure Japan's leaders that the United States recognized them as "our senior partner in Asia."[23]

Allison worried that Hatoyama's diplomacy represented an opening gambit in a bid by Japanese conservatives to free themselves from "unilateral dependence on the U.S." Although partly a normal evolution, Allison predicted that the pace and direction of disengagement, unless altered, would eventually carry Japan toward neutralism or a still more antagonistic position. More than anything else, the friction caused by the "unequal" security treaty infuriated the Japanese. Unless American leaders moved quickly to renegotiate the 1951 agreement, the ambassador warned, Japanese resistance would inevitably render it useless.

Although Hatoyama was expected to leave office after concluding an agreement with the Soviets, Allison reported that the same problems would persist regardless of who served as prime minister. Only "quiet, informal, private talks based on personal trust" between Japan's leaders and American officials (such as himself) could avert further deterioration.

Political development during December 1956 appeared to confirm Allison's analysis. As decided by LDP leaders months before, Hatoyama resigned as prime minister following the agreement with Moscow. The death of two senior faction leaders upset plans for a brokered succession. In a hotly contested party election, the ideologically conservative but nationalistically inclined Ishibashi Tanzan outpolled Kishi Nobusuke to win the LDP party presidency and the right to head a new government.

Ishibashi's victory sent shivers through diplomatic circles. For example, Howard Parsons, the director of the State Department's Office of Northeast Asian Affairs, told a British diplomat that the Americans "had put their money on Kishi" and were shaken when the wrong horse had won. They hoped that by serving as foreign minister Kishi would "put some brake on Ishibashi." "If we are lucky," Parsons added, "Ishibashi may not last too long."[24]

The Americans considered Ishibashi a "headstrong . . . rabble rouser" who (unlike Kishi) had "never got over the personal affront of having been purged during the occupation." His independent brand of conservative thought struck many in Washington as anti-American. Ishibashi's desire to expand trade and possibly establish diplomatic ties with China set off alarm bells. State and Defense officials feared he would encourage protests against the continued occupation of Okinawa. Ishibashi's attitude during Assistant Secretary of State Walter Robertson's recent visit to Tokyo, when he put the American "on notice" that the "era of more or less automatic Japanese compliance with American wishes on China was over," seemed a portent of things to come. To make matters worse, Ishibashi took power just as the British threatened to scuttle CHINCOM limits on trade with China.[25]

Had Ishibashi implemented these policies, relations between Japan and the United States might have faced an early crisis. Concern over events in Tokyo prompted the NSC's Operations Coordination Board to expand efforts to influence Japanese opinion by placing "favorable news and features in the Japanese press, periodicals, radio, and television" that stressed the importance of close ties with the United States. However, Parsons's hope that the new prime minister "may not last too long" proved prescient. Less than two months after he took office, Ishibashi's declining health forced his resignation. In February 1957, LDP Diet members voted, to Washington's relief, to select Kishi Nobusuke as prime minister.[26]

As a rising star in the Ministry of Commerce and Industry during the 1930s, Kishi had worked closely with the *zaibatsu* and the Japanese military to promote industrial development in Manchuria. He also became a golfing partner of American Ambassador Joseph C. Grew. As a member of General Tojo's cabinet, Kishi co-signed the declaration of war against the United States in December 1941 and later served as wartime head of the munitions ministry.

After Japan's surrender, Occupation authorities purged, arrested, and held Kishi in Tokyo's Sugamo Prison from 1946 to 1948 as a suspected Class A war criminal. While incarcerated, he befriended fellow inmate Kodama Yoshio, a figure with underworld connections who had amassed wealth and influence in China by supplying raw materials to the Japanese war machine. After their release in the late 1940s, Kodama emerged as a grey eminence in the world of conservative politics, supplying money and underworld muscle for promising politicians.

Harry Kern, Eugene Dooman, Compton Packenham, and other members of the influential American Council for Japan, who recalled Kishi's prewar friendship with Joseph Grew, took him under their wing even before he was depurged in 1953. They introduced him to American visitors, tutored him in English, and arranged for his travels in Europe and the United States.

Kishi regained financial solvency through the intervention of Fujiyama Aiichiro, an old friend and prominent industrialist who appointed him to the board of several companies. (Kishi repaid the debt in 1958 by appointing his patron foreign minister.) After being "depurged" in 1953, Kishi reentered politics and became secretary-general of the Democratic Party. Following the conservative merger in 1955, he emerged as a powerful factional leader in the LDP. Unlike Yoshida, whose power rested on support from the old aristocracy and financial interests, Kishi drew strength from heavy industry, extreme nationalists, and underworld elements. He favored dismantling many Occupation reforms, revising the constitution, accelerating rearmament, and providing state support for industry. Like most Japanese, Kishi favored trade with China. But, unlike Ishibashi, he would not defy Washington's prohibition on formal links to the Beijing regime and risk losing the vital rewards of the Pacific alliance.

Kishi had impressed Americans since his rehabilitation in the late 1940s. As we will see, he established a covert financial and political relationship with the CIA after becoming prime minister. He often acted as a conduit between embassy staff in Tokyo and conservative leaders. In July 1955, as secretary-general of the Democratic Party, he provided information about the negotiations between the Liberals and Democrats to form a new party. Kishi forecast a November merger agreement, with the new party committed to constitutional revision, repeal of liberal Occupation laws, a more active anti-Communist foreign policy, accelerated rearmament, and greater reliance on central economic planning.

Before becoming prime minister, Kishi briefed embassy officials about his plans to raise campaign funds. He would press large businesses to "subscribe" to party economic and political reports, with the cash going into central coffers. Special subscriptions would be levied before elections. This would give party leaders greater control over Diet members while making it unnecessary for candidates to solicit money individually.

The funding proposal constituted one element in his plan for electoral reform. Kishi informed the Americans he would promote changes in the election law to create small, single-seat constituencies. Campaign finance and electoral reforms, he predicted, should assure the nascent LDP control of the Diet.

With Kishi's spirits buoyed by several "king size scotch-and-sodas," he told embassy counselor George A. Morgan that five politicians (Ogata

Taketora, Ikeda Hayato, Sato Eisaku, Kono Ichiro, and Miki Takeo), as well as himself, would become prime ministers. (All except Ogata and Kono did.) He also admitted his continuing "dream" of Pacific expansion. To solve Japan's population and economic problems, Kishi told Morgan, the United States should purchase New Guinea and Borneo. "With U.S. capital and machinery and Asian manpower, the islands and their enormous resources would be developed" to save Japan from the threat of communism.[27]

Although Kishi's rise to power pleased American diplomats, they continued to hear echoes of Allison's warning about the Nationalist trend in Japanese foreign policy. Unless the United States ameliorated the widespread dissatisfaction with its subordinate status, Japan might eventually "slip away." The Eisenhower administration addressed this challenge in its evolving economic policy. It now had to adjust its security relations to political realities within Japan.

8 *THE STRUGGLE TO*

REVISE THE SECURITY

TREATY, 1957–60

*I*N 1957, Hollywood released a film version of *Sayonara*, James Michener's best-selling novel about American military personnel in Japan during the Korean War. Starring Marlon Brando as air force pilot Lloyd Gruver, the story centered on the redemptive power of love between Japanese women and American soldiers. One of the protagonists, Joe Kelly, commits suicide along with his bride when his callous superior officer threatens to transfer him out of the country. In Gruver's case, a submissive "golden skinned" lover, along with a dose of Japanese culture, transform him from a coarse bigot to a champion of interracial harmony.[1]

During the Occupation, American military authorities discouraged soldiers from marrying Japanese women, although about 6,000 did so anyway. It required a special act of Congress, the War Brides Act of 1945, to permit Asian wives and children of military personnel to enter the United States. Liaisons with American soldiers were as often a source of shame and resentment among Japanese as the "healing" process described by Michener. A notorious example of conflict caused by a soldier's treatment of a Japanese woman occurred on January 30, 1957, when Army Specialist 3/C William S. Girard shot to death a woman collecting brass scrap on an American firing range in central Japan.

Japanese and American witnesses confirmed the "facts" of the case. Girard had been participating in a small-unit firing exercise at Camp Weir. About two dozen Japanese scrap collectors had followed the American unit to gather expended brass shell casings. During a break, Girard and another soldier were told to guard a machine gun. While doing so, Girard tossed several shell casings in the direction of the scavengers and motioned for two of them, a man and a woman, to retrieve them. As they approached, Girard yelled at them to run, placed an expended cartridge in the grenade launcher attached to his rifle and fired twice, striking the woman in the back as she fled, killing her.

Socialist politicians and the Japanese press condemned the killing as a typical, if extreme, act of arrogance by a de facto army of Occupation. Members of Congress, the midwestern press, and a surprisingly vocal public portrayed Girard as a victim of zealous ingrates. When President Eisenhower waived legal jurisdiction in the case, he was accused of betraying principles of justice and pandering to Tokyo. At the height of the controversy, which coincided with a visit to Washington by Prime Minister Kishi, Dulles feared that a "wave of anti-Japanese sentiment," unlike anything seen since 1945, might lead to public protests.

Speaker of the House Sam Rayburn urged Eisenhower to cancel Kishi's visit. On June 27, 1957, the House Foreign Affairs Committee reported out a bill introduced by Ohio Republican Frank T. Bow that would overturn all "status of forces" agreements to deny Japan and other countries legal jurisdiction over American servicemen stationed abroad. Despite Eisenhower's vigorous opposition, Republican House leader Joseph W. Martin and Senate Minority leader Everett Dirksen predicted congressional passage. The "issue was so hot," they told Eisenhower, "Congress might even override a presidential veto."

As Eisenhower pondered the jurisdictional question, Ambassador Douglas MacArthur II warned from Tokyo that unless Girard was handed over to local authorities, "vital interests" not only with Japan but "throughout free Asia" would be jeopardized. The president concluded that enactment of the Bow bill or his refusal to surrender Girard would lead Japan and other nations to demand the departure of American troops from their soil. Angered by what he saw as political posturing, Eisenhower complained to a friend that only an abysmal misunderstanding of Japan's value to the United States could account "for the fact that we seem to be trying to make a national hero out of a man who shot a woman—in the back at something like ten to fifteen yards distance." A face-saving solution to the Girard case calmed tempers, but the incident spurred Eisenhower to reexamine the security pact with Japan.[2]

Along with restrictions on China trade, the security treaty and the presence of several hundred thousand American troops remained the most contentious issue between Japan and the United States during the late 1950s. When Eisenhower took office in January 1953, about 210,000 American service personnel plus dependents were stationed in Japan. Even as Japan's economy recovered, the wide gap between the living standards enjoyed by these Americans—compared to their hosts—provoked envy and resentment. Since 1945, some 25,000 Japanese women had married GIs. This, along with rampant prostitution around military bases, grated on Japanese sensibility. Disputes over wages paid to household servants and civilians employed on bases, resentment over the acquisition of farmland for military airfield extensions, the continued occupation of Okinawa and other small islands, and transgressions by off-duty soldiers that ran the gamut from traffic violations to assault and murder contributed to the emotions surrounding the Girard case.

The status of forces agreement in effect since 1953 gave Japanese courts jurisdiction over American military personnel accused of crimes committed while *off duty*. In practice, military authorities retained jurisdiction in most cases. As Eisenhower noted, "Out of fourteen thousand cases since 1953 in which Americans were subject to trial in Japanese courts, the Japanese had voluntarily relinquished jurisdiction in 13,642—or 97 percent." Even in the 358 cases tried before local courts, the sentences handed down were generally lighter than the equivalent punishment meted out by American military tribunals. Nevertheless, the special legal status accorded GIs reinforced a sense of inequality and added to the many resentments associated with the security treaty.

As a former theater commander in Europe, Dwight Eisenhower recognized these problems more clearly than many Americans. Also, the administration's evolving defense strategy known as the "New Look" stressed the role of air power and nuclear weapons over ground and conventional forces. As the United States adopted a policy of massive nuclear retaliation to deter aggression, the 200,000 troops stationed in Japan became a strategic anachronism. These factors prompted Eisenhower to gradually reduce ground forces, halving the number in Japan by the end of 1956.

The Japanese government, in the person of Foreign Minister Shigemitsu, made its first serious effort to alter the security treaty in August 1955. As we noted earlier, Shigemitsu urged Dulles to amend the 1951 pact as part of his attempt to steer a more independent course between the Soviet Union and the United States. Dulles insisted that Japan speed rearmament and expand its regional defense commitment before asking Washington to amend the treaty. Two years later Prime Minister Kishi Nobusuke resumed the quest.

Even before the Girard incident, many Japanese voiced frustration with the terms of the 1951 agreement. Written during the Korean War and tolerated as the price to be paid for ending the Occupation, the treaty reflected the imbalance of power between the two signatories. American forces stationed in Japan were empowered to intervene in domestic affairs but had no obligation to defend the country. The treaty contained neither a time limit nor any provision for consultation or revision. It gave Japan no say over the stationing of nuclear weapons on its soil and allowed the United States complete freedom to use bases and troops in Japan to intervene in other countries.

In 1957, while Prime Minister Kishi toured Southeast Asia to drum up business and divert attention from opposition demands for closer ties with China, a delegation of Japanese Socialists visited Beijing. There, Mao Zedong denounced the security treaty as an infringement on national sovereignty, called for its abrogation, and offered to sign a nonaggression pact with Tokyo. Many Japanese quietly agreed with Mao's assessment.[3]

Observing the mood in Japan, the NSC concluded early in 1957 that the "major U.S. objective—a firm alliance in the Pacific—is not being achieved." Japan's tendency to "drift away" resulted, in part, from decreasing economic and diplomatic dependence on Washington as Japan rebuilt its economy and national pride. But it also reflected a "failure to develop mutuality as shown by subtle but unmistakable evidence that Japan's leaders" were unsatisfied by how the United States treated their country. Although the Japanese realized they were "not as yet strong enough militarily and industrially to dispense with the present U.S. defense arrangement," they chafed under the terms of the security treaty and had begun "seriously talking about 'adjusting' relations with the United States in the direction of 'greater equality'." The NSC study cautioned that unless Washington revised the security treaty, "basic U.S. interests with respect to Japan" would be endangered.[4]

The close relationship that evolved between the new ambassador to Tokyo, Douglas MacArthur II (a career diplomat, nephew of the Occupation-era general, and member of the inner circle of Eisenhower and Dulles advisers) and Kishi eased many strains that developed as the two sides reviewed the treaty. Recalling the broadly felt anger toward the security treaty he encountered on his arrival in Tokyo in February 1957, MacArthur acknowledged that Japanese of all political stripes "thirsted for being treated on the same basis of equality that we treated other allies." He added, when "a treaty which is in force becomes considered by one of the parties to that treaty as not only not in its own interest, but inimical to its own self-interest, the treaty isn't really worth very much. Because if you ever had to apply it and get cooperation from the other side, you wouldn't get it."[5]

Beginning with their first meeting, Kishi impressed the ambassador as someone with whom he could "do business." MacArthur arranged for Eisenhower to extend an invitation for the prime minister to visit Washington. Kishi repaid the vote of confidence by initiating frequent confidential meetings with the ambassador. In their talks he spoke of the "distrust of and ambivalence toward the United States" voiced by growing numbers of Japanese. This attitude stemmed from "resentment against Japan's subordinate position under the security treaty," a desire to recover Okinawa, and "dissatisfaction over the embargo" against China. "Many Japanese," he explained, believed Washington "wanted a war aimed at overthrowing the Communist bloc powers by force" and feared being drawn into a disaster because of American bases on their soil.

Kishi convinced MacArthur that the United States had reached a "turning point" with Japan and that unless it accommodated demands for change, America's position would gradually erode "in an atmosphere of acrimony and mounting hostility." The ambassador argued that these complaints were not leftist propaganda, but the subject of discussion "at the highest levels of the Japanese government." He urged Eisenhower and Dulles to make Kishi's coming visit an opportunity to place the "relationships between Japan and the United States in the security and economic fields on a really equal basis." Failure to move forward might bring the Socialists to power. Even if Kishi and the conservatives held on, public opinion would push Japan "progressively into neutralism."[6]

Dulles at first resented the warning. He told MacArthur that although he looked forward to an "exchange of respective viewpoints" during Kishi's visit, he did not intend to discuss specific changes in the security treaty. Since the "American public was unaware of the existence of any problem" with the treaty he had authored, it would neither understand nor approve renegotiating the pact. Dulles wanted Kishi told not to expect rapid changes and chided MacArthur by advising "less frequent meetings" between the ambassador and prime minister.[7]

In addition to Dulles's reluctance to open talks on the treaty, tension over the Girard case complicated planning for the summit. The killing occurred on January 30 and for the next four months a joint committee in Japan debated who had jurisdiction. For a soldier on a rest break to entice and shoot a scavenger, the Japanese insisted, did not conform to "official duties" as described by the status of forces agreement. This made Girard subject to Japanese, not American, justice. In May, army authorities waived jurisdiction, but secured a secret promise from the Japanese that Girard would be charged with the "least serious offense" possible.

This action elicited a storm of protest in Congress, angry newspaper editorials, and a round of fingerpointing between the State and Defense Departments. Each agency suggested that while they would have preferred to retain American jurisdiction, the other wanted to appease the Japanese. Politicians and editorialists demanded that Girard be tried by a U.S. court martial.

Congressman Bow, author of the bill revoking status of forces agreements, described Girard as a model soldier defending army property against a thief. A dozen representatives spoke in agreement. Several senior Republicans told Eisenhower they considered Japanese demands to try Girard an insult to Americans. Numerous midwestern newspapers took up this theme. On May 19, for example, the *Cleveland Plain Dealer* editorialized that although "we want to get along with Japan," to "sacrifice one American soldier in the interest of maintaining amicable relations with our former enemy is monstrous, morally wrong and wholly indefensible." Press accounts portrayed Girard as a victim deprived of basic legal rights. A poll taken in June in Minnesota revealed that a remarkable 95 percent of respondents claimed to have heard of the case and nearly 60 percent opposed his trial by a Japanese court.[8]

Eisenhower ignored this outcry and rejected advice that he reassert American jurisdiction over Girard. In a meeting with legislative leaders on June 4 and at a news conference the next day, the president argued that in contrast to accounts that portrayed the killing as an accident, Girard had "gone out of his way to 'manufacture' ammunition" used to assault the woman. He also noted that sentences handed down by Japanese courts against American soldiers were generally "lighter than the sentences meted out by our courts-martial." The "Japanese had acted very splendidly" in observing the status of forces agreement and he would not intervene. The president then told Ambassador Asakai Koichiro that to secure both "individual justice" for Girard and the "continuance of the satisfactory relations between" the United States and Japan, he would leave the case in Japanese hands.[9]

In June 1957, Girard's lawyers secured a federal court order barring his transfer to Japanese authorities. The Justice Department immediately appealed to the Supreme Court. On July 11, the high court overturned the previous decision and affirmed Eisenhower's right to turn Girard over to the Japanese. His trial began on August 26. The verdict announced on November 19 found Girard guilty of "causing bodily injury resulting in death." He received a three-year suspended sentence and was expelled from Japan. The army discharged him in December.

Kishi's visit to Washington coincided with the excitement over the Girard case and prompted Eisenhower and Dulles to ameliorate bilateral tensions. For example, when the British abandoned the CHINCOM restrictions in June 1957, Eisenhower practically encouraged Japan to follow suit. As he put it to Ambassador Asakai, he did not like embargoes and thought "it was wise to trade as much as possible with practically all nations."[10]

As the date of Kishi's visit neared, Dulles, too, softened his stand on the security treaty. He told his aides, he was "at the point of having to make a Big Bet" and wanted to know if they agreed with his inclination to "put our money on Mr. Kishi." Frank Nash, a special consultant Dulles had sent to Tokyo, responded that Kishi was not only the "best bet," but the "only bet we had in Japan." But growing irritation with such things as trade restrictions, the security treaty, and the Girard case, Nash reported, would force the United States to make a "real pitch to line him up on our side." Changing his tune, Dulles spoke of the need to revise the 1951 treaty as a mutual security agreement. This meant reducing American troop levels and consulting Japan about the use of bases and stationing of nuclear weapons.

Even before Kishi arrived, Dulles and Eisenhower decided to withdraw from Japan 60 percent of all American military personnel, including most ground troops, as soon as possible. Remaining forces, the president suggested, might be placed under joint control. Even the Joint Chiefs, Admiral Radford reported, had decided it was better for the Japanese to "decide for themselves" the pace of rearmament than for Washington to impose a timetable.[11]

In briefing the president for meeting the prime minister, Dulles praised Kishi as the "strongest Government leader to emerge in postwar Japan." As a good friend of the United States, he was determined to put relations on a more equal basis. Dulles admitted that while the existing security treaty had served both countries well, the "time had come to take the initiative in proposing a readjustment" to replace it. He proposed

telling Kishi that Washington supported changes and would begin negotiations following the summit. MacArthur made a similar point, telling
Eisenhower that unless the United States satisfied Japanese complaints,
"within five years" they would drift toward neutralism or "even turn to
work with the Communists."[12]

Kishi's discussions with Eisenhower and travel in the United States
went well. Demonstrations over Girard fizzled. Kishi addressed both
houses of Congress, spoke to the National Press Club, and golfed with
Eisenhower (at an otherwise racially segregated club). He fulfilled a boy-
hood dream by throwing the first pitch at a game between the New York
Yankees and the Chicago White Sox. Quite a second inning for someone
who had co-signed the declaration of war against the United States in
1941!

The prime minister affirmed to Eisenhower Japan's policy of "anti-
communism on the international side" and "close cooperation with the
United States." If the Socialist Party came to power, he warned, these policies would "come to an end." This made it "essential" for America that the
Liberal Democratic Party continue in power. To assure LDP rule, "certain
things" had to be "rectified," starting with the security treaty. Kishi urged
that 7,000 Bonin Islanders who were forcibly moved to Japan in 1945 be
allowed to return home, that U.S. military authority on Okinawa be
reduced, and that the United States help to promote trade expansion in
Southeast Asia and China. Eisenhower pledged his serious attention on all
points. Admiral Radford and Dulles delivered harangues about the Communist military threat, but seemed neither surprised nor angry when Kishi
blandly promised to enhance Japan's defenses where possible.[13]

Dulles and Kishi discussed security issues for several hours on June 20
and 21. For openers, the secretary announced that Eisenhower had decided
to remove most ground forces from Japan and Kishi was welcome to take
the credit. But Dulles probably had ulterior motives in making this concession. Before engaging in a detailed discussion of defense matters, he "had
something that he . . . wanted to say to the prime minister." In agreeing to
the meeting, he "assumed" Kishi's government "desired to continue its
close and intimate relationship with the United States" and basically
"shared our estimate of the danger from Soviet and Chinese Communism,
and that these present talks were not designed just to ease the United
States out of Japan because Japan did not want us with them." If this were
not so, and Kishi preferred that "we divorce ourselves from Japan," the
Americans would "accommodate ourselves to that wish." Rather than
"impose" policy on a reluctant ally, Dulles said he was prepared to
"develop Australia as an industrial base in place of Japan."

Kishi assured Dulles that he and the LDP were "absolutely" committed to "close cooperation" with the United States. The Socialists, on the
other hand, would change things "completely" if they took power. The
"problem" for both nations was "how the conservative party can be continued in power on a long-term basis." Kishi defined revision of the security

treaty as a critical issue in Japanese domestic politics. With American support, the conservatives could use it to contain the left.[14]

Dispensing, as Dulles put it, with "all the niceties of diplomatic usage," the two men set out to find common ground. Kishi insisted on "the right of consultation concerning the disposition of United States forces in Japan," a provision to clarify the "relationship of the Security Treaty to the UN Charter," and "a clear date . . . for the expiration of the treaty." Dulles offered to consult except in emergency situations and saw no problem in informing the United Nations of "any actions taken under the Treaty" that affected international peace and security. He could not accept a five-year time limit, he explained, because any substantive change to the existing treaty required Senate ratification. Dulles offered to exchange letters in which the United States stated it had no desire to continue the treaty indefinitely and was prepared to alter it as regional circumstances changed. He would also promise "publicly" that American forces in Japan would never intervene in domestic affairs, "except at the express request of the Japanese government."[15]

Kishi proposed forming a bilateral consultative committee "to consider improvements in the implementation of the treaty." This would placate Japanese opponents without the need of dragging contentious issues before the Senate. Dulles agreed, although he had a more restrictive view of the committee's role. The secretary of state listened politely, but made no commitments, while the prime minister called for repatriating Bonin Islanders, reducing American authority in Okinawa, paroling war criminals, limiting atomic tests, and financing trade expansion in Southeast Asia.[16]

Crafting a joint communiqué proved tricky. Kishi proposed referring to "a high-level committee" empowered to discuss "basic matters." Dulles retorted that he agreed to a committee empowered only to discuss the deployment of forces within Japan and make reports to the United Nations. They settled on announcing the formation of a group to "study problems arising in relation to the Security Treaty."A similar dispute arose over the promise to "consult" on the disposition of American forces. Kishi believed this referred to the movement of forces in and out of Japan and to other countries. Dulles said it applied only to the relatively noncontroversial question of shifting forces within Japan. These conflicting views revealed a deep divide. As Kishi observed, the "most troublesome thing in Japan in connection to the Security Treaty was the fear that Japan could be gotten into a state of war involuntarily" through action taken by U.S. forces in Japan.

Dulles believed that in the absence of a powerful Japanese military committed to regional defense, the freedom to use American troops and bases in Japan was the main reason for the security treaty in the first place. He would not promise to seek approval from or even notify Tokyo about military operations. He went no further than to promise that, under normal circumstances, Washington would not act "in any way that was abrupt or lacking in the normal courtesy between friendly governments."

Dulles also refused to endorse increased Sino-Japanese trade. Although Eisenhower had encouraged Kishi to pursue this, Dulles mocked Japanese belief in what he called the "miraculous virtue" of China. He insisted on replacing references to China with a bland statement acknowledging Japan's need "to increase its trade" with the world. Kishi's proposed reference to the "ultimate" return of the Bonin and Ryukyu Islands to Japan also irritated Dulles. When the prime minister noted that Dulles himself used this phrase at a recent press conference, the secretary replied that this "showed how dangerous press conferences were." Kishi then suggested bringing their disputes to the president.[17]

Eisenhower resolved the impasse by asking Kishi and Dulles what they meant respectively by "ultimate" and "residual." Since, he observed, the United States intended some day to return Okinawa and, in practice the two definitions meant pretty much the same thing, why not use the term "residual" sovereignty and define it along the lines desired by the Japanese?

Once he caught his boss's drift, Dulles declared that the "truly important matter" was not the text of the communiqué but the "purport of what was happening." Both sides had come away assured that the security treaty would operate in a more bilateral way despite the difficulty of formal amendment. Japan and the United States were committed to a relationship of "real mutuality and real cooperation." In an obvious, if condescending, effort to flatter, Dulles repeated that he and Eisenhower were "making a big bet" on Kishi whose performance, they hoped, would justify their trust.[18]

The numerous references by MacArthur, Dulles, and Eisenhower to bets and investments in Kishi were more than rhetorical flourishes. After his visit, Kishi and his brother, Finance Minister Sato Eisaku, opened a dialogue with American officials regarding LDP finances. In July 1958, for example, Sato met secretly with Stan Carpenter, first secretary of the embassy, to plead for campaign funds. Complaining that the Communists and Socialists had access to "substantial" sums of money from China and the Soviet Union, Sato tried, as MacArthur phrased it, "to put the bite on us."

Sato told Carpenter that the LDP had established a "secret organization" of "top business and financial leaders in Japan" to fund election campaigns. Unfortunately, these sources were temporarily tapped out, even though the LDP faced elections for the Diet upper house. Pleading poverty and warning of a leftist victory, Sato asked "if it would not be possible for the United States to supply financial funds to aid the Conservative forces in this constant struggle against Communism." As cover, a Japanese middleman could handle the payments.[19]

Although Carpenter and MacArthur rebuffed this solicitation, it came as no surprise. Sato, MacArthur revealed, had discussed covert funding with American officials several times during the previous year. The ambassador shared Sato's concerns about the series of Diet elections expected during 1958–59. Organized labor and the Socialists still posed a threat to conservative rule, he reported. Despite Kishi's popularity in Washington, the prime minister proved a lackluster campaigner and MacArthur pressed

Dulles to authorize actions to bolster the LDP and Kishi's party faction. These included getting South Korea to grant Japan more liberal fishing rights, encouraging Vietnam and Indonesia to reach reparations agreements with Tokyo, delivering speeches promoting markets for Japanese exports, financing Southeast Asian development, speeding the release of war criminals, and allowing at least some Bonin Islanders to return home. While unstated, MacArthur lobbied for providing covert campaign funds as well.[20]

During the final months of 1957 and early 1958, MacArthur, Dulles, and Eisenhower undertook several well-publicized efforts to bolster Kishi's fortunes. They approved a decrease in Japan's military expenditures for the coming year and held out a promise of gradual relaxation of military control in Okinawa, both highly emotional issues among the Japanese.[21]

The president also authorized the CIA to initiate a covert program in Japan. As Alfred C. Ulmer, Jr., a CIA officer who controlled many operations in Japan from 1955 to 1958 put it, "we financed" the LDP. The CIA "depended on the LDP for information" and used secret payments to recruit allies within the party. By the early 1960s, annual payments of between $2 and $10 million to the party and individual politicians had become "so established and so routine," reported Assistant Secretary of State for Intelligence Roger Hillsman, that they were a normal part of bilateral relations.

The money supplied by the CIA was used in a variety of ways, beginning with the May 1958 campaign for the lower house seats in the Diet. State Department and intelligence analysts feared that the Socialists might make significant inroads and that Kishi's "pro-American" faction would fare poorly compared to their competitors within the LDP. Campaign funds were channeled through a select group of LDP party leaders to Diet candidates considered especially friendly to the United States. Additional money was spent acquiring political intelligence that could be used against the Socialists. Some Socialist Diet candidates, judged relative moderates, received funds to improve their position within the party. As one CIA participant recalled, acquiring "assets" within the JSP as well as "obstructing the Japanese opposition" was "the most important thing we could do." Although the payments were modest in comparison to the larger scope of Japanese-American financial ties, they helped buttress Kishi's fortunes in the Diet lower house election of 1958 and the upper house contest of 1959. Payments to LDP and Socialist politicians continued for at least a decade.[22]

Hopeful that LDP gains in the Diet election scheduled for May 1958 would set the stage for movement on the treaty, MacArthur pressed Dulles to adopt a flexible position. He criticized the Joint Chiefs and Assistant Secretary of State Robertson who urged linking treaty revision to speedier rearmament and Japanese agreement to play a military role in East and Southeast Asia. As the ambassador put it in a letter to Dulles, Japan's long-term cooperation in achieving a "balance of power . . . against the Soviet

Union and Communist China" depended on far more than unrestricted base rights or Japanese rearmament. Japan's economic growth and political stability constituted its greatest contribution to containment. A "truly mutual" security treaty would go far toward "wiping out latent doubts over where Japan's basic loyalties lie" and would affect the "alignment of other free Asian countries."

Most Japanese, MacArthur argued, demanded no more—or less—control over the use of American bases and troops on its soil than did the British or Italians. There was a "universal desire among the Japanese to liberate themselves" from what they and everyone else saw as a "genuinely unequal" relationship. Making Japan a consulting partner, MacArthur predicted, would assure its cooperation in regional security and possible permission to stockpile nuclear weapons on military bases. Efforts to preserve the current treaty would only foster "neutralism." The "best," if not only, "chance" to continue to use Japan for military support and deployment purposes in East Asia, the ambassador concluded, was to approach Kishi immediately after the May 1958 election and work with him to revise the treaty.[23]

The results of the May 1958 Diet election pleased the Eisenhower administration (which had helped pay for it) and the LDP. Instead of projected losses of twenty or thirty seats, the LDP slightly increased its majority to 287 members, as compared to 166 for the Socialists. Not only had the leftward trend of electoral politics been arrested, but Kishi's faction also increased its strength within the party. The prime minister added loyalists to his cabinet and prepared to press forward on the treaty question.

MacArthur informed Dulles that the "time ha[d] now come" to deal with "basic security problems." The Japanese, he speculated, might be more flexible than the Americans. He particularly worried that the military establishment was so intent on retaining unilateral "rights" that they were oblivious to the fact that such rights would soon become "totally unenforceable." Like it or not, the United States would have to accommodate Japanese views on nuclear weapons, deployment of forces, and limiting the geographical scope of a new treaty. If Americans did not bend "we will lose our shirts."[24]

MacArthur's concern about the military proved on target. John Steeves, the political adviser to the commander in chief of the Pacific area, alerted State Department officials that defense planners envisioned a new treaty with Japan that he considered "unrealistic beyond description." They spoke of expanding privileges "far beyond what we now enjoy under the Security treaty and the Administrative agreement." Even moderate elements hoped to retain a free hand to deploy troops from Japan and maintain nuclear weapons in the country. They even suggested making a new treaty conditional on Japan's amending its constitution's no war clause.[25]

While the American military nurtured these dreams, Foreign Minister Fujiyama Aiichiro told MacArthur that recent Soviet technological triumphs, such as the testing of long-range missiles in the Pacific and the launching of *Sputnik*, made the Japanese jittery. They doubted the "advisability of depending on U.S. deterrent power" and also feared that even a local conflict in the Asia-Pacific region would draw Japan into an unwanted war.

By late August, MacArthur recommended that instead of amending the current pact, Washington negotiate a completely new "mutual security" treaty. The United States would have to abandon its unilateral rights and accept the fact that the Japanese military would defend only its own national territory. Holding out for more would achieve less. Socialist as well as conservative Diet members had already introduced proposals to restrict the import of nuclear weapons and block the combat deployment of American forces from Japanese bases. Only by moving toward a new treaty, MacArthur reported, would Kishi be able to deflect these pressures.

In September 1958, MacArthur returned to Washington in advance of a visit by Fujiyama. He persuaded Dulles to support his position and try to bring the military establishment around. The ensuing debate resembled the civilian-military conflict that preceded the 1951 treaty.[26]

MacArthur and Dulles told Defense Department representatives that the United States required from Japan a "relationship broader than a mere military alliance." To achieve the fundamental goal of assuring Japan's alignment to the West, Washington had to accommodate Japanese demands to restrict the treaty area, limit the introduction of nuclear weapons, and consult over the combat deployment of American forces. Military officials expressed concern that "consultation" would, in effect, allow Japan to veto American actions in the Taiwan Strait and elsewhere in East Asia. MacArthur countered that the military's rigidity would "drive Kishi out of business," lose "one of the four major industrial complexes" of the world, and prompt other Asians to "run foot races to Peiping." Ultimately, when Eisenhower and Dulles took a stand in favor of accommodation, the Joint Chiefs and Defense Department gave their grudging approval to negotiations.[27]

Fujiyama conferred with Dulles on September 11 and they quickly agreed on the need to replace the current treaty. Japan, the foreign minister explained, wanted to retain an American defense commitment. However, both constitutional and political realities mandated that Japanese military forces could only be used within the nation's territorial limits, not elsewhere in Asia. The new treaty must provide for consultation regarding the introduction of nuclear weapons or the deployment of American forces outside Japan. Dulles accepted these points and promised to move forward after speaking with military advisers and selected senators.[28]

Despite efforts by the Defense Department and Joint Chiefs of Staff to impede revision, by October 5, 1958, MacArthur and Fujiyama had a draft treaty ready for Kishi's inspection. MacArthur made clear to the Japanese that the Eisenhower administration, because of its faith in Kishi, was prepared to surrender privileges and accept a limited military commitment from Tokyo to assure the "closest possible relations with the Japanese government."[29]

Although the draft addressed many points of conflict, several substantive and political problems surfaced. Foreign ministry personnel raised several questions about the treaty's geographical scope. For example, they objected to the implication that Japan would be required to help defend Okinawa and the Bonins while these islands remained under American control. Tokyo also desired more effective consultation over troop deployment and the introduction of nuclear weapons, and insisted on revising the unpopular administrative agreement. In addition, political developments in Japan forced Kishi to ask more from the Americans.

In October 1958, the prime minister submitted to the Diet a Police Duties Performance Bill that authorized preventive action against potential lawbreakers. Socialist legislators, the labor movement, and even some conservative politicians condemned this as an undemocratic attempt to intimidate unions, antinuclear activists, and critics of the security treaty. Street protests and disruptive behavior by Socialist Diet members impeded a vote on the police bill and, in November, forced its withdrawal. Kishi's retreat emboldened rivals within the LDP and energized citizens opposed to a military pact in any form.

Following the police bill fiasco, Kishi and Fujiyama told MacArthur that LDP infighting prevented adoption of a unified party position on the treaty. So-called mainstream (pro-Kishi) and anti-mainstream factional leaders disagreed over whether to include the American-controlled Ryukyu and Bonin Islands within the treaty area. Some felt the pact should run for ten years, others felt for less. These were important questions, but the contention among faction leaders had more to do with a desire to wound Kishi than improve treaty terms.

Outside the party leadership, a growing number of Japanese feared that the United States had inserted treaty language referring to the "western Pacific" or "Far East" to obligate Japan to intervene in the Taiwan Strait or Southeast Asia. Given the current military tension between China and the United States over the Nationalist-held offshore islands, public opinion ran strongly against committing Japan to defend anything more than its home territory. Kishi's secret discussions with some right-wing Socialists suggested that they might tacitly support treaty revision as long as defense obligations applied only to Japan.

The prime minister concluded that a unified LDP policy would probably not be possible before early 1959. When asked by MacArthur if he still thought he could win Diet passage of a treaty, Kishi predicted violent opposition from the Japanese Socialists and thought it might be necessary to "call out the Self-Defense Force." But, he assured the American envoy, he would get Diet approval.

To assist Kishi's effort in forging a party consensus, MacArthur urged Dulles to agree to changes in the administrative agreement and concede the point that Japan need only defend the home islands. The important thing, after all, was that American forces would continue to enjoy Japan's goodwill and access to its logistic facilities. MacArthur even backed Kishi's demand that the agreement dating from 1951 authorizing U.S. forces in Japan to be utilized in Korea be subject to consultation with Tokyo. When the Pentagon objected, MacArthur told Dulles that if combat forces in Japan were deployed to Korea without consulting Tokyo, "We would be out of business here . . . in a matter of hours."

Dulles (suffering from the fatal cancer that led to his resignation in April 1959 and death in May) approved nearly all MacArthur's recommendations. In all likelihood the secretary of state saw completion of a revised treaty as one of his major legacies. This disposed him to grant MacArthur broad authority to pursue whatever deal had a chance of getting through the Diet.[30]

As Kishi hoped, in April 1959, a majority within the LDP reached a consensus on treaty terms. Base rights would be granted to the United States out of a mutual desire to maintain "international peace and security in the Far East." However, Japanese and U.S. forces in Japan were obliged to respond to armed attack only "in the areas under the administration of Japan"—in effect, the home islands. Kishi and Fujiyama bowed to popular pressure and insisted on revision of the administrative agreement.

This generally pleased MacArthur, but he objected bitterly to calls for renegotiating the administrative agreement. If the provisions governing military personnel and the use of bases were subject to "prolonged and perhaps acrimonious debate," the "entire idea of a new treaty los[t] its attractiveness" to the United States, he warned. Changes in the administrative agreement, he made clear, would have to be settled before the security treaty was signed and submitted for ratification.[31]

Kishi focused his considerable bureaucratic prowess on maintaining unity within the LDP. To assure Diet support for the treaty, he forged alliances with some critics and stripped others of party and government posts. He implied that ratification of the new treaty would cap his career and that he might step down after seeing it through. Out of pique, several of Kishi's rivals visited Moscow and Beijing in hope of achieving a breakthrough with the Soviet Union or China that would undermine support for the new treaty. But none of his opponents could halt Kishi's drive.

In June 1959, an LDP victory in upper house elections, assisted again by covert American funding, prompted Kishi to reshuffle his cabinet and reward pro-treaty factions. Nevertheless, the complexity of revising portions of the administrative agreement that dealt with civil, criminal, tax, postal, and commercial rules applying to American military personnel, as well as the need to clarify the treaty area, and rules for consultation and nuclear weapons, took until early January 1960 to complete.[32]

The central issues of prior consultation in case of combat deployment of American forces from Japan and the introduction of nuclear weapons proved so controversial that they were not openly addressed in either the treaty or administrative agreement. Japanese negotiators insisted that consultation included the right to approve or disapprove of deployments and the stationing of nuclear weapons. The Americans refused to concede a veto.

When it became clear that the Diet would insist on Japan retaining the right of approval, the two sides fell back on an indirect formula. They resolved that following a proposed signing ceremony between Kishi and Eisenhower in January 1960, the president would issue a statement that "the U.S. Government had no intention of acting with respect to the matters involving consultation in a manner contrary to the wishes of the Japanese government."

At the insistence of the Defense Department, MacArthur was authorized to reach a secret understanding with Kishi that allowed American naval vessels and aircraft "transiting" Japan to carry nuclear weapons. (Nuclear weapons on Okinawa were unaffected.) These and related secret agreements resulted in bombs and components occasionally being stored on barges located near American naval bases. The Japanese government would assert that since Washington had never requested permission to introduce nuclear weapons, and since Tokyo granted no permission, no nuclear weapons were in Japan.[33]

During the final stages of negotiation, a well-publicized criminal trial along with sharp debate in the Diet revealed mounting misgivings about the entire security relationship. The so-called Sunakawa case attracted international attention on March 30, 1959, when the Tokyo District Court acquitted seven anti-base activists charged with trespassing on a U.S. airfield outside the town of Sunakawa. The indictment dated back to July 1957 when 300 labor and student activists protested requisition of farmland to extend a runway. Judge Date Akio dismissed the case on the grounds that the security law protecting foreign bases violated Article IX of the Japanese constitution prohibiting maintenance of war potential. If the presence of U.S. troops violated the constitution, any law protecting foreign bases lacked validity. This ruling, which called into question the entire security relationship, shocked both the Japanese and American governments.

Kishi ordered an immediate appeal to the Supreme Court, while 280 volunteer lawyers for the plaintiffs considered the case a critical test. Pressed for quick review, the high court held six open hearings before issuing a decision on December 16, 1959. Holding that the lower court had erred, the Supreme Court ordered the case returned for retrial. The justices decreed that Article IX barred Japanese, not foreign, war potential. Without ruling directly on the constitutionality of the security treaty or of Japan's own Self-Defense Forces, the court described these as political matters best settled by the Diet and voters.[34]

The current treaty's narrow escape from judicial scrutiny coincided with Diet review of the still-incomplete new security treaty that began on October 28, 1959. Socialist members questioned Kishi and Fujiyama sharply about the precise meaning of the terms "Far East," and "consultation," and the circumstances in which American combat forces could be deployed. In this early round, the two officials offered evasive, sometimes contradictory, responses.

Kishi made matters worse by simultaneously introducing a bill to fund $55 million in reparations to South Vietnam. The agreement with the

Saigon regime, reached the previous May, led Socialist deputies to protest what they called illegal payments to a puppet regime. On November 27, after much shoving and pushing among members on the floor of the Diet, the LDP majority moved to close debate, prompting a mass walkout by the Socialists. With only the LDP majority present, and a coalition of anti-treaty groups demonstrating outside the building, the Diet approved reparations. The controversial behavior by both sides influenced Diet handling of the security treaty debate.[35]

Early in January 1960, Japanese and American negotiators completed revisions of both the security treaty and administrative agreement. This, Foreign Minister Fujiyama explained, "marked the end of the postwar period as far as Japan's diplomacy was concerned."[36] Kishi decided to fly to Washington to sign the documents at a White House ceremony. Ambassador MacArthur and Kishi believed that Eisenhower's personal stamp of approval would boost the prime minister's popularity and assure quick Diet ratification of the treaty. Kishi was so certain that the Japanese public, media, and LDP would embrace the treaty that he insisted on affixing his own signature to the document, rather than allowing Foreign Minister Fujiyama to do so.

Nevertheless, as Kishi prepared to leave for Washington, he and his treaty faced mixed portents. Some 30,000 treaty opponents demonstrated in Tokyo while a radical Marxist splinter of about 2,000 students—members of the Zengakuren, the All Japan Federation of Student Self-Government Associations—trooped to the airport late on January 15 hoping to prevent the prime minister's plane from taking off. In the predawn hours of January 16, riot police smashed through barricades erected inside the Haneda airport terminal and arrested nearly a thousand demonstrators. With the terminal and runway cleared, Kishi left for Washington. But instead of heralding a new era, the fight over the treaty produced the most bruising episode in postwar Japanese-American relations.[37]

9 *POLITICS AND SECURITY:*

THE TREATY CRISIS OF 1960

DURING the spring and summer of 1960, the Pacific alliance nearly came apart at the seams. Kishi's efforts to push the revised security treaty through the Diet provoked violent opposition within the parliament and on the streets of Tokyo. The United States had agreed to treaty revision to signify its desire to play a reduced role in Japanese internal affairs, but found itself forced back to the center of domestic politics. American efforts to promote in Japan a consensus on security and anti-Communism, resembling that in West Germany, were frustrated by the refusal of the Japanese Socialists to behave like their German Social Democratic counterparts. To salvage the security treaty, Washington saw no alternative except to continue efforts to undermine the Socialists and bolster the LDP.

Eisenhower and Kishi considered the new security pact a step toward institutionalizing a partnership of equality while preserving U.S. military and base rights. The revised treaty eliminated the provision for American military intervention in Japan, allowed either side to terminate the agreement after ten years, and stipulated consultation before combat deployment of U.S. forces from Japanese bases or the introduction of nuclear weapons. Japan was required to respond to attacks only within its own territory, was relieved of the obligation to contribute to American defense costs, and received an American pledge to expand trade and economic development. The new administrative agreement resembled that applied in the NATO countries.

Prime Minister Kishi received a welcome in the United States on January 19, 1960 in sharp contrast with his riot-scarred departure from Tokyo. *Time* magazine placed on its cover a portrait of a smiling Kishi against a background of humming industry, while *Newsweek* trumpeted the arrival of a "Friendly, Savvy, Salesman from Japan." Dismissing his critics as a disgruntled rabble manipulated by Moscow and Beijing, *Newsweek* declared that Americans admired a "patriot and a fighter." The man who signed the declaration of war against the United States in 1941 and spent three years cleaning latrines in Sugamo prison under investigation for war crimes had proved himself one of the "free world's most durable leaders."

The news weeklies heralded Japan's emergence as a great economic power, blending coverage of the treaty signing with descriptions of what *Newsweek* called the "busy skilled Islands of Nippon." Kishi's transformation, from militarist to statesman, the reports stressed, signified a new era in bilateral relations. According to *Time*, Kishi's "134-pound body," packed "pride, power and passion—a perfect embodiment of his country's amazing resurgence." *Newsweek* highlighted Japan's booming technology exports to the United States—epitomized by the ubiquitous Sony transistor radio—along with the new security treaty, as affirming America's alliance with the "economic powerhouse of Asia." The treaty and expanding trade, *Newsweek* predicted, would spark a "new wave of prosperity" on both shores of the Pacific.[1]

Nearly all media accounts praised the treaty. Newspapers described it as an "exemplary document" that marked the "beginning of partnership in economic and military affairs which can have profound and salutary effect on future Asian development." The *New York Times*, *Herald Tribune*, and Hearst press praised Kishi's "political courage as well as realistic good sense in committing Japan to firm alliance with the West, rather than neutralism."[2]

In Washington, Kishi conferred with Eisenhower, Secretary of State Christian Herter, and other officials. He exchanged signed texts of the Treaty of Mutual Cooperation and Security, a revised administrative agreement, and related documents. As promised, the president released a statement declaring that the United States had "no intention of acting in a manner contrary to the wishes of the Japanese Government" on issues involving "prior consultation under the treaty." Both leaders agreed that economic expansion in general, and bilateral trade in particular, were of "paramount importance" to the "well-being and progress of both countries." Eisenhower accepted an invitation to visit Tokyo in June, following an anticipated trip to the Soviet Union. Japanese officials announced that Crown Prince Akihito would, in turn, visit the United States. Kishi hoped the momentum provided by treaty ratification and Eisenhower's visit would enhance his chance to win another term as prime minister in the fall of 1960.[3]

Kishi's visit, American diplomat David Bane told a British colleague, had gone exceptionally well. The prime minister's "disarming frankness" charmed the president, who staked "a good deal on Kishi's reliability and staying power." While Eisenhower may not have "actually said, as he did of Mr. Nixon in 1952 'he's my boy' . . . the atmosphere seems to have been much the same." Bane admitted it was probably a "failing of the United

States to forget and forgive too soon, and that he sometimes envied [the British their] longer memories, both of men and policies." But in "Japan as elsewhere," one had to "work with the material on hand."[4]

Although the new treaty eliminated many of the "unequal" provisions of the 1951 pact, it did little to placate Socialist opponents. They considered foreign forces in Japan a violation of the constitution and a threat to security. The mere presence of American troops and equipment, critics charged, increased the chance of conflict with China and the Soviet Union and the danger Japan might be dragged into an unwanted and disastrous war.

Soviet and Chinese reactions to the treaty confirmed this fear. Three days after Kishi's return from Washington, Soviet Foreign Minister Andrei Gromyko warned Japan's ambassador in Moscow that "in conditions of a modern rocket-nuclear war all Japan with her small and thickly populated territory, dotted . . . with foreign war bases, risks sharing the tragic fate of Hiroshima and Nagasaki in the very first minutes of hostilities." Condemning the pact as a provocation against the Soviet and Chinese peoples, the Kremlin withdrew its standing offer to return the Habomai and Shikotan Islands once Japan and the Soviet Union signed a peace treaty. The Soviets then fired an ICBM test missile directly over Japan en route to its Pacific touchdown. China stepped up its verbal attack on the "Kishi clique of war criminals" who risked involving Japan in an imperialist war on America's behalf.[5]

As he prepared to submit the treaty for ratification, Kishi considered dissolving the Diet and calling a snap election. If, as likely, the LDP retained its majority, he would be in a strong position to secure approval. Two factors dissuaded him. The State Department cautioned that any delay in ratification might prompt the Senate to postpone action until after the summer 1960 recess, by which time the American presidential election would be in process.

In fact, the treaty was not a partisan issue and the Senate practically ignored it. In January 1960, Assistant Secretary of State J. Graham Parsons briefed J. William Fulbright, Chair of the Senate Foreign Relations Committee, and described the pact as the "culmination of a historical process" that began with Japan's surrender. Parsons confided to Fulbright that a secret deal with Tokyo permitted U.S. forces in Japan to "react instantaneously without consultation" in case of renewed Communist attack in Korea. He may have mentioned the secret agreement on the "transit" of nuclear weapons. Fulbright "expressed no objections." His colleagues only cared about avoiding another "Girard case."[6]

When Yoshida Shigeru, now over eighty years old, endorsed the treaty, Kishi felt certain he would have broad-based LDP support without calling for an election. Yoshida had initially opposed treaty revision, concerned that Washington would press Japan to commit its military power in Southeast Asia. When this provision was not included, Yoshida decided to support the pact rather than risk having the Socialists make a snap election a referendum on the treaty. In return for his cooperation, Yoshida expected to influence the selection of Kishi's successor. His protégés included two current cabinet members, MITI minister Ikeda Hayato and Finance Minister Sato Eisaku, who was also Kishi's brother. Like their mentor, they pledged that their Diet factions would support the treaty.

With Yoshida, Ikeda, and Sato on board, Kishi concluded he had sufficient strength to allow Diet debate to continue through April and then force a vote in the lower house thirty days before the scheduled May 26 end of the current Diet session. Japanese law stipulated that once the lower house of the Diet approved a treaty, it came into effect thirty days later, with or without the approval of the upper chamber, so long as the Diet remained in session.

American diplomats considered it ironic that treaty approval hinged on support by Yoshida, whom they had helped drive from office in 1954 because of his opposition to rapid rearmament. Kishi and MacArthur agreed that "Yoshida has been of inestimable value" in lining up LDP factions behind the treaty. Eisenhower acknowledged this early in May when he agreed to meet the former prime minister later that month in Washington. This meeting assumed critical importance when developments in Japan jeopardized the treaty.[7]

Bitter divisions among the Socialists strengthened Kishi's hand. The merger of right and left Socialist parties in 1955 produced a shaky marriage. The left-wing faction, linked to the Sohyo labor federation, cooperated uneasily with right-wing Socialists whose power base lay within the more moderate Zenro labor federation. For a time, the hope of winning a Diet majority obscured their doctrinal differences. But setbacks in the lower and upper house elections of 1958 and 1959 strained Socialist unity. The fissure widened during 1959 when Zenro refused to join the People's Council opposed to treaty revision and Sohyo accused the more moderate labor federation of trying to steal union members. In December 1959, right-wing Socialist leader Nishio Suehiro bolted the Japan Socialist Party (JSP) and soon organized the Democratic Socialist Party (DSP) with 37 seats in the Diet lower house and 16 in the upper, compared to the JSP's 128 and 69.

The JSP and Sohyo adhered to a Marxist ideology of class struggle while the DSP and Zenro advocated the type of bread-and-butter labor activism familiar to Americans. They discouraged militant strikes and mass agitation against the security treaty. The DSP favored gradual, negotiated loosening of the security relationship with Washington. Since 1958, the United States and the LDP had encouraged the Socialist split by providing secret financial support to Nishio and to the Zenro labor federation. Kishi and Ikeda supplied funds to and maintained contacts with key DSP members in expectation that some might support treaty revision or at least not disrupt efforts at Diet ratification.[8]

The Japanese business community emerged as Kishi's strongest ally on treaty revision. The major business federations condemned treaty opponents as pro-Communist and warned that failure to revise the security relationship threatened Japan's economic survival. They particularly appreciated the treaty preamble that contained a commitment to "encourage economic cooperation" and "promote conditions of economic stability and well-being" between Japan and the United States. The communiqué issued in Washington by Kishi and Eisenhower had stressed the importance of "trade among free nations" and Japan's key role in the "economic development of free Asia." These sentiments reflected the business federations' goal of boosting trade with the United States and Southeast Asia and resisting protectionist pressure in Congress.[9]

Opposition to the treaty came from a broad, diffuse movement that reflected a sometimes bewildering array of tactics and goals. Anti-treaty sentiment coalesced during 1959 among Socialists in the Diet, the Sohyo labor federation, the small Japan Communist Party, intellectuals and university professors, and the radical Marxist but anti-JCP Zengakuren student movement. These groups united loosely under the banner of the People's Council for Preventing Revision of the Security Treaty, usually referred to by its Japanese acronym, Ampo. Ampo members disagreed forcefully over tactics as well as goals. Some opposed the new treaty as a threat to peace; others hoped to use the anti-treaty movement to topple Kishi, improve ties with China, oppose "U.S. imperialism" or even, in the case of the Zengakuren, set the stage for a revolution within Japan. In practice, most opponents disliked Kishi and LDP rule more intensely than they reviled the security treaty itself. They feared Kishi would parlay successful treaty ratification into renewed efforts to expand police power, crack down on organized labor, stifle government workers, and amend the constitution.[10]

Their fears had a real basis. The anti-treaty, anti-Kishi movement coincided with what proved to be the last large labor struggle in post-Occupation Japan. During the spring of 1959, miners at the Miike coal mine, a subsidiary of the Mitsui Company, went on strike against efforts to downsize operations by firing surplus workers. In January 1960, the company, supported by the business community and government, locked out strikers in an effort to break the radical union and speed the nation's shift from coal to petroleum. The confrontation continued for nine months.

Since treaty ratification required a simple majority vote of the lower house of the Diet, and given the LDP's commanding majority of 288 seats compared to the JSP's 128 and DSP's 37, approval seemed certain. In fact, the style of deliberation in the Diet, as well as the intense factionalism within the LDP, created major impediments.

Kishi's rivals within the LDP (including Kono Ichiro, Miki Takeo, and Matsumura Kenzo) had only minor substantive objections to the treaty. They did, however, have an interest in complicating its ratification. If the treaty won quick Diet approval, Kishi stood a good chance of winning a third term as LDP president and prime minister. If the treaty barely scraped through, Kishi's grip on power could be broken, opening a path for others.

The Japan Socialist Party remained unalterably opposed to treaty revision on both principle and political grounds. It confirmed this position in March 1960 when members selected Asanuma Inejiro as party chairman. Asanuma was well known for his proclamation in Beijing a year before that U.S. imperialism was a common enemy of both the Japanese and Chinese people.

The Democratic Socialists, whose small presence in the Diet could not directly influence the outcome, were courted by both the LDP and JSP. The DSP opposed the treaty as presented, but hinted they might find it acceptable if it were amended further. More important, the party pledged to observe normal parliamentary procedure. Even if they voted not to ratify, DSP members intended to observe Diet process and not participate in a boycott.

Kishi squandered his chance of securing Democratic Socialist support by insisting that the Diet not amend the treaty but vote it up or down as received. The JSP countered with a strategy of parliamentary delay and intense questioning designed to highlight ambiguities in treaty language. They hoped to force debate beyond April 26, a month before the scheduled end of the regular Diet session on May 26. Then, even if the lower house approved the treaty, there would be fewer than the required thirty days for automatic ratification without upper house action. This presumed that the Diet session would not be extended beyond May 26. The JSP hoped to bottle up the treaty and make it the focus of the next election.

Hearings on the pact were held by special committees of the lower and upper houses between February and May 1960. When Kishi, Fujiyama, and other government spokesmen testified, Socialist members focused their attack on ambiguous language relating to the geographic scope of the Far East, the circumstances under which U.S. forces in Japan could be sent into combat outside Japan, the meaning of prior consultation, and Japan's right to veto U.S. troop and nuclear deployments.

Kishi and Fujiyama brought trouble on themselves by first saying that the "Far East" included parts of China and Siberia, and then limiting it to the area around Japan and territory controlled by the Republic of Korea and the Republic of China. This imprecision troubled even some supporters. Critics argued that the treaty ran counter to the cold war thaw prevailing since Soviet Premier Nikita Khrushchev visited the United States in 1959.[11]

The People's Council coordinated activities by labor, student, intellectual, antinuclear, and other treaty opponents. Peaceful demonstrators and petitioners appeared sporadically at the Diet compound all spring, with large rallies beginning on April 26. Most of Japan's major newspapers also opposed the treaty. They wanted it rewritten to give Japan more control over American forces and demanded that Japan have the right to approve, not merely consult, on policy matters. The press considered the pact's ten-year duration too long and accused Kishi of showing insufficient "sincerity" in dealing with other parties. As the *Asahi Shimbun* declared in an editorial summarizing its objections, "for the sake of the people," the Liberal Democrats ought to bring the parties "together and forge a mutually satisfactory policy."[12]

Kishi's plan to allow the opposition to talk itself out before forcing a vote thirty days before Diet adjournment foundered when the April 26 deadline passed without action. A week later, after an American spy plane disappeared over the Soviet Union, the treaty's prospects took a sharp turn for the worse.

On May 1, a U-2 reconnaissance aircraft based in Turkey and piloted by Francis Gary Powers crashed deep within Soviet territory after being damaged by a missile. Eisenhower had approved the risky mission to gather intelligence that he hoped would make the case in favor of reaching an arms control agreement with the Soviets at the upcoming Paris summit. He guessed, correctly, that the Russians had not deployed the large missile force they boasted of and that proof of this would allow him to neutralize critics of arms control. Instead, the ill-fated flight buried détente.

When the plane failed to arrive at its destination, Washington released a statement referring to a lost weather-research aircraft. A few days later, Moscow retorted that it had bagged a spy plane. (Despite assurances given to the president that neither pilot nor plane could survive a crash, Powers had parachuted to safety, fallen into Soviet hands, and confessed his spy mission.) After the Eisenhower administration dismissed the Kremlin charges as Communist propaganda, Khrushchev exhibited portions of the wrecked aircraft, then trotted Powers out before startled observers.

On May 16, the Paris summit collapsed when Eisenhower refused to apologize to Khrushchev for the U-2 intrusion or pledge an end to overflights. This debacle soured Soviet-American relations, halted progress on a nuclear test-ban treaty, and raised the specter of more intense rivalry between the two power blocs. All this alarmed the Japanese who knew U-2s operated from local bases.[13]

The U-2 incident galvanized the treaty debate in Japan by arousing near panic about the consequences of retaining American air and naval bases on Japanese soil. As most Japanese quickly learned, the United States flew U-2 aircraft out of Atsugi airfield near Tokyo. (In September 1959, engine trouble forced one of the distinctive "black jets" to make an emergency landing at a civilian airport. Although U.S. military personnel sealed off the site, a Japanese journalist reported the episode and some questions were raised in the Diet and press.) In the wake of the May 1 shootdown, China charged that U-2s from Japan routinely violated its airspace. Khrushchev threatened a "shattering blow" with nuclear-tipped rockets against any country from which American aircraft intruded into Soviet airspace.[14]

The Eisenhower administration's plodding response maximized the negative impact of the U-2 incident within Japan. On May 7, the State Department issued a bland statement acknowledging that the United States had made flights of unarmed U-2 aircraft for legitimate intelligence gathering "along the frontiers of the Free World for the past four years." At best a half truth, many of the missions crossed freedom's frontier. The next day, an air force spokesman stated that although U-2 aircraft had been stationed in Japan for several years, all were currently grounded. This hardly allayed fears of future spy flights provoking Soviet attack.

The U-2 incident fed public suspicions of American-backed conspiracies. During 1960, author Matsumoto Seicho's serialized book *Dark Mist over Japan* became a best-selling account of purported plots by U.S intelligence agencies dating from the Korean War. A popular *Asahi* columnist, Aramaki Hideo, accused the Japanese government of acting like "an American branch store" and ignoring national interest. Public anger grew so intense that on May 9 Ambassador MacArthur informed Herter and Eisenhower that the treaty was doomed unless they could "assure Kishi and his government that U-2 flights from Japan would make no illegal overflights of foreign airspace" in the future. For good measure, Washington should claim that "no such overflights had been conducted in the past."

Herter authorized MacArthur to tell Kishi that henceforth the United State would not undertake peacetime U-2 spy missions from bases in Japan without explicit permission from the Japanese government. Admitting that American claims not to have flown earlier spy missions were likely to be received "with some doubt," Herter insisted that all past U-2 operations from Japan were for "legitimate scientific purposes" and none had engaged in "intelligence overflight missions." At this point, Kishi was so beleaguered by criticism for allowing past U-2 operations that he expressed "deep and heartfelt thanks" to Eisenhower for authorizing what struck most Japanese as a misleading statement.[15]

By the middle of May, the U-2 flap pushed the Democratic Socialists back into a tactical alliance with the JSP, which opposed both extension of the Diet session and treaty ratification. Their delaying tactics, combined with foot-dragging by the LDP factions most eager to wound Kishi politically, stalled ratification. MacArthur tried to counter conservative bickering by meeting privately with faction leaders and encouraging them to stand with Kishi and the United States in support of the treaty.

Encouraged by the ambassador's effort, Kishi took bold action. On May 19, he proposed a fifty-day extension of the current Diet session. When lower house Speaker Kiyose Ichiro called for a vote on the question, a number of Socialist legislators staged a sit-in outside his office. That evening, the chairman of the committee holding hearings on the treaty called a snap vote to report out the document, prompting a walkout by opposition members. Unchallenged, the LDP-controlled committee endorsed the treaty and sent it to the full Diet. Shortly before midnight on May 19, Speaker Kiyose summoned police to clear away the legislators barring his way to the Diet floor. After reaching the rostrum, he moved for a fifty-day extension of the Diet session. With only Liberal Democrats present, the resolution carried. Just past midnight, on May 20, the same Diet members approved the treaty. Now, even without approval by the upper house, the pact would come into force on June 19.[16]

Kishi's parliamentary maneuver outraged not only treaty opponents but most of the Japanese press and a broad spectrum of ordinary citizens. The *Asahi Shimbun* denounced the LDP's "undemocratic act" as a case of "violence of the majority." Many believed Kishi's determination to halt debate and push the treaty through on a midnight vote was a ploy to achieve ratification before Eisenhower arrived on June 19. An *Asahi* column compared the prime minister to a "retainer performing tricks before his master." In the politically charged atmosphere, Kishi's perceived effort to curry favor with a foreign leader by defying parliamentary custom diminished, rather than enhanced, his stature among Japanese. Opponents demanded the prime minister's resignation and recision of the vote to extend the Diet session. This would block automatic ratification of the treaty. The JSP began an indefinite boycott of the Diet and threatened mass resignation of its elected representatives. Removing Kishi and forcing a general election, as much as opposition to the treaty per se, became a rallying cry among the Socialists, the press, and the People's Council following the Diet actions of May 19 and 20.[17]

MacArthur was more concerned about Kishi's loss of support within the LDP than about opposition strength. From his contacts among factional leaders, the ambassador learned that even Ikeda—Yoshida's protégé—had discussed the need to replace the prime minister. Massive protest rallies outside the Diet, the Socialist boycott, press criticism, and loss of LDP support, MacArthur worried, might force Kishi to resign before June 19, when the treaty would automatically come into effect. If that happened, he considered it "difficult to believe that final ratification would not be very seriously jeopardized."

MacArthur's anxiety increased after meeting with JSP leader Asanuma on May 25. Asanuma called for postponing the president's visit because it would be used to legitimize Kishi's undemocratic action. The ambassador angrily rejected this advice. Instead, he tried to persuade Ikeda to defer any move against Kishi until after June 19. MacArthur met secretly with Ikeda's son-in-law, Kondo, on May 23, and told him that American leaders were "deeply disturbed" at reported efforts to force Kishi's resignation. The ambassador wanted Ikeda to publicly declare that "there should be no Diet dissolution" or effort to unseat Kishi "until the [security] treaty had entered into effect." MacArthur added that the American government "hoped Ikeda would one day be prime minister," but feared that if he "became responsible for the failure of the treaty," a "cloud would be cast over his reputation." Kondo carried the warning to his father-in-law who sent word that he would "abide by the commitment he made to [MacArthur] on May 11 to ensure ratification of the treaty."[18]

To firm up Ikeda's support, MacArthur asked that a State Department official contact Yoshida—then in New York—about his protégé's contact with anti-Kishi forces. This "played into the hands of pro-Communist and neutralist elements in Japan" who hoped to topple Kishi and kill the treaty. Yoshida should be told that if the treaty went "down the drain," it would be the "greatest victory Communists could gain in Asia and a terrible blow not only to U.S.–Japan relations but particularly for Japan itself."[19]

Secretary of State Herter broached this with Eisenhower, who promptly decided it "was a good idea" that an "approach be made" to Yoshida. Richard Sneider, a Japan desk officer who had served under MacArthur, met with Yoshida. On May 26, at a White House meeting, Eisenhower spoke personally with the former prime minister about the need to stiffen Ikeda's spine. Yoshida contacted Ikeda and promptly informed Herter that the "situation was in hand."[20]

During the next few weeks, the security treaty as well as Kishi's political future remained open questions. In Tokyo, anxious American diplomats and intelligence officials pressed conservative politicians to arrange an orderly succession to Kishi and not jeopardize Japan's Western orientation. Treaty opponents demanded Kishi's resignation, recision of the Diet vote for the treaty, cancellation of Eisenhower's visit, and new elections. Some Liberal Democrats opposed to Kishi tacitly encouraged radical treaty foes in a bid to force the prime minister's resignation. But the massive protests in Tokyo mounted by treaty opponents began to worry them.

Although the June 19 presidential visit to Tokyo had been designed to celebrate a revitalized alliance, it became a rallying cry for those opposed to the treaty and LDP rule. Dragging Eisenhower into a bitter fight among the Japanese hardly seemed designed to improve bipartisan relations.

Following the May 20 vote approving the treaty, the Socialist Party boycotted Diet proceedings. The JSP, anti-treaty organizations, and most of the national press denounced the "tyranny" of the Liberal Democrats as a perversion of democracy, demanded Kishi's resignation, and called for a delay in implementing the treaty until a new round of Diet elections. Opinion polls published in the *Asahi Shimbun* on June 2 and 3 indicated that just over half the Japanese public opposed Kishi's actions and favored a cabinet change. Because polling techniques were crude, both questions and answers were susceptible to varied interpretation. Criticism of Kishi did not necessarily indicate support for the JSP or strong opposition to the treaty.[21]

Kishi insisted he had followed the law and pressed for upper house ratification of the treaty by mid-June. This would put the treaty in force well before automatic ratification on June 19, the day Eisenhower was scheduled to visit Tokyo. A pro-treaty vote, followed by a presidential visit, Kishi hoped, would energize his supporters and provide momentum for his campaign to win another term as party leader and prime minister. But Kishi misjudged the depth of resentment felt by the public about his Diet maneuvers, the growing mood among LDP leaders that he had become a liability, and Washington's waning faith in his value as an ally.

Almost daily after May 20, tens of thousands of treaty opponents demonstrated outside the Diet compound and U.S. embassy. These boisterous and well-organized protests, called *demo* in Japanese, filled their ranks with university students and union members. Participants chanted "Down with the Treaty," "Dissolve the Diet," and "Overthrow Kishi." Despite the

General Douglas MacArthur, Supreme Commander for the Allied Powers in Japan, 1945–1951. His hope for an early peace treaty with Japan to boost his presidential ambitions was frustrated by the Truman administration. (Courtesy of the Harry S. Truman Library)

John Foster Dulles shakes the hand of Prime Minister Yoshida Shigeru at the signing of the treaty of peace with Japan on September 8, 1951 in San Francisco. Secretary of State Dean Acheson *(on right)* and others look on. (Courtesy of the National Archives)

President Dwight D. Eisenhower and Vice President Richard
M. Nixon discuss the itinerary of Nixon's upcoming trip to South-
east Asia and Japan, October 1953. (Courtesy of the Dwight D.
Eisenhower Library)

President Eisenhower chats with Prime Minister Yoshida Shigeru
in the White House, November 1954. Eisenhower and Dulles
rebuffed Yoshida's plea for increased economic aid. (Courtesy of
the Dwight D. Eisenhower Library)

President Eisenhower and Prime Minister Kishi Nobusuke relax during their June 1957 meeting in Washington. In the wake of this visit, Eisenhower authorized the CIA to begin funding Kishi's supporters. (Courtesy of the Dwight D. Eisenhower Library)

President Eisenhower and Prime Minister Kishi sign the revised Treaty of Mutual Cooperation and Security between the U.S. and Japan, January 19, 1960. Ambassador Douglas MacArthur, II, stands directly behind the president and Secretary of State Christian Herter sits on the left. (Courtesy of the Dwight D. Eisenhower Library)

President John F. Kennedy seated with Japanese Prime Minister Ikeda Hayato, June 20, 1961. At this meeting, Kennedy committed the United States to buy more Japanese exports. Standing *(from the left):* Ambassador Asakai Koichiro, Secretary of State Dean Rusk, Minister of Foreign Affairs Kosaka Zentaro, Ambassador Edwin O. Reischauer, interpreter James Wickel. (Courtesy of the John F. Kennedy Library)

President Lyndon B. Johnson makes a point to Japanese Prime Minister Sato Eisaku, November 11, 1967. LBJ refused to return Okinawa before the end of the Vietnam War. (Courtesy of the Lyndon B. Johnson Library)

Ambassador Edwin O. Reischauer, who questioned the wisdom of administration policy in Asia, calls on President Johnson in July 1966. LBJ soon replaced him. (Courtesy of the Lyndon B. Johnson Library)

President Johnson confers with his hawkish ambassador to Japan, veteran diplomat U. Alexis Johnson, June 1968. (Courtesy of the Lyndon B. Johnson Library)

President Richard M. Nixon and Prime Minister Sato at their first summit meeting, November 19, 1969. Nixon's promise to return Okinawa pleased Sato. (Courtesy of the National Archives)

National Security Adviser Walt W. Rostow confers in July 1966 with Wakaizumi Kei, a Japanese academic who often served as Prime Minister Sato's secret emissary. Wakaizumi negotiated the abortive textile deal with Henry Kissinger in 1969. (Courtesy of the Lyndon B. Johnson Library)

Former Prime Minister Kishi served as a link between the LDP and the American government during the 1960s and 1970s. His meeting with President Nixon on October 22, 1971, was one of many between the two veteran politicians. (Courtesy of the National Archives)

President Nixon greets Prime Minister Tanaka Kakuei at a Rose Garden ceremony at the White House, July 31, 1973. Scandals later forced both leaders to resign. (Courtesy of the National Archives)

President George Bush and Prime Minister Miyazawa Kiichi confer in Tokyo, January 1992. Miyazawa was Yoshida's last protegé to serve as prime minister. At a dinner honoring Bush, the president fell ill with the flu and collapsed on Miyazawa. (Courtesy of the George W. Bush Library)

President Ronald Reagan and Prime Minister Nakasone Yasuhiro (with Secretary of State George Shultz looking on) relax at Camp David, April 13, 1986. Mutual distrust of the Soviet Union solidified their friendship. Meanwhile, Japan's exports to the United States surged and the American trade deficit reached new heights. (Courtesy of the Ronald Reagan Library)

anti-treaty focus, participants showed no hostility toward American military personnel, diplomats, tourists, or journalists they encountered. With one exception, the *demos* remained nonviolent. The Sohyo labor federation supported the demonstrations with general strikes on June 4, 15, and 22 during which walkouts by transport workers halted commuter trains in and around Tokyo.

Alarmed by the intensity of the opposition, and eager to secure tangible signs of American support, Kishi's close ally, LDP Secretary General Kawashima, appealed to MacArthur for renewed infusions of cash. At a meeting on May 23, Kawashima portrayed the treaty debate in Japan as a struggle for supremacy between "supporters of the U.S.S.R. and supporters of the United States." The Soviets and Chinese Communists, he alleged, were "working with all their might" and "pouring in a great deal of money" to defeat both Kishi and the treaty. The Kishi faction "needed money to wage the ideological and political struggle" required to secure the treaty. American funds, secretly channeled thorough private business groups, would be used to "establish a student group to fight Zengakuren" and to wage a publicity campaign in favor of the security pact that most major newspapers opposed.

MacArthur responded cautiously to this appeal, telling Kawashima "he did not see any possibility of providing such funds, although he would keep the problem in mind." Interpreting this as a coded call for more details, Kawashima suggested that Washington mask payment as "profits on commercial transactions" channeled to the Federation of Economic Organizations, or Keidanren. MacArthur then suggested that Kawashima call on Keidanren Vice President Uemura who coordinated business contributions to the LDP. He did so that same day and a few weeks later the CIA began funding a political campaign along the lines proposed by Kawashima.[22]

By the end of May, Secretary of State Herter sent word to Tokyo that Eisenhower would postpone his visit to Tokyo if this would defuse tensions. MacArthur had favored a delay, but now worried that this would prove a "mortal blow" to Kishi and be seen in Japan as a "victory for pro-Communist and anti-American forces." Eisenhower had the ambassador query the prime minister on a "purely personal basis" and when Kishi proposed to go ahead, the president agreed.

Although opinion in Washington varied about the wisdom of the visit, concern that cancellation would lead to Kishi's immediate ouster persuaded Eisenhower to stay the course. MacArthur influenced the president by endorsing Kishi's claim that the Chinese and Soviets directed the Tokyo protests. Eisenhower worried that the security treaty and the future of Japanese-American relations hung in the balance. Moreover, failure to arrange an "orderly transition in Tokyo" could affect the U.S. presidential election. This placed an added premium on the visit.[23]

Although the American public paid little attention to the president's itinerary, his selection of sites fueled resentment among many Japanese. Originally, Eisenhower planned to stop in Tokyo following a trip to the

Soviet Union. The U-2 and Paris summit debacles in May led Khrushchev to cancel his invitation. Eisenhower then arranged to visit the Philippines, Taiwan, South Korea, and Okinawa en route to Japan. The trip now seemed more an inspection of forward military bases than a "goodwill" tour.[24]

The NSC met on May 31 to discuss the turmoil in Japan. CIA representative Robert Amory, Jr., reported that while only a minority of Japanese actively opposed the treaty, the public had lost faith in Kishi. Fellow Liberal Democrats doubted he retained an ability to govern. In fact, Amory reported, Kishi counted "on the President's visit to Japan to restore his prestige" and make it possible for him to stay in office. Although Amory reassured Eisenhower that Kishi's LDP rivals "had no substantive objection to the security treaty," they wanted him replaced. The president probably faced no physical danger in Japan, but his visit had become a tug-of-war between those trying to force Kishi from office and those wanting to keep him in power. This "would be quite a goodwill visit," Eisenhower remarked sarcastically."[25]

By early June, leading Senate Democrats, including Mike Mansfield of Montana, Hubert Humphrey of Minnesota, John Stennis of Mississippi, Warren Magnuson of Washington, and the chair of the Foreign Relations Committee, J. William Fulbright, publicly urged the president to stay out of Japan. In private, Eisenhower questioned the visit and seemed especially disturbed that Kishi was "using the President for an internal thing." The point of the trip, Eisenhower told Herter, was to "pay respect to a sister democracy," not to "appea[r] as a supporter of the security treaty or Kishi or anything else." It was a "sorry thing" to contemplate speaking before the Diet with "armed guards at the door."[26]

Testimony by Herter and aides before the Senate Foreign Relations Committee on June 7, 1960, centered on Eisenhower's visit rather than the security treaty. (The committee earlier held brief hearings in which Herter admitted that "prior consultation" meant, in fact, prior approval by Tokyo.) State Department officials acknowledged that it was unfortunate that the visit had been linked to Kishi's political fortune. But cancellation in the face of Red protests "would have very unfortunate repercussions in the whole Far East." All agreed that so long as the president faced no personal danger, he should go to Tokyo.[27]

MacArthur's reports accused the Soviet Union and China of "committing all their available reserves" to the "present internal struggle in Japan" to defeat the treaty, topple Kishi, and prevent Eisenhower's visit. Many dissident LDP leaders, he admitted, also urged postponing the visit in hope of bringing Kishi down. Despite the ambassador's claim that Communists controlled the protests, he noted the absence of "revolutionary or deep anti-American fervor . . . even among some of the Zengakuren students," the most radical treaty foes. He predicted the Zengakuren activists would demonstrate against James Hagerty (Eisenhower's press secretary) when he arrived on June 10, but would probably behave with greater restraint toward the president. To sway opinion, MacArthur warned Japanese newspaper editors that he would view interference with the visit as a victory for Communism.

MacArthur reported that "certain members of the LDP are working quietly . . . with important groups who . . . spontaneously wish to give the president a warm welcome." These "friendly demonstrators" included firemen, veterans, religious groups, and right-wing students. The ambassador did not elaborate, but gangsters (yakuza) composed a major component of this promised security force. In fact, Kodama Yoshio, Kishi's old friend and fellow inmate in Sugamo prison, took charge of its organization.[28]

The tension among the president's staff surfaced during an NSC meeting on June 8, shortly before Eisenhower was scheduled to depart for East Asia. CIA director Allen Dulles reported that out of pique over the president's intended visit to Taiwan, the Chinese Communists had increased their shelling of Nationalist-held offshore islands and claimed numerous American violations of Chinese airspace and territorial waters. In Japan, Dulles predicted, the best to be hoped for was automatic ratification of the treaty on June 19, followed by Kishi's resignation and replacement by an elder statesman, possibly Yoshida.

Although intelligence reports revealed no plot to attack the president in Japan, Eisenhower worried that the "situation was really getting difficult." Vice President Nixon, recalling the busloads of schoolchildren brought out to greet him in 1953, predicted a "great demonstration of popularity for the president when he visited Japan." But Nixon may have guessed what kind of welcoming committee MacArthur, Kishi, and Kodama had recruited, since he spoke of the "major danger" of embarrassing the president if "those Japanese friendly to the U.S. . . . attack[ed] the Leftist demonstrators" along the parade route.[29]

On June 9, Eisenhower gamely told congressional leaders that he intended to travel to Japan because an America president should never be frightened away from his duty by a "bit of name calling." Most of the press agreed that "cancellation would be interpreted as yielding to Communist-inspired pressure" or "mobocracy." The next day's events in Tokyo forced an agonizing reappraisal.[30]

On June 10, Presidential Press Secretary James Hagerty and Appointments Secretary Thomas Stephens traveled as an advance party to Japan. That afternoon MacArthur met them at Tokyo's Haneda airport where 10,000 demonstrators had massed. The protestors did not interfere with the Americans as their limousine left for the embassy. However, as they exited the airport, several thousand Zengakuren student radicals surrounded the vehicle, slashed its tires, smashed windows, and began to rock it back and forth. Several dozen Socialist Diet members stood by watching, later explaining they hoped to hand Hagerty a petition. For unknown reasons (some Americans suspected that Kishi's rivals had plotted to embarrass him), Japanese police did not arrive on the scene for about fifteen minutes. Embassy officials learned of the incident almost immediately and braced for an attack on the compound by preparing to destroy sensitive materials.

In fact, Zengakuren demonstrators neither harmed nor threatened Hagerty's party during the hour-long confrontation. At one point a demonstrator bumped a Secret Service officer and apologized profusely. Japanese police easily cleared a path for a Marine helicopter to pick up the party and fly them to the American embassy. Whatever the Zengakuren students intended, MacArthur considered the incident a godsend. He reported that pictures of the confrontation, replete with "action shots that will be quite graphic" would have a "most salutary and helpful result" and "be a major setback for the Communist cause in Japan." The local press did, in fact, criticize the students' behavior. As one newspaper put it, "unless the Japanese people start behaving like adults" they would "never be allowed to make their appearance on the international stage."[31]

When, following the Hagerty incident, a quarter million anti-treaty demonstrators massed outside the U.S. embassy in Tokyo, Herter and Eisenhower lost faith in MacArthur's judgment. In a message to the ambassador approved by the president, Herter ridiculed the inability of Japanese police officials to protect the visiting Americans. If anything vaguely similar occurred during the president's visit, "it might destroy at one blow the whole edifice of the close friendship" built between Japan and the United States during the past ten years.

Since the president did not want to "enter into an internal quarrel or . . . find himself used as a symbol of contending forces in a nation which he is trying to assure of America's friendship," Herter instructed MacArthur to prod Kishi into requesting that the visit be postponed. If the prime minister insisted on going ahead, he must be told that the evolving security situation would dictate a final decision. By now, Herter made clear, the administration had shifted its interest from goodwill to damage control. He suggested that MacArthur and Kishi develop a plan to blame "Socialists and their Communist instigators" for the violence in Japan and the cancellation of the president's visit.[32]

MacArthur conferred with Fujiyama and Kishi on June 11 and 12, telling them that if "anything should happen to the President or there should be a bad incident it would be a disaster." He demanded more forceful policing and explained that the issue now went beyond the security treaty or even Kishi's political survival. The Soviet Union and China, with the tacit cooperation of intellectuals, the press, labor leaders, students, and cowardly business leaders, were attacking the "parliamentary system in Japan." The government had an obligation to suppress mob rule.

While promising beefed-up security, Kishi unveiled a plan to calm tempers. He proposed to recess the Diet for a few days and meet with the heads of the Socialist and Democratic Socialist parties, Asanuma and Nishio. He would invite them to join in a pledge to receive Eisenhower peacefully. (Nishio accepted the proposal issued on June 13, but the Socialist leadership refused to call off protests unless Kishi first promised to resign, rescind the treaty vote, and call new elections.) Kishi decided to assess the security situation over the next few days and then decide whether the president's visit should be canceled.

Instead of bringing the security treaty before the Diet's upper house, Kishi settled for automatic ratification on June 19, thirty days after lower house approval. MITI Minister Ikeda elaborated on Kishi's proposal, telling MacArthur that the cabinet was considering calling a Diet recess from June 17 through 23. The ambassador worried that a recess might create an excuse to delay final treaty ratification.[33]

In a last attempt to persuade Eisenhower to come to Tokyo, MacArthur detailed the extraordinary security measures Kishi was prepared to implement. In addition to 25,000 policemen assigned to protect the president, the government would deploy "welcoming groups, consisting of numerous civic organizations, business groups, Boy and Girl Scouts, and friendly elements along the route." "Auxiliary forces" composed of "30,000 young men of various athletic organizations" strongly opposed to Zengakuren students "would assist the police." Two-thousand troops from the Self-Defense Force would also be placed on standby duty.[34]

The athletic "auxiliary forces" were, in fact, Kodama's recruits from numerous right-wing groups, including the New Japan Council, the All-Japan Council of Patriotic Organizations, the Japan Veterans League, and religious sects. Kodama also tapped several thousand street vendors and members of crime syndicates to staff his private security force. Referring to the gangsters by their Japanese name, one wag claimed Kodama had organized "Yakuza for Ike."[35]

Even while touting these security measures, MacArthur began to prepare a postmortem on Kishi. Leftist agitation, Liberal Democratic factionalism, and the prime minister's own failure of leadership, he reported to Washington, had made Kishi "the focal point of blame for everything that is wrong in Japan." Acknowledging that Kishi could not continue as prime minister, MacArthur had already suggested to members of Kishi's cabinet that he announce his retirement "after treaty ratification" both by Japan and the U.S. Senate, about a week hence.

The timing was critical because some LDP leaders spoke of compromising with treaty opponents by dissolving the Diet and scheduling elections after ratification on June 19 but before the exchange of ratification instruments between the two governments. This would leave treaty implementation in limbo.

The ambassador devoted increased attention toward selection of Kishi's successor. Since Yoshida controlled enough LDP votes to play the role of kingmaker, Kishi and other faction leaders were courting him. The former prime minister had just returned to Tokyo from the United States and Europe and MacArthur joined LDP leaders lined up at his door. When they conferred on June 20, Yoshida brushed aside the ambassador's suggestion that he replace Kishi on an interim basis, but indicated that he favored selection of Ikeda or Sato.

Despite the botched handling of the treaty, both ordinary and influential Japanese, MacArthur insisted, hoped to maintain close security and economic links to the United States. Convinced that the JSP and Sohyo labor leaders would not attack Eisenhower, and that the special security measures Kishi arranged would be adequate, on June 15 the ambassador appealed a final time for the president to visit Tokyo. A few hours later, a bloody riot inside the Diet compound forced MacArthur to abandon his position.[36]

On the night of June 14, the most radical element among the Zengakuren students raised the stakes in the anti-treaty campaign by marching on the Diet. The next evening, during a large but peaceful demonstration outside the parliament compound, several thousand Zengakuren activists ignored the pleas of Socialist Diet members and broke through the gates around the Diet building. During an all night battle with police, 600 students were injured and one female student was either trampled or choked to death.[37]

The night of violence and death did not prevent the automatic ratification of the treaty but it did end any consideration of a presidential visit. On June 16, after conferring with MacArthur, Kishi formally requested that Eisenhower "postpone" his trip to Tokyo. The president learned of the request while delivering a speech in Manila and issued a statement condemning the actions of a "violent minority" in Japan.[38]

Kishi spent the night of June 18–19 holed up in his official residence, ignoring pleas from police that he go into hiding before the site was "attacked by a mob" gathering outside. The prime minister replied that "as long as the security treaty revision was realized, I do not mind being killed." Moments after midnight on June 19, LDP Secretary General Kawashima spoke with Kishi, urging that he now resign to "stabilize the people's sentiments." Kishi refused to relinquish power until the United States and Japan exchanged ratified copies of the treaty.

In Washington, the Senate Foreign Relations Committee approved the pact on June 14. The full chamber voted on June 22, by 90–2, to ratify the treaty. After scurrying around Tokyo in secret to get needed signatures, on the morning of June 23, Fujiyama met secretly with MacArthur at the foreign minister's residence. Still fearing an attack, Fujiyama prepared a plan for the two men to scramble over a rear wall if a mob broke in. However, no opponents showed up and they exchanged signed copies of the treaty. Kishi then announced his resignation.[39]

As Eisenhower feared, he was blamed for the upheaval in Tokyo. James Reston, the respected *New York Times* political reporter, commented that "at best the United States has lost face, at worst it has lost Japan." Senate Majority Leader and presidential hopeful Lyndon B. Johnson claimed that "Mr. Khrushchev's political ju-jitsu" had virtually forced Americans out of Japan. The Minnesota Democrat, Senator Hubert Humphrey, accused Ambassador MacArthur and the Department of State of "playing politics in support of Kishi." Editorials in many newspapers described events in Japan as a "serious challenge to American prestige and a threat to our entire position in Asia." The "Kremlin's triumph," opined syndicated columnist Joseph Alsop, "cannot be concealed by any amount of Byzantine twaddle about defeat in Japan being balanced" by Eisenhower's warm reception in Manila. A number of papers and commentators warned that America's "whole global system of bases may be undermined by Communist victory in its relentless campaign to weaken and ultimately destroy the free world defense system."[40]

Although press accounts suggested that skillful diplomacy could salvage Japan, the CIA warned that after treaty ratification and Kishi's resignation, the Japanese left would attempt to make the country "ungovernable" and render the treaty worthless. To prevent this, Eisenhower authorized the intelligence agency to take actions to block anarchy and a drift toward neutralism before the next general election, expected in the fall.

By utilizing its financial leverage with the LDP, the CIA worked to assure Kishi's quick replacement by a more moderate conservative leader. Yoshida might fill this role on an interim basis, succeeded by one of his protégés, such as Ikeda. MacArthur had broached these options with Yoshida on June 20.

The need to encourage stability led the CIA to fund "moderate" elements within the LDP who were deemed more responsive to demands by the Japanese electorate for progressive domestic policies. The agency also increased its assistance to DSP leader Nishio Suehiro and other moderate Socialists, with the aim of creating an influential Japanese Social Democratic Party along European lines. In the medium term, the CIA hoped to move the center of Japanese politics closer to the middle and away from the extremes of right and left. To stabilize Japan immediately, friendly or CIA-controlled media would be used to criticize treaty opponents and stress the importance of strong ties to the United States. Finally, to neutralize the Zengakuren student radicals, the agency funded right-wing action groups.[41]

On June 21, Ikeda passed word to MacArthur that with Yoshida's support he expected to succeed Kishi soon and doubted that the LDP would need to select an interim leader. To reassure Washington of where he stood, Ikeda boasted that "only the support of his faction [had] made it possible for the government to get the treaty through the Diet." He counseled the Americans not to worry about the possibility of JSP and LDP anti-mainstream collusion to force Kishi's resignation before the exchange of treaty ratifications. Ikeda predicted the Democratic Socialists would collaborate with the LDP mainstream to prevent this "because he was responsible for [DSP leader] Nishio receiving substantial financial support." MacArthur again described Ikeda as "far the best successor to Kishi for he believes staunchly in Japanese-American partnership and is militantly anti-Communist as is his preceptor, Yoshida."[42]

Kishi's resignation on June 23 cooled the political temperature in Tokyo and even moderated the ambassador's outlook. MacArthur previously warned of Chinese and Soviet control of the anti-treaty movement.

On June 24, he admitted that many "non-Communist elements took part in demonstrations against Kishi's 'undemocratic and authoritarian' action on May 19 in the Diet." The "unpopularity of Kishi, not the security treaty, was the major issue" mobilizing many Japanese. "Suicidal factional strife" within the LDP, he added, contributed as much to the collapse of parliamentary rule as sabotage by the left.

MacArthur now claimed that basic economic and security policies toward Japan were successful. More Japanese felt positive about their relationship with the United States than had been true in 1957 when he arrived in Tokyo. They recognized the critical importance of exports to America and, even if uncomfortable with being forced to choose sides in the cold war, preferred a U.S. to a Soviet security umbrella.

Conservative infighting, random events like the U-2 shootdown, Kishi's lack of popularity and mismanagement of the treaty ratification process, rather than a Communist conspiracy, the ambassador admitted, had contributed to a crisis atmosphere. But the "hard-core of conservative middle-of-roadism" in Japan remained "basically unaffected by recent events." Whoever succeeded Kishi would continue to represent this "dominant conservative force."[43]

For once, the ambassador made an accurate prediction. After the treaty came into effect and Kishi tendered his resignation, nearly all public protest ceased. On June 24, Yoshida publicly endorsed Ikeda's candidacy to head the LDP. On July 14, after much internal maneuvering, the party elected Ikeda president and the Diet, with the Socialists again present, confirmed him as prime minister four days later.

In accord with the CIA program, press treatment of the new government changed dramatically. Foreign Minister Kosaka Zantaro told American officials that "business elements in the newspaper world" were reducing leftist influence. The "banks, paper mills, and the advertisers," he explained, demanded that newspaper owners "exert a more moderating influence on their papers." Personnel changes among the political reporting staffs of the three large national dailies muted criticism of Ikeda and the security pact.[44]

In an article similar to many in the major national dailies, the *Mainichi Shimbun* on July 4 ran a lead story under the headline "U.S. Aid Bolsters Japan's Economy." Japanese economic growth might be the envy of the world, the paper reported, but no one should "forget the tremendous U.S. economic assistance . . . that has made Japan's miraculous postwar rehabilitation possible." Since 1945, American aid, raw materials, military procurements, loans, and investments had created the foundation of Japanese recovery. Also, by promoting a liberal international trade environment, the United States cleared a path for future Japanese economic growth. Despite the "recent unpleasant incidents" concerning the security treaty, the *Mainichi* concluded, "economic relations between the two countries will never deteriorate to any serious degree."[45]

As prime minister, Ikeda shifted attention away from contentious foreign policy issues to domestic concerns. Shelving Kishi's plan to expand police powers, he pledged to "promote parliamentary government through mutual cooperation with the opposition." In the waning days of Kishi's rule, when asked by an aide how, as prime minister, he would restore public trust, he answered "Isn't it all a matter of economic policy?" On taking office, he endorsed the goal of "income doubling" within a decade, a plan conceived by his economic adviser Shimomura Osamu. If GNP grew by an average of 7.2 percent annually—below the rate of the past several years—by 1969 Japan's national income would double. (Helped by rising exports to the United States, Japan averaged 10.4 percent economic growth during the 1960s, easily surpassing Ikeda's goal.) By August 1960, opinion surveys found that 51 percent of the Japanese public supported the new prime minister. The dispirited strikers at the Miike coal mine abandoned their struggle as Ikeda's power took hold, dealing a blow to militants in the labor movement. On a symbolic level, cordial ties with the United States were bolstered by Crown Prince Akihito's September visit to the United States where Eisenhower hosted a state dinner in his honor.[46]

Without Kishi as a target, the anti-treaty coalition dissolved. The Socialists, Communists, and radical students blamed each other for the failure to block the new security pact. Rightist violence replaced daily leftist demonstrations. Even Kishi fell victim to this when a disgruntled extremist stabbed him in the leg during an LDP meeting shortly after he resigned as prime minister. The most spectacular right-wing attack was the assassination of Socialist Party leader Asanuma by a seventeen-year-old student on October 12, 1960, during a party meeting. Although the JSP accused the United States of encouraging this violence, it offered no proof.

Leftist squabbling, a robust economy, CIA-supplied campaign funds, and Ikeda's popularity contributed to LDP victory in the November 1960 Diet election. The Conservatives gained thirteen seats, for a total of 296, winning 57.6 percent of the vote. The JSP won 145 seats with 27.5 percent of the vote. Their twenty-three-seat gain came largely at the expense of the Democratic Socialists who, despite American support, failed to attract many votes.[47]

The Eisenhower administration's final assessment of U.S. policy toward Japan, drafted by the National Security Council in the midst of the treaty crisis, reflected a cautious optimism confirmed by the results of the November Diet election. American policymakers continued to view Japan—like China—through lenses crafted in the early cold war. Japan remained one of the world's four major industrial complexes and the only highly industrialized nation in the Asian-African area. If its strength were "harnessed to Communist Bloc power," the NSC warned, "the world balance of power would be significantly altered." American access to logistic facilities and bases was "indispensable to an economical and effective defense of the Far East." Because of Japan's "critical dependence upon the United States for defense and trade," American policy would "have a crucial bearing" on preserving its free world orientation.

While the NSC noted Japan's remarkable economic growth, it worried that dependence on international trade and foreign raw materials—factors over which "Japan itself has little direct control"—left the country vulnerable. More than any other ally, Japan's stability rested "upon the United States not only as its most important source of industrial raw materials and largest single market but also for leadership in fostering liberal trade policies throughout the free world and particularly among the industrialized nations of Western Europe." Any deterioration in the terms of trade would push Japan's political and business leaders to "consider a shift toward reliance on the Communist Bloc." Ultimately, the NSC concluded, Japan's pro-Western orientation required a "fair and reasonable share of the U.S. market and other Free World markets."[48]

In December 1960, as a new president prepared to assume office, MacArthur offered a similar assessment of Japanese-American relations. He concluded a laundry list of self-congratulatory achievements by stating:

> Japan's most vital self-interest and its strongest tie with the free world is trade. The American market is essential and as long as Japan's daily bread depends largely on our cooperation and friendship, we do not believe a majority of conservative Japanese people will wish to chase the Communist rainbow.

Offering advice he himself would have been wise to follow, MacArthur urged president-elect John F. Kennedy to "view Japan as an equal, whom we respect and not as a formerly occupied country that we expect to follow along in our wake."[49]

10 *THE NEW FRONTIER*

IN THE PACIFIC

THE three years that followed the security treaty crisis proved unusually convivial. Chastened by the upheaval of 1960, President John F. Kennedy and Prime Minister Ikeda Hayato shifted the focus of bilateral relations away from military issues and back toward trade, a subject in which both sides perceived mutual advantage. Like Eisenhower, Kennedy believed that increasing economic interdependence would link Japan more firmly to the Western alliance. And, like his mentor, Yoshida Shigeru, Ikeda recognized that only the United States could provide the outlet for trade expansion on which Japan's export-oriented economy and conservative hegemony depended. The appointment of an exceptionally able ambassador to Tokyo, Edwin O. Reischauer, improved contacts between both countries. Disagreements over China, Okinawa, and trade continued during the early 1960s, but Washington and Tokyo contained them without harming the alliance.

Although Eisenhower had feared the treaty crisis would become a major issue in the presidential election, Ikeda's quick restoration of order removed Japan from American headlines. Democratic candidates linked the treaty riots to a general malaise attributed to Eisenhower–Nixon foreign policy, including the U-2 shootdown, Paris summit failure, Cuban Revolution, and "missile gap." Harvard Professor Edwin O. Reischauer set the standard for informed criticism in an article he published in the influential journal *Foreign Affairs*. The "dean" of America's academic Japan experts complained that the Eisenhower administration's handling of the security treaty, its emphasis on Japan as a military ally, and its close tie to Kishi had alienated the bulk of otherwise friendly Japanese. It was a grave mistake to dismiss Japanese anger with America as a Communist plot.

Frustration with the United States was rampant among the "bulk of Japan's intellectuals and college students—that is, the would-be ideological pathfinders and the generation to which the future of Japan belongs." Only skillful diplomacy could restore this "broken dialogue."[1]

President John F. Kennedy, widely traveled and urbane, had only limited and unpleasant associations with Japan. As a young naval officer in 1943, a Japanese destroyer sank his PT boat. His rescue of fellow crewmen, depicted in a later popular account, *PT 109*, established his heroic legend. Shortly before this near-fatal encounter, Kennedy served aboard a supply ship under Japanese air attack. During a lull in the battle, he later recalled, "a Jap parachuted into the water." As the American ship approached him, "he suddenly threw aside his life jacket . . . pulled out a revolver" and began firing "at our bridge." Kennedy had been "praising the Lord and passing the ammunition," but the action of the lone Japanese "sitting in the water, battling an entire ship" amazed the Americans. They returned fire wildly and ineffectively until an "old soldier . . . picked up his rifle, fired once and blew the top of his head off." As the airman sank, "we hauled our ass out of there." To Kennedy, the Japanese flier's devotion "brought home very strongly how long it is going to take to finish the war."[2]

Remarkably, neither Kennedy nor his close aides who fought in Europe or the Pacific came away embittered. New Frontiersmen such as Lyndon Johnson (whose plane came under Japanese attack near New Guinea during an inspection trip to the Pacific), Dean Rusk (who served in the China–Burma–India theater), George Ball (who assessed strategic bombing damage in Germany and Japan), Walt Rostow (an OSS analyst who selected air targets over Germany), and Roger Hillsman (a commando who fought the Japanese in Burma) greatly admired the postwar achievements of Germany and Japan and recognized their centrality to the cold war. In interviews with the Japanese TV network NHK and the *Mainichi Shimbun* newspaper soon after his inauguration, Kennedy spoke approvingly of a Japan "destined to rule" the economy of the Asia/Pacific region and stressed the "great benefits" future trade held for America and Japan.

Early in his administration, the president stanched efforts by Democratic Representative John F. Baldwin to bar Defense Department purchases of Japanese products and a related proposal by Leo O'Brien to enact a law to "observe December 7 each year as 'the day that will live in infamy.'" In a thinly veiled effort to defend domestic textile producers, O'Brien charged that Japan had not apologized for its attack and still bore America ill will, as proven by the events in Tokoyo of June 1960. The congressman decried policies that left American markets vulnerable to another sneak attack. Writing for Kennedy, presidential aide Lawrence O'Brien informed the representative: "I suppose that all of us feel the same about December 7, 1941." However, in 1961, "we are now trying to improve Japanese–American relationships, and I doubt that calling the Japanese names each year is calculated to achieve that purpose."[3]

The president's determination to maintain close ties with Japan extended into the area of covert support for the LDP. Assistant Secretary of State for Intelligence Roger Hillsman learned in February 1961 about the secret payments authorized by Eisenhower since 1958 that provided several million dollars annually to the LDP and DSP. When Hillsman questioned the wisdom of continuing this program, a CIA briefer told him as well as National Security Adviser McGeorge Bundy and Bundy's assistant, Walt Rostow, that it was their choice:

> it is a going thing—Eisenhower decided to do it and you can't reverse that. All you can do is cut it off now or let it die gradually. If you cut it off now there is a big danger that it will become public. If it becomes public . . . it will greatly damage U.S.–Japan relations, it will hurt the LDP seriously, it will strengthen the Communist Party of Japan.

Kennedy accepted Hillsman's advice that the payments "be allowed to continue and gradually [be] cut down." This pleased the CIA officer who predicted that the operation would not "become public for thirty years and by that time no harm will be done."[4] Selectively assisting candidates became routine during the 1960s. For example, during a discussion in 1965 about a "secret action plan" to influence elections on Okinawa, senior State Department and Army officials agreed that "permitting the Japanese LDP to handle the [U.S.] money" was "the most effective way" to assure favorable outcomes in contested elections.

Kennedy's strong belief in the benefits of free trade shaped his administration's broader approach to Europe and Japan. Not only was Japan America's second biggest export market, but the trade balance between the two nations continued to run strongly in favor of the United States, approaching a billion dollar surplus in 1960–61. Ambassador MacArthur, who returned to the State Department as an adviser on European affairs, and George Ball, the undersecretary of state for economic affairs, stressed these points.

MacArthur informed Kennedy that although the Japanese political scene had stabilized, LDP factionalism remained a threat to conservative rule. Taking a broader view than he had while in Tokyo, MacArthur admitted that not only the Communists and Socialists, but important elements among the press, the intelligentsia, and the LDP deeply resented Japan's lockstep cooperation with the United States. Much of this criticism centered on policy toward Communist China. Historical and cultural ties as well as China's "trade-baited diplomacy" exercised a powerful attraction, especially among smaller industrial firms. Even "responsible" LDP leaders like Ikeda, who understood the American policy of isolating China, feared the political consequences of "blind subservience" to the United States.

Japan, MacArthur told Kennedy in a meeting in April 1961, was too big a consumer of U.S. exports, too vital a site of military bases, and too important a factor in American efforts to spur the economic and political development of Southeast Asia to alienate. He worried that protectionist pressures in Congress could quickly push Japan toward the Communist bloc. If faced with rising trade barriers, the "Japanese would not commit suicide," he explained, but would "end up where and with whom she can earn a living." Kennedy promised to divert efforts by Congress to restrict imports "in such a way that Japan would not be penalized or hurt."[5]

That same day, the president hosted a group of Japanese business leaders in the White House. In a spirited presentation, he told the delegation that he "recognized Japan lived by trade" and consequently favored an "expansive rather than a restrictive" trade policy. In contrast to American cloth producers and members of Congress who blamed the industry's problems on Japan, Kennedy praised Japan's record of voluntary exports restraints and blamed exporters like Hong Kong for disrupting the American market.

On May 2, the president announced a program to assist the modernization of the domestic textile industry. He also called on importing and exporting nations to convene a meeting in Geneva to address immediate and long-term conflicts. Rejecting demands that he impose unilateral quotas, Kennedy warned that doing so risked "serious economic, political, and even security problems."[6]

Kennedy was determined to avoid action that might cloud his scheduled meeting in late June with Prime Minister Ikeda Hayato. Administration officials made a forceful case for expanding, rather than restricting, bilateral trade. The president's foreign policy advisers all concluded that increasing Japan's exports to the United States would deflect pressure within Japan for expanded trade with China and enhance Japan's identification with the West.

Early in 1961, the China issue reemerged, in the words of one diplomat, as the "main external preoccupation of both Government and Opposition" in Japan. With the security treaty and Kishi out of the way, and as China's relations with the Soviet Union deteriorated, Chinese Premier Zhou Enlai expressed renewed interest in trade with Japan. He announced that even in the absence of government-to-government agreements, he saw no reason why private contracts with "friendly" Japanese firms and individuals could not be negotiated. By the time Ikeda came to Washington, Japan and China were exchanging goods valued at about $2 million per month. Foreign ministry officials queried British diplomats about how to retain America's friendship while expanding trade with China.

Since 1958, Chinese officials had limited their contact largely to members of the Japan Socialist Party. Lately they began to cultivate Ikeda's rivals within the LDP. American diplomats reported that this tactic had "drastically increased the pressures already upon Prime Minister Ikeda to change . . . the policy of no initiatives toward Peiping which he inherited from his conservative predecessors." The Socialists and dissident LDP members charged that by following Washington's lead blindly, Japan faced "isolation in East Asia" and diminished economic opportunity. Kennedy's advisers feared the China issue could potentially "rupture Japan's alignment with the United States and the Free World."[7]

Ikeda responded cautiously to domestic pressure. He eased currency controls to permit cash exchanges—rather than barter—with China, but hesitated to move further before meeting Kennedy. As early as April 1961, during a brief trip to Tokyo, Walt Rostow heard appeals from several Japanese business and academic representatives, including the brother of Foreign Minister Kosaka Zentaro, to relax U.S. restrictions on allied trade with China.[8]

Kennedy's effort to improve relations with Japan received critical support from his ambassador. Sending Harvard professor Edwin O. Reischauer—whom he never met—to Tokyo proved a deft move. The idea came from James C. Thomson, a former instructor at Harvard who now worked for Undersecretary of State Chester Bowles. Kennedy had assigned Bowles to fill major diplomatic posts and he, at Thomson's behest, recruited Reischauer. Secretary of State Dean Rusk mistrusted the professor's relatively dovish views on China and opposed the appointment. But strong support from the Chairman of the Senate Foreign Relations Committee, J. William Fulbright, saved the nomination.

During confirmation hearings in March, Fulbright's backing proved invaluable. Reischauer did not hide his belief that the Unite States should reconsider its nonrecognition of China. When an unfriendly senator tried to highlight the difference between this view and that voiced by Rusk and Kennedy, Fulbright cut off discussion by declaring that the nominee had urged recognition only before the Korean War. Although, as Reischauer later admitted, he "did in fact favor moving toward recognition," he decided that "silence on my part would be the better part of wisdom." The nomination then moved quickly through the Senate.[9]

Born in Japan of missionary parents, and possessing a lifelong interest in cultural diplomacy, the new ambassador devoted himself to restoring what he called the "broken dialogue" between Americans and Japanese. This required overcoming the "residues of racial prejudice, wartime hatreds and cultural unfamiliarity." Many Japanese felt "helpless and resentful in their dependence on the United States." They feared being dragged into a new war in Asia. By the same token, Reischauer felt that most Americans took Japan for granted as a cold war ally.[10]

After assuming his post in April 1961, the ambassador spoke often before Japanese audiences and insisted that the United States was not as aggressive or militaristic as widely depicted. Far from endangering peace in the region, America's military presence in Japan and the western Pacific stabilized Asia and protected Japan. In less public forums, he argued that America's security umbrella restrained right-wing elements in Japan who favored large-scale rearmament. Most Japanese, Reischauer believed, saw the United States as "more powerful and domineering than it actually was, while most Americans saw Japan as less cooperative and far less important than it was."

Unlike Ambassador MacArthur, who had conferred almost exclusively with LDP politicians and business leaders, the new envoy and the staff he brought to Tokyo reached out to a broad array of Japanese. Reischauer recruited a few Japanese-speaking scholars from Harvard as liaisons to student and intellectual groups. In 1962, he brought John Emmerson to Tokyo as his chief deputy. The Japanese left admired Emmerson because of his work with Japanese POWs in China during World War II and his effort to free political prisoners early in the Occupation. His appointment troubled Japanese rightists.[11]

The ambassador and his staff reached out to opposition Diet members, labor activists, student groups, and others who considered the embassy hostile territory. Reischauer and his Japanese wife, Haru, herself an accomplished journalist and granddaughter of Meiji-era Finance and Prime Minister Matsukata Masayoshi, appeared frequently on Japanese television. He chatted informally in Japanese, traveled widely, and usually charmed audiences.

Reischauer made the phrase "equal partnership" a hallmark of his tenure in Tokyo, often working it into speeches and official communications. He used it in the sense of getting rid of the "Occupation psychology" that persisted in Japan–United States relations and pressing Japanese to regard themselves as capable of playing an important role in world politics. When President Kennedy adopted the phrase, the Japanese press began referring to this as the "Kennedy–Reischauer offensive."[12]

Shortly after his arrival, Reischauer oversaw the settlement of a pair of disputes left unresolved since 1952. On June 8, the United States agreed to pay Tokyo $8 million in compensation for Japanese who had been displaced from the still-occupied Bonin Islands, including Iwo Jima. Two days later, the governments agreed that Japan would repay, over a fifteen-year period, $490 million of its $2 billion Occupation-era GARIOA debt. Japanese negotiators urged the United States to apply the bulk of the money toward economic development aid to Southeast Asia. Reischauer designated $25 million of the payment for cultural exchange programs (which assisted creation of the Japan Foundation), but bristled when the State Department tapped the fund for embassy entertainment.[13]

The ambassador's success eased the work of the State Department Japan specialists and White House national security staff preparing for Ikeda's visit. "Basically," they informed the president in a briefing, "Japan is in good shape." Amid an economic boom, popular sentiment was "more friendly toward the United States than at any time in recent years." Still, "serious uncertainties" clouded the future. The Socialist appeal to fears of war and the popular desire to establish relations with China threatened LDP hegemony. The best way to quash this danger, Kennedy's advisers reasoned, was to "tie Japan's economy more fully with that of the West" and enhance the "sense of partnership between Japan and the U.S." Integrating Japan with the West would soften and make more manageable inevitable differences over China, Okinawa, nuclear testing, and American military intervention in Laos and Vietnam. It would also undermine those Japanese who criticized the alliance with the United States.

Deputy National Security Adviser Walt Rostow and State Department Japan expert Richard Sneider, along with Reischauer, played key roles in preparing Kennedy for his talks with Ikeda. In the short run, Rostow explained, "the problem is nationalism, in the longer run, neutralism." The president needed to "reassure Japan of its status as a senior partner of the United States" and guarantee "fair treatment in trade." As far as possible, Kennedy should accommodate "Japanese nationalist desires on such matters as trade with Communist China and our administration of the Ryukyus." Rough spots could be smoothed over by creating joint cabinet-level committees on trade, cultural, and scientific exchanges and by demonstrating that Washington considered Tokyo a "senior partner."

Like most civilian and military advisers, Rostow considered it vital to maintain control of Okinawa. To mitigate resentment, he urged Kennedy to reaffirm Japan's residual sovereignty, permit the Japanese flag to be flown above public buildings, and cooperate with Tokyo to improve the Ryukyuan economy.

Concerning China, Rostow urged tactical flexibility without fundamentally changing the American position. Recent analyses suggested that even if most trade restrictions were lifted, Sino-Japanese commerce would remain small. Thus, maintaining restraints on Tokyo would prove counterproductive. Rostow recommended that the president tell Ikeda that while "we recognize Japan may trade with Communist China," he should insist that trade "not involve political concessions by Japan" or any change in Japan's support for the American effort to keep China out of the United Nations.[14]

The State Department's top Japan officer, Richard Sneider, offered similar advice. During the "next few months," he informed Kennedy, Ikeda would succeed or fail in taking control of the LDP based on his ability to "still the efforts of his factional rivals" and demonstrate his "effectiveness in dealing with the crucial relations with the U.S." Successful talks with the president would "dramatically bolster his prestige among the Japanese public" and "silence the critics of his policies" by demonstrating his ability to shape the views within the "senior councils of the Free World." If "events should conspire to rob his trip of this aura," Ikeda would be "forced into retirement" and replaced by a politician less pro-American. Reischauer agreed and stressed to Kennedy the value of using the word "partnership" in his dealings with Ikeda.[15]

Ikeda arrived in Washington with little fanfare. *Time* magazine's brief treatment typified press coverage. "There is nothing particularly wrong with U.S.–Japan relations these days," *Time* reported, so "there was nothing urgent about . . . the visit to Washington of Japan's Prime Minister Ikeda." He came to "score points at home . . . where he is not very popular." *Time* and other journals stressed that the prime minister came to Washington with a single point. He "count[ed] on continued prosperity to keep his nation in the free world camp." To double national income in ten years, Japan had to boost exports to the United States "by at least 5 percent a year." Trade restrictions would "hurt the Japanese economy—and that economy is vital to Far East stability."[16]

Kennedy followed these recommendations during his talks with Ikeda on June 20 and 21. Eager to assist the prime minister's goal of "income doubling," the president pledged to "maintain a liberal trade policy" despite a "very tough fight on this question" from "protectionist elements" in the textile industry. Kennedy noted that Japan bought much more from the United States than it sold, and acknowledged its special need for trade. Japanese textile exporters, he told Ikeda, "suffered from the voluntary quota program on textiles instituted in 1957." Kennedy and Undersecretary of State George Ball assured the prime minister that their proposal for a short-term textile agreement, followed by negotiations for a new multilateral export policy, would expand Japan's access to both the U.S. and European markets. One of the few disagreements between the two leaders involved Ikeda's suggestion that the United States and Japan cooperate in expanding economic assistance to Southeast Asia. Despite increasing American military aid to the region, the president declined to participate.[17]

Kennedy and Ikeda reportedly "hit it off very well." The president's support for trade expansion "deeply impressed and reassured" the prime minister. Creation of joint economic, cultural, and scientific committees convinced the Japanese public and press that the United States attached "considerable importance to Japan as a major partner" and viewed this partnership "as considerably broader than a military alliance."

Ikeda especially appreciated Kennedy's pledge to "pursue liberal trade policies looking to an orderly expansion of trade." Among other things, it provided him with cover to follow the American lead on China. Ikeda told Kennedy that while Japan hoped to "engage in at least as much trade [with China] as the Western European countries are currently doing," Tokyo would continue to separate trade and politics. In short, Japan would not recognize the PRC and would cooperate with the United States in "keeping the Chinese Communists out of the UN." The president's staff expressed gratitude that in return for permitting the display of Japanese flags over Ryukyuan public buildings, the celebration of Japanese holidays, and increased economic aid to the Ryukyus, Ikeda promised to "avoid actions likely to stimulate reversionist pressures" and other moves to "infringe on [U.S.] administration" of Okinawa.[18]

The Okinawa Problem

Although conflict over the reversion of Okinawa did not become a crisis during the Kennedy years, it held considerable emotional and military importance. In the opinion of most Japanese, the Occupation era had not fully ended in 1952. The Ryukyu Islands—dominated by Okinawa with a population of nearly one million people—had been part of Japan since the late nineteenth century. The last great battle of the Pacific War had been fought on Okinawa, a killing field on which 12,000 Americans and at least 150,000 Japanese soldiers and civilians perished. After 1945, U.S. military planners envisioned Okinawa as a base for controlling a future Japanese threat. As the cold war developed, the island, along with bases in the Philippines, became a pivot for containment of Communism in Asia.

In 1951, the Department of Defense vetoed the return of Okinawa to Japan by asserting its critical importance for operations in Korea and security in the western Pacific. The peace treaty acknowledged Japan's "residual sovereignty" over the Ryukyus and nearby Bonin and Volcano Islands, but deferred their return until the threat to peace in the region had receded. During the 1950s, Eisenhower and Dulles rebuffed efforts by Japan to recover Okinawa. By 1960, the network of naval, air, logistic, and intelligence facilities on the island constituted the largest American base network in the Asia/Pacific region.

Ikeda raised the Okinawa issue during his meeting with Kennedy. The Japanese left had long called for the island's return while the LDP deflected pressure by pointing to Soviet seizure of the Kuriles and the disputed islands off Hokkaido. But this sophistry did not stop frequent complaints from Okinawan farmers about inadequate compensation for land taken by the air force for runway expansion or the fact that, as Japan began to prosper, the Ryukyus remained an impoverished backwater. Like the security treaty in 1960, Okinawa had incendiary potential.

Following Ikeda's visit, Kennedy heard warnings along these lines from George Ball and Edwin Reischauer. Ball, accompanied by National Security Council staff member Carl Kaysen, visited Okinawa in July 1961, while traveling to Tokyo. Until then he had thought of the island "merely as a major World War II battlefield." Now he observed "our vast stores of supplies and the proprietary manner in which our military administered the island." With Japan an ally, Ball thought it "preposterous" that "we should still be treating [Okinawa] as our colony." The military's monopoly of power and lack of concern for local sensibilities created a situation "tailor made to generate trouble between Tokyo and Washington." How, Ball asked, could the United States decry European or Soviet colonialism "yet persist in similar practices in Okinawa?" He immediately alerted Kennedy of the "dangers implicit in our position."[19]

Reischauer visited the Ryukyus shortly after Ball had. He discovered that the High Commissioner, Lt. General Paul Caraway, viewed the consulate on Okinawa with contempt. The general, who impressed the ambassador as a "rigid, bull-headed man," described the Ryukyus as "essential to America's future military position in the western Pacific." He would tolerate no diplomatic meddling. Caraway feared the eventual loss of American bases in Japan and, even sooner, limits on freedom to operate those bases. He spoke of the Japanese government as his "chief challenger for control of Okinawa" and accused the ambassador and his staff of "conspiring with the Japanese in this." The general described Reischauer as a "menace, because he thinks he knows everything." The ambassador had "a lot of information" but "he knows nothing."[20]

In words that reflected wounds left festering since the Pacific War, Caraway stated that:

> Japan, its people, political and economic structure, and its government are tough physically and are equally tough minded. . . . Japan was wholly expansionist in the 1930s, and indeed to the end of World War II—and beyond. The Japanese still cannot believe that the United States could have been so foolish as to set them up in business again [or] that the United States could be so timorous . . . in asking that this country have a fair shake from Japan in the Western Pacific.

Convinced that American dominance in the Pacific depended less on political or economic power than on its ability to focus overwhelming military power quickly, Caraway warned that surrendering any control of Okinawa would blunt this edge.[21]

Reischauer rejected this thinking as mean-spirited and shortsighted. The claim that Okinawans favored American military rule and had no interest in self-determination was clearly false. Okinawans had some cultural and linguistic distinctions, the ambassador knew, but considered themselves Japanese. Nearly all of them favored reversion. This sentiment would inevitably become a trenchant political issue in Japan. Reischauer urged Kennedy to allow Okinawa greater autonomy and cooperate with Tokyo to improve living standards.[22]

Responding to pleas by Ball and Reischauer, in November 1961, Kennedy appointed Carl Kaysen to head a task force on the Ryukyus. Early the next year, the group made a compelling case for reform of the military administration. They urged greater home rule for Okinawans, election of a local chief executive, transfer of authority from American military to civilian administrators, and cooperation with Tokyo in improving the local economy.[23]

Although Kennedy endorsed these proposals and reaffirmed Japan's residual sovereignty in the Ryukyus, General Caraway remained an obstacle to change. He raised numerous objections to implementing the reform proposals and interfered with efforts by Japan to provide economic assistance. Reischauer found himself in the "ridiculous position" of having to lobby with the Japanese government to minimize its assistance in face of Caraway's opposition. Not until the summer of 1964, when General Albert Watson II, replaced Caraway as High Commissioner, did the situation improve. By then, the escalation of the Vietnam War and Japan's growing assertiveness turned demands for Okinawa's reversion into a major problem for Presidents Johnson and Nixon.

The China Problem

Shortly after Kennedy's death, NSC staffer James C. Thomson noted that there existed "only one important matter on which the U.S. and Japan do not basically see eye to eye—China." Despite American pressure, bonds of culture and trade continued to pull Japan toward the Asian mainland. All Japanese knew "that for better or worse Mainland China is going to be a few hundred miles away forever" and "Japan must live with it as best it can."[24]

Concern over Tokyo's interest in closer ties with China remained a sore point between the United States and Japan during the 1960s. A few officials, including Chester Bowles, James Thomson, and ambassadors John Kenneth Galbraith and Edwin Reischauer, favored new approaches toward China, such as cultural exchanges, famine relief, and admitting Beijing to the United Nations under a "two Chinas" formula. An aide to Reischauer recalled that up to 1963 the ambassador received only one serious rebuke from Washington. When he told a group of Japanese that decisions on diplomatic ties with China were up to them, Secretary of State Rusk sent the ambassador a cable that said "No, they aren't."

President Kennedy hinted at reassessing the nonrecognition policy, but never budged. China's support for guerrillas in Laos and Vietnam, its October 1962 border war with India, and its nuclear weapons development program affirmed Kennedy's belief that China threatened American interests and allies. Not even the vituperative Sino-Soviet split altered his view. As Kennedy and Rusk saw it, the Communist fissure proved that the Soviets could neither abide nor control Mao Zedong. Beijing's rhetoric so alarmed Kennedy that in 1962–63 he weighed broaching with the Soviets plans for a joint attack on China's nuclear weapons development facilities.[25]

Most Japanese feared and disliked the Soviet regime, but had a more benign view of China. They believed that nationalism, rather than Chinese meddling, accounted for most of the unrest in Southeast Asia. Kennedy and his aides could scarcely believe it when the Japanese government and public sided with China in its border dispute with India. Even a large part of the Liberal Democratic leadership and business community viewed Chinese Communism as something of a transitory phenomenon with which Japan could profitably co-exist. Ikeda told Kennedy during their June 1961 meeting, "Japan historically and traditionally has had special relations with the Chinese continent" and these would continue.

By 1962, the economic impact of China's break with the Soviet Union led Beijing to seek greater trade with Japan. That fall, several prominent LDP officials, retired bureaucrats, and Japanese businessmen traveled to China to explore commercial possibilities. In September 1962, Ikeda reportedly told one such group, "My position compels me to keep my 'face' directed toward the U.S. So will you represent my 'face' toward China?"

Talks between Zhou Enlai and Matsumura Kenzo, a senior LDP member, produced an agreement to promote trade and "normalization of relations, including political and economic relations." To dampen American reaction, Foreign Minister Ohira told journalists that visits to China by Japanese politicians and businessmen, and any trade agreements they reached, were strictly private in nature.[26]

Despite such disclaimers, Assistant Secretary of State Averell Harriman expressed official distress. Speaking before the Japan-U.S. Society in Washington on September 26, 1962, Harriman noted that Japan had achieved economic recovery "practically without any trade with mainland China." Although some Japanese believed that future prosperity required expanded contact with China, Harriman urged the Japanese government to recognize that Free World trade was "the trade you can count on." China, he warned, used trade as a political weapon. "Great opportunity for increased development in free world trade" existed between Japan and the West, Harriman asserted, but dallying with China would jeopardize this.[27]

Ikeda tried to blunt American criticism by pointing out that no serving government officials had signed agreements with China and that structural limits would restrain two-way trade. The Chinese would want "to buy a lot from Japan," he observed, but "what would Japan buy from Communist China?"[28]

Nevertheless, in November, steel executive and former MITI official Takasaki Tatsunosuke signed a memorandum with PRC representative Liao Chengji to create a new framework for Sino-Japanese trade. The so-called L-T trade consisted of a five-year agreement to engage in at least $100 million trade per year. Japan would export steel, fertilizer, agricultural chemicals, farm machinery, and industrial equipment, while China sold food and raw materials. Chinese trade representatives could open offices in Tokyo while bureaucrats on leave from MITI would serve in Beijing.

The United States grudgingly accepted this development, but still tried to discourage Japan from assisting Chinese economic development. Assistant Secretary of State Hillsman urged Japan not to extend trade credits, deferred payment rights, or long-term financing to China, all considered forms of aid, not trade.[29]

While cautious about provoking a showdown with Tokyo over trade, the Kennedy administration tried to enlist Japan in a more active military and political offensive against the PRC. American officials cited the brief border war fought between China and India in October 1962 as a reason to mistrust Beijing. In November, Harriman met with Shiga Kenjiro, Director General of the Japanese Defense Agency. Given India's experience, Harriman asked, did Japan now realize that China posed "a greater danger than that emanating from the Soviet Union?" Only a "united and military strong Free World" could stop Beijing. This argument failed to resonate among Japanese who recalled India's refusal in 1951 to sign the San Francisco peace treaty. Moreover, even the Nationalist regime on Taiwan supported China's claim to disputed territory held by India. Shiga criticized the "arrogant attitude" of India's leaders who refused Beijing's offer to negotiate the dispute. Most Japanese, he added, felt "considerable resentment" against India.[30]

Kennedy went further than Harriman in remarks to a meeting of the joint United States–Japan trade and economic committee on December 3, 1962. He told the group, which included several members of Ikeda's cabinet, that "the major question facing us today is the growth of Communist forces in China, and how to contain Communist expansion in Asia." He asked for suggestions about "what the United States and Japan as allies can do, and what roles they can play in order to prevent Communist domination of Asia."

Although the Japanese press and government spokesmen dismissed Kennedy's appeal as "personal sentiment" that required no response, Secretary of State Rusk tried to sell the idea to Foreign Minister Ohira Masayoshi, Vice Foreign Minister Takeuchi Ryuji, and Ambassador Asakai Koichiro at a private meetings two days later. After a century of friendship with China, Rusk complained, Americans "now felt like jilted lovers." In light of China's falling out with the Soviet Union and fight with India, he wondered where Japan stood. Takeuchi answered obliquely. Japan, he noted, had fought two wars with China but most Japanese considered themselves the aggressors. In contrast, they "looked on the Russians as the aggressors" in the wars fought with Japan. Asakai observed that while Americans tended to like Russians but hate Chinese Communists, "in Japan the situation is exactly reversed."

To Rusk's astonishment, the Japanese officials he spoke with "agreed that India had got its just deserts" at the hands of the Chinese army. Asakai added that Japan was under pressure to "make a deal with Communist China before it becomes a nuclear power." The Communists pointed to the "traditional friendship between the United States and China and warned Japan not to be caught off guard by America's temporary disaffection from China."

Foreign Minister Ohira volunteered the most worrisome "personal opinion." He believed the United States "should leave Communist China alone." A flustered Rusk retorted that the United States would "leave the Chinese Communists alone when the Chinese Communist leave others alone." As long as Beijing threatened Southeast Asia and India, Washington would resist.[31]

Washington's attempt to inhibit Sino-Japanese contact soon took a new form. At the end of December, Harriman told a Japanese newspaper that under current international conditions, the United States was in no position to expand its purchase of Japanese products. Washington then floated a proposal to impose new restraints on cotton textiles. Early in January, the Kennedy administration requested the right to send nuclear-powered submarines on port calls to Japan. (American and Japanese spokesmen implied that the ships carried no nuclear weapons, although, as Reischauer knew, the oral agreement of 1960 allowed the transit of nuclear weapons through Japan.) At a meeting of the joint security consultative committee on January 19, 1963, American officials repeated their warning about China's nuclear weapons program and urged Japan to cooperate against this threat.[32]

Ikeda deftly sidestepped American demands. His government delayed for several months approving the nuclear submarine visits by insisting on elaborate safety assurances. The prime minister characterized Kennedy's call to contain China as a statement of principle in opposition to territorial expansion. It had no bearing on Japan's policy of promoting economic and cultural ties with China. By August 1963, Ikeda felt confident enough to approve sale of a rayon factory to the People's Republic with financing provided by Japan's Export-Import Bank.[33]

Anticipating Washington's anger at the decision to provide credit to China, a Japanese foreign ministry official urged the United States to tolerate this and future deals, not on economic grounds, but as part of a strategy to encourage political moderation in China. Many Japanese, he added, saw a "racist element" in Moscow's break with Beijing. They also "tended to attribute a racist motive to Washington's 'sympathy' with Moscow" and hostility toward China. By accepting Japan's initiative, the United States could refute this belief and speed change within China.[34]

Although what Rusk called the "aid not trade" deal to finance sale of the rayon factory threatened to become a major problem between Tokyo and Washington, Taiwan's vitriolic reaction forced the United States to mediate on Japan's behalf. Jiang Jieshi's Nationalist government denounced the deal as tacit recognition of the PRC. Jiang issued a litany of complaints, even accusing Japan of responsibility for the Communist revolution in China because of its 1937 invasion. Taiwan recalled its ambassador from Tokyo, canceled government contracts with Japanese businesses, organized violent demonstrations outside the Japanese embassy, and threatened to break diplomatic relations with Tokyo. During late 1963 and early 1964, the American government worried that these actions might backfire, provoking Japan and other Asian-African states to support China's entry into the United Nations. In May 1964, tempers cooled after Ikeda sent Yoshida Shigeru to Taibei on a fence-mending mission. He delivered a letter—an update of his 1951 epistle—to the Nationalist government promising that Japan would neither recognize the PRC nor use government funds to finance trade.

This appeased Taiwan but infuriated China—which promptly canceled several contracts with Japan and ceased negotiations on other deals. In November 1964, Sato Eisaku replaced the ailing Ikeda as prime minister. Representing elements within the LDP that were less enthusiastic about trade with China, Sato pursued a more restrained policy. Shortly after Sato took office, Mao launched the Cultural Revolution. Maoist radicals stressed economic self-reliance and contempt for Sato's pro-American policies. Although Japan became China's biggest trading partner after 1965, the forces unleashed by the Cultural Revolution halted progress toward normalization of relations. Even as Washington escalated the war in Vietnam partly out of fear of China, China's self-imposed isolation reduced it as a source of tension between Japan and the United States.[35]

The Trade Issue

For many American policymakers and representatives of certain industries, Japan's export challenge proved more vexing than disputes over China or Okinawa. Japanese textile exports to the United States had been a political hot potato since the 1950s. The Eisenhower and Kennedy administrations beat back several efforts to limit Japanese sales. In February 1961, for example, the Amalgamated Clothing Workers Union called on its members to refuse to cut Japanese cloth imported after May 1. The union complained that Japan's annual sale of some 60,000 mens' suits exceeded the 1957 voluntary restraint formula and threatened American jobs. In fact, since American companies produced twenty million suits annually, Japanese imports hardly dented the market. Although Kennedy persuaded the union to call off its boycott, he faced a chorus of complaints from the industry.

George Ball, undersecretary of state and Kennedy's point man on textiles, recalled that dealing with demands for quotas caused him "more personal anguish than any other task I undertook during my total of twelve years in different branches of the government." As a presidential candidate, Kennedy had promised to help the textile industry and, following his election, the industry "promptly demanded that he redeem his promise." Basically a free trader but still a politician, the new president appointed a Cabinet Committee on Textiles sympathetic to industry demands for quotas, as well as a special trade representative, George Ball, who opposed trade restrictions.[36]

Following Kennedy's May 1961 proposal for a textile conference in Geneva, the administration agreed to raise by about 5 percent the level of cotton goods Japan could export to the United States in the coming year. Even though Tokyo had urged a 30 percent increase over the level permitted by the 1957 voluntary agreement, the Japanese press, government, and industry praised the spirit of Kennedy's approach. In contrast, 33 senators and 122 representatives complained in a letter to the president that his program, which focused on cotton textiles, ignored the threat posed by foreign woolens and synthetics. Even though Japan's share of the American market had fallen relative to exporters such as Hong Kong, members of Congress and industry critics continued to blame Japan and complained that the administration proposal raised, rather than lowered, Japanese export levels.[37]

On July 21, the United States and fifteen trading nations reached a short-term multilateral agreement on cotton textiles, effective for the twelve months beginning October 1. The interim pact imposed no firm limits on cotton imports into the United States, but allowed Washington to call on any signatory to restrain textile sales at the previous year's level if the

United States determined that rising sales were "disrupting its markets." The Japanese reluctantly agreed to accept a small increase (5 percent to 10 percent) in its voluntary export restraint level in return for a U.S. promise to seek a 30 percent reduction in Hong Kong export levels. American negotiators pressed Tokyo to accept by warning that failure to reach an interim agreement would "generate insuperable pressure from a wide range of other domestic interests which find imports from Japan disturbing or disruptive."[38]

Ball devised the so-called orderly marketing procedure to counter protectionist demands from American producers. He believed that structural problems, outdated technology, and self-inflicted inefficiencies, not foreign competition, caused most of the problems faced by domestic producers. Instead of trying to resuscitate a dying patient through quotas, Congress should allow the domestic manufacturing base to shrink to a sustainable size. American capital could then either be channeled toward textile manufacturing in developing countries where it could profit from low labor costs or shifted toward domestic investment in "capital intensive and knowledge intensive industries and services that befitted a nation with an advanced economy."[39]

Ball feared that imposing quotas would "make a mockery of our concern for the Third World and our commitment to free trade." He ridiculed contentions by trade associations that the domestic apparel industry was "essential to national security." Did they believe "naked American soldiers would be easier to shoot than fully clothed enemies?"

In preparation for negotiating the short-term agreement in Geneva, Ball traveled to Tokyo. There, Reischauer described the special economic and political importance of the textile issue to Japan. The two men discussed organizing a "Pacific Community," composed of the United States, Japan, Australia, and Canada, as a counterpart to the European Economic Community. Although the concept never materialized, Ball departed convinced that Japan's special trading needs must be accommodated by the United States. Compared to other textile exporters, Japan had suffered disproportionately by agreeing to the 1957 voluntary export restraints. The July 1961 short-term agreement reflected Ball's sympathy for Japan, as did his subsequent effort to shape the administration's broader textile and trade policies.

Ball argued for subordinating tariff and textile issues to strategic concerns. For example, when the U.S. Tariff Commission recommended imposing an "escape clause"—an action required when foreign sales of a particular product reached a "peril point" threatening domestic producers—to limit carpet imports, Ball urged that Kennedy deny the request. In return for salvaging a few million dollars in domestic carpet sales, Ball warned, Washington risked alienating two key allies, Belgium and Japan.

Putting the issue in context, he noted that Belgium already blamed the United States for forcing it to leave the Congo and resented Washington's recent effort to bring down the Belgium-backed breakaway regime in the

Congo's mineral rich Katanga province. Now, faced with a Soviet challenge in Berlin and complex negotiations of a long-term textile and tariff agreement with the European Economic Community, Washington needed Belgium's support. If the U.S. barred carpets, Belgium might scuttle European cooperation on these more critical issues.

If "relations with Belgium are difficult," Ball told Kennedy, "relations with Japan are even more sensitive." The Japanese already resented the fact that while they had accepted modest export increases under the terms of the interim textile agreement, the United States had done little to enforce the 30 percent reduction imposed on Hong Kong. Action against carpets might jeopardize Japan's assistance in reaching a long-term textile agreement. Since Japan's trade deficit with the United States approached $800 million in 1961, Ball considered it "quite irrational" to alienate Japan "over only a few million dollars in trade."

Imposing additional trade barriers, he asserted, contradicted the "substantial assurances" Kennedy gave Ikeda of American determination to pursue liberal commercial policies. Ball thought it especially misguided to contemplate retaliatory action on the eve of the first meeting of the new U.S.-Japanese Economic Committee. "We would do well," he cautioned, "to remember that it was only fifteen months ago that Communist-inspired mobs in Tokyo caused the cancellation of President Eisenhower's visit." Kennedy's meeting with Ikeda, and Reischauer's "brilliant efforts" in Tokyo had repaired much of that damage. Imposing the escape clause on carpets would only convince the Japanese that "we talk a good game but do not play it." Ball persuaded Kennedy to reject the Tariff Commission's recommendation, but he worried that a succession of such cases would imperil bilateral relations.[40]

With the dramatic changes in the world economy evidenced by creation of the European Economic Community, Japan's industrial growth, and economic expansion in the Third World, Ball sensed the time had come to initiate a broad revision of tariff and trade policy. Instead of negotiating item-by-item tariff reductions with individual countries, he proposed that Kennedy seek authority from Congress to negotiate substantial across-the-board tariff reductions with American trading partners. This would rationalize world trade and assure the most effective use of capital. The president embraced the idea and it eventually won congressional approval as part of the Trade Expansion Act of 1962, enacted in October. By 1963, this resulted in lowering tariffs on a broad range of Japanese and European products.[41]

The Joint Economic Committee held its first meeting in November 1961 in Hakone, Japan. Secretary of State Rusk, flanked by four cabinet members and numerous technical experts, reassured the Japanese of Washington's good intentions. Japanese delegates noted that during the past year Japan purchased nearly $1 billion more annually from the United States than Americans had from Japan. To redress this imbalance, they called for encouraging the flow of Japanese goods into the American market.

The Americans countered that the trade surplus ignored the substantial sums spent by the United States to maintain military bases and personnel inside Japan and failed to account for American expenditures elsewhere in Asia that financed the purchase of Japanese goods and services. American officials also urged Tokyo to abandon restrictions on foreign imports and investments as a way to counter protectionist pressure within the United States.

Despite these different perspectives and the fact that few specific decisions emerged, Reischauer judged the conference, as well as follow-up meetings by the joint scientific and cultural committees, a "great success." The Japanese press gave the event extensive coverage, telling the public that for the first time "genuine and equal consultation had taken place on economic matters of mutual concern." The ambassador reported that the conference buttressed Ikeda's "partnership" diplomacy with the United States and at "the very least won time" for the prime minister's income-doubling plan to take effect. Japan's faith in American dedication to "liberal trade policy" had been sustained, Reischauer noted, but still remained shaky. It would "hardly survive" if Congress or the U.S. Tariff Commission adopted protectionist measures.[42]

Kennedy put the Hakone discussions in the best possible light, telling journalists attending a November 9, 1961, press conference that the conclave assured an "American-Japanese partnership" in trade. Japan played a "key role in the economy of Asia and Free World economic objectives depended in a very important extent on her cooperation." He minimized the importance of Japanese trade barriers and disputed complaints that Japanese exports hurt domestic industry.

During the next two years, the administration's basically pro-Japanese trade policy took some slight detours, largely in response to pressure from domestic textile producers. For example, early in 1962, the administration floated the idea of imposing a "cotton equalization tax" on Japanese textiles. Since, the argument ran, the Agriculture Department subsidized the price of raw cotton sold by American farmers to Japan, a tax on finished textiles exported to the United States would compensate domestic manufacturers for the higher costs they incurred compared to Japanese mills. Japanese officials retorted that while Japan sold about $71 million of finished textiles to the United States in 1960–61, it had purchased $251 million of raw cotton. The proposed tax would penalize Japanese producers for taking advantage of an opportunity promoted by the American government and, the foreign ministry warned, force Japan to halt talks on a long-term textile agreement.

Reischauer and Ball sympathized with the Japanese contention that such a tax represented a "reversal of the Hakone spirit" and jeopardized Japanese participation in a long-term textile agreement in the final stage of negotiation. Japan had made the issue "a test of our faith," Ball informed Kennedy, and imposition of the tax would have "disastrous consequences." Kennedy followed this advice. His assurance of continued access to the American market contributed to achieving a five-year textile agreement in

Geneva in February 1962. The pact allowed Japan and other exporters about 6 percent annual growth in sales to the United States. To placate domestic producers, it extended the "orderly marketing procedure" formula that Ball had authored.[43]

The liberalization of American trade policy coincided with major Japanese economic initiatives. As part of the effort to double national income, the Ikeda cabinet committed substantial funds to modernization of Japan's industrial base. Following the type of investment strategy Ball recommended, Japanese economic planners gave special assistance to capital-intensive sectors of the economy and innovative technology. Easy credit and priority access to foreign exchange went to companies prepared to modernize automotive production, as well as the manufacture of electronic goods, synthetic fibers, and petrochemicals.

The introduction of Honda and Yamaha motorcycles and Toyota automobiles to the American market between 1961 and 1964 typified this trend. In 1966, six years after the first of these motorcycles arrived, they sold 400,000 units, about 85 percent of total U.S. sales. In 1964, Toyota test-marketed fifty Corona sedans in California. By 1973, Toyota sold a quarter of a million vehicles to Americans.

While assisting the high-technology, high-value-added export sector, Japanese planners applied negative economic levers to phase out industries that relied on the export of high-volume, labor-intensive goods, such as cotton textiles, which elicited the most serious foreign complaints. Linking innovative technology to export promotion became a key Japanese economic strategy.[44]

These policies, along with access to the American market and new opportunities in Southeast Asia, contributed to real GNP growth within Japan averaging 10 percent annually between 1960 and 1965, double that of the United States. Japan achieved an annual export growth rate of about 17 percent during the 1960s, also double that of the United States. Japan's trade deficit with the United States declined sharply and, by 1965, Tokyo ran a surplus for the first time since World War II.

U.S. Merchandise Trade with Japan (in millions of dollars)

	Exports	Imports	U.S. Surplus/Deficit
1961	1,837	1,055	782
1962	1,574	1,358	216
1963	1,844	1,498	346
1964	2,009	1,768	241
1965	2,080	2,414	-334

Source: Statistical History of the United States, From Colonial Times to 1970

As Kennedy and his advisers hoped, Japan's high rate of export growth created a new dependence on American raw materials and consumers. At least until 1965—when Japan first ran a substantial surplus in its U.S. trade account—this pleased most American officials. Japan seemed a model of rapid, capitalist development and a critical pillar of stability in East Asia. Washington mildly pressed Tokyo to drop restrictions on imported goods, abandon currency controls, and eliminate barriers to foreign investment. On balance, the political and strategic stability that evolved in Japan barely a decade after the end of the Occupation seemed an achievement to boast about, not a problem to solve.

Aside from his initial meeting with Ikeda and support for the trade expansion efforts of Ball and Reischauer, Kennedy devoted limited attention to Japanese affairs. This relative lack of attention often left Reischauer frustrated by what he considered high-level indifference to Japan. Perhaps because no critical issues arose during the early 1960s, Japan barely warranted mention in the memoirs written by the president's aides, aside from Ball and Reischauer. Because of his frosty relations with Dean Rusk, Reischauer had difficulty getting senior officials to discuss Japan policy with him or to accept invitations to visit Tokyo.

Reischauer scored a victory in February 1962 when the president's brother, Robert Kennedy, visited Tokyo. The attorney general arrived en route to Indonesia, on a mission to curb efforts by Indonesia's President Sukarno to seize part of Malaysia and Dutch colonial territory in Southeast Asia. Much to Reischauer's surprise, Kennedy informed the embassy he wanted a "full and meaningful schedule" during his stop in Tokyo. Taking him at face value, Reischauer arranged activities from 8 A.M. through 10 P.M. Kennedy returned the draft with a request to fill the 6 A.M. to 8 A.M. slot. When Kennedy reached Tokyo, he was taken to ice skate early in the morning with a workingman's club, followed by a meeting with a youth group and participation in a judo match.

Despite threats of protest by campus radicals, Kennedy insisted on speaking to university students. Addressing a large and initially hostile audience at Tokyo's Waseda University, he astounded hecklers by inviting them to join him on the stage for an impromptu debate. He so charmed the students that they concluded the evening by singing the university theme song for the American. Japanese television broadcast the event, which proved a public relations triumph.

Reischauer recalled that the visit "changed my status in Washington completely." Henceforth, "I had a powerful friend there and a direct channel to the President." Robert Kennedy returned to Tokyo in 1964, again to meet with Sukarno, and repeated his bravura performance at Waseda.[45]

Economic growth, an export boom, embassy-sponsored programs to bring industrialists, labor union officials, students, and intellectuals on tours of the United States, along with the favorable publicity generated by events like the Kennedy visit, restored the dialogue Reischauer valued. In 1962, the official Communist Party newspaper, *Akahata*, condemned his achievements as a major threat to all leftists within Japan. In October, a lead editorial introduced a week-long series of articles on the threat posed by the "The Kennedy–Reischauer Line." *Akahata* declared:

> One year and a half since the arrival of Ambassador Reischauer in Japan, the sinister hand of America's strategy toward Japan—the Kennedy-Reischauer Line—has been steadily extending, with military bases as the axis, from the fields of culture, ideology, education, and science to the field of the labor movement. American imperialists are not only undertaking intelligence activities through armed forces, police, and espionage networks, but also "inviting" Japanese scholars, cultural men, and labor union representatives to America or sending many old Japan hands into Japan to work on the top and middle ranking leaders of cultural and educational institutions and strengthen ideological maneuvers toward the leaders of labor unions and democratic organizations.

Akahata criticized the JSP and its labor allies for allowing themselves "to be utilized as a convenient foothold for these maneuvers." Reischauer's plot to "tame Japan's leftist forces through his affable manners" had proved both dangerous and effective. Non-Communist journalists marveled at the success of the "Reischauer offensive," reporting that it "created panic" among the radical left and right.[46]

This atmosphere of goodwill even permeated the monster film genre. In 1963, the Toho studio released *King Kong vs. Godzilla*, in which Godzilla emerged from the Arctic Ocean and attacked the northern island of Hokkaido—just as the Soviets might in case of war. King Kong, a monster from the South Pacific linked symbolicly to the United States, galantly assisted the Self-Defense Forces on Hokkaido. This metaphor reversed past criticism of American military policy and celebrated the security treaty as Japan's salvation.

In November 1963, Kennedy tentatively decided to visit Japan, Southeast Asia, and Australia early the next year. Roger Hillsman proposed that he use the trip to promote the theme of a new "Pacific partnership that joins the developed countries of the Pacific"—such as Japan, Australia, and the United States—with the "less developed countries in a coordinated program of nation building." This would link "two major components" of U.S. policy in Asia—"deterrence of Communist aggression" and "nation building, the construction of a viable system of free-world societies through economic and technical assistance." Echoing a decade-old theme, Hillsman envisioned Japan playing a special role of "consultation and collaboration" in the "development of free Asian societies."[47]

Less than three weeks later, an assassin killed Kennedy. Had he lived, his visit to Japan—the first by a serving president—would probably have been a great success. Public support of the Pacific alliance had rebounded since 1960 and the trade boom had alleviated many internal stresses. Kennedy yielded slightly on Okinawa and did not push too hard on China. With Vietnam a mere cloud on the horizon, Kennedy had achieved the goals set by Eisenhower before the 1960 crisis. But soon, the war in Southeast Asia rekindled nearly all the earlier problems with a vengeance.

11 *THE UNITED STATES, JAPAN,*

AND THE VIETNAM WAR,

1964–68

THE Vietnam War, fought, in part, for and from Japan, had nearly as dramatic an impact on Japanese-American relations as the Korean conflict did. In addition to its military and political consequences, the war hastened Japan's emergence as a global economic power. Japan's role as a logistic base and tacit ally in the war revived a massive anti-American protest movement, compelled the Johnson administration to make numerous concessions on issues such as trade, China, and Okinawa, and contributed to a dramatic transformation in the relationship between the two allies.

On the eve of the escalation of the Vietnam War, almost no one in Washington or Tokyo predicted its impact on the Pacific allies. Early in 1964, when the Department of State prepared an interagency appraisal of "The Future of Japan," it speculated that over the next decade Japan would become increasingly "strong, confident and nationalistic." Pro-Western conservatives were likely to retain control, "possibly alternating power" after 1970 with "socialist governments of considerably more moderate hue than today's Japan Socialist Party." America could live with these changes and "indeed benefit from them."

Developments since 1960, the Department stressed, "proved the soundness of our policies." The Kennedy administration's trade and security initiatives promoted "moderating trends on the left" and a more socially conscious attitude within the LDP. With "discreet encouragement," Japan might even agree to take a more active role in promoting regional security. Nevertheless, the "prime requirement of a healthy course of developments in Japan" remained the "rate of growth of Japan's foreign trade." Japan would cooperate on issues such as China, Okinawa, and

Southeast Asia so long as the United States maintained a liberal trade policy. On the other hand, if it were denied "opportunities to expand its sales in the U.S. market," Japan would neither achieve "minimum economic goals" nor be of much help in Asia. "Firm Executive Branch resistance" to protectionist pressure was required to assure Japanese–American cooperation.

The report offered a sensible caveat. Any ten-year estimate must allow leeway for unpredictable elements such as "earthquakes and typhoons" that marked the natural order and for sudden and unforeseen political events, such as the Lucky Dragon "fallout excitement, the Girard Case, and the Security Treaty turmoil."[1]

As the State Department predicted, Japan's economy not only grew but exceeded the analysts' most optimistic estimates. A more socially conscious LDP retained firm control and continued to ally itself closely with the United States. Disputes over China and Okinawa were contained within reasonable bounds. However, not a single Japan specialist guessed that the war in Vietnam would have a determining impact on relations with Japan and the rest of Asia.

Even those closest to the decision to escalate the Vietnam War tended to misperceive its impact. Walt Rostow, for example, assured Lyndon Johnson in 1966 that in addition to "real progress" in the administration's overall foreign policy, it was "clear that a good part of your administration's place in history will consist in the reshaping of Asia and our relations in it." Rostow's prediction proved true, although hardly in the sense that he meant it.[2]

In May 1961, Vice President Lyndon B. Johnson returned from a tour of Southeast Asia to report to President Kennedy about the growing threat posed by China and regional Communist insurgencies. Johnson asserted that "the battle against Communism must be joined in Southeast Asia with strength and determination . . . or the United States, inevitably, must surrender the Pacific and take up our defenses on our own shores." If Communist forces overran mainland Southeast Asia, the "island outposts— Philippines, Japan, Taiwan—have no security and the vast Pacific becomes a Red Sea."[3]

By the 1960s, calculations of Vietnam's value still contained a large dose of the "domino theory" proclaimed by Eisenhower in 1954. As the "superdomino," Japan had to be buffered from a Communist breakthrough in Southeast Asia. Thus, General Maxwell D. Taylor, Chairman of the Joint Chiefs of Staff, asserted in January 1964 that the loss of South Vietnam would influence the judgment of all non-Communist Asia, including Japan, as to the value of "U.S. resolution and trustworthiness."[4] Credibility like rice, rubber, and tin, was a strategic commodity the United States could not afford to squander.

Although Japanese leaders shared elements of this vision, they continued to doubt the wisdom of American efforts to contain China and escalate the war in Vietnam. This divergent outlook surfaced early in 1964 when, in the wake of Kennedy's death, Secretary of State Dean Rusk visited Tokyo.

In talks with Prime Minister Ikeda and Foreign Minister Ohira Masayoshi, Rusk tried to reenlist Tokyo in Washington's campaign to isolate the PRC.

The French decision of January 1964 to recognize the People's Republic of China encouraged the Japanese to hope the American-led nonrecognition policy had begun to crumble. It also aroused latent fear that the United States might make its own deal with China and cut Japan out. Rusk pounced on Ohira's suggestion that the time had come to discard old approaches. Washington, he insisted, bore no responsibility for the fact that China engaged in "conspiratorial and subversive activities throughout the world." Its "militancy, both in doctrine and in action," and its aggressive behavior in Southeast Asia and the Formosa Strait, made it impossible to deal positively with Beijing. According to Rusk, even the Soviet Union feared the prospect of "800 million Chinese armed with nuclear weapons." This specter prompted Moscow to sign a limited test ban treaty with Washington. If China made the Soviets tremble, Rusk implied, Japan should be terrified.[5]

Ohira dismissed this argument as "rather stiff." Pressing Japan to "follow the same course," he warned, would have an "undesirable" effect. Rusk deprecated Japan's interest in trade and cultural contact with China as "nostalgia." Ohira should consider Tokyo's prospects, given China's threat to "Korea, Formosa, Vietnam, Cambodia, Thailand, and Indonesia." As Rusk saw it, Japan prospered from, then criticized its ally's policy in Asia. The United States, he stated bluntly, could "pull out of [Southeast Asia today] and we will survive, but Asian countries will not survive."[6]

Rusk called on Japan to expand its armed forces and double the $100 million it spent annually on American military equipment. Beside improving security, this would help offset the dollar drain caused by foreign defense expenditures. It would silence critics who complained that Japan failed to carry its weight as an ally. "It is not easy," Rusk explained, to "draft a boy from a Kansas farm or a Pittsburgh factory in order to send him to Japan as a rifleman when Japan has a population of 95 million people."

Ikeda, an alumnus of the Yoshida school, parried this criticism. If Japan purchased additional military equipment, it would need to buy from domestic, not foreign, manufacturers. Ikeda attributed Japan's positive relations with most of Asia to the fact that "it no longer had a great army." Expanding the Self-Defense Force would jeopardize this. Southeast Asia might look to the United States "for its basic military security," but it looked to "Japan to perform a mission in the economic field."[7]

Latent tensions over China, Vietnam, defense spending, and the balance of payments increased as the Vietnam War expanded. Reischauer, who admired Ohira and Ikeda, and disagreed with the administration's view of the Chinese threat to Asia, tried to mediate the differences. He recalled that often, after presenting the "official" position on these subjects, he confided to Japanese officials and journalists that as a "scholar" he personally supported opening ties with China and favored a negotiated settlement in Vietnam. This buffered some of the tension between Washington and Tokyo. Ironically, an attack on him by a deranged Japanese also cushioned relations.[8]

On March 24, 1964, as Reischauer stepped out of the embassy, a young man with a knife slashed him. The attacker, motivated by delusions, not politics, was subdued at the scene. Although the wounds appeared superficial, Reischauer received a transfusion of hepatitis-tainted blood. He suffered both immediate and long-term complications as well as a lengthy hospital stay.

Reporting to Washington from his hospital bed, Reischauer described the "shame and fear of adverse repercussions" felt by Japanese officials and ordinary citizens. The attack elicited national remorse, "even though the stabbing was a fluke, without any meaningful relation to current issues." The Japanese press described him as the "best-loved representative ever sent to Japan" and called on the nation to apologize collectively.

While Reischauer recuperated, Richard Nixon—in Tokyo as a representative of Pepsi-Cola—turned up at his bedside. In several conversations that foreshadowed later policy moves, Nixon spoke "forcefully of the desirability of recognizing Peking, sounding, the ambassador noted, for all the world like [Harvard professor of Chinese history] John Fairbank." Upset by Washington's refusal to reevaluate its containment policy in Asia, even though the "American public had been ready for this for some years," Reischauer found Nixon good company. He recalled with considerable bitterness that neither Rusk nor Johnson sent him a personal note during his convalescence. This departure from their normal graciousness suggested that the president and secretary of state could not abide the ambassador.[9]

The Japanese, to be sure, sent mixed messages about Vietnam and China. For example, in July 1964, shortly before the Gulf of Tonkin incident, Fukuda Tokuyasu, then Director General of the Japan Defense Agency, told Secretary of Defense Robert S. McNamara that Japan "very much appreciated the U.S. efforts in Southeast Asia." Still, he thought it would be difficult to "maintain control of such an area solely through military means." Intervention ran counter to the region's nationalist sentiment and made it easy for the Communists to "twist" American motives.

McNamara asked about the "effect on Japan" if the United States "lost in Vietnam" and a "Viet Cong government took over." Fukuda thought this might lead to some additional Communist expansion in Southeast Asia and the loss of trade opportunities for Japan. The Japanese left would renew protests against the security treaty. McNamara wondered if this would push Japan closer to China. While Japan might increase trade with Beijing, Fukuda did not foresee any basic policy change. Describing South Vietnam as a "bonfire which is close," Fukuda offered his "personal" view that Japan should do everything possible to help the United States "put it out." But, he added, "Japan's new constitution and domestic attitude inhibit actions in this regard."[10]

Fukuda's two cheers for American policy typified the ambivalence of the Japanese government. Ikeda and his successor, Sato Eisaku, voiced approval of American action, hinted at political and economic alternatives, and made clear that Japan could not play any part in the conflict. Citing the no-war clause of Japan's constitution and domestic opposition to intervention, officials simultaneously endorsed and distanced Japan from American policy. The Johnson administration tried to nudge Tokyo toward greater cooperation on Vietnam by granting it a variety of concessions. Sato—younger brother of Kishi Nobusuke—who succeeded the ailing Ikeda as prime minister in November 1964, proved a master at this game. Another disciple of Yoshida, Sato balanced American pressure to become more involved in Vietnam with complaints of domestic critics that he conceded too much.

When Sato took office, the Japanese public expressed an all-time high approval rating of the United States. Forty-nine percent of those polled in one sample described America as the foreign nation they most respected, while only 4 percent indicated dislike. During the next several years, this approval rate plummeted. By the early 1970s, a mere 18 percent of Japanese named the United States as their most admired country. Although a number of factors, including violence in American society, racial conflicts, trade disputes, and surging Japanese pride affected this outlook, disaffection over Vietnam proved the most salient issue.

In preparation for a meeting between Sato and Johnson in January 1965, each side exchanged "talking papers." Japan submitted positions on Okinawa and the Bonin Islands, China, and defense policy. But, as Sato told Reischauer, these were "surface views" that would do "little damage if leaked to the public." Japan's ambassador, Takeuchi Ryuji, speaking to Rusk, revealed what he considered the main point for discussion: "Many Japanese were worried over Japan's economic future" and feared that Johnson "would not pursue as liberal trade policies as President Kennedy." The American report said almost nothing about trade. It focused on China's October 1964 nuclear test explosion and highlighted the danger posed by Chinese "expansionist pressures against bordering countries especially in Southeast Asia." Trade or diplomatic concessions to Beijing, the Americans warned, would encourage Chinese aggression. The president also wished to discuss how Japan could assist efforts to defend South Vietnam and improve relations with South Korea. "Because of limitations in [the president's] time," Sato was told, economic problems would be discussed by "other high officials in Washington."[11]

Although President Johnson accorded Prime Minister Sato the formalities of a state visit, he spent less than two hours talking with Sato during January 11 to 14, 1965. The president's remarks followed the points already sent to Tokyo. The "heart of the matter" was Sato's cooperation in keeping China out of the United Nations and encouraging a peace settlement between Japan and South Korea. Partly to save an estimated $1 billion over the next few years, Washington urged Japan to assist Korea economically.[12]

Sato avoided talking about China by noting Japan's separation of politics from trade. He asked if the United States intended to stay in Vietnam.

Johnson pledged "not to withdraw" in the face of Communist threats. Sato applauded this "determination to maintain a firm stand" and repeated "his desire that we hold out." Why then, Johnson shot back, were "all our friends . . . under the bridge or hiding in caves" when he asked for assistance? The United States had already spent $4 or $5 billion in Vietnam, but "we seem to be alone." Where "were Britain, Japan, and Germany?" Johnson thanked Sato for giving medical aid to Saigon, but the time had come for him to "show the flag." If Japan "got in trouble, we would send our planes and bombs to defend her." America was "in trouble in Vietnam" and the question was "how can Japan help us?"

The president backed this appeal with some arm-twisting. Every day he "confronted a number of senators who jump down his throat because of problems arising from Japanese" textile and electronic exports. The president wanted help solving this problem "for he had 50 senators after him on it." Sato doubted Japanese textiles had much of an impact and asked why American politicians always focused on what Japan sold to the United States, never what it purchased.[13]

Johnson assigned his aides to thrash out policy details with Sato. Rusk spoke with passion about the Chinese threat to Southeast Asia and the need to isolate China. Sato agreed to follow Washington's political lead on China, at least for the time being, and sign a peace treaty with South Korea. He promised to give more than "moral support" for American efforts in Southeast Asia but suggested nothing beyond the $1.5 million in medical, technical, and financial assistance already provided South Vietnam and Laos.

Washington granted Sato's request to expand the role of the joint consultative committee on Okinawa, so long as it did not limit military freedom of action. Rusk also approved a long-standing request by Tokyo to allow visits by former Japanese residents to gravesites on the American-occupied Bonin Islands. The secretary of state proposed negotiations on several economic issues, including Japanese requests for expanded air routes to the United States, revision of a Pacific fishing pact, and reconsideration of the interest equalization tax first imposed in 1963 that discouraged American investment in Japan. Rusk also promised to press Congress to repeal the Saylor Amendment that restricted the purchase of Japanese mass transit equipment with federal funds. Most of these issues were resolved to Japan's satisfaction.[14]

Although the Johnson administration remained adamantly opposed to any dealing with China, a hint of flexibility emerged during a conversation between LDP Secretary General Miki Takeo and Vice President-elect Hubert Humphrey. Discussing ways that Japan and the United States might alleviate Asian poverty and promote democracy, Humphrey voiced sympathy for the Japanese argument that trade "could act to reduce some of the aggressive, militant spirit of Communist China." Speaking "individually," the vice president suggested that Japanese trade with China "could be a positive factor." Although Humphrey spoke for himself, Miki and Sato may have interpreted this as subtle encouragement of their policy.[15]

The communiqué that emerged from the Washington visit reflected both Johnson's desire that Japan endorse American policy toward China, Vietnam, and Okinawa, and Sato's determination to avoid commitments. They agreed that American military bases on the Ryukyu and Bonin Islands were vital for the "security of the Far East." When conditions were right, the islands would revert to Japanese control. Meanwhile, they would expand joint efforts to improve the welfare of the inhabitants. Johnson and Sato affirmed their diplomatic support for Taiwan, but the prime minister defended Japan's right to trade with China. "Continued perseverance would be necessary for freedom and independence in South Vietnam," Sato agreed, but again he avoided any commitment.[16]

Two weeks later, Japan donated 11,000 radios to South Vietnam. This failed to impress Washington. State and Defense officials proposed an incentive for Tokyo to support Saigon more actively. It offered "certain U.S. military equipment" to Japan on "exceptionally favorable terms" and promised to significantly boost American military procurement from Japanese industry "in return for additional Japanese grant aid to Southeast Asia." The United States would provide air defense missiles to Japan and place orders for vehicles, aircraft parts, and the overhaul of navy vessels with Japanese firms if Tokyo gave Vietnam and "one or more non-Communist countries" in Southeast Asia military and economic aid. The more aid Japan provided Vietnam, the larger the American grants to and procurement in Japan would be.[17]

This appeal—which paralleled Johnson's Many Flags program (discussed later) designed to recruit Asians to fight in Vietnam—failed to sway the Japanese. The encouraging words spoken by Sato and other Japanese visitors to Washington became vague expressions of sympathy on their return to Tokyo. For the duration of the war, Japan confined its direct aid to South Vietnam to medical and humanitarian assistance. Bandages and radios were mere tokens, Johnson complained, "what I am interested in is bodies."[18]

In February 1965, the United States began sustained bombing of North Vietnam. That summer, as the Saigon regime teetered on the brink of collapse, Johnson dispatched the first contingent of combat troops to South Vietnam. Nearly a half million followed.

Despite Johnson's frustration with Sato, the prime minister personally supported American policy in Vietnam. He certainly believed that Japan's access to the American market, its best chance to recover Okinawa, and ability to trade with China hinged on remaining in Washington's good graces. As evidence of his loyalty, Sato permitted American forces nearly unfettered use of bases in Japan and Okinawa. Although this cost him some domestic support, it paid strong political and economic dividends.

During most of Sato's nearly eight years as prime minister (1965–72), he dominated the normally fractious LDP. The death of several rivals early in his tenure and bitter rifts within both the Socialist and Communist parties divided the opposition. Nevertheless, the Vietnam War, in

Reischauer's words, "cast a dark shadow over all Japanese-American relations" after 1965.[19]

Even Japanese leaders who supported Johnson's policies were troubled by America's failure to consult with Tokyo in advance of the initial decision to bomb North Vietnam. The periodic use of airfields on Okinawa for B-52 raids proved especially upsetting. Sato informed Reischauer that although he did "not question in any way the right of the U.S. to use Okinawa" as a staging site for B-52 attacks, he harbored "deep personal concern regarding the adverse impact this action" would have in Japan. Reischauer, too, cautioned Washington that use of the Okinawa bases handed "the left a sizeable club with which to beat the Sato administration." Linking Sato, Vietnam, and Okinawa "in this dramatic manner could provide the Japanese Left the key missing element—a sense of direct Japanese involvement—in their current effort to convert Japanese public concern over Vietnam into massive indignation and action against our security relationships with Japan including the Okinawa base."[20]

Sato made recovery of the Ryukyus one of his major goals. But he could not escape the anger many residents of Okinawa felt toward American use of airfields to bomb Vietnam. When he visited the island in the summer of 1965, instead of being cheered for expanding home rule and improving living standards, demonstrators chased Sato onto an American base where he took refuge.

The Johnson administration believed a commitment to Vietnam would reassure Japan. However, the escalation during 1965 provoked more anxiety than confidence. NSC staffer James C. Thomson recalled that, as the war expanded, a Japanese official "told me a wondrous thing that made my hair stand on end. . . . 'We tried that twenty years ago, and it was a terrible mistake to do.'"[21]

Although Johnson, McNamara, Rusk, and Bundy argued that expanding the commitment to Saigon was vital in preserving American "prestige" and "credibility" among its allies, George Ball cited Reischauer's views to challenge this assumption. At a critical White House meeting in July, Ball urged withdrawing from Vietnam in part because even Japanese leaders sympathetic to American goals think "we are propping up a lifeless government [in Saigon] and are on a sticky wicket." If forced to choose "between a long war and cutting our losses, the Japanese would go for the latter." A stalemate, Ball predicted, would damage American credibility far more than a voluntary withdrawal. This appeal had virtually no impact on Johnson.[22]

Japanese of varied political outlook saw the Vietnam War, like the Korean conflict, as something of a proxy struggle between the United States and China. Japanese Socialists and Communists opposed the Korean War but could do little about it under Occupation constraints. Conservatives and business interests supported the war's results, if not purpose. The contempt many Japanese felt for Koreans probably mitigated any feelings of sympathy.

The Vietnam War coincided with resurgent Japanese nationalism and struck a strong emotional cord. Opinion surveys revealed that a broad spectrum of Japanese sympathized with Vietnamese nationalism and viewed the United States as a bully. Many saw a similarity between their own disastrous effort to dominate Southeast Asia and American policy. Recalling the horrors of air attacks on Japanese cities created empathy with Vietnamese victims.

The Sato government tried to accommodate Washington's war plans without provoking too much domestic criticism. The government often cited anti-war sentiment as a reason for not doing all its ally asked. When the air war against North Vietnam began in February 1965, Foreign Minister Shiina Etsusaburo described American action as "justified" self-defense. On February 14, Shiina told the Diet that the United States could utilize its bases in Japan for "routine operations" in Vietnam, so long as they were not used directly for combat. (Bases in Okinawa could be used without restriction.) In practice, planes and ships destined for combat in Vietnam were free to operate from Japan as long as combat orders were not issued until they departed Japanese territory.

Sato also stretched the geographical limit set in 1960 that had excluded Indochina from the Far Eastern security zone covered by the United States–Japan treaty. He permitted Japanese merchant sailors to serve on U.S. military transports carrying weapons to Vietnam. The security treaty evolved into a document facilitating American operations in Southeast Asia.[23]

When Japan's national newspapers and television news coverage began to criticize American strategy and tactics in Vietnam, the Johnson administration reacted sharply. During April and May 1965, Henry Cabot Lodge, William Bundy, and Walt Rostow visited Tokyo to firm up official support for the war. Former ambassador MacArthur and Undersecretary of State Ball told the Senate Foreign Relations Committee that Japanese journalists distorted the truth because hundreds of Communists worked for the *Asahi* and *Mainichi,* two of Japan's largest papers. Whatever the senators made of this explanation, it caused an uproar in Japan. Reischauer, worried that Americans might believe the Red subversion argument, dispatched a "very strongly worded telegram to the State Department" that detailed the "extremely adverse reactions in Japan to the American bombing of North Vietnam."[24]

Nevertheless, the high-level lobbying persuaded Japanese officials to proclaim allegiance to American policy. The National Liberation Front in South Vietnam, abetted by North Vietnam and China, an LDP spokesman announced, had violated the Geneva accords and bore responsibility for the war. On May 7, 1965, Foreign Minister Shiina told the Diet he considered U.S. bombing of North Vietnam "proper" and pledged to cooperate under the terms of the security treaty "because America is taking these military actions on behalf of the peace and security of the Far East." That same day Sato told an LDP forum that the Japanese should complain less about U.S. escalation and worry more about "Red Imperialism."[25]

Disagreements over Vietnam strained but never fractured the ruling coalition. During 1965, LDP Diet members organized a dominant 160-member "Asian Problems Study Group," affiliated with the prime minister. Members believed that Japan's interests were best served by supporting American actions in Asia. They favored keeping China out of the United Nations, retaining close ties with Taiwan and South Korea, and endorsing Washington's Vietnam policy.

The smaller 100-or-so-member "Asian-African Problems Study Group" voiced misgivings about American policy and favored a negotiated solution in Vietnam. However, the group cared more about expanding trade and political contacts with China than opposing American policy in Southeast Asia. These factions chastised each other and sometimes sent rival delegations to Vietnam, China, and Korea. But neither considered Vietnam an issue over which to bolt the LDP. This paralleled the situation of most Japanese, a majority of whom felt uneasy about cooperation with Washington, but continued to send LDP majorities to the Diet.[26]

Discontent with the war had an important, if secondary, impact on Japanese-American relations. Running B-52 raids out of Okinawa proved especially unsettling to Japanese opinion. While in the United States during August 1965, Reischauer complained to State Department officials that use of the Okinawa bases needlessly offended Japanese sensibilities. He told an audience in Boston that the "loss of our close relationship with Japan because of Vietnam would be much more disastrous than anything that might happen in Vietnam itself except a world war."[27]

Reischauer felt ambivalent about escalation. Although he doubted the Chinese threat to Southeast Asia and favored negotiation over expansion of the war, once escalation began, he "accepted the administration's argument that the quickest way to end the war was to force North Vietnam by military might to desist from trying to conquer the South." Only half persuaded by his own argument, Reischauer often found himself defending policies he judged neither effective nor moral. In the spring of 1965, he challenged Washington's Red-baiting attack on Japanese press coverage of the Vietnam War. In October 1965, however, he echoed the administration's charge and accused Japan's leading newspapers and journalists of serving as mouthpieces for Red propaganda. At the end of the year, after visiting Saigon, he concluded privately that critics of the South Vietnamese regime were correct.[28]

Reischauer's criticism of Japanese war opponents coincided with attacks by Assistant Secretary of State William Bundy, the *New York Times* columnist James Reston, and Philip Quigg, deputy editor of the influential journal *Foreign Affairs*. All chastised Japan's politicians and intellectuals for their "dangerously mistaken" view of China, failure to support and assist the American effort in Vietnam, and reluctance to play a greater military role in Asia. These bitter exchanges, Reischauer lamented, eroded much of the goodwill he had cultivated since 1961.[29]

In January 1966, President Johnson sent Averell Harriman and Vice President Hubert Humphrey as special envoys to Tokyo. Both encouraged

Sato to send emissaries to neutral and Communist countries in pursuit of peace in Vietnam. However, Harriman made clear, any settlement must be based on "America's position of strength." Humphrey took a conciliatory approach, urging the prime minister to "take a more active role in Southeast Asian development" and promote a "greater Japanese presence and participation in South Vietnam." The vice president suggested that "the Japanese might wish to provide full medical services for one or more provinces in Vietnam." Little came of these ideas.[30]

The Japanese business community, concerned about American trade retaliation, urged Sato to placate Washington. Early in 1966, the prime minister issued public statements critical of China's nuclear program and recent H-bomb test. He restricted government credit to Beijing and barred a Chinese trade delegation from visiting Japan. Foreign Minister Shiina announced that in light of the security treaty, "Japan was not in a neutral position vis-à-vis the United States and North Vietnam." America fought to "maintain the security of the Far East" so Japan "had an obligation to furnish facilities and territories for this purpose."[31]

China lost no time in alerting Japan to the risks it courted by following the American lead in Vietnam. In February 1966, a ranking Chinese official asked a member of Japan's trade office in Beijing to pass a warning "to the Japanese foreign office." If, during the air war against North Vietnam, the official stated, "the U.S. bombs China, unfortunately the U.S. is out of our reach. We are not able to return the blow. However, it is not impossible for us to reach Japan." The threat, American analysts agreed, sought to "push Japan toward a neutralist position and use Japan to restrain the scope of U.S. action."[32]

American escalation, Tokyo's acquiescence, and Chinese threats incited an anti-war movement among university students and intellectuals. *Beheiren* (Citizens' Federation for Peace in Vietnam) opposed the war both on pacifist grounds and out of concern that Japan would be dragged into the conflict because of its security ties with the United States. *Beheiren* favored peace in Vietnam, self-determination for the Vietnamese, and cessation of Japanese complicity in the war. The movement maintained a separate identity from the Socialist and Communist parties, which opposed the war on more ideological grounds and saw the nonpartisan anti-war activists as something of a threat to their following. *Beheiren* leaders and publications accused the Sato government of being a co-conspirator with, not a passive accomplice to, the war. *Demos* in front of the U.S. embassy became so frequent by mid-1965 that riot police assumed a nearly permanent presence. Between 1965 and 1970, some eighteen million Japanese demonstrated against the Vietnam War.[33]

Opinion surveys during the period 1965 to 1968 found a sizeable majority of Japanese opposed to bombing Vietnam and expanding the ground war. Respondents sympathized with the Viet Cong goal of toppling the Saigon regime. By 1968, at the height of American escalation, two-thirds of Japanese polled favored adopting a more neutral foreign policy. Only 20 percent wanted to continue the security treaty with the United States after 1970 when it could be ended. (Support for the alliance increased in 1969 when Nixon began removing troops from Vietnam.)

Despite these trends, neither grassroots nor elite opposition to the war ever threatened Sato's domination of the LDP or the party's monopoly of power. The anti-war movement failed to arouse the depth of passion that the anti-security treaty movement had in 1960. Many Japanese opposed the war, but still voted for the LDP.

The structure of Japanese politics and the LDP further mitigated the impact of the anti-war movement. Prime ministers were chosen by Diet members, not voters. LDP faction leaders controlled blocs of Diet members in the bargaining process that resulted in selection of a party leader/prime minister. Party barons and their followers forged and broke alliances to gain control of cabinet posts, patronage, and rewards for constituents and campaign donors. Whenever possible, they avoided embracing popular causes or grappling with divisive issues. The Vietnam War was not so overwhelming a concern among voters as to force the LDP to take heed of anti-war sentiment or risk losing its Diet majority.

Moreover, continued covert CIA financing of friendly Japanese politicians and publications muted criticism of American policy. As the war in Vietnam escalated, the United States spent about $1 million annually in subsidies to sympathetic newspapers and magazines and to individual members of the Democratic Socialist and Liberal Democratic parties. Americans made a special effort to influence politicians on Okinawa where popular opposition to the use of bases for Vietnam operations piggybacked on demands to return the island to Japanese control. A "secret action plan" provided cash to sympathetic politicians in elections held in 1965 and 1968. Even Ambassador Reischauer, a mild critic of the CIA subsidies, recognized the importance of keeping the lid on in Okinawa. In discussing the plan with military officials, his concern focused on assuring that leading national figures in "the Japanese LDP [rather than the party's Okinawa branch]" served as the primary conduit of American funds. This was "the most effective way" to assure both success and stealth. Deputy Undersecretary of the Army John M. Steadman agreed that secrecy was critical because if the "U.S. is caught with its hand in the cookie jar there will be a serious blow up in Japan."[34]

The American Military in Japan

In 1952, over 200,000 American military personnel remained on nearly 3,000 bases and installations in Japan. These numbers shrank steadily over the next decade. By 1964 (excluding facilities and personnel on Okinawa, 45,000 military dependents, and the sailors of the Japan-based Seventh Fleet), the United States maintained in Japan twelve large bases, 136 other facilities, and 46,000 military personnel. Half of them were in the air force and the remainder divided between the army, navy, and marines. Even as the Vietnam War expanded, U.S. force levels in Japan continued to decline.

By the mid-1960s, the United States all but abandoned its effort to promote large-scale Japanese rearmament. The self-defense forces totaled around 250,000 throughout the decade. In place of size, the Defense Department pressed Japan to improve the quality of its air and maritime forces. As a result, Japan's military evolved into an efficient defense force with little offensive capability.

The repair, communication, ammunition and oil storage, and recreational facilities the U.S. military retained in Japan were critical components of Asian defense strategy. These installations, along with those in Okinawa, Guam, South Korea, Taiwan, and the Philippines, formed a coordinated network east of Hawaii. Bases on Okinawa were especially vital to the air war in Vietnam. One million military transport and combat flights originated in the Ryukyus between 1965 and 1973. KC 135 tanker planes refueled B-52 bombers flying from Guam to Indochina, and the B-52s sometimes flew directly from the Ryukyus. Unrestricted by the 1960 security treaty, American forces stored chemical and nuclear weapons on Okinawa. Nearly three-fourths of the 400,000 tons of supplies required each month by American troops in Vietnam passed through the warehouse and port facilities on the island. Small wonder that beginning in 1965 the Defense Department referred to Okinawa as the "keystone of the Pacific," even placing the logo on local license plates. In December of that year, Admiral U.S. Grant Sharp, commander of Pacific forces, declared that "without Okinawa we couldn't continue fighting the Vietnam War."[35]

As the Vietnam War escalated, American analysts noted that Japan served "as host for this country's second largest foreign base establishment, after that in Germany." Air force and marine units in Japan and Okinawa filled "a key role opposite the growing power of Communist China and the Soviet Far East." By "making it unnecessary for Seventh Fleet vessels to return to Hawaii or the West Coast for maintenance and repair," American naval bases in Japan "save us hundreds of millions of dollars a year in peacetime, and would have even greater logistics value in certain kinds of war situations, as the Korean War showed." Ammunition and equipment storage sites, repair facilities, and an industrial infrastructure all made Japan the linchpin for the U.S. defense posture in East and Southeast Asia. A Senate subcommittee on military preparedness concluded in April 1966 that "it would be very difficult to fight the war in Southeast Asia without [bases] at Yokosuka and Sasebo."[36]

Although the security treaty barred the United States from introducing nuclear weapons to Japan without permission, the secret protocol of 1960 permitted nuclear-laden planes and ships to "transit" through the country. American war plans and informal procedures followed by local commanders stretched this loophole even further. Air force transport planes stationed on Pacific islands were assigned, in case of a war alert, to transport nuclear weapons to U.S. air bases in Japan without obtaining Tokyo's approval. The weapons would then be deployed against targets in Northeast Asia.[37]

While visiting Japan in the early 1960s as a Rand Corporation analyst working on a Pentagon study, Daniel Ellsberg uncovered a more serious violation of the security treaty. The small marine air base at Iwakuni, on the Inland Sea, had a handful of planes assigned to attack some two dozen targets in North Korea, China, and the Soviet Union. The marines arranged with local navy officials to store nuclear bombs on an LST barge (the "San Joaquin County") semi-permanently moored a few hundred yards offshore. If needed, the motorized barge would approach the beach and send its bombs ashore on amphibious tractors directly to the marine airfield. Neither civilian nor military commanders in Washington seemed aware of this. Navy records, Ellsberg discovered, listed the LST as docked in Okinawa. The arrangement was "regarded as super-secret from the Japanese" and from civilians in the Pentagon.

The barge's vulnerability to sabotage and the high risk of public disclosure of its cargo prompted Ellsberg to criticize the operation as harebrained. Exposure might bring down the Japanese government, lead to a rupture in diplomatic relations, or even drive Japan toward neutralism. Given the marginal importance of the targets assigned to the marine planes, Ellsberg described the situation to Assistant Secretary of Defense Paul Nitze and Defense Secretary Robert McNamara as the "most fantastically irresponsible action it was possible to imagine." But when they pressed the navy to remedy the problem, top admirals denounced "civilian meddling" and McNamara dropped the subject.[38]

The nuclear weapons barge remained in place until the spring of 1966 when someone—perhaps Ellsberg—leaked word to Reischauer who was stunned by the information. In the best of circumstances, it represented a treaty violation and breach of trust. Should its presence be revealed amid the rising tide of anti-American, anti-Vietnam War protests, he warned, it would ignite a "dangerous political explosion." Reischauer grew livid when Secretary of State Rusk nonchalantly told him "that he thought I had known about the vessel" and tacitly approved. The envoy threatened to resign unless Rusk ordered its swift removal. Rusk complied, but the incident widened the gulf between the two men.[39]

By this time, Reischauer found it nearly impossible to defend the Asia policies of the Johnson administration. His rapport with Japanese intellectuals had been eroded by their opposition to a Vietnam policy he only half believed in. Even before this latest incident, he decided to quit his post and return to Harvard during the summer of 1966. Once again, however, Rusk and Johnson stymied his effort. Declining to accept in a timely manner his request to resign, the president and secretary of state waited until July and then called Reischauer back to Washington for consultations.

Johnson met with Reischauer for an hour on July 22. The ambassador hoped to speak about the damage America's China and Vietnam policies were doing throughout Asia. But Johnson delivered a harangue about anti-war senators who undermined his policies. Dispirited, Reischauer left the White House and ventured to the Senate where he shared his doubts with Senator J. William Fulbright and other members of the Foreign Relations Committee. Three days later, the State Department announced his resignation and the selection of career diplomat U. Alexis Johnson as ambassador to Tokyo.[40]

The war dogged Reischauer's final days in Tokyo. At farewell receptions he attended, "groups of vociferous young Americans and Japanese" stood at the entrance to the buildings "shouting protests against America's Vietnam policies." At one event the protestors even included "an acquaintance," Professor Howard Zinn of Boston University. Reischauer could "never forget him wildly beating on a drum in an effort to spoil the party given in Haru's honor."[41]

Japan and the Economic Dimensions of the Vietnam War

The Vietnam War had a greater economic than political impact on Japan. Defense industries which had been in the doldrums since the mid-1950s expanded rapidly as the Pentagon procured Vietnam-related material in Japan and surrounding countries. Military orders encouraged technological transfer and innovation. With American industry producing at full capacity, ever higher levels of Japanese exports found a permanent niche in the U.S. consumer market. The expenditure of billions of war-related dollars in Taiwan, South Korea, Singapore, Thailand, the Philippines, and Hong Kong sparked a regional boom that also benefited Japan.

Japanese and American government agencies and private banks used different criteria in calculating the war's economic impact on Japan. The Ministry of International Trade and Industry had the best data, but issued the most conservative analyses in order to dampen charges of war profiteering. United States Treasury officials used numbers close to the mid-range estimates of the Japanese Finance Ministry and private banks. All calculations came on top of the $340 million "base" level of U.S. procurements in Japan in 1964. They also accounted for the fact that exports to the United States and Southeast Asia were on an upward curve when escalation began.

MITI data for 1965 to 1972 indicates that Japan earned at least $7 billion in "extra" sales of goods and services related to Vietnam. This included $1.77 billion in direct procurement by U.S. forces in Japan; $2.83 billion in indirect procurement by Vietnam and countries such as South Korea, Taiwan, and the Philippines; and almost $2 billion in indirect procurement in terms of additional exports to the United States made possible by the war. Japan earned at least $1 billion per year and possibly as much as $1.5 billion from the Vietnam War.[42]

MITI Estimates of Japan's Earnings from Vietnam War, 1965-72 (in U.S. dollars on top of 1964 base of $340 million)

	1965	1966	1967	1968	1969	1970	1971	1972
Direct procurement	6	134	188	251	303	323	28	285
Exports to U.S.	—	55	246	369	438	371	256	162
Indirect procurement by Asian nations	77	256	392	444	517	404	400	400
Totals	83	445	826	1,064	1,258	1,098	937	847

MITI officials minimized Vietnam's impact by comparing war orders to total GNP. They noted that Korean-era procurement totaled about $1.8 billion in an economy only a sixth as large as that of Japan in the Vietnam era. Procurement at the peak of the Korean War represented nearly 60 percent of the value of all Japanese exports, while during the Vietnam War they were about 12 percent of total exports. But however calculated, Vietnam had a huge impact on the pace and direction of economic growth.

Initial Vietnam procurement included such items as rubber boots, sandbags, and barbed wire. By 1966, the Army Procurement Agency in Japan (APA) expanded its purchases to cotton cloth, rubber, petroleum, cement, sheet iron, motorcycles, synthetic fibers, transceivers, canned and instant foodstuffs, electronic equipment, as well as watches and cameras, presumably intended as gifts for GIs to purchase at post exchanges. By 1967, APA purchases included equipment needed for the repair and construction of roads, rail lines, and harbors. That year, the APA bought over 200 railway freight cars from Japanese manufacturers.

Although Japanese industry refrained from selling weapons or munitions for use in Vietnam, petrochemical companies enjoyed a brisk trade in "precursor" chemicals used to manufacture napalm, TNT, and other explosives. In the late 1960s, these sales totaled between $150 and $300 million per year. Electronic manufacturers, such as Sony, built no weapons but sold the APA guidance systems used in military aircraft, missiles, and bombs. MITI deleted many of these sales from its procurement calculations, claiming that it lacked detailed knowledge about the total value or end use of material sold privately to the U.S. military.[43]

Japan accrued another benefit from recreational (R&R) spending by Americans. Between 1966 and 1969, about 50,000 military personnel stationed in Southeast Asia visited Japan annually. Hotels and travel agencies bid for contracts to serve the troops brought in on air charters for five-day stays. Hotels provided a billet, loaned the soldiers civilian clothes, and arranged for their entertainment, somewhat as had been done during the early Occupation. Each servicemen spent about $100 per day, earning Japan a minimum of $25 million a year.[44]

War-related procurement in Asia proved as beneficial to Japan as direct American purchases. Taiwan, South Korea, Thailand, Hong Kong, and the Philippines received large orders from the United States and, often, cash payments for sending troops to Vietnam. To fulfill procurement contracts, these countries purchased machinery and semiprocessed materials from Japan. The value of these orders exceeded that of direct procurement within Japan. Meanwhile, general exports from Japan to non-Communist Asia increased from $2 billion in 1965 to $6 billion in 1972. MITI estimated that 20 percent of this astounding growth was generated by the war.

The dollars earned by Southeast Asian countries from U.S. procurements after 1965 fueled a regional boom in consumer purchases, with Japan the main beneficiary. Japanese consumer exports to South Vietnam increased from $35 million in 1965 to $223 million in 1969. Exports included trucks, buses, cars, motorcycles, clothing, and electrical products. Small companies such as Honda discovered a lucrative niche market selling light motorcycles to South Vietnam. By the late 1960s, U.S. Ambassador Ellsworth Bunker referred to Saigon as "Honda-ville." In any case, South Vietnam was only Japan's *seventh* largest regional trading partner. By the early 1970s, over 20 percent of Japan's exports went to Asia, its second biggest market after the United States. Much of Japan's earnings from this trade flowed back into the region in the form of investments, grants, and loans.[45]

President Johnson's effort to enlist allied support for the war provided an additional spur to regional growth. The Many Flags Program begun in 1965 brought troops from Australia, New Zealand, the Philippines, Thailand, and South Korea to Vietnam. Several hundred Chinese Nationalist pilots, technicians, and guerrillas operated secretly in South Vietnam as something of a counter to the Chinese logistic troops in North Vietnam. Some 7,500 Australian and 500 New Zealand soldiers fought beside the Americans as allies. Troops from other Asian countries were virtual mercenaries.

Civilian and military officials in South Korea, the Philippines, and Thailand saw the Vietnam War as a business opportunity. President Ferdinand Marcos of the Philippines relished the prospect of marketing his army and civilian workers to the Vietnam effort after he received assurances from Vice President Hubert Humphrey, visiting Manila, that "we rewarded our friends." With no apparent sense of irony, Marcos told Humphrey that "there is no price too high to pay for freedom," and then demanded an average of $26,000 for each of the 2,200 Filipino soldiers sent to Vietnam. Arguing that Washington had treated him less generously than it did South Korea and Japan, the Filipino leader insisted that U.S. contractors in Vietnam hire at least 5,000 Filipino civilians, that the Pentagon reequip units of the Philippine army, and that Washington increase economic and military assistance to Manila as part of a package deal to send combat troops.[46]

Thailand, too, reaped a bountiful harvest from cooperating with the Vietnam War effort. Out of gratitude for sending a small number of troops to Vietnam, Washington provided Bangkok with an annual stipend of $50 million. It paid the Thai army an additional $100 million between 1965 and 1971 for contributing troops to the CIA-run "secret army" fighting in Laos. In return for allowing the U.S. air force to mount nearly 75 percent of its bombing runs over North Vietnam from Thai air bases, the Johnson administration doubled the level of economic and military aid to Bangkok.[47]

South Korea benefited most of all from these arrangements. In return for the United States providing lucrative procurement contracts, equipping and paying troops sent to Vietnam, and allocating funds for the modernization of the Korean army, the military government in Seoul agreed to send up to 50,000 Korean soldiers to South Vietnam at a given time. Some Koreans remained until the Saigon regime collapsed in 1975. All told, about 300,000 Korean soldiers served in Vietnam. The United States also hired 16,000 Korean civilians to work in Vietnam.

Korean firms received contracts to do such varied tasks as produce weapons and cart away Saigon's garbage. Dollar remittances from Korean soldiers and civilians rose as high as $200 million annually in 1969, about 20 percent of Seoul's foreign currency revenue. Between 1966 and 1970, South Korea earned at least $1 billion for services rendered in or for Vietnam.[48]

Few Americans knew—or cared—about these payments to Asian nations. It was assumed that they shared American values and concerns about Vietnam and, as allies, pitched in to help. Johnson praised them as "staunch allies" who "volunteer[ed]" to fight for the Free World."

The flood of dollars into Korea and Southeast Asia funded activities as varied as a vast sex industry for GIs on R&R, light manufacturing, and a new consumer export market for Japan. It stimulated the kind of regional growth Americans and Japanese had talked about since the late 1940s. With its advanced economy and geographic proximity, Japan harvested a great number of American dollars from throughout Southeast Asia and used them to modernize factories at home and invest in regional resources.

Vietnam spending benefited Japan in one additional way. As the war expanded, American industry produced at almost full capacity. Domestic manufacturers could not simultaneously satisfy military orders and burgeoning demand for such items as machine tools, steel, petrochemicals, consumer electronics, domestic appliances, textiles, and automotive parts. Shortages and inflation were averted in industries such as steel—which operated at full capacity in 1968–69—primarily because Japan (and other) exporting nations filled the gap.

Japanese exports to the United States in 1965 totaled $2.4 billion. By 1969, they had doubled and by 1972 quadrupled to over $9 billion. A significant amount of this increase could be attributed to trade opportunities created by production shortages in America. After the war ended, Japan retained most of its new market share in Southeast Asia and the United States. While world trade tripled in value during the 1960s, Tokyo's exports increased sixfold. The chronic trade and balance-of-payments surplus with the United States originated during this period. Beginning in 1965, Japan's global foreign trade (exports and imports) and international

U.S. Merchandise Trade with Japan (in millions of dollars)

	Exports	Imports	Balance
1964	2,009	1,768	+241
1965	2,080	2,414	-334
1966	2,364	2,963	-599
1967	2,695	2,999	-304
1968	2,954	4,054	-1,100
1969	3,490	4,888	-1,398
1972	4,965	9,064	-4,099

Source: Statistical Abstract of the United States, 1970–80

payments balance (trade, services, capital transfers, etc.) both shifted to a strong surplus. The 1964 global foreign trade surplus of $377 million approached $9 billion in 1972. Between 1965 and 1969, Japan's trade surplus with the United States alone ballooned from $334 million (on two-way trade of about $4.5 billion) to almost $1.4 billion (on two-way trade of about $8.5 billion). By 1968, American officials realized the economic shift generated by the war in Vietnam approached crisis proportions.

Diplomatic Damage Control, 1967–68

When U. Alexis Johnson took over the Tokyo embassy in October 1966, he recognized that the fabric of economic and security ties between Japan and the United States had frayed badly since his predecessor had "restored the broken dialogue." Johnson served in Tokyo in the 1930s and during a lifetime in the foreign service had been posted throughout Asia. Before his appointment to Japan, he was deputy undersecretary of state. His spirited support for the Vietnam War convinced Rusk and President Johnson that he would represent administration priorities better than Reischauer had.

As the ambassador saw it, Japan thrived on American trade and security "benefits," but shunned "responsibility." He blamed the growing trade imbalance on "restrictive quotas" placed on the import of high-technology products, unfair limits on investments by American firms, and a "deeply ingrained patriotic chauvinism" that led Japanese consumers to shun foreign goods. Johnson charged that Japan violated the free trade principles of GATT and treated the United States "something like an underdeveloped country, purchasing agricultural products in return for its manufactured goods."[49]

The ambassador pressed the Sato government to reduce tariffs and restrictions on foreign investment. By 1968, Japan eliminated many of the most bothersome barriers. Although more American products entered Japan, Japan's exports grew at a faster pace, widening the trade imbalance between the two countries.

Security issues proved as vexing as trade. Japan thrived under an American-provided defense umbrella, Johnson noted, but its leaders did little to supplement American efforts on their behalf. He wanted to resolve three critical questions: (1) the status of the Bonin and Ryukyu Islands, (2) the future of American bases in Japan and the mission of the Self-Defense Forces, and (3) Japanese attitudes toward the Vietnam War. Continuation of the security treaty beyond 1970 (when either party could withdraw after a year's notice) required resolution of these issues.

Although the tiny Bonin Islands (which included Iwo Jima) had mostly symbolic importance, the Ryukyus possessed both military and political value. Okinawans had grown increasingly restive under American control and all of Japan's political parties demanded reversion to Japanese control.

Because of their "insular" nature, Johnson complained, most Japanese perceived little military threat to themselves and lacked capacity to think "responsibly" about security. Although they relied on a U.S. nuclear umbrella, the Japanese people as a whole viewed American bases on their soil as "something of a nuisance, a humiliation, and a lightning rod that might involve them in hostilities not of their own choosing." In short, the bases were a source of "small daily irritations and of large strategic risk." While Johnson insisted that the Japanese "who mattered," including bureaucrats, business executives, and LDP leaders, privately supported American containment efforts in Vietnam, China, and Korea, they were too insecure to proclaim it. Johnson favored returning Okinawa to Japan in part because this would compel Tokyo to think about defending its outlying territory.[50]

The Vietnam conflict shaped Japan's views on American bases, Okinawa, and continuation of the security treaty. At the same time, Johnson acknowledged, "Japan was vital to our effort in Vietnam." It provided "ports, repair and rebuild facilities, supply dumps, stopover points for aircraft, and hospitals for badly wounded soldiers." Japanese laborers performed the "great bulk of this work for which we spend several billion dollars each year." He made it his mission to "promote Japanese understanding and support of our involvement," for its own sake and to push Japan to "think more precisely about the kind of Southeast Asia it wished to see."[51]

Shortly before Johnson went to Tokyo, former National Security Adviser McGeorge Bundy prodded the president to act on Okinawa. Like the ambassador, Bundy predicted that settlement of the question would make Japan more cooperative and committed to Asian security. The "desirable trade," he told Walt Rostow, his successor, "would be one which restored Japanese civil government in Okinawa while insuring explicit Japanese acceptance of whatever military rights we need there." Unfortunately, the United States required "nuclear rights in Okinawa and . . . it will be hard for the Japanese to grant them explicitly." The president took Bundy's advice, creating a Ryukyu Islands Study Group to formulate a way to accommodate the demands of the Japanese and U.S. military needs.[52]

While most diplomatic officials and Defense Secretary McNamara favored flexibility on the Ryukyus and Bonins, the armed services opposed any change in the status quo. According to Johnson, the navy objected to giving up control of the Bonin Islands (with its sixty-five enlisted men, navigation station, and war memorial) because "the Navy's basic position was that we should not give up anything anywhere that might someday possibly be useful." Naval planners insisted that in case of the loss of Japan, Okinawa, Taiwan, and the Philippines, the Bonins would then become a vital outpost. Johnson retorted that if the navy was run out of all these spots, the Bonins would be irrelevant. Nevertheless, the Joint Chiefs of Staff insisted on unfettered control of Okinawa and the Bonins, including the right to store nuclear weapons.[53]

Despite the military's hard line, the president and his civilian advisers recognized the potency of the Okinawa issue among the Japanese and Sato's need to show results from his pro-American/pro-Vietnam stance. The administration cobbled together its position in the fall of 1967 just in advance of visits to Washington by Foreign Minister Miki Takeo and Prime Minister Sato.

Although such key advisers as McNamara, Rusk, Rostow, U. Alexis Johnson, and Treasury Secretary Henry Fowler agreed that Miki and Sato had to show results, they hoped to make Japan "pay" for American concessions on Okinawa and the Bonins. For example, Rostow outlined to the president a "mutually advantageous package deal" involving the return of the Bonins and talks on Okinawa in return for Japan buying more American goods and increasing aid to the Asian Development Bank and United Nations. McNamara urged Johnson to listen politely to Japanese proposals but explain that reversion of Okinawa must be related to larger, "fundamental issues" such as the attitude of Congress and the American public, the extension of the security treaty beyond 1970, retention of U.S. bases in the Ryukyus, a large increase in Japan's purchases of American military equipment, and reducing Japan's balance-of-payment's surplus with the United States. Rostow and McNamara described Okinawa as a lever to lighten the "very heavy political and economic costs of providing security to" the Far East.[54]

On August 31, 1967, the National Security Council endorsed McNamara's view. The president's advisers agreed that the reversion of Okinawa and the Bonins must be linked to Japan carrying a heavier economic and political burden in Southeast Asia, cooperating in efforts to contain China, improving the balance-of-payments problem, buying more U.S. military products, and granting continued base rights on Okinawa.[55]

In mid-September when Japan's foreign and finance ministers arrived in Washington for a joint cabinet meeting, Treasury Secretary Henry Fowler presented them with a plan to reduce Japan's balance-of-payments surplus with the United States by $500 million over the next year. It called on Japan to liberalize trade and investment policies while selling more to Europe and less to the United States. The administration also urged Tokyo to increase funding for the Asian Development Bank and raise its aid to Indonesia and South Vietnam. By linking these issues to the reversion of Okinawa, the administration hoped to reduce pressure on the dollar and commit Japan to a greater regional role.[56]

Recognizing that President Johnson wanted Japan to pay a price for "forward movement" on the Ryukyus and Bonins, Sato tried to demonstrate his allegiance to American policy. Shortly before his November 1967 meeting with Johnson, he toured Southeast Asia and made a symbolic show of visiting Saigon. He hinted that it might be possible for American forces on Okinawa to retain nuclear weapons after the island's return to Japan. The restrictions mandated by the security treaty might be phased in, permitting unfettered use of the Okinawa bases during the Vietnam War. Sato floated these ideas to encourage Johnson to set a date for reversion.[57]

During the Washington summit, Secretary of Defense McNamara, rather than the president, took the lead in pressing Sato to move in the desired directions. He cautioned the prime minister that the balance-of-payments issue had become a domestic political problem, with Americans "restive and unwilling to carry the burden themselves" of defending Japan. With the United States "spilling blood," McNamara wanted to know "why Japan, India, and Western Europe did not believe it important to contribute" more financially and materially to the U.S. effort in Vietnam. If he hoped to avoid trouble, Sato must "work toward a greater political and economic role, and ultimately, a military role in Asia."

After assuring McNamara that most Japanese appreciated the American effort in Vietnam, even if the constitution barred direct assistance, Sato steered the discussion toward Okinawa. The defense chief took a tough line, stating that return of the island was inevitable, but only after Japan agreed to "permit the U.S. to operate in the Ryukyus in ways which might ultimately involve operations requiring nuclear weapons to be placed there and combat operations to be conducted from there." This left Sato pleading for at least a face-saving agreement on the principle of reversion, with a base deal to follow.[58]

Although President Johnson spurned Sato's appeal to specify a tentative date for the return of the Ryukyus, he publicly declared that the islands should be returned "within a few years"—a phrase the Japanese translated as "two or three years." Sato acknowledged that American bases in the Ryukyus "continue to play a vital role in assuring the security of Japan and other free nations in the Far East." Both sides deferred the delicate questions of whether nuclear weapons would be retained on Okinawa and if American bases there would be subject to the same controls as bases in Japan proper. In the interim, both governments agreed to improve living standards on the Ryukyus. Japan promised to try to reduce its balance-of-payments surplus with the United States and boost economic aid to Southeast Asia. Johnson urged Tokyo to assist Saigon in creating an "educational television" system akin to PBS in the United States.[59]

In a gesture designed to help Sato at home—especially given the lack of progress on Okinawa—Johnson agreed to immediate talks to return the Bonin Islands to Japan. Since no Japanese currently lived on these islands, and fewer than 100 American military personnel staffed navigational facilities there, this seemed a simple task. Both sides underestimated the complexity of returning these specks of land to Japan. The American battle monument on Iwo Jima presented an emotional obstacle. Millions of Americans recalled the stirring photograph—and later statue—of marines unfurling the banner as they captured Mount Surabachi. American negotiators proposed returning all the Bonins *except* Iwo Jima, or returning it too, but declaring all of Iwo Jima an American military base to assure preservation of the war memorial. The Japanese protested that this negated the whole point of reversion.

The Americans then suggested that a U.S. flag be maintained on Iwo Jima after the island's return to Japanese control. But under pressure from those who claimed he had not pushed hard enough to recover Okinawa, Sato insisted that the American flag had to go. In June 1968, after months of wrangling, the two sides struck a compromise. Japan agreed that the United States could retain a symbolic bronze flag on Iwo Jima in place of an official cloth flag.[60]

At the end of 1967, the Johnson administration could point to modest improvement in its relations with Japan. Although the export surplus with the United States continued to grow, Tokyo made some efforts to ease balance-of-payment strains. Japan continued to provide token support in Vietnam, deferred its demand for return of Okinawa, and refrained from expanding trade or diplomatic ties with China. Since the Vietnam War was the source of so many problems with Japan, the president and his advisers believed that with victory in sight, better relations were assured.

Walt Rostow articulated the administration's optimism. During a dinner at the British embassy, he compared Lyndon Johnson's decision to make a stand in Vietnam to the "British decision to face World War II after the German invasion of Poland." The "noisy but small" number of domestic critics failed to realize that the American "way of life, our future position in the world, and, in particular, our whole position in Asia" depended on victory in Vietnam. Progress had been slow, Rostow noted, "but it was progress nonetheless."[61]

The Tet offensive unleashed by the Viet Cong in February 1968 shattered both the illusion of military success in Vietnam and the consensus that allowed Johnson to escalate the war. Although Tet cost the Viet Cong dearly, it dramatically altered American opinion. On March 31, the president announced his decision to reduce air attacks against North Vietnam, attempt direct negotiations with the Communist side, and not seek reelection.

The Japanese were as stunned by this news as most Americans were. With what U. Alexis Johnson called a "liberal assist from the American press," the Japanese public interpreted it as a "major reversal of policy and a declaration that [America] was seeking to get out of Vietnam instantly regardless of the consequences. Johnson's decision not to run impressed Japanese as a de facto "resignation to admit a mistake in policy."[62]

Since the Vietnam War had been viewed as a proxy struggle between the United States and China, the offer to negotiate directly with Hanoi aroused suspicion in Tokyo. U. Alexis Johnson reported the belief that Washington might abandon its policy of military containment in Asia and move "towards an accommodation with China, again leaving the Japanese government out on a limb." He assured the Japanese that no one in Washington "favored detente with Peking." Nor would a future president "take such a radical step without including our most important Asian ally."[63]

During the final year of the Johnson administration, Japanese-American relations seemed driven more by chance than design. The crash of an American fighter plane on Kyushu, radiation leaked by a visiting nuclear submarine, a port call by the nuclear-powered aircraft carrier *Enterprise*, the opening of a hospital to treat soldiers wounded in Vietnam, and use of Okinawan air bases for B-52 attacks in Vietnam all became occasions for demonstrations against the war and the American military presence in Japan. North Korea's seizure of the American electronic spy ship *Pueblo* in January 1968 increased Japanese concern about being dragged into regional conflict through its American connection.

These incidents, along with race riots and political violence in the United States and the tortured American effort to begin peace talks with North Vietnam, stimulated renewed doubts among both Japanese Socialists and the LDP about the value of the Pacific alliance. During the spring and summer of 1968, Japan specialists in the Department of State and the Tokyo embassy circulated to President Johnson and his top aides warnings about fissures opening between Japan and the United States.

The Japanese, these diplomats reported, might be "brewing up one of their periodic convulsions reminiscent of 1960." After four years of stability, Sato faced renewed challenges within the LDP, a public tolerant of "extra-legal protests" against the American military presence, and a "coalescing issue involving relations with the U.S.—the Okinawa problem." If momentum to return Okinawa faltered, Japan might move in the direction of a "serious reappraisal of our relationship," perhaps even refusing to extend the security treaty after 1970.[64]

Sato's strategy of cooperation with the United States seemed less attractive now that many influential Japanese had "second thoughts about American staying power in Asia." Trade and payment problems, the Tet offensive, the *Pueblo* incident, racial and social unrest, an "abrupt shift into de-escalation and negotiations with Hanoi," and President Johnson's withdrawal from the presidential race were "cited as evidence of American weakness" and instability. Foreign Minister Miki Takeo—a rival of

Sato—had even called for ending Japan's "excessive dependence" on the United States.

The tensions might subside once Sato solidified his grip within the LDP or was supplanted by a rival. Still, Okinawa remained "one potential" problem that might drive the Japanese "off the reservation." Conservative Nationalists, the Socialists, and anti-war activists might make "common political cause" to demand the island's return and gut the security treaty with the United States. Should the economy deteriorate, the United States pull out of Asia or adopt "protectionism," the "cumulative effect could conceivably be to set Japan again on the introverted, irrational course it followed in the 1930s."[65]

President Johnson and such advisers as Walt Rostow refused to admit they had presided over an erosion of American will, power, and wealth. Yet they understood that Washington could no longer assume the full political and economic burdens of containment in Asia. At the same time, they resented Japanese carping at incidents involving American personnel in Japan, Tokyo's reluctance to share defense burdens, and the doubts voiced about the future value of the American alliance. Instead of criticizing the United States, they wanted Japan to assume its fair share of the costs of containment. Even then, although only implicit in the Johnson administration's final actions, the United States would need to rethink its approaches to Vietnam and China.

Secretary of State Rusk felt compelled to dispel talk of American "weakness" in a meeting with Japan's vice minister of foreign affairs. The United States "is not a sick society," he told a skeptical Ushiba Nobuhiko in June 1968; rather, it had been asked to "carry more of the psychological and political burden than we should." The American people could no longer "accept the role of unilateral policemen" in defending Asian allies. The "key question for them is who else will share these responsibilities."[66]

Prompted by Rostow, President Johnson sent a message along these lines to Tokyo. If "our relationship was to survive in the long run, the Japanese would have to overcome their one-sided view of that relationship." Americans had paid a heavy price defending South Vietnam and garrisoning Asia. It had kept "an arm around the Japanese and held an umbrella over them for a long time." The Japanese government must understand that the time was long overdue for Japan to "contribute to Asian security."[67]

U. Alexis Johnson pushed this theme to audiences in Japan. He criticized Japanese restrictive trade policy, small defense expenditures, and failure to rectify a growing balance-of-payments problem. American bases in Japan and Okinawa, he declared, were vital to Japanese security.

The Japanese government announced its intention to continue the security treaty beyond 1970 but, like the public, remained ambivalent on defense matters. Sato was noncommittal about the post-reversion status of Okinawan military bases, even though return of the island hinged on an acceptable formula. In September 1968, when the Defense Department proposed returning control of several dozen American bases to Japan, Tokyo balked. Supposedly, the self-defense forces lacked funds for their operation. Only Johnson's threat to embarrass Sato by publicizing the refusal to recover the bases led to a settlement.[68]

Richard Nixon's election as president in November 1968 pleased diplomats in Tokyo and Washington. He promised to end the Vietnam War and reexamine policies in Asia through a fresh lens. In fact, the "shocks" that Nixon administered to Japan caused the most dramatic strains in bilateral relations since the end of the Occupation.

12 THE "NIXON SHOCKS"

AND THE TRANSFORMATION

OF JAPANESE-AMERICAN

RELATIONS, 1969–74

IN a somber speech to the Diet in January 1972, Prime Minister Sato declared that "drastic changes in world conditions" during 1971 had "put Japan in a difficult international situation." A sense of "uneasiness and "irritation" were "pervasive among the Japanese people." Given Sato's normal reserve, this had to be counted as a blunt, emotional statement.[1]

What Sato lamented were several shocks—*shokku*, in Japanese— administered by Richard Nixon challenging the strategic and economic relationship that prevailed between the United States and Japan since the Occupation. The American commitment to the containment of China (and, by extension, Vietnam), a strong dollar, and liberal trade had long served as pillars of security and an engine driving Japan's economic growth.

The 1971 jolts culminated a process begun when Johnson capped escalation of the Vietnam War in 1968. Nixon continued the changes by reducing the American military presence in Asia, pulling back from Vietnam, opening ties with China, cutting the dollar's link to gold, and imposing restrictions on imports. His pursuit of a new structure of peace stemmed from the fact that the United States could no longer afford the old structure. When Nixon took office, not only had the Soviets achieved a rough strategic parity with the United States, but the economic policies of European allies and Japan threatened American prosperity. As the trade deficit grew and the dollar weakened, Washington's global influence waned.

Nixon and his advisers used a military lexicon to describe the economic threat to America. In the spring of 1971, Secretary of Commerce Maurice Stans reportedly declared that "the Japanese are still fighting the war. Their immediate intention is to try to dominate the Pacific and then

[210]

perhaps the world." In August, as foreign pressure to redeem dollars for gold increased, Secretary of the Treasury John Connally told Nixon that the government "can't cover our liabilities—we're broke; anyone can topple us." Nixon later described his "New Economic Policy" of 1971 partly as an effort to "stick it to the Japanese."[2]

In pursuing détente with the Soviet Union and China, the United States acknowledged its inability to shoulder the costs of containment in both Europe and Asia. The so-called Nixon Doctrine, the return of Okinawa to Japan, strategic arms control, the liquidation of the war in Vietnam, import restrictions, and the new economic policy were all attempts to assure an orderly transition as the United States entered a period of relative decline and reduced its military presence in Asia.

The Nixon Administration and Japan

Throughout nearly six years in office, Richard M. Nixon centralized the foreign policy apparatus under his control. Presidential aides directed most initiatives and none wielded more authority than National Security Adviser Henry A. Kissinger. Like Nixon, Kissinger held a dim view of diplomats and usually ignored Secretary of State William Rogers. As Undersecretary for Political Affairs, U. Alexis Johnson remarked, the State Department moved from "the center of things" to the periphery. Although Johnson tried "to shield the Department from the pummelling that rained down upon it" from the White House, Kissinger, with Nixon's encouragement, "certainly enjoyed putting the boot in State whenever possible."[3]

As vice president and then as a business representative of Pepsi-Cola and other multinational firms during the 1960s, Nixon enjoyed a comfortable relationship with Japanese officials. He visited Tokyo frequently and felt confident of his ability to cooperate with LDP leaders. In an article entitled "Asia After Vietnam" published in the October 1967 issue of *Foreign Affairs*, Nixon stressed the importance of America's Asian allies doing more to defend themselves against "China's ambitions." Repeating a view expressed during his 1954 visit to Tokyo, Nixon lamented Japan's constitutional restraints on rearmament and urged Tokyo to behave like a great power. This included acquiring nuclear weapons.[4]

In his initial talks with the NSC staff, the new president touched on the need to reassess Japan policy. He recalled the anti-treaty crisis of 1960 and described Okinawa as a powder keg that might explode at any time. He revealed a desire to return control of the Ryukyus to Japan under favorable terms in order to retain base rights on Okinawa. As one NSC staffer put it, Nixon understood the Americans had to "make the case" the Japanese would accept.[5]

Kissinger shared Nixon's views on Okinawa, but did not see Japan as critical to U.S. security. He found Japanese diplomats difficult to relate to, complaining that they were "not conceptual," lacked long-term vision, and made "decisions by consensus." They were, he mocked, "little Sony sales-man." Chinese leaders such as Zhou Enlai fascinated Kissinger, but Japan-ese officials seemed "prosaic, obtuse, unworthy of his sustained attention." Worst of all, Kissinger complained, "every time the Japanese ambassador has me to lunch he serves Wiener schnitzel."

Because Kissinger paid relatively less attention to Japan, the State Department enjoyed more influence over policy than it did with other major nations. As one diplomat observed, Kissinger preferred not to grap-ple with a problem "until there is a crisis." He dealt with Okinawa because Nixon considered it a priority, but let career diplomats negotiate the details of reversion. Most Japan policy issues, especially economic ones, bored or confused him.[6]

Kissinger attributed initial missteps in dealing with Japan to the fact that "neither I nor my colleagues possessed a very subtle grasp of Japanese culture and psychology." This caused "some unnecessary shocks" to Japanese sensibilities. Another problem was that international economics had not been his "central field of study." Once he learned that "key eco-nomic policy decisions are not technical but political," he claimed to have "built an extraordinarily close relationship" with Japan.[7]

Largely because of Nixon's and Kissinger's indifference to economic problems, the administration ignored emerging monetary and trade prob-lems. Roger Morris, a member of the NSC staff, recalled that of more than 140 National Security Study Memoranda (NSSMs presented options for presidential consideration) prepared during the first three years of the Nixon administration, only one dealt with international monetary policy and three or four with other economic questions. Economic policy, Morris surmised, "enjoyed equal rank with U.S. policy in Haiti" but less than Peru. Kissinger's "profound lack of knowledge and interest in economics," Morris contends, led him to view trade matters as "low policy" unworthy of attention. Another NSC staff member compared discussing economics with Kissinger to discussing military strategy with the pope. Kissinger rec-ognized that several departments and agencies had authority over trade and monetary matters. With Nixon's backing, he enjoyed near monopoly control over security issues. Jousting with the Treasury, Commerce, and Agriculture departments and the Federal Reserve would likely overextend his power.

Undersecretary of the Treasury Paul Volcker recognized this early on. Instructed to report regularly on international monetary policy to Kissinger (rather than to the secretary of the treasury), he ignored the order. No one complained since "papers on the intricacies of international monetary affairs ended up at the bottom of Kissinger's in-tray, assuming they ever got that far."

Nixon shared what Roger Morris called Kissinger's "parochial" out-look on foreign economic policy. Both men measured power by a military rather than an economic calculus—and by that assessment, Japan hardly merited the rank of great power. By delegating trade and monetary issues to subordinates, or ignoring them entirely, they made a solution to emerging problems all the more difficult.[8]

Okinawa, the Nixon Doctrine, and Textiles

In January 1969, the NSC began a review of relations with Japan. Focusing on Okinawa, it concluded that a violent incident on the island could unhinge security relations with Japan and endanger the U.S. defense position in the Pacific. Japanese public and political opinion demanded reversion of the Ryukyus and control over remaining American bases. In March 1969, Prime Minister Sato told the Diet he would make the return of Okinawa free of nuclear weapons his first order of business with the new administration.

In Washington, only the Joint Chiefs of Staff voiced serious opposition to reversion. They "considered our Okinawa bases to be of inestimable value," not just for current operation in Indochina, "but for our whole strategic position in the Pacific." Yet, even the Joint Chiefs recognized the need to return the Ryukyus. By talking tough, they hoped to force Nixon and the Japanese to meet their demands. These included use of Okinawa bases for combat operations in Vietnam, a right to reintroduce nuclear weapons to Okinawa in an emergency, and Japan's acknowledgment that under the security treaty it had a stake in the security of Taiwan and South Korea.[9]

Nixon and Kissinger heeded the Joint Chiefs' call, but worried that unless Washington moved quickly on Okinawa, Japan might not extend the security treaty beyond 1970. Kissinger ordered plans prepared for reversion on terms favored by Japan. According to NSC staffers Morton Halperin and Roger Morris, both the president and his national security adviser disliked the Nuclear Non-Proliferation Treaty signed by Lyndon Johnson and thought it inevitable that countries such as Israel and Japan should develop their own atomic arsenals. In the case of Japan, this would moot the issue of nuclear storage on Okinawa and force Tokyo to assume greater responsibility for its own and regional defense. In March 1969, the NSC staff reported to Kissinger and Nixon that because "pressures in Japan for reversion [of Okinawa] were now unstoppable," the risks of maintaining the status quo far "outweighed the military cost of having somewhat less flexibility in operating the Okinawa bases under Japanese sovereignty." A refusal to accept Japanese demands might result in "losing the bases altogether," both in the Ryukyus and Japan.[10]

The Joint Chiefs hoped to link Okinawa reversion to a promise from Japan that American forces on the island were free to mount operations in defense of South Korea, Taiwan, and Vietnam. Undersecretary of State Johnson cautioned the Joint Chiefs that "it was an illusion to think we would have any freedom of action whatever, on Japan or Okinawa, if the local population was hostile to us no matter what 'fine print' was included in our agreements."

On April 30, 1969, Nixon settled on a formula that combined the Pentagon and NSC approaches. The United States would return Okinawa if the Japanese government granted general approval for American forces based there and in Japan proper to carry out regional defense. In NSDM 13, Nixon resolved he was "prepared to consider, at the final stages of the negotiations, the withdrawal of [nuclear] weapons while maintaining emergency storage and transit rights, if other elements of the agreement were satisfactory."[11]

On June 3, 1969, Hedrick Smith reported in the *New York Times* that Nixon had decided to return Okinawa and withdraw nuclear weapons from American bases there. Nevertheless, Prime Minister Sato hesitated to meet with Nixon without assurance that Okinawa would be returned without nuclear weapons. To move negotiations forward, NSC staff member Morton Halperin met informally with a Japanese diplomat and hinted broadly that if Sato came to Washington, he would not be disappointed.[12]

Japanese-American negotiations on Okinawa began in earnest in June 1969 and continued through the Nixon–Sato summit that November. Ambassador Armin H. Meyer, assisted by State Department Japan specialists Richard Sneider and David Osborn, met regularly in Tokyo with the staff of the foreign ministry. Secretary of State William Rogers and Undersecretary U. Alexis Johnson conferred several times with Japanese Foreign Minister Aiichi Kichi. Having set the parameters, Kissinger and the NSC staff allowed the State Department to work out the details concerning issues such as the future of Voice of America transmitters on the island, the status of American-owned businesses, and the amount Japan should pay for roads and other facilities built by the United States.[13]

Essentially, the United States wanted a broad measure of operational control over bases on Okinawa, but would accept limits to secure this. Japan desired the restoration of sovereignty over Okinawa and the right to impose conditions on use of American bases. In return for the withdrawal of nuclear weapons, Tokyo would grant Washington latitude to use the Okinawa bases for operations in Vietnam, Korea, or Taiwan.

To facilitate compromise, U. Alexis Johnson suggested that Nixon and Sato conclude their upcoming summit with a joint communiqué announcing the return of Okinawa by 1972 with American bases on the island subject to the terms of the United States–Japan Security Treaty that barred storage of nuclear weapons on Japanese soil without prior approval. To placate the Joint Chiefs, Sato would announce that the security of South Korea was "essential" to Japan and that of Taiwan "important." If, at the time Okinawa reverted to Japan, the Vietnam War continued, Tokyo agreed "reversion would be accomplished without affecting the United States' efforts to assure the South Vietnamese people the opportunity to determine their own political future without outside interference." In effect, U.S. forces could continue combat operations.

In addition to the formal communiqué, Sato would deliver a speech—prepared in consultation with Johnson—declaring that if the United States required Japanese bases to meet an armed attack on Korea, the Japanese government "would decide its position positively and promptly." The prime minister would also promise that Japan would take a "positive attitude" toward the use of bases to defend Taiwan. Although not legally binding, these assurances went well beyond previous commitments to regional security.[14]

As diplomats worked on the details of the Okinawa deal, Nixon took a lengthy trip though Asia, timed to coincide with the Pacific touchdown of the Apollo 12 lunar mission. On July 25, at a press briefing in Guam, the president issued a rambling statement on future security policy that his aides soon dubbed the "Nixon Doctrine." The president drew attention to the American "role in Asia and the Pacific after the end of the war in Vietnam." Warning against isolation, he pledged to honor existing security pacts with Asian nations and promised to provide material support to resist aggression. But American ground troops would not be on call to fight another Vietnam-type war. The United States would resist nuclear intimidation by the Soviet Union or China, but Asian nations would have primary responsibility for their own defense. As the president explained sometime later, the "biggest reason for staying on in Vietnam" as long as he did "was Japan." It and other Asian allies had to be reassured that the "Nixon doctrine is not a way for us to get out of Asia, but a way for us to stay in."[15]

The president and Congress shared the belief that America's allies in both Europe and Asia must carry a larger share of the common defense burden. As Japan's trade surplus increased, American industries clamored for protection against allegedly unfair foreign competition. In the late 1960s the business press coined the pejorative term "Japan, Inc." to describe government–industry collusion to promote exports and close domestics markets to foreign competition.

Kissinger's economic adviser, C. Fred Bergsten, alerted him to the danger of rival bureaucrats seizing the protectionist banner and limiting NSC influence. To prevent this, Kissinger forwarded to Nixon a proposal by Bergsten to systematically press Japan to liberalize foreign investment rules, restrain textile exports, and allow more imports. The president returned Kissinger's memorandum with the comment: "capital liberalization is not important to us politically. We have to get something on textiles."[16]

For Nixon, textiles were a domestic political issue, not an international economic one. As a candidate in August 1968, he promised a group of textile executives that, if elected, he would "take the steps necessary to extend the concept of international trade agreements [i.e., quotas]" to synthetic fibers, as had been done with cotton goods. In fact, Japanese synthetics had a small impact. Textile and apparel imports from Japan constituted 1 percent of American textile production and only 4 percent of total Japanese textile output. Most inexpensive imports came from other Asian producers.

In 1969, about 2.5 million Americans worked in the textile and apparel industries, with plants located heavily in the South. This resonated with

Nixon's "southern strategy" to win nomination in 1968. To undermine the appeal of California governor Ronald Reagan among southern Republicans, Nixon courted Senator Strom Thurmond of South Carolina. Thurmond proved a key ally at the nominating convention and introduced candidate Nixon to his own contacts among textile producers. In exchange for his pledge to limit imports, the American Textile Manufacturers Institute contributed money to Nixon's election fund and promised future donations once he delivered. During the 1968 campaign, Nixon blamed Democrats for not protecting the industry against unfair competition.[17]

Textiles were only one of several products, including shoes, steel, and electronics, that faced stiff challenges from Europe and Asia. Although Nixon had generally supported free trade, following his election he singled out the textile industry as facing a "special problem which has caused great distress" to both producers and wage earners. He demanded that Japan accept "voluntary restraints" on its synthetic exports, similar to the agreement limiting cotton goods. Nixon favored voluntary action to preclude having Congress set quotas he could neither control nor take credit for. Arkansas Democrat Wilbur Mills, the powerful head of the Ways and Means Committee and a presidential aspirant, threatened to push a quota bill through Congress unless Nixon acted quickly.[18]

In March 1969, Nixon designated Maurice Stans, his former campaign finance director and now Secretary of Commerce, to lead textile negotiations. Stans sought to fulfill the pledge to the textile industry and boost his own standing in the administration by securing a deal. He and his aides believed that success required keeping the "softies" in the State Department out of negotiations. As one observer put it, Stans decided to visit Japan to "lay down the law" and demand "unconditional surrender."[19]

Not surprisingly, he received a chilly reception in Tokyo in May 1969. Foreign ministry officials preferred to delay textile talks until settling the Okinawa question. Textile manufacturers and their allies in MITI (the powerful Ministry of International Trade and Industry) ridiculed the notion that Japan's 1 percent share of the U.S. synthetic fiber market justified quotas. Newspapers and public opinion polls called on the Japanese government to end its reflexive subordination to the United States and resist calls for voluntary trade restraints. Stans left Tokyo complaining of rude treatment. His hosts criticized his vulgarity.[20]

During the next several months, MITI and Commerce Department working groups could not even agree on a formula for measuring the impact of Japanese textile exports. Stans accused the Japanese of bad faith and on October 2 American negotiators handed them an aide memoir drafted in the Commerce Department, but reflecting the views of American textile producers. It proposed an export restraint formula with "comprehensive ceilings," sublimits in different product categories, a five-year term, and no annual increases. The Japanese rejected this, but offered to begin multilateral talks in Geneva under GATT rules. Stans insisted on bilateral talks in Geneva. Anxious to avoid a breakdown on the eve of the

Nixon–Sato meeting, Tokyo agreed to start talks in Geneva on November 17, just before the Washington summit.[21]

Kissinger hoped to avoid involvement in the "low policy" issue of textile quotas. However, when Nixon told him "in no uncertain terms that he meant to have a textile agreement and that as a Presidential Assistant I was to contribute to the objective," he relented. Kissinger played a key role in textile negotiations through his contacts with a private emissary designated by Prime Minister Sato. The Japanese go-between (whom Kissinger called "Mr. Yoshida" but who later revealed himself to be Professsor Wakaizumi Kei, an academic friend of Sato) worked with Kissinger to solve textile and nuclear issues before Nixon and Sato met.

In Kabuki theater, special actors called *kuroko* (black veils) move across the stage arranging scenery and assisting other performers. Although visible, their black robes render them "unseen" by the audience. In the Japanese political world, *kuroko* refers to behind-the-scene intermediaries who arrange deals. In the Okinawa and textile negotiations, Japanese practice, Kissinger's own penchant for using a "back channel," and Nixon's dread of face-to-face argument coincided.

The intermediaries began serious talks in September 1969. Kissinger presented the Commerce Department plan to "Yoshida" and stressed that an agreement must follow it closely. "Yoshida" indicated that Sato would accept these terms if Nixon promised the non-nuclear return of Okinawa. Kissinger took to the idea of sorting out the textile and Okinawa issues through a brokered compromise. Nixon hated face-to-face bargaining and would appreciate his aide clinching the deal before Sato came to Washington. Kissinger hoped this would free him to focus on the "high policy" issues worthy of attention. Nixon endorsed the approach, telling Kissinger, "Let's try to get it done and not fool around with the State Department."[22]

In the three months before Sato's visit, Kissinger and "Yoshida" thrashed out terms for resolving the Okinawa and textile issues. While American officials made no secret that they intended to return the Ryukyus, they stressed that the terms of reversion depended on progress in related talks. As Kissinger put it, Nixon could resolve the nuclear question to Japan's satisfaction once Japan resolved the textile question to his.

Although use of the "black veil" had potential advantages—such as allowing each side to float trial balloons without fear of embarrassment—Kissinger lacked technical knowledge about textiles and served only as a conduit for the Commerce Department. "Yoshida" (and Sato) were so anxious to achieve a breakthrough on Okinawa—and avoid accusations that they sold out the textile industry to do so—that they accepted the American formula without consulting or informing Japanese manufacturers and government ministries whose cooperation was required for implementing the plan.

The deal unraveled before it was sealed. On November 17, two days before the prime minister arrived in Washington, "Yoshida" placed what Kissinger described as a "frantic phone call." Sato, he explained, could not announce an export restraint deal at the summit. He would implement the agreement, but for political reasons the settlement must appear to emerge later from the textile talks in Geneva or from negotiations among diplomats in Washington.[23]

Compared to textiles, talks on Okinawa went smoothly. "Yoshida" and Kissinger agreed that Nixon would offer to withdraw nuclear weapons from Okinawa provided they could be reintroduced in an emergency. Sato would reject this, but agree that in an emergency the United States could "raise the question" of reintroduction. Nixon would "accept Sato's compromise," meeting both sides' needs. Nixon still insisted that Sato sign a secret agreement on emergency reintroduction of nuclear weapons.[24]

The Nixon–Sato Summit

Nixon, a friend of Sato's older brother, Kishi Nobusuke, got on well with the visiting prime minister. With the main points already settled, the two leaders could share credit for resolving the status of Okinawa. Sato promised to extend the security treaty for a "considerably long period" beyond 1970 and noted that the return of Okinawa would dispose Japanese opinion toward playing a greater security role in the Pacific. To facilitate high-level contact, they agreed to install a "hot line" between Tokyo and Washington.

Nixon offered to return Okinawa to Japan by 1972. Technical negotiations on legal, financial, and military questions for implementing the return would begin at once. (A technical agreement was signed on June 17, 1971; the Senate confirmed the treaty in November; reversion occurred on May 15, 1972.) The United States would retain military bases in the Ryukyus "without detriment to the security of the Far East" or interference with the ability of the United States to defend the "countries of the Far East including Japan." Nixon pledged to recognize the "particular sentiment of the Japanese people against nuclear weapons," but reserved the right to request their reintroduction to Okinawa in an emergency. Wakaizumi Kei, an aide to Sato and the prime minister's back channel to Kissinger, later confirmed that Sato had signed a document authorizing the reintroduction of nuclear weapons into Okinawa in an emergency.

Richard Sneider, a State Department Japan specialist and former NSC staff member then serving as Deputy Chief of Mission in Tokyo, recalled that Nixon linked his offer to remove American nuclear weapons from Okinawa with a broad hint to Sato that the United States would "understand" if Japan decided to "go nuclear." The president's views echoed remarks Kissinger made to his staff the previous spring. The State Department interpreter present at the meeting found this discussion so troubling that he notified his senior colleagues about what Nixon said. Sneider later told Seymour Hersh that Nixon and Kissinger "thought they were being cute" by encouraging a change from American to Japanese nuclear weapons on Okinawa.

Sato, who in 1967 codified Japan's "Three Non-Nuclear Principles (Japan would not manufacture, possess, or introduce to its territory nuclear weapons—but would rely on the U.S. nuclear deterrent to counter "international nuclear threats"), reported that Nixon "confused" him. To "clean up the mess," career diplomats "quietly sabotaged" the gambit by telling the Japanese "they'd misunderstood what Nixon and Kissinger were saying." Sato probably understood the president's intent, since shortly after the summit he signed the Nuclear Non-Proliferation Treaty that committed Tokyo *not* to develop nuclear weapons. The real "misunderstanding" between the leaders related to textiles.[25]

Roger Morris reports that as formal talks concluded, "Nixon asked Sato to meet him and Kissinger alone in an anteroom of the Oval Office." The president raised a "necessary private agreement" related "informally" to Okinawa reversion. Nixon explained that the Pentagon, Congress, and other groups considered his return of Okinawa a "give-away." As compensation, he asked Sato to affirm the textile limits informally agreed to by his go-between.

Although one NSC staff member characterized Sato's response as "a bit Delphic" (something like "I will do my best to solve the problem"), Kissinger and Nixon believed he pledged to do so. Sato, Kissinger insisted, "took full responsibility," saying "it was his personal credo and vow to keep his word" and "committed his sincerity and all his efforts" to carry out the textile agreement. Nixon "said that was good enough for him," and shook Sato's hand.[26]

As planned, Sato delivered a speech to the National Press Club in which he pledged that Japan would respond "promptly and positively" to an American request to utilize Okinawa bases for the defense of South Korea and Taiwan. The prime minister spoke of a "New Pacific Age" with the "two great nations across the Pacific," of quite different ethnic and historical backgrounds, on "the verge of starting a great historical experiment in working together for a new order in the world." This coincided with Nixon's call for Asian allies to shoulder more responsibility for regional security. Few Americans recognized that most Asians cringed whenever a Japanese leader spoke of a "new order" in the Pacific. China charged that "American imperialists" and "Japanese reactionaries" had hatched "a new war plot."[27]

Sato expressed "deep gratitude" to Nixon for his "magnanimous" decision returning Okinawa. The president described the agreement as heralding "a new era . . . between the United States and Japan, in our relations not only bilaterally in the Pacific but in the world." Nixon told his cabinet to leak word that his predecessors could not have achieved the Okinawa deal because they "didn't have the confidence of the people or the world leaders." This should give "liberals something to think about."

In December 1969, proclaiming he had finally ended the era of foreign occupation of Japanese soil, Sato parlayed the Okinawa agreement into victory in a snap election to the Diet's lower house in which Liberal

Democrats and allied independents won 303 of 486 seats. Nixon, too, boasted in a Foreign Policy Report of February 1970 that the Okinawa settlement was "among the most important decisions I have taken as president." In a private discussion with members of Congress, Nixon predicted that Japan had finally shed its reluctance to involve itself in world affairs and he "wouldn't be surprised if in five years we didn't have to restrain them."[28]

The Textile Trap

Despite apparent success, Nixon grew increasingly bitter toward Japan during the first months of 1970. His discomfort reflected frustration with Sato's failure to implement the textile settlement. Kissinger and "Yoshida," with Sato's subsequent approval, had agreed that Japan would restrain exports of synthetics for a five-year period. Following the December 1969 Diet election, American and Japanese textile delegations in Geneva were supposed to "negotiate" an agreement along Commerce Department guidelines. This would shield Sato from charges that he sold out textile interests to recover Okinawa. Sato insisted that the official record of the Washington summit not mention textiles, but "Yoshida" assured Kissinger that Sato "would honor the understanding." U. Alexis Johnson (in Washington) and American textile negotiators (in Geneva) would propose export controls that actually exceeded the Commerce Department formula. The Japanese would balk. The Americans would then introduce the Commerce Department terms that the Japanese would formally accept.

The problem with this "Kabuki Play," as Kissinger called it, was that Sato neglected to share the script with key Japanese players, including the ministries of finance, international trade, and foreign affairs, and the textile industry. When U. Alexis Johnson and American negotiators in Geneva (who also knew little of the deal and were upset by the "extreme" American terms) presented the initial harsh demands, they were promptly rebuffed. But then so were the supposedly acceptable fallback provisions. When Johnson probed for an explanation, Ambassador Shimoda in Washington, MITI Minister Ohira Masayoshi, and Japanese textile manufacturers all denied knowledge of a deal.

In January 1970, in a cabinet shuffle, Sato replaced his LDP rival Ohira with an ally, Miyazawa Kiichi. Nixon and Kissinger hoped this would solve the problem. But Sato kept Miyazawa in the dark and the new MITI chief announced that until Washington provided evidence of injury caused to America by Japanese textiles, the two sides had nothing to discuss. With the Nixon–Sato deal in tatters, Japanese and American negotiators exchanged charges of duplicity. Senator Strom Thurmond even suggested that Congress delay the return of Okinawa until Japan met American demands.[29]

Japanese trade and foreign office officials not directly concerned with textiles feared the deterioration of relations or even a trade war if Congress passed quota legislation. To avert this, in March 1970, Tokyo indicated a willingness to impose selective controls on textile exports in cases where the U.S. Tariff Commission (rather than GATT) documented injury.

Washington responded cautiously. Pepsi-Cola chairman David Kendall, a friend of Nixon's and leader of a free trade lobbying group, visited Tokyo and floated a plan resembling Japan's recent offer. Treasury Secretary David Kennedy also spoke with Sato in Tokyo about the importance of reaching an agreement. The prime minister "apologized for placing President Nixon in a difficult position," but added that it was "difficult for him to control the situation." Ambassador Shimoda in Washington then suggested a one-year deal along the lines proposed by Kendall with future export levels to be negotiated after tempers cooled. Nixon seemed interested until Maurice Stans denounced the plan as too weak. The Commerce Secretary then announced that the administration had reached the "end of the line" and would tolerate no more "arrogance" from Tokyo. Unless Japan accepted American demands, Nixon would support a tough quota bill in Congress.[30]

On cue, House Ways and Means Committee Chair Wilbur Mills introduced a quota bill on April 13. It called for restrictions on both textiles and footwear tied to 1967–68 import levels. Quota increases were subject to growth in domestic sales. The law exempted from these limits countries that negotiated voluntary restraint agreements with the United States. Introduction of the bill opened the flood gates for proposals to impose quotas on a wide range of goods from Japan, Hong Kong, Taiwan, and South Korea.

Nixon's anger with Japan surfaced indirectly on April 27, 1970, three days before the U.S. invasion of Cambodia. Reflecting on recent accomplishments, Nixon told Kissinger that "we have been praised for all the wrong things." Nearly everyone applauded the Okinawa agreement, efforts to control nuclear and chemical weapons, and the Nixon Doctrine. But now that he was "finally doing the right thing" (attacking North Vietnamese and Viet Cong strongholds in Cambodia), he anticipated nothing but criticism.[31]

Despite their posturing, neither Mills nor Nixon favored action by Congress. They hoped that the threat of legislation would prompt "voluntary" compliance, but feared loss of control in case Congress interceded. Each wanted to take sole credit for helping American industry. For his part, Stans feared that congressional action would diminish his value to Nixon.

Stans warned Kissinger and Nixon that Japan presented a comprehensive economic challenge. Textiles only exemplified the fact that since the cold war began "overriding weight . . . has been given in our policy formulation to geo-political and military factors to the subordination of economic/financial considerations." Japanese industry prospered because of a "complex set of unwritten government-business-banking relationships which determine the direction and pace of Japanese trade and investment." Stans urged action to force Japan to change or for America to act similarly.[32]

Even while condemning Japanese practices, Stans maneuvered to bring Japan back to the bargaining table. He dispatched his own "black veil," business consultant Ralph Reid, who had worked closely with Miyazawa during the Occupation, to tell the MITI minister that he would accept a short-term compromise. A hopeful Miyazawa returned to Washington on June 22, 1970.

In a misguided show of intimacy, Stans invited Miyazawa to negotiate in his Watergate apartment whose walls were decorated with big-game trophies shot on safari. Like many Japanese, Miyazawa considered dead animals and those who handled them ritually unclean. The mood deteriorated when Stans served lunch under the maw of mounted lions and wildebeests.[33]

Instead of a one-year plan Reid had spoken of, Stans proposed a strict five-year export limit. Miyazawa decided the two sides were operating "on different wavelengths." Although Kissinger, U. Alexis Johnson, and other "moderates" proposed compromise formulas, Stans would have none of it. He insisted on a multiyear scheme with rigid triggers and subceilings. On Miyazawa's third day in Washington, Stans embarrassed the envoy further by pulling a document out of his pocket that he called the "Sato memo" of November 1969. How, he demanded to know, could Miyazawa defy his prime minister's pledge. Miyazawa retorted that since no such agreement existed, Stans had cited a forgery. When Stans dragged U. Alexis Johnson into the fray, Miyazawa asked if he "believed there was . . . a Prime Minister's Memo." Johnson knew Sato had agreed to something like Stans's document, but realized Miyazawa knew nothing of it. To spare the envoy further humiliation, Johnson denied knowing that such a document existed. Miyazawa then fled Washington and chances for a negotiated solution seemed dead.[34]

The Japanese press described the impasse as a victory. The *Asahi Shimbun* editorialized on June 26 that the breakdown of talks "turned out to be the first instance in which Japan rejected a U.S. demand, and could be considered the first example of 'independent foreign policy' in the postwar Japanese history of economic diplomacy." It urged Sato to build on this "independent posture" as the "cornerstone of its economic diplomacy of the 1970s."[35]

Nixon responded by sending Stans before the House Ways and Means Committee to endorse Mills's quota bill. By the time the committee completed a draft in August, the proposed law reduced imports of synthetic textiles 40 percent below the 1969 level—unless voluntary agreements were negotiated before it took effect. As the Japanese pondered this threat, American officials demanded that Japan liberalize regulations on imports of foreign capital and products. To make a point, the government imposed a limit on Japanese television imports pending an inquiry into alleged violations of American anti-dumping laws.[36]

In September, Nixon's chief domestic adviser, John Ehrlichman, accompanied George Shultz, head of the Office of Management and Budget, to

Tokyo for consultations with Japanese officials on a variety of economic issues. Although their talks with Miyazawa and others did not focus on textiles, the MITI minister was "super critical of Stans" and insisted that he not play "any further effective role" in the negotiations. Sato also passed the word that he wanted to meet personally with Nixon. The president replaced Stans as textile negotiator with White House aide Peter Flanigan and agreed to meet Sato at the end of October. Although Nixon kept open negotiating channels, his view of Japan grew more critical. At this time, a "high American" official, widely believed to be the president, told journalists that the United States–Japan Security Treaty was designed, in part, to "police Japan against turning communist or returning to militarism."[37]

Before the meeting with Sato, Flanigan redrafted the American position on import restraints and passed it to Sato via a new Japanese intermediary who had hooked up with Kissinger. The plan envisioned a three-year ceiling on twenty textile categories (based on 1968–69 export levels) with no quota shifting among categories. Export levels could be raised if the market grew. Kissinger described this as the administration's best and final offer. With no agreement, Nixon would push for passage of Mills's bill.[38]

Nixon and Sato, with Kissinger, Foreign Minister Aiichi Kichi, and Ambassador Ushiba Nobuhiko present for parts of the discussion, conferred on October 24. They covered a variety of topics, including Southeast Asia, the Nixon Doctrine, Okinawa, environmental pollution, economic relations, and China (Nixon insisted he contemplated no change in policy and would keep Tokyo "fully informed") before turning to textiles. When Sato broached the subject, Nixon remarked that the issue had been settled the year before. Their agreement only remained to be implemented.

Sato apologized for the delay and restated a desire to settle the dispute. Kissinger then pulled the Flanigan proposal out of his pocket and asked Sato if the terms were acceptable. The prime minister agreed to all the major points, asking Nixon how soon he wanted to finalize a settlement. The president "replied it would be nice if the issue was resolved before the November 3 congressional election." When Kissinger went over the draft with Sato, the prime minister's aides voiced some technical objections. Sato pointed to the document and said, "This is what I wanted. This is fine, leave it as it is." Accordingly, the joint communiqué implied that a textile agreement was imminent.[39]

Although Sato must have understood exactly what he agreed to, he again refused to confide in cabinet or industry representatives. When Sato met with Japanese textile producers on returning from Washington, they spoke so vehemently against voluntary controls that he declined to admit that he had twice promised Nixon he would impose them. Flanigan then received a Japanese plan that improved on previous offers, but fell short of Sato's promise.[40]

The deadlock spurred House passage of Mills's quota bill by a vote of 215–65 on November 19, 1970. When opposition arose in the Senate, Nixon threatened to call Congress into special session to act. However, by the

Christmas recess, Senate opponents effectively killed the textile bill by attaching it to a controversial welfare reform package.

Despite legislative failure, the Japanese foreign ministry—which, unlike MITI, favored compromise—intervened. In December, Ambassador Ushiba and Flanigan drafted a compromise plan. But just as a settlement appeared possible, Nixon retreated, concerned that American textile producers would denounce him. In January 1971, he renewed demands that Tokyo accept stringent export limits.[41]

On March 8, as Nixon muttered darkly about "the Jap betrayal," representatives of the Japanese textile industry announced that they and Wilbur Mills had agreed on a three-year voluntary export restraint program that precluded any need for a government-to-government agreement. Mills told Flanigan that he thought the president would support the private deal since it got both of them off the hook of the quota bill they secretly opposed. But when the *Washington Post* and the *New York Times* praised Mills for "an achievement on a grand scale" that no one else had the "mix of talent, outlook, and power" to achieve, and after American textile spokesmen attacked the deal as too lax, Nixon reacted with fury.

Sato had not only failed to deliver on his promise, but had rewarded Nixon's Democratic rival. On March 11, the president denounced the Japanese industry plan as lacking "the terms essential to the United States." Japan, he informed Sato, must either negotiate with the administration or face quota legislation. To retrieve the initiative, Nixon named a new negotiating team, including Peter Peterson as adviser on international economic affairs and former Secretary of the Treasury David Kennedy as textile negotiator.[42]

By this time, the textile impasse merged with the Okinawa issue and the Senate's desire to reassert treaty power. The draft agreement to return the Ryukyus was nearly complete in February 1971 when Foreign Relations Committee Chairman J. William Fulbright notified Secretary of State William Rogers that any settlement must be "submitted in the form of a treaty" to the Senate. Since the administration had intended to seek some form of congressional approval, Rogers replied positively to Fulbright on March 10.

American journalists and Japanese officials mistook this as a ploy to pressure Tokyo on textiles. Senator Strom Thurmond made the linkage explicit in a speech delivered on June 16, 1971, the day before the signing of the Okinawa treaty. He complained that Japan was "asking a big favor" on Okinawa but offered nothing on textiles. Arguing that the issues were "interrelated," he demanded a quid pro quo. Although not unhappy that Tokyo thought he encouraged Thurmond, the president kept the issues separate.[43]

Nixon's rejection of the Japanese industry plan initiated the most difficult period in bilateral relations since the end of the Occupation. To salvage a deal with Nixon, Sato reshuffled his cabinet early in July. He named two LDP faction leaders who hoped to succeed him, Fukuda Takeo and Tanaka

Kakuei, as heads of the foreign ministry and ministry of international trade and industry, respectively, and urged them to work for a solution. But just as they assumed their posts, Nixon delivered twin shocks—his July 15 announcement of a planned visit to China followed by his August 15 decision to cut the dollar loose from gold, impose an import surcharge, and force the upward valuation of the yen. He also threatened to impose textile quotas under the terms of the Trading with the Enemy Act.

The China Shock and Triangular Diplomacy

Asakai Koichiro, Japan's ambassador in Washington during the 1950s and early 1960s often spoke of a recurring dream. He imagined waking to news that the United States abruptly recognized China without informing Japan. This scenario, dismissed by American officials as a fantasy, became known in diplomatic circles as "Asakai's Nightmare." The events of July 15, 1971, made him seem a visionary. As Undersecretary of State U. Alexis Johnson noted, Kissinger's "passion for secrecy, combined with his contempt for the [State] Department and disdain for the Japanese, threw a devastating wrench into our relations with Japan on the question of China."

Nixon's and Kissinger's interest in opening a dialogue with China reflected deeper changes in the cold war. On taking office, both men recognized that the Soviet Union had or would soon achieve a rough nuclear parity with the United States. Instead of a costly and probably futile effort to restore superiority, they sought to moderate Soviet behavior through economic and political incentives broadly labeled "détente." These included negotiated limits on strategic weapons, increased trade and technology transfer, and recognition that the Soviet Union had legitimate global interests.

As Washington cultivated a more cooperative relationship with Moscow, it found that the political and economic policies of its allies often clashed with American interests. Tension within the NATO and Pacific alliances coincided with the demise of the Sino-Soviet bloc. In March 1969, the protracted war of words between Moscow and Beijing escalated into a series of border skirmishes. This schism created an opportunity for the United States to play off the Communist rivals against each other, assuming Washington had some leverage with the People's Republic of China. Following the border clashes, Nixon and Kissinger concluded that improved ties with China might constrain Soviet behavior and impel both rivals to cooperate with the United States or risk isolation.

Only a few months after taking office, Nixon urged Kissinger to "plant that idea" as a way to prod Moscow. "I think that while Gromyko is in the country would be a very good time to have another move toward China made," he told Kissinger in September 1969. With the United States in a balancing position, Kissinger later remarked, "each communist power [had] a stake in better relations with us." The leverage gained through this triangular diplomacy with Moscow and Beijing might also hasten an end to the Vietnam War (through Soviet or Chinese pressure on North Vietnam), provide Washington with greater influence over Japan, and facilitate an orderly reduction of U.S. military power in Asia.

Just as fear of Chinese expansion initially prompted American intervention in Vietnam, a desire to assist Chinese resistance to Soviet pressure increased the administration's determination to speed a settlement in Vietnam. In effect, Nixon began to apply his "doctrine" of reduced involvement in Asia before, rather than after, "victory" in Vietnam. As Kissinger elaborated, the "China initiative . . . restored perspective to our national policy." It reduced "Indochina to its proper scale—a small peninsula on a major continent." The "drama" of opening ties with China would "ease for the American people the pain that would inevitably accompany our withdrawal from Southeast Asia."[44]

In an odd symmetry, a China weakened by the cultural revolution sought American assistance in balancing Soviet and Japanese challenges. Following the August 1968 Soviet invasion to crush Communist reform efforts in Czechoslovakia, the 1969 Sino-Soviet border clashes, and the redeployment of substantial Soviet forces to the disputed frontier, Chinese leaders feared an assault by their former ally. Japan's growing wealth and assertiveness—brought home by Sato's affirmation in 1969 of an interest in the security of South Korea, Taiwan, and Vietnam—raised the added specter of a rearmed, expansive Japan.

Since the Korean War, American military deployment in Asia had a primary goal of containing China. Nixon's gradual withdrawal of ground troops from Indochina, his decisions to return Okinawa and encourage Japan to play a regional security role, the Nixon Doctrine, and Washington's pursuit of détente with the Soviet Union foretold a diminished American security role in the Asia/Pacific region. Because the retreat of American power coincided with a growing Soviet threat, Chinese strategists who previously feared a U.S. victory in Vietnam now agonized about the consequences of a defeat. America's retreat would leave China caught between the Soviet Union and Japan. As Nixon and Kissinger hoped, Mao's determination to protect China outweighed his disdain for capitalism, solidarity with Hanoi, mistrust of the United States, and drive to regain Taiwan.[45]

During 1969 and 1970, the administration signaled a desire to improve ties with China. Nixon and Kissinger used the periodic talks held in Warsaw between the American and Chinese ambassadors to encourage a dialogue. In September 1970, Nixon told a reporter for *Time* magazine of his interest in visiting China. Mao responded in December, informing American journalist Edgar Snow, in an interview printed in *Life*, that he "would be happy to talk to" Nixon, "either as a tourist or as president." Kissinger then opened a secret communication channel (excluding the State Department) to China through Pakistani and Rumanian officials.

On June 2, 1971, after almost two years of secret exchanges, Zhou Enlai invited Kissinger to come to China to arrange a presidential visit. Kissinger described the message as "the most important communication that has come to an American president since the end of World War II." Nixon told his aides that "fundamental shifts in the world balance of power made it in both [nations'] interest to have relations." Faced by the Soviets on one border, a Soviet-backed India on another, and Japan to the Northeast, which could "develop [military power] fast because of its industrial base," China sought protection from the United States. Mao and Zhou still demanded that "the U.S. should get out of the Pacific" but, Nixon surmised, they really "don't want that."

As United States military power in Asia receded, the president explained, Japan would "either go with the Soviets or re-arm," two bad alternatives from China's perspective. He believed that with a little tutoring Mao and Zhou would agree that continued U.S. military presence in Japan, Korea, and Southeast Asia was "China's [best] hope for Jap restraint."[46]

On July 9, while visiting Pakistan, Kissinger feigned stomach trouble, dropped out of sight, and flew in a Pakistani airliner to Beijing. He and Zhou Enlai spoke for seventeen hours over two and one-half days. Amid rote posturing, philosophizing, and light repartee on both sides, Kissinger offered Zhou the single thing he believed motivated China—"strategic reassurance, some easing of their nightmare of hostile encirclement." As proof of American goodwill, he provided communication intercepts and satellite pictures of Soviet military deployment along China's border. Zhou recited what Kissinger called the "Chinese Communist liturgy," demands that the Americans abandon Taiwan, pull out of South Vietnam, and cease assisting a "militaristic Japan." But, over lunch, the Chinese premier assured Kissinger that these minor impediments need not delay improved ties or a presidential visit.[47]

On the day Kissinger returned to the United States from China carrying an invitation for Nixon's visit, the president mused to H. R. Haldeman that in politics "everything turns around." China "made a deal with us" due to "concern regarding the Soviets," their former ally. He had "fought the battle for Chiang" and Taiwan since the 1950s and had "always taken the line that we stand by the South Koreans, and we stand by the South Vietnamese, etc." How "ironic" that he, like Mao Zedong and Zhou Enlai, was the "one to move . . . in the other direction." Rapprochement with China, Nixon predicted, would "change the world balance" and "shatter old alignments." The "pressure on Japan," might even push it toward an "alliance with the Soviets." Moscow, Nixon predicted, would try to redress the Asian power balance by "moving to Japan and India." (Soviet Foreign Minister Andrei Gromyko flew to Japan in the wake of Nixon's announcement, but his refusal to even discuss return of the northern territories blocked reconciliation.)

Nixon acknowledged it might take some effort to "reassure Pacific allies we are not changing our policy" or selling out old friends "behind their backs." But they must be made to understand that while there was "validity ten years ago to play the free nations of Asia against China," America could now "play a more effective role with China rather than without."[48]

Nixon the politician saw as much advantage in the China initiative as did Nixon the statesman. To make certain he received maximum credit for the breakthrough, the president prodded his staff to keep Kissinger under wraps and away from journalists when he returned from Beijing. Nixon not only kept news of the approach to China secret from the Department of State and America's allies before his public announcement on July 15, but wanted steps taken to ensure that no prominent Americans—and certainly no Democratic politicians, such as Senator Edward Kennedy—traveled to China before he did. He spoke of his pending trip as something "good to hit the Democrats with at primary time." The NATO allies and Japan would be told of the initiative by telephone, just before the president went public.

Late on July 14, General Alexander Haig, Kissinger's deputy, summoned U. Alexis Johnson to Nixon's home in San Clemente, California. When he arrived the next day, NSC aide Winston Lord casually told him the president was about to make a live television announcement that Kissinger had returned from China with an invitation for Nixon to visit Beijing. Johnson grew frantic that no one had alerted Japan. In fact, Nixon personally vetoed a suggestion to send Johnson to Tokyo twenty-four hours before a public disclosure. Just minutes before Nixon's address, Johnson reached Japan's ambassador in Washington, Ushiba Nobuhiko, by telephone. When told the purpose of the call, the envoy cried out: "Alex, the Asakai nightmare has happened."

In Tokyo, three minutes before Nixon's speech, Kusuda Minoru, Sato's secretary, encountered the prime minister emerging from a cabinet meeting that had reaffirmed Tokyo's support for Taiwan and South Korea and informed him of the president's action. Just a week before, Defense Secretary Melvin Laird had assured Sato that Washington contemplated "no basic change" in China policy. Now, in shock, Sato mumbled to his aide "Is that really so?" Ambassador Armin Meyer failed to get even a three-minute warning. He knew nothing until he heard Nixon's speech on the radio while having a haircut.

When Kissinger and Nixon "embarked on a period of rapturous enchantment with China," U. Alexis Johnson complained, they shoved "our most important ally in Asia . . . to the back burner." Although they never officially linked their handling of the China issue to the textile dispute, Nixon and Kissinger approved journalist Henry Brandon's attribution of motive. In a book based on interviews with both men, Brandon wrote: "Angry that the Japanese government, despite its promise to do so, did not place voluntary restraints on its exports, Mr. Nixon deliberately affronted Japanese Premier Sato by giving him no hint of his new policy toward China."[49]

Although most Japanese favored broader contact with China, Nixon's calculated insult stung deeply. Sato issued a statement welcoming the

Sino-American dialogue "in the interests of world peace." Japan, he noted, had long favored closer ties with China. In private, Ambassador Meyer reported, most LDP leaders were "upset as hell" and doubted that "Sato could last" after the humiliation inflicted by Nixon. Although Nixon sent the prime minister a note pledging to "work closely with you on China policy," his actions mocked the promise. "I have done everything" the Americans "have asked," a tearful Sato told visiting Australian Labor leader Gough Whitlam, but "they have let me down." Among Nixon's cabinet, only the long-ignored Secretary of State, William Rogers, expressed sympathy for Sato, suggesting that "lots of mood music" be played to soothe him.[50]

The fact that, while Washington and Beijing opened lines of communication, Sino-Japanese relations deteriorated, magnified the shock of Nixon's action. Chinese leaders expressed alarm over Japan's rapid economic growth and rising military budget. (Defense spending hovered near 1 percent of the GNP, but rapid economic expansion led to increased defense spending. Between 1960 and 1970, military expenditures rose from $508 million to $1.5 billion per year.) They particularly disliked Sato's assertion of Japan's security interest in South Korea, Taiwan, and Vietnam, as expressed in the Okinawa communiqué of November 1969. The Chinese press denounced "criminal plots" among counterrevolutionaries in Japan and America, "reactionary policies of the Sato Cabinet," and attempts by Tokyo to rebuild the "Greater East Asia Co-Prosperity Sphere."

In April 1970, Zhou Enlai and North Korean strongman Kim Il-sung jointly declared that "Japanese militarism has revived and has become a dangerous force of aggression in Asia." They accused Sato's government of "directly serving U.S. imperialism in its war of aggression against Vietnam," of plotting with Washington a new war against North Korea, and of "attempting to include the Chinese sacred territory of Taiwan in their sphere of influence." Zhou announced new guidelines governing Sino-Japanese trade. China would no longer trade with Japanese companies investing in Taiwan and South Korea, manufacturing arms for the American war effort in Southeast Asia, or engaged in joint ventures with American firms.[51]

Sato urged Japanese business leaders to resist Chinese pressure and cited Nixon's assurance that Washington contemplated no change in China policy. Nevertheless, demands from business groups anxious to enter the largest market of Asia and from a wide spectrum of political opinion persuaded nearly half the members of the Diet to join the nonpartisan Parliamentarians League for the Restoration of Ties with China. Despite this, Sato held the line against Beijing, resisted efforts to seat the PRC in the United Nations, and dismissed all hints that Washington might alter its China policy. Even when Zhou Enlai told a Japanese trade negotiator in the spring of 1971 that China and the United States might soon begin a serious dialogue independent of Japan, Sato paid no heed.[52]

Ironically, Nixon and Kissinger may have used the threat of a nuclear-armed Japan to put pressure on China to accept U.S. terms for cooperation.

During Kissinger's secret trip to Beijing of July 9 to 11, 1971, Secretary of Defense Melvin Laird visited Tokyo. Through his own sources, including documents pilfered by Kissinger aide navy yeoman Charles Radford and passed on to the Joint Chiefs of Staff, Laird learned of the secret approach to China and later claimed he passed word of this to a Japanese defense official shortly before Nixon revealed it. (This contradicts the assurance he gave Sato on July 5 that Washington was *not* about to change tack.)[53]

In public as well as private talks, Laird berated Japan for demanding the removal of nuclear weapons from Okinawa. Instead of limiting American security efforts, Japan should provide military assistance money to Southeast Asian countries and boost its own military capacity, starting with development of an ABM system to counter a future Chinese threat. He and his aides hinted that Washington favored a nuclear-armed Japan. Kissinger claimed these remarks were unauthorized and undermined his effort with China.[54]

In a deposition given in June 1975 to the Watergate Special Prosecution Force, Nixon contradicted Kissinger. When asked about Radford's theft of NSC documents, the former president, a prosecutor told Seymour Hersh, grew animated. "Radford knew everything"; he was "in on all the meetings." Nixon explained that during their initial contact with China, he and Kissinger warned that if the PRC did not agree to strategic cooperation against the Soviets on American terms, they would encourage Japan to develop nuclear weapons. In Nixon's words, "We had these tough negotiations with China over the Mutual Defense Treaty . . . with Japan. You have to be tough. And we told them that if they tried to jump Japan then we'll jump them." Nixon reportedly said, "We told them that if you try to keep us from protecting the Japanese, we would let them go nuclear." He boasted of "'put[ting] it to' the Chinese like someone out of Hell's Kitchen."[55]

Laird's remarks in Tokyo add credibility to Nixon's later account. Possibly, Laird, Kissinger, and Nixon played "good cop/bad cop" to encourage a more cooperative attitude in Beijing. After all, the last thing China wanted was a nuclear-armed Japan as it tried to enlist American support against the Soviets. On July 5, 1971, four days before Kissinger's visit to China, Zhou struck journalist Ross Terrill as "very agitated indeed about Japan." In an interview, Zhou accused Washington of conspiring to revive "Japanese militarism" and assisting Tokyo's acquisition of tactical nuclear weapons. The Chinese prime minister repeated this assertion after Nixon's announcement of July 15. In a discussion with journalist James Reston in August 1971, Zhou warned that Nixon's promotion of Japanese rearmament, along with the withdrawal of U.S. forces from Indochina, encouraged the revival of Japanese militarism. He depicted Japan's civilian nuclear industry as conspiring to build atomic warheads as part of a plan to dominate Southeast Asia.[56]

In the months leading up to Nixon's February 1972 visit to Beijing, Chinese propaganda and diplomatic messages suggested that, aside from the Soviet buildup, nothing was more worrisome than "Japanese expansionism." Beijing accused Tokyo of planning to take advantage of America's retreat from Vietnam by asserting economic hegemony over Southeast Asia. This played to economic and political strains between Tokyo and Washington. According to *The People's Daily*, "Japanese militarists" hoped to "make a comeback by relying on U.S. imperialism, [while] the latter strives to tighten its control over Japan economically, politically, and militarily by fastening her firmly to its war chariot." In a warning to Tokyo, the paper noted that the United States had no real "wish to see an independent, prosperous, and shiny Japan in Asia." It called Japan a "close partner" but stood "ready to betray her at any time."[57]

Japan's ambassador in Washington, Ushiba Nobuhiko, responded to these allegations by accusing Beijing of pandering to the fear of militarism to "isolate Japan" and drive a wedge between the Pacific allies. China hoped to make Washington more dependent on Beijing for strategic cooperation against the Soviet Union. In an unusually blunt public statement, he contrasted professional diplomats such as U. Alexis Johnson and Marshall Green who understood this ploy, and amateurs such as Nixon and Kissinger, whom China manipulated.[58]

Japan–United States Economic Conflict

The tears shed by Sato over Nixon's treatment reflected both a personal betrayal and a belief that Japan, having sailed loyally in the wake of America's China policy for two decades, deserved better. Over the next few months Nixon hurled additional lightning bolts at Tokyo. His decision to end the dollar's convertibility into gold, force a revaluation of the yen, levy a surcharge on imports, and threaten to impose textile quotas—the New Economic Policy—set Japan's leaders further back on their heels.

In addition to the stalemated textile negotiations and the ballooning American balance-of-payments deficit that approached $29 billion by the end of 1971, the United States experienced its first overall merchandise trade deficit—$2.27 billion—in nearly a century. The deficit with Japan alone in 1971 swelled to $3.2 billion, on two-way trade of almost $11.5 billion.

Japan was America's second biggest export market (after Canada), taking 11 percent of all U.S. exports. The United States absorbed 31 percent of Japan's exports. The structure, as much as size, of the trade deficit upset Americans. Japan's $7.3 billion of exports to the United States consisted mostly of manufactured goods such as textiles, steel, electronics, and, increasingly, automobiles. These competed directly with domestic American production. In contrast, unprocessed food and industrial raw materials made up two-thirds of America's $4.1 billion in exports to Japan. The remainder included capital equipment not manufactured in Japan.

American business executives and politicians complained that collusion among Japanese politicians, bureaucrats, and business elites produced this structural imbalance. According to this view, the all-powerful Ministry of International Trade and Industry, relying on an array of formal and informal powers, coordinated a predatory trade strategy of export promotion and protection of the domestic market.

On June 6, 1971, in response to complaints about continuing restrictions, Sato approved an eight-point program to liberalize rules on foreign trade and investment in Japan and provide more assistance to developing countries. Although informal barriers persisted, Japan's formal restrictions were not much different from those of Western Europe. Because the reform package ignored textiles and did not bring down the overvalued yen, the Nixon administration dismissed its significance.[59]

Spokesmen for industries that competed directly with Japanese exports complained the loudest. Elly R. Carraway, Jr., president of Burlington Industries, a large textile producer, told a Senate subcommittee in May 1971 that the United States was on the "brink of defeat" in a trade war. A few months later, he claimed that Japan had pursued "a brilliant plan" to dominate the world economy. Ford Motor Company executive Edsel B. Ford, II, cautioned shareholders that the onslaught of Japanese automobile exports would inevitably transform the United States into a service economy. Featured articles in *Time, Newsweek,* and *Forbes Magazine* during the spring of 1971 all used military and racial terminology to warn of the threat posed by "Japan, Inc." *Newsweek* spoke of Japan's "massive invasion of the world automobile market." *Time*'s description of Japan's "business invasion" portrayed America as locked in a struggle with a "mighty industrial economy that has been shaped by Oriental history and psychology." It quoted a "member of the Nixon Cabinet" (probably Maurice Stans) as saying: "The Japanese are still fighting the war, only now instead of a shooting war it is an economic war. Their immediate intention is to try to dominate the Pacific and then perhaps the world." A Harris poll conducted that spring revealed that although American consumers liked Japanese products, 66 percent favored greater restrictions on imports. By July 1971, top congressional Democrats, including Henry Reuss of Wisconsin and Wilbur Mills, endorsed legislation to suspend dollar–gold convertibility and impose an import surcharge in response to Japan's allegedly unfair trading practices.[60]

At the normally sedate meetings of the United States–Japan Businessmen's Conference during 1971, Americans criticized their counterparts harshly. At the September gathering, Japanese delegates listened in stunned silence as a crooner performed "Import Blues."

> I got the import blues . . . and I got 'em bad.
> I'm a cotton mill man . . . and my heart is sad.
> I used to work six days a week, sometimes more . . .
> Now its three day a week . . . and I sure am sore.
>
> I'm good at my business, a weaving hot shot
> And still I ain't got . . . a heckuva lot.
> I've made big money at the weaving trade
> But now, the people of Jay-Pan have it made.

They make cheap-john goods in a sleazy style
And ship these goods to the whole world wide.
And my little wife . . . well . . . she runs to the store
Gobbles 'em up, and says you gonna get more?

She bought me a shirt that was import made
And I got mad . . . because it hurt my trade.
She bought a Jap-made mini, way 'bove the knee . . .
You should have seen it after it was washed.[61]

Nixon's anger toward Japan increased when his new textile negotiator, David Kennedy, failed to win concessions after visiting Tokyo several times during the spring and summer of 1971. Kennedy told Nixon that America's "future economic and political relations with the Asian as well as the Europeans" hinged to a large degree on success with textiles. The issue went "far beyond a political problem affecting Southern politics" or one industry, White House aide Harry Dent told the president in July. His "prestige was on the line around the country." Alexander Haig urged getting "tough with the Japanese." Economic adviser Peter Peterson warned Nixon that unless he moved immediately to impose export restrictions, American textile producers "would go to Wilbur Mills and try to work out a deal with him." He would harvest the credit, leaving Nixon "the hostage of Wilbur Mills on this critical issue." Most of the president's advisers urged that he act unilaterally to restrict textile and additional Japanese exports and Nixon sent Sato yet another personal plea.[62]

By July 1971, the textile dispute blended into the broader economic problem faced by the United States. Because of large balance-of-payment deficits, faith in the dollar as the world's "reserve currency" had declined steadily. The $25 billion held abroad by central banks and governments, especially in Great Britain, France, Germany, and Japan, far exceeded the value of the $11 billion gold reserve that backed them. Although no one expected a rush to exchange these dollars for gold, at some point faith in the nation's credit could erode enough to cause a panic. If foreign banks holding dollars demanded payment in gold, the Treasury could cover less than half the claims. Trade and payment problems also contributed to a sluggish economy, inflation, and job losses.

Nixon's chief economic advisers, OMB director George Shultz and Treasury Secretary John Connally (who assumed the post in March 1971), blamed the trade and payments deficits on America's trading partners. Undervalued yen, marks, and francs, they argued, made foreign goods artificially cheap in the United States and American products unnaturally expensive abroad. They proposed to raise the value of the yen and mark to make dollars—and American exports—cheaper. Nixon's economic advisers also criticized the allies for imposing a variety of regulatory barriers to American exports and refusing to pay a fair share of defense costs. Influenced by Undersecretary of the Treasury Paul Volcker and his staff, Connally urged the president to force the upward valuation of foreign currencies, impose restrictions on imports, levy an import surcharge, suspend dollar–gold convertibility, and make the allies assume a greater share of the defense burden.[63]

Connally, a silver-tongued Texas Democrat drifting toward the Republican Party, beguiled Nixon during 1971. Kissinger believed his "swaggering self-assurance" fulfilled "Nixon's Walter Mitty image of himself." Connally boasted to Kissinger that "you will be measured in this town by the enemies you destroy. The bigger they are, the bigger you will be." When asked by a journalist what qualified him for the Treasury post, Connally quipped "I can add." He told former NSC staffer C. Fred Bergsten that his "philosophy" of international economic policy was "all foreigners are out to screw us and it's our job to screw them first." His panache impressed Nixon so much that in July 1971 he told his staff to "figure out how the hell we can get [Vice President] Agnew to resign early" so that Connally could assume the job. Nixon called the Texan "my logical successor."[64]

As pressure on the dollar increased during the summer of 1971, Nixon instinctively attacked the messenger. He told aide Frederick Malek to purge a "Jewish cabal" in the Bureau of Labor Statistics whom he blamed for reporting bad economic news. When this gambit went nowhere and reports circulated that the British were about to redeem some $3 billion dollars for gold, Nixon assembled his domestic political and economic advisers at Camp David on August 13 to 14. The meeting, economic aide Herb Stein told speechwriter William Safire, was the "most important weekend in economics since March 4, 1933" when Franklin Roosevelt closed the nation's banks.

Connally controlled the agenda.* The country, he warned, "can't cover our liabilities—we're broke; anyone can topple us anytime they want." Only bold action would mobilize domestic support and force the upward valuation of foreign currencies. There were no options to discuss, Connally argued, since "we don't have alternatives." With the nation's assets "going out by the bushel basket," the president would soon be "in the hands of the money changers."

If Nixon failed to act, his aides warned, Wilbur Mills and congressional Democrats would seize the initiative. The president rejected Arthur Burns's suggestion to create a bipartisan commission for developing an emergency economic program. As their price for cooperation, Nixon predicted, the Democrats would demand that a "bi-partisan group of senators go with me to China—no way!" He then agreed to "close the gold window" (ceasing to exchange dollars for gold), levy a 10 percent surcharge on most imports (in order, Nixon explained, to "get leverage over the Japanese"),

---

* Those present included Nixon, George Shultz, John Connally, Maurice Stans, Pete Peterson, Peter Flanigan, Herbert Stein, Federal Reserve Chairman Arthur Burns, Chairman Paul McCracken of the Council of Economic Advisers, and speechwriter Wiliam Safire. Kissinger, about to leave for Paris to meet with North Vietnamese officials, was not "part of the program."

impose a temporary domestic wage-price freeze, provide investment incentives to industry, and reduce federal spending.[65]

The "Japs, Russians, Chinese, and Germans," Nixon told his aides, retained a "sense of destiny and pride" while Americans seemed to lack the will to compete. He urged his speechwriters to think of Franklin Roosevelt as they drafted a declaration of a "new economic policy" that prompted every American "to be the best he can be."[66]

On the evening of August 15, 1971—the anniversary of V-J Day—in language borrowed from FDR, Nixon told a national radio and television audience that "We are going to take action—not timidly, not half-heartedly, and not in piecemeal fashion." The times required a "a new economic policy for the United States" to fight "unemployment, inflation, and international speculation." He stressed determination to "protect the dollar from the attacks of international money speculators" and called on the nation's trading partners to "set straight" the values of their currencies before he dropped the import surcharge. America, Nixon declared forcefully, would no longer "compete with one hand tied behind her back."

These initiatives were more of an effort at image building and an attempt to force a change in exchange rates than a strategy for reform of the international monetary and trade system. But given Japan's level of dependence on the American market, they had a dramatic impact. Just as the opening to China overturned the political ground rules of the Pacific alliance, the new economic policy undermined the foundations of postwar economic relations. The China shock had injured Japan's pride, but the economic shock, as Nixon admitted to his aides, was designed in large part to give Japan an overdue "jolt."[67]

The president's public announcement of his new economic policy did not dwell on the legal basis for imposing an import surcharge that violated GATT rules. In a written directive, Nixon proclaimed a "national emergency" that empowered him to take action to "strengthen the international economic position of the United States." This authority derived from the Trading with the Enemy Act, passed by Congress in 1917, and amended shortly after the Japanese attack on Pearl Harbor. It allowed the president in time of war or declared emergency to regulate the importation of "any property in which any foreign country or a national thereof has any interest." Although White House spokesmen downplayed this basis for placing a surcharge on European imports, Nixon instructed them to publicize use of the Trading with the Enemy Act "only for textiles—i.e., Japs."[68]

Once again, Ambassador Meyer learned of the president's imminent announcement from a Tokyo radio station. He reached Secretary of State Rogers by telephone and pleaded with him to inform Prime Minister Sato of what lay ahead. Rogers arranged to speak with Sato shortly before the president's address. Because of difficulty locating an interpreter, he informed Sato of Nixon's intention only ten minutes before the rest of the world—a seven-minute improvement over the China shock.

Nixon encouraged domestic support for his program with thinly veiled attacks on Japan. Addressing the national convention of the Veterans of Foreign Wars in Dallas on August 19, he warned that "history" was "strewn with the wreckage of nations that were rich and that fell before people that were less rich and considered to be inferior to them intellectually and in every other way, because the rich nations, in their maturity, lost their drive, lost their desire, lost their dynamism, lost their vitality." Nations that the United States assisted after World War II had become "our strong competitors economically." Nixon claimed the new economic policy would inspire "a new birth . . . of vitality" and a "new desire to be just as good, just as efficient . . . just as strong as we need to be." To make certain Americans knew whom to blame, he called the economic threat "far more serious than the challenge that we confronted even in the dark days of Pearl Harbor."[69]

In the two weeks after Nixon's declaration of the new economic policy, Japanese finance ministry officials thought that the administration primarily wanted to halt the outflow of gold, not drive up the value of the yen. To prevent an upward valuation that might hurt exports, Japanese officials attempted to maintain the existing yen-dollar exchange rate of 360 to 1 by buying over $4 billion at the old rate. Soon, it became impossible to sustain the dollar's value this way and Tokyo accepted a de facto upward float of the yen.

Japan's uncertainty stemmed partly from American design. Connally believed a period of confusion would erode foreign resistance to currency revaluation. He offered few specific proposals to America's anxious trading partners. Nixon, influenced by Connally, added to the uncertainty by stating in mid-September that a revision of exchange rates alone would not be sufficient to end the import surcharge. He demanded that America's allies agree to share defense costs, restrain their exports, and eliminate non-tariff barriers to U.S. exports. Connally and Volcker informed the Europeans and Japanese that the United States required a package of trade and currency reforms that would achieve a $13 billion improvement in the U.S. balance of payments.[70]

Toward an Economic Armistice

When Japanese and American cabinet ministers gathered at Williamsburg, Virginia on September 8-10 for their eighth bilateral meeting, monetary and trade issues dominated their discussion. But, as a Japanese official recalled, each country's delegates "talked along parallel lines and never met."

Secretary of State Rogers insisted that "any country in chronic surplus as Japan is" was obliged to increase imports, eliminate export incentives, and revalue its currency "to bring its global balance of payments into equilibrium." Rogers called on Japan to go beyond its effort of June 1971 and eliminate all restrictions on imports and foreign investment, increase its foreign assistance, and assure orderly marketing of its exports.

Connally demanded that Tokyo carry out a large upward valuation of the yen, settle the textile dispute on American terms, and reduce both tariff and non-tariff barriers to American imports. The last point he stressed as most important.

Foreign Minister Fukuda Takeo and Finance Minister Mizuta Mikio interpreted economic data and trends rather differently. They insisted that Tokyo had already implemented most of Rogers' demands and denied that Japan's "current balance of payments is in basic disequilibrium." Instead of trying to force Japan to increase the value of the yen and limit exports, Fukuda suggested that the United States devalue the dollar and correct its own balance-of-payments problem "through domestic means such as fiscal and monetary measures." In his own allusion to Pearl Harbor, he warned that Nixon's import surcharge might initiate a wave of global protectionism similar to what preceded the Second World War.

The gulf between the allies showed in other areas as well. Rogers pressed Japan to co-sponsor a "two-Chinas" resolution designed to retain a UN seat for Taiwan when, as expected in October, member states voted to admit the People's Republic of China into the world organization. Despite sympathy for Taiwan, the Japanese government doubted that the American salvage effort would succeed. Tokyo had no desire to endorse a doomed policy certain to enrage China. Fukuda refused to commit Japan and, instead, pressed Rogers to send the Okinawa treaty to the Senate for speedy ratification.[71]

Although it was a very small part of the larger economic picture, the textile dispute continued to unnerve officials. Japanese producers complained that Nixon's threat to impose textile quotas on top of the general import surcharge was "totally barbarian." If the surcharge continued, they threatened to end the modest export restraint program begun in the spring.

Foreign Minister Fukuda—one of two leading candidates to succeed Sato—recognized that this dispute had assumed an exaggerated significance in both countries. He publicly called on Japanese textile interests to accept a government-to-government agreement as the price of stabilizing Japanese-American relations. His major rival, MITI Minister Tanaka Kakuei took an opposing stand. Tanaka told Maurice Stans that since Washington provided no evidence that Japanese textiles had injured American industry, further export restraint was not justified.[72]

Despite this bravado, Tanaka conferred secretly with David Kennedy the day before the Williamsburg meeting convened. He promised to reopen textile talks and seek agreement along the lines proposed by Washington. Kennedy warned Tanaka that unless a deal was signed by October 15, Nixon would impose unilateral quotas under the Trading with the Enemy Act.

The MITI minister devoted himself to deliver what Sato twice promised. He planned to negotiate secretly with the Americans, extract some concessions, and then bow before overwhelming force. At Williamsburg, the two men agreed that Tanaka would initially reject American demands, only to be served with an ultimatum threatening unilateral action by October 15. This ultimatum or *kurofune* (literally, "black ship," referring to the steam-powered warships Commodore Perry flaunted to extract concessions from Japan in 1853) would serve as Tanaka's cover. He would pound the table, demand concessions, but finally accept Washington's terms. At the close of the Williamsburg meeting, Kennedy told Nixon that Tanaka would cooperate and that a textile agreement was "in the bank."

As part of the charade, however, Nixon and Kissinger received Foreign Minister Fukuda at the White House on September 10 and warned him that it would become "impossible to restrain the explosive forces building up" over textiles beyond October 15. Unless a government-to-government agreement was approved by then, Nixon threatened unilateral action. When the foreign minister took the unpopular position of urging Japanese textile executives to approve such negotiations, Tanaka—engaged in secret talks of his own—criticized Fukuda for caving in to Washington. When the MITI minister privately voiced concern that accepting American terms would end his career, David Kennedy retorted that their subterfuge, if successful, "will make you prime minister."[73]

To prevent Tanaka from trying to extract concessions, Kennedy avoided dealing with him directly. He went into virtual hiding on a military base in Guam and sent an assistant, Anthony Jurich, to arrange details of an agreement with Japan and with representatives of South Korea, Taiwan, and Hong Kong. Jurich arrived in Tokyo on September 20 and, as arranged, delivered an ultimatum stating that unless Japan and the three other Asian exporters agreed by October 1 to import restraints, the United States would utilize the Trading with the Enemy Act to impose quotas effective October 15.

When word of the ultimatum leaked, the Japanese and American press criticized Nixon's threatened use of the wartime act. An editorial in the *New York Times* on September 24, entitled "More Ugliness to Japan," blamed the "White House ultimatum" for "unwisely accelerat[ing] the downward spiral in America's relations with its chief Asian ally." Ohya Shinzo, president of the Japan Textile Federation agreed, calling Jurich a "ninja," a phantom who performed evil under the cloak of darkness.[74]

Although Tanaka and Jurich missed the October 1 deadline, they made progress toward a deal. Nixon repeated his determination to impose quotas, but expressed private relief that "the Japs look serious on textiles and yen both," making it less likely he would need to carry out his threat.[75]

On September 21, at roughly the same time as he threatened to invoke the Trading with the Enemy Act against Japan, Nixon sent the Okinawa reversion treaty to the Senate. The president discouraged efforts to link a ratification vote to acceptance of American trade demands. The treaty won easy passage (84 yes to 6 no votes) on November 10, 1971. Reversion took place on May 15, 1972.

On September 26, in another conciliatory sign, the president and first lady flew to Anchorage, Alaska, to greet Emperor Hirohito whose plane made a one-hour refueling stop en route to Europe. Nixon described this first meeting between a sitting president and Japanese emperor as a "historic" event and a "spiritual bridge spanning East and West."

Meanwhile, Tanaka struggled to win approval of a trade deal from the Japanese Textile Federation and other business groups. In early October he secured the grudging acceptance of textile producers by pledging a relief package to compensate them for lost exports. The powerful Federation of Economic Organizations (Keidanren) then weighed in. In order to eliminate the import surcharge that hurt all Japanese exports to the United States, the federation endorsed Tanaka's plan. On October 13, Kennedy flew to Tokyo. He and Tanaka initialed an agreement on October 15, only hours before the imposition of quotas.[76]

The wool and synthetic textile agreement (signed officially on January 3, 1972, but effective for three years beginning October 1, 1971) contained aggregate limits, category caps, controls on shifting among categories, and a 5 percent annual growth factor. At first glance, this resembled the initial demands of Nixon and Stans. However, the agreement utilized a substantially higher base-year quota than the original scheme. For example, the 1969 plan allowed first-year sales of 448 million square yards of synthetic material. The 1971 pact permitted Japan to sell 954 million square yards the first year, or more than twice as much.

Nevertheless, both Nixon and American manufacturers applauded the settlement. White House aide Peter Peterson, speaking for the president, called the understanding a "hopeful sign of the continuation of our good relations with Japan in the future." It demonstrated that "vigorous competitors in the free world can cooperatively work out their differences" and prevented the "erection of permanent walls around the United States."

American textile producers rewarded Nixon handsomely. On April 6, 1972, the day before a new law took effect requiring the detailed disclosure of campaign contributions, textile executive Roger Milliken handed Maurice Stans (by then chief fund-raiser for Nixon's reelection) $363,000 in cash and checks gathered primarily from southern mills. Another $150,000 followed by November.[77]

Editorials in the *New York Times* and the *Washington Post* denounced the textile deal. On October 16, the *Times* charged that the "agreement bludgeoned out of the Japanese . . . represented a victory on the part of President Nixon and the Southern textile industry, but at a cost of America's long-range international political and economic interests that has yet to be fully calculated." It quoted a senior Japanese official as saying, "It's going to be bad, very bad. People here just won't forget how this was done." A *Post* editorial of October 18 called the settlement an example of "international economic policy at its worst." It caused a "maximum of rancor and distrust abroad with a minimum of benefit at home." It had "everything to do with the electoral votes of the Carolinas next year and nothing to do with economics."

Ultimately, the textile deal had little market impact. Other Asian producers quickly stripped Japan of its comparative advantage in textiles. By 1973,

Japan imported more synthetics than it exported, its sales to the United States fell below quota, and Osaka mill owners joined Americans in demanding restraints on Asian competitors. In this light, Nixon's July 31, 1973 remarks to Prime Minister Tanaka Kakuei ring especially odd. At a White House reception, the president claimed Tanaka and he had "not haggled over what is the textile quota going to be" as might "a couple of desert rug merchants." While others wasted time dealing with the "murky, small, unimportant vicious little things," they concentrated on "building a better world."[78]

Economic and Diplomatic Aftershocks

During the autumn of 1971, Nixon, Connally, and Kissinger made progress toward an agreement to revalue world currencies. At a series of meetings of finance ministers and their deputies in London, Paris, Tokyo, Rome, the Azores, and Washington between September and December, the United States and its major trading partners discussed new methods of setting currency values and exchange rates. Meanwhile, Japanese trade officials and business analysts concluded that their exports could tolerate a rise in the yen's value if Washington eliminated the 10 percent import surcharge.

Nixon and Connally defended their confrontational approach during a meeting with Republican legislators on November 16, 1971. Connally argued that for the first time in twenty-five years a president fought "for the equity of the American businessmen in the world market." America's trading partners, especially Japan, "had been riding the U.S.—a good horse—to death in the postwar years." The "goddamn State Department," Nixon added, "hadn't done its job" but "we're changing the rules of the game." Both men argued that "economic nationalism" was the "proper tack for GOPers to take." In one of his ironic compliments to his early political enemies, Nixon explained that "what we want is a New Deal, a Fair Deal for America in the World."[79]

The process culminated on December 17, 1971, at a conference held in the Smithsonian Institution in Washington among the so-called Group of Ten, the major Western European powers plus Canada, Japan, and the United States. Delegates agreed to a devaluation of the dollar by about 9 percent (by raising the price of gold to $38 per ounce) and upward valuation of the yen by 16.9 percent, the mark by 13.5 percent, and the franc by 8.5 percent. Currency values would be permitted to fluctuate in a range up or down 2.5 percent. The yen–dollar exchange rate fell from 360 to about 308 to 1. As part of the deal, Washington dropped the import surcharge.

Nixon took much of the credit for the achievement. Speaking to the delegates at the Smithsonian conference, he praised the accord as the "most significant monetary agreement in the history of the world . . . indeed the most significant event that has occurred in world financial history." When a Japanese delegate rose to dispute this claim, Connally gaveled the proceedings to an end.[80]

Undersecretary of the Treasury Paul Volcker shared the silenced delegate's skepticism. As Nixon spoke, he muttered to an aide, "I hope it lasts three months." Six months later, the British broke the Smithsonian formula by allowing the value of the pound to float outside the stipulated limit. When informed that Italy might follow suit, Nixon remarked to his staff—and to a hidden microphone—"I don't give a fuck about the lira." By February 1973, the "most significant monetary agreement in the history of the world" had collapsed. Thereafter, the value of all major currencies floated on the basis of supply and demand.

The belief among Treasury officials and academic economists that floating currency rates and a rising yen would spur American exports and solve the trade and payments deficits proved—in the long run—false. During 1972, the trade deficit grew more slowly and during 1973 it declined because of such factors as the rising yen and a steep increase in oil prices after the October 1973 Arab–Israeli war. After 1975, American consumers purchased Japanese automobiles and electronic goods in ever-increasing volume.[81]

Gyohten Toyoo, a finance ministry official in 1971, believed that the shocks that summer convinced his colleagues that the "Nixon administration was thinking about the possibility of using Communist China as a counterweight to Japan in post-Vietnam Asia." Kissinger and Connally, the Japanese concluded, achieved a "meeting of the minds" and acted in tandem to "pull the rug out from under Japan." Just as the Nixon administration relied on triangular diplomacy to influence Soviet behavior, the Americans seemed to be "playing a kind of China card to Japan." In fact, Nixon had just spoken in these terms to British Prime Minister Edward Heath. The "Japanese are all over Asia like a bunch of lice," he complained, and somehow must be fit into a post-Vietnam framework.[82]

Although the reaction among LDP faction leaders to the Nixon shocks varied, most recognized that Sato's days in power were numbered along with the "San Francisco" system that defined Japan's place in the world for two decades. In the scramble to achieve Sino-Japanese rapprochement, LDP stalwarts pushed aside the Socialists who had urged such a policy since 1951. Corporations, anxious to claim a piece of the China market, severed ties to Taiwan and accepted Zhou Enlai's "Four Conditions" for trade.

Hori Shigeru, LDP secretary general spoke for many party elders in December 1971 when he wrote that the *Pax Americana* had run its course. Japan's strategic and economic ties to the United States remained important,

Value in Millions of Dollars of U.S. Imports from and Exports to Japan, 1969–73

	1969	1970	1971	1972	1973
Imports	4,888	5,875	7,259	9,064	9,676
Exports	3,490	4,652	4,055	4,965	8,313
Deficit	-1,398	-1,223	-3,204	-4,099	-1,363

Source: Statistical Abstract of the United States, 1970–80

but not paramount. In 1945, the United States became the predominant world power. The world revolved around an American axis, allowing Japan to "re-emerge from the depths of misery brought on by defeat and achieve her present position by striving earnestly to adjust her policies to those of the American-dominated world order." But the world had "ceased to revolve around an American axis" and "entered a tri-polar, or a five polar era." For Japan, Hori wrote, friendship with the United States remained "vital." It was necessary to consolidate this friendship even further "to promote our development and prosperity." At the same time, it was "necessary for us to recognize, once again, that Japan is an Asian nation."[83]

Although Sato probably agreed with this assessment, his desire to retain American goodwill and reluctance to cut old ties to Taiwan constrained his action. Despite his initial reluctance to follow the American lead, by the time the United Nations voted on the China question on October 26, 1971, Sato supported the doomed American effort to preserve a seat for Taiwan as well. Concern over Okinawa as well as the economic crisis influenced this decision. At the time of the UN vote, the Senate was poised to take final action on the Okinawa treaty and Nixon continued to push on textiles, currency values, and the import surcharge. By allying Japan with the United States on Taiwan, Sato hoped to assure passage of the Okinawa treaty and moderate Washington's economic pressure.

Even as the prime minister placated Washington, he dispatched intermediaries to China during October and November in the hope of arranging a rapprochement. But his reluctance to recognize the PRC as the sole, legitimate government of China with authority over Taiwan or to abrogate Japan's peace treaty with Taiwan angered Beijing and doomed an early Sino-Japanese rapprochement.[84]

Anxious to know where Japan stood in American strategic thinking, Sato met Nixon in San Clemente on January 6 to 7, 1972, a month before the presidential visit to China. His arrival coincided with a newspaper column by Jack Anderson that included a cable to Washington from Ambassador Meyer discussing a conversation with Foreign Minister Fukuda and his own views on China policy. Meyer had cautioned Nixon and Kissinger against trying to "persuade the Chinese that the United States–Japan security relationship had a restraining effect on Japanese 'militarism.'" The Chinese, he predicted, would report this to Japan in hope of driving a wedge between Tokyo and Washington—and making each more dependent on Beijing. Meyer also urged Nixon to refrain from announcing any major policy changes while in China. If the president recognized the PRC or broke relations with Taiwan before conferring with Japan, the LDP's faith in America might crumble completely. Without the steadying effect of the security treaty, Sato's successors might reject strategic cooperation with the West and "decide to develop an autonomous nuclear force de frappe."[85]

In probing Nixon for an indication of future American action, Sato admitted that the "shock of the announcement" on China the previous July "ran much deeper than the President could even imagine." Perhaps, following the president's upcoming visit to China, Kissinger could "stop off in Japan," providing "he didn't have a stomach ache." Nixon's remarks did little to comfort Sato. The president reaffirmed the security commitment to Japan, admitted his intent to expand ties with China, and promised not to abandon Taiwan. He hoped the Japanese would not "crawl" or "engage in an obvious race to Peking," meaning, of course, a race to upstage him. Japan, Nixon argued, should play a military as well as economic role in Asia, suggesting, yet again, that it reconsider its attitude toward nuclear weapons. He also pushed for a promise to buy more American-built jets. Sato agreed to assign MITI minister Tanaka to work on aircraft purchases, but refused to yield on nuclear weapons. The Diet and the Japanese public overwhelmingly opposed them, while Soto had all he could handle refuting Chinese accusations of resurgent militarism. Turning the tables, he requested that Nixon state publicly that "the United States would not provide Japan any nuclear weapons" and that Japan had "no other recourse except the United States nuclear umbrella."[86]

On February 21, 1972, Nixon hurtled down the stairway of his plane at Beijing's airport to shake the hand of Zhou Enlai. Ushered into Mao's presence a few hours later, he spoke eloquently of his own journey from anti-Communism to China. What brought old adversaries together was "recognition of a new situation in the world and a recognition on our part that what is important is not a nation's internal political philosophy. What is important is its policy towards the rest of the world and towards us." Both China and America worried about Soviet behavior and the future of Japan. Why, he asked rhetorically, did the Soviets have "more forces on the border facing you" than facing Western Europe? Sino-American differences over Taiwan, Korea, and Indochina paled in comparison.

Nixon countered criticism of Japanese militarism by asking if China really preferred "for Japan to be neutral and totally defenseless." Would China not benefit from Japan's maintaining "defense relations with the United States?" Without the security treaty, he cautioned, America would "have no influence" in Tokyo. Without a U.S. military presence in Asia and Japan, "our protests" about Japanese or Soviet behavior "no matter how loud, would be like firing an empty cannon. We would have no effect because thousands of miles away is just too far to be heard."[87]

Mao enjoyed talk of artillery. "Generally speaking," he declared, "people like me sound a lot of big cannons." He recited a Maoist slogan ("The whole world should unite and defeat imperialism, revisionism, and all reactionaries and establish socialism"), then "laughed uproariously at the proposition that anyone might take seriously a decades-old slogan scrawled on every public poster in China." To Kissinger this showed Chinese leaders "were beyond ideology in their dealings with us." Fear of the Soviets "had established the absolute primacy of geopolitics" and led to a "tacit nonaggression pact with us."

Neither Nixon nor Kissinger have revealed what promises they made to win Chinese approval of the formula to deal simultaneously with Beijing and Taipei. Besides agreeing that Taiwan was part of China, Nixon secretly pledged that after reelection he would formally recognize the PRC, break diplomatic ties with Taiwan, and take unspecified steps to prevent Japan from dominating Taiwan.[88]

During his week in China, Nixon stated that America's alliance with Japan was in China's interest since it "guaranteed that we would be a major factor in the Western Pacific to balance the designs of others, and would keep Japan from pursuing the path of militaristic nationalism." This held true for U.S. troops and bases in the Philippines and South Korea as well. In a remarkably nimble reversal of twenty years of cold war rhetoric, Nixon claimed the American base network in Asia could protect China from current or future threats from the Soviet Union and Japan.[89]

Mao and Zhou denied hostile intentions toward Japan or South Korea, but complained that Tokyo and Seoul struck military postures hostile toward China. In banquet toasts of February 27, Nixon and Zhou pledged to oppose efforts by any country to establish hegemony in the Asian-Pacific region. The Shanghai Communiqué of February 28, 1972, contained a brief mention of America's chief Asian ally: "The United States places the highest value on its friendly relations with Japan" and would continue to "develop the existing close bonds." The Chinese noted their opposition to the United States–Japan Security Treaty, condemned "the revival and outward expansion of Japanese militarism," and endorsed "the Japanese people's desire to build an independent, democratic, peaceful and neutral Japan."[90]

Regardless of the details of the Nixon–Kissinger–Mao–Zhou discussions, Nixon's signature on a document that contained these criticisms of Japan stung Sato. At a press conference after release of the Shanghai Communiqué, Sato mumbled to reporters that Nixon "called this a major event of the century," then stalked out of the room. A subsequent briefing in Tokyo by Assistant Secretary of State Marshall Green and talks between Kissinger and Ambassador Ushiba in Washington provided little comfort. The Americans denied making any secret deals with China and pledged that Washington would honor its Asian commitments.[91]

In March 1972, Nixon stunned Tokyo again. The Tiaoyu (Senkaku, in Japanese) Islands consist of uninhabited rock on the continental shelf between Okinawa and Taiwan, claimed by both Tokyo and Taipei. When oil was found in the area in 1970, China asserted ownership. Following Nixon's trip to Beijing, the State Department modified its endorsement of Japan's claim in favor of a more ambiguous stand. This, Sato guessed, foretold what Nixon and Mao were up to.

The Nixon shocks of 1969–72 and their aftermath strained but never severed the tie between Japan and the United States. Both nations remained so mutually dependent that not even the strategic and economic jolts of 1971–72 broke the bond. Over the next two decades, détente and renewed cold war, Japanese trade expansion and American economic decline, created new conflicts as well as surprising sources of strength that sustained the Pacific alliance.

EPILOGUE—

ALTERED STATES:

FROM COLD WAR TO

NEW WORLD ORDER

N*IXON'S* economic shock, along with divisions among the Liberal Democrats over how to respond to the China opening, shaped the struggle to succeed Sato as prime minister. In a larger sense, Washington's foreign policy initiatives during the early 1970s signified the beginning of the end of the special dependency relationship that had prevailed between the United States and Japan since the Occupation. Over the next twenty years, the changing nature of the cold war, the evolution of a new world economy, and domestic forces would transform the Pacific alliance.

Minister of International Trade and Industry, Tanaka Kakuei—dubbed the "computerized bulldozer" because of his tenacity, unusual flare for publicity, and contempt for bureaucrats—easily outflanked his main Liberal Democratic rival, Foreign Minister Fukuda Takeo. Buoyed by the slogan "Don't miss the boat to China" and by a plan for massive domestic economic development, Tanaka won the LDP presidency and premiership in July 1972.

Like Nixon and Kissinger, Tanaka distrusted career bureaucrats and diplomats. He circumvented the foreign ministry by dispatching business leaders and members of opposition parties to sound out the Chinese on their terms for rapprochement. Zhou Enlai proved eager to accommodate Tanaka. In a humiliating rejection of the Japanese left, Zhou revealed that China no longer opposed the United States–Japan Security Treaty. If Japan recognized the PRC as the sole legitimate government of China and severed diplomatic ties with Taiwan, Zhou offered to drop demands for war reparations and tolerate Japan's continued commercial relations with Taiwan.[1]

On August 31, 1972, Tanaka conferred with Nixon in Honolulu. He told the president he intended to establish full diplomatic ties with China, but promised to maintain the security treaty with the United States. Tanaka also informed Nixon of a move designed to placate American criticism of Japanese trade practices. All Nippon Airlines would purchase twenty-one L-1011 passenger aircraft from the Lockheed Corporation in a deal valued at $400 million.[2]

This arrangement, whether or not Nixon knew, was part of a larger kickback scheme. In November 1974, Japanese journalists revealed that during the previous decade Lockheed had paid about $12 million in bribes to Japanese middlemen, often through Kodama Yoshio—Kishi's underworld patron and the organizer in 1960 of "Yakuza for Ike"—to promote sales of fighter and passenger aircraft. The money flowed up and down the LDP food chain. Tanaka resigned in December 1974 and was convicted of bribery in 1983. In February 1976, Senator Frank Church held hearings on the incident. This led to passage of the Foreign Corrupt Practices Act that made it a crime for American companies to bribe foreign officials.[3]

In 1972, however, Tanaka rode high in public opinion. When he departed Tokyo for China on September 25, Diet members from all parties cheered him on. The prime minister, who first visited China in 1940 as a soldier in the Imperial Army, was greeted at the Beijing airport by a delegation of Communist notables and a People's Liberation Army chorus singing "Three Main Rules of Discipline, Eight Points of Attention," a Communist battle hymn from the war of resistance against Japan. Over the next several days, Tanaka and Zhou Enlai agreed to terminate the state of war between their countries and establish full diplomatic ties. Tanaka expressed "regret" for past injuries inflicted on China and Zhou agreed to drop war damage claims. Japan recognized the PRC as China's sole legitimate government whose territory included Taiwan. Both sides promised not to seek hegemony in the Asia-Pacific region and to oppose such efforts by others. They planned to negotiate a treaty of peace and friendship, although it took until 1978 to do so. Tanaka believed he had set a winning course politically and hoped that increased trade with China would wean Japan from dependence on the United States.[4]

As both Washington and Tokyo hoped, China's official view of Japan changed rapidly. Foreign Minister Ohira Masayoshi told Nixon that the Chinese described the United States–Japan Security Treaty as "not at all" a problem for the PRC. After a February 1973 visit to the PRC, Kissinger noted in a report to Nixon that when the United States and China initiated direct contact in July 1971, Mao and Zhou had urged American "withdrawals from Asia," characterized "Japan–U.S. military ties [as] at a minimum unhelpful," told us to "get out of Korea," worried about Taiwan, cared nothing for Europe, and still considered the United States "capable of colluding with the USSR, Japan, and India to carve up China."

Eighteen months later, Kissinger reported, Mao and Zhou had a completely altered outlook. Like Nixon, they hoped to see the Indochina War end quickly, with Vietnam outside the Soviet orbit. The Chinese not only ceased complaining about resurgent militarism in Japan, but praised Tokyo as an incipient ally. Zhou now agreed that Japan's defense treaty with the United States "braked militarist tendencies" and gave Tokyo an "indispensable sense of security." Mao and Zhou actually admonished the United States for appearing to slight the Japanese. During Kissinger's trips to Asia, Mao asserted, he must spend more than a single day in Tokyo. A pro forma stop there after visiting China "isn't very good for their face," he explained. Sounding uncannily like John Foster Dulles, the two old revolutionaries encouraged Kissinger to organize an "axis" that included Japan, Pakistan, Iran, Turkey, and Western Europe to restrain Soviet expansion.[5]

Soviet leaders feared creation of just this kind of hostile coalition. In hopes of diverting Japan from cooperation with China and acquiring hard currency, the Russians offered Japan an opportunity to participate in the exploitation of Siberia's vast oil, gas, and timber resources. Prime Minister Tanaka visited Moscow in September 1973, but concluded no major commercial agreements. Like most Japanese, he considered Russians a "backwards" type of European who posed more of a threat to Japan than China did. Tanaka hesitated to cooperate in Siberia without American encouragement or participation. Continued Soviet refusal to return the disputed northern territories, as well as the massive sums required for Siberian development, tempered Japanese enthusiasm. Tanaka and his successors limited participation in ventures with Moscow.[6]

In contrast, the Japanese government encouraged investment in South Korea and Southeast Asia. During the 1970s, Japan became the major outside investor in both areas, displacing the United States. At the beginning of the decade, Japan's share of foreign investment in Southeast Asia was about 15 percent, compared to America's 36 percent. By 1976, the Japanese share grew to 36 percent, while the American share slid to 26 percent. By the end of the decade, about 20 percent of Japan's entire annual overseas investment went to Southeast Asia.[7]

It seemed likely that the bruising Nixon shocks and Tanaka's approach to China would widen the division between the United States and Japan. A *Yomiuri Shimbun* poll of LDP candidates running for Diet seats in December 1969 (just after the Okinawa agreement) revealed that 99 percent strongly supported maintaining the alliance with the United States. By the time of the December 1972 general election, however, a poll found that only 44 percent of Liberal Democratic candidates expressed great enthusiasm for the alliance. Nearly half favored revising or abrogating the pact.[8]

Despite this view, a variety of forces tempered nationalist and anti-American impulses within the LDP, with the result that Japan remained tethered within the American orbit. Even though there was overwhelming public approval of the opening to China, less than three months later, in December 1972, Tanaka's party suffered a reversal. The LDP went into the election with 297 Diet seats yet emerged with only 271. The Socialists and Communists made strong gains at the expense of the Liberal Democrats and minor parties.

Ironically, American détente with China and the Soviet Union undermined the conditions that gave birth to the Pacific alliance and the Liberal Democratic Party. As international tensions and the threat of war abated, Japanese voters began to look at opposition parties with renewed interest. LDP leaders wondered if the Socialists might become the ultimate beneficiary of the withering away of the cold war.

This prospect discouraged Japan's political and business elites from pursuing anti-American or pro-neutralist agendas despite their anger at Nixon and a sense that American policy had become undependable. Although China and a peaceful Southeast Asia held great commercial promise, in the near term nothing matched the American market. Tanaka and his LDP successors through 1993 saw no alternative but to ride what remained of the cold war wave in tandem with the United States. This seemed safer than undermining the strategic and economic consensus on which their rule had relied for a generation. It sustained the Pacific alliance through the era of détente in the 1970s, renewed cold war in the 1980s, and increasing trade friction in the 1990s.

The Impact of the Yom Kippur War and Oil Crisis

Prime Minister Tanaka hoped to reduce Japan's dependence on exports to the United States—a source of growing political and economic tension at home and abroad—through a massive internal development scheme. His plan, discussed in a campaign book entitled *Building a New Japan: The Remodeling of the Japanese Archipelago*, included construction of two dozen new urban and industrial centers linked by rapid rail lines, highways, tunnels, and bridges. Vast public works would create a huge internal market for domestic manufacturers. Unfortunately for Tanaka, economic and military developments frustrated his vision.

Japanese government and business officials worried that the yen–dollar revaluation agreed to at the 1971 Smithsonian conference would impede exports and plunge the country into recession. During 1972–73, however, Japan's current accounts surplus increased. Although the rate of export growth to the United States slowed, America's overall trade position barely improved. In order to redress the trade imbalance, the Nixon administration renewed demands for further upward valuation of the yen. Tanaka deflected some pressure by rewarding a few American firms, such as Lockheed, with contracts. But, as one finance ministry official recalled, the prime minister "was far more occupied with his grandiose plan to remodel Japan [by building new cities and bullet train lines] than any questions of the further revaluation of the yen."[9]

Time began to run out for Tanaka early in 1973. In February, the Smithsonian exchange rate agreement collapsed. Thereafter, currencies were largely free to "float" in value, based on market forces. The yen found a value of 257 to 264 to the dollar, about a 17 to 20 percent appreciation. This boosted the value of dollars held by Japanese but crimped exports a bit. War in the Middle East and the resulting oil crisis played greater havoc with Japan's economy.

On October 6, 1973, after prolonged tension, Syrian and Egyptian forces attacked Israeli positions in the territories occupied by the Jewish state since the June 1967 Arab–Israeli War. The fighting lasted just over two weeks before a UN-imposed cease fire took effect on October 22. Two days later, a Soviet threat to send troops to Egypt led Nixon to place U.S. forces on a special alert. Whether Nixon acted primarily to deter the Soviets or in hope of regaining domestic support that had eroded during the Watergate scandal remains unclear. Although Moscow backed down and the Egyptians and Syrians ultimately failed to recapture much territory, the Arabs took pride in their initial military drubbing of the Israelis. They also discovered how to use petroleum as a weapon.

During October and November, panic buying and spot shortages allowed Arab oil-exporting states to raise oil prices from about $3 to $12 per barrel. They also slashed petroleum sales by at least 25 percent to "unfriendly" countries who either assisted Israel militarily or failed to support a UN resolution calling on Israel to return all territory captured in 1967 as a prerequisite for peace talks. Either because they agreed with the Arab position, or simply hoped to safeguard fuel supplies, on November 6, 1973, all the countries of Western Europe, except for the Netherlands, demanded that Israel surrender land occupied since 1967. Arab oil ministers called on Japan to follow the European lead before the end of November or face stiffer sanctions.[10]

Angered by what he perceived as selfish desertion by the NATO allies in the face of Arab radicalism, Kissinger (now Secretary of State) flew to Asia to consult with China and Japan. Fearful that the Soviet Union might utilize the oil crisis to neutralize Europe and unleash its power against China, Mao Zedong told Kissinger on November 12, 1973, that Japan must play a key role in defending Asia. In an elaboration of the views he expressed the previous February, Mao described Japan as "insecure and sensitive" because of world events. He would "see to it that China did not force Tokyo to choose between the U.S. and China," as that would polarize Japan and promote reactionary nationalism. Both Washington and Beijing, Mao explained, must discourage a "free floating Japan playing off other countries against each other." The Japanese were "afraid of you," Mao told Kissinger, and must be reassured of their primacy in the Pacific alliance.[11]

Flying from Beijing to Tokyo in November 1973, Kissinger found the Japanese not so much disagreeing with the substance of American efforts in the Middle East as fearful of the consequences of following in their ally's wake. Japan depended upon imported petroleum for about 75 percent of its energy needs. Of that, some 85 percent came from Arab and Persian Gulf states. The quadrupling of oil prices after the October war pushed up Japan's energy import tab from $4.5 billion in 1972 to $21.2 billion in 1974.

Unlike the case with the European allies, Kissinger believed that Japanese leaders had no principled objection to American policy in the Middle East. But to guarantee access to petroleum supplies they felt compelled to shift toward a pro-Arab, anti-Israel stance. Japan, he observed, "could not risk simply being an appendage to American diplomacy." In contrast to the Europeans, who genuinely "disagreed with the United States," the Japanese "needed to make a record, not conduct a policy."[12]

Tanaka, who spoke with unusual directness for a Japanese politician, cited statistics on Japanese trade and resources to justify a show of "sympathy" with the Arab cause. If the United States guaranteed Japan's petroleum needs, Tanaka explained, he could resist Arab pressure. But Kissinger's refusal to do so left him little choice. The more circumspect foreign minister, Ohira Masayoshi, explained in a delicate way why Tokyo had to move toward the Arab position to assure oil deliveries. Recalling Ohira's argument with a mix of appreciation and condescension, Kissinger observed that "in its silken, soft, insinuating way Japan, largely under Ohira's guidance, had brought us with a minimum of friction to a position that it considered essential to its national interest and domestic stability without threatening the essence of the Japanese-American relationship."[13]

Japan's internal dialogue was a bit less "silken" than Kissinger imagined. The oil crisis spurred panic among consumers and industry. Tanaka and Ohira remained unsure of how far to go in distancing Japan from the United States. MITI minister Nakasone Yasuhiro, leader of a powerful LDP faction, demanded that Japan make a deal with the Arabs and show that "the era of blindly following [the United States] had come to an end."[14]

Nakasone carried the day. At the end of November, Japan followed the example of Western Europe by calling on Israel to withdraw from all territory seized since 1967 and recognize the "legitimate rights of the Palestinian people." Delegations from the ministries of finance, foreign affairs, and international trade hastened to the Middle East where they donated $5 million to Palestinian relief efforts and offered generous loans, investments in joint ventures, and technology transfers to several Arab states. On December 25, 1973, Arab oil ministers moved Japan to their list of "friendly" nations and restored oil sales. Expressing greater sympathy toward Japan than the Europeans, Kissinger released a statement declaring that while he did not agree with Tokyo's pro-Arab tilt, he "understood the circumstances that impelled it."[15]

Although Tanaka's action restored the flow of oil to Japan, the huge rise in energy costs (from $4.5 billion in 1972 to $21.2 billion in 1974), combined with a steadily appreciating yen, threw Japan into recession. Not only were funds unavailable to finance the prime minister's internal development scheme, but Japan needed a much larger supply of U.S. currency to pay for dollar-denominated oil imports. This played havoc with Tanaka's desire to reduce exports to the United States and make up the difference with domestic expansion. As had been true since the Occupation, Japanese stability and growth remained dependent on the American market.

Despite the admiration for Chinese and Japanese leaders Kissinger professed in his memoirs, his contemporary views were less sympathetic and reflected his belief that realpolitik, not morality, dictated national behavior. According to Seymour Hersh (who obtained notes taken during a briefing the secretary of state gave to the Joint Chiefs of Staff in March 1974), Kissinger returned from recent trips to Beijing and Tokyo deeply suspicious of both powers. The "Japanese," he asserted, "are mean and treacherous but they are not organically anti-American; they pursue their own interest." The United States must maintain a balance in Asia or "Japan could be a big problem."

In contrast, Kissinger said, the Chinese "would kill us if they got the chance and would pick up Japan if they thought they could get away with it." Fortunately, their fear of the Soviet Union forced them to cooperate with Washington. Kissinger predicted Japan, prodded by the oil crisis, would "go nuclear at some time." The Chinese "would worry if the Japanese began to increase their defense expenditures." That would be all right, he concluded, so long as Japan did so "without [the United States] being publicly linked to it." Ultimately, it was in America's interest to keep Japan and China concerned about the other.[16]

These geopolitical nostrums seemed distant from Japanese domestic politics. In December 1974, Tanaka fell victim to the Lockheed bribery scandal and an economic recession caused by the rising value of the yen and a quadrupling of world oil prices. Four weak Liberal Democratic prime ministers (Miki Takeo, Fukuda Takeo, Ohira Masayoshi, Suzuki Zenko) succeeded him, each in power for barely two years. Only in 1982, when Nakasone Yasuhiro became party leader, did Japan reassert a clear role in world affairs. Even this proved a temporary respite. After Nakasone's departure in 1987, a half dozen LDP prime ministers led the government for short periods before the party collapsed in 1993.

The Perils of Détente, 1974–80

Japan occupied a small niche in the foreign policy agenda during the brief presidency of Gerald Ford (August 1974–January 1977). Deciding "it was about time" an American president visited Japan, Ford accepted an invitation Tanaka had originally extended to Nixon. However, he considered the visit "more ceremonial than substantive," in contrast to the "weightier measures" he dealt with in "South Korea and Vladivostok." When he met the prime minister, Ford said little in response to Tanaka's concern that Washington might "impose new quotas upon a variety of Japanese goods." Ford rushed through their talks, visited Kyoto's shrines, and flew off to Seoul.[17]

Despite twenty years of anxiety about Southeast Asian dominos, the North Vietnamese victory of May 1975 caused barely a ripple in Japan. Hanoi's military success did not extend beyond the Indochina peninsula.

In a supreme irony, Beijing took the lead in restraining Vietnamese regional muscle flexing, fearful that its erstwhile ally had allied itself too closely with Moscow. Japan, in turn, became a strong supporter of ASEAN, a political and economic organization of non-Communist Southeast Asian states.

Aside from the brutal conditions within Khmer Rouge-controlled Cambodia during the late 1970s, and an outflow of refugees, East and Southeast Asia remained relatively stable. President Jimmy Carter relished the opportunity to place the region on a backburner after two decades of American obsession. From 1978 on, however, Japan's rapidly growing trade surplus, along with its reluctance to boost defense spending despite the collapse of détente, strained relations between Washington and Tokyo.

In an effort to reduce trade friction, Carter assigned former Democratic Party Chairman Robert Strauss as Special Trade Representative to press Japan to import more American products. In July 1978, the United States, Japan, and other GATT members approved a "framework of understanding" providing for 30 percent tariff reductions. Despite concessions by Japan, America's annual merchandise trade deficit with Japan grew from just over $5 billion in 1976 to nearly $10 billion in 1980. An increasing portion of this end of the decade imbalance stemmed from Japanese automobile exports, which already accounted for about 10 percent of all cars sold to Americans.

If Soviet-American détente had continued after 1978, and if the Liberal Democrats had overcome their chronic distrust of the Soviet Union, Japan might have continued its gradual disengagement from the U.S. security system and sought to balance its diplomatic, security, and trade relations more equitably among China, the United States, and the Soviet Union. While doing so, Tokyo could still have consolidated its strength in Southeast Asia and pursued a self-interested policy in the Middle East. The Self-Defense Forces, while no match on paper to the larger armed forces of its Communist neighbors, benefited from high morale, modern equipment, and the difficulty of mounting an amphibious assault. By the late 1970s, they possessed the ability to repel a limited conventional attack from either China or the Soviet Union. Backed by a highly productive military-industrial complex, the Self-Defense Forces had the potential to become a military establishment capable of both national defense and regional influence. The collapse of détente mooted these options and halted the process of Japan's gradual disengagement from its alliance with the United States.

During 1978 to 1979, both the Carter administration and its Republican critics saw the hand of the Soviet Union (or its Cuban proxy) in political upheavals in Central America, Poland, Sub-Saharan Africa, Iran, and Afghanistan. These regional conflicts, along with allegations that Moscow had cheated on arms control agreements, all but ended efforts at serious cooperation between the superpowers. Beginning under Carter and accelerating in the Reagan administration, the United States pursued a military buildup designed to reestablish strategic superiority over the Soviet Union, reassert control over the Western alliance, reimpose authority in the Mid-

dle East, and consolidate strength in the Pacific through strategic cooperation with both China and Japan. In both Western Europe and Japan, Conservative governments eager to cooperate with the United States assumed
power.

In the spring of 1978, the Carter administration moved closer to China.
National Security Adviser Zbigniew Brzezinski described the PRC as a
"central element" in global security policy and Undersecretary of State
Richard Holbrooke urged Tokyo to coordinate an anti-Soviet strategy with
Washington and Beijing. In December, President Carter announced that the
United States would recognize the Beijing regime as the sole legitimate
government of China, severing its formal ties and defense treaty with Tai-
wan. Congress, however, passed the 1979 Taiwan Relations Act establishing a framework for future trade and diplomatic contact and promising
American assistance if China tried to forcibly take the island.

Early in 1979, when China launched a brief border war to "punish"
Vietnam for its recent incursion into Cambodia where it ousted the brutal—but pro-PRC—Pol Pot regime there, Washington endorsed the attack.
The United States also applauded the conclusion of the Sino-Japanese
Treaty of Peace, Friendship, and Mutual Co-Operation in 1978. Closer ties
between the two Asian powers, along with Tokyo's acceptance of a treaty
clause opposing "hegemony" (code for Soviet expansion) in Asia, suggested Japan would assist China's anti-Soviet efforts and divert exports
from the U.S. market to China.

Yet, even as administration leaders applauded these moves, Democratic and Republican members of Congress criticized Japan for spending too
little on its own defense while profiting from a comparatively "free ride"
under the American security umbrella. In 1978, Congress adopted the first
of many resolutions calling on Tokyo to increase defense expenditures.

In December 1979, the Japanese government announced it would
barely increase defense spending during the coming year. This action, coming in the wake of crises in Afghanistan and Iran, angered both National
Security Adviser Brzezinski and Secretary of Defense Harold Brown, who
condemned Tokyo publicly. Japan, Brown declared, faced "steady
increases in Soviet military power" and was "more dependent than most of
the other industrialized democracies on oil from the Persian Gulf."
Although Japan could easily afford to spend more on defense, the
"increase contemplated in the December 29 budget proposal is so modest
that it conveys a sense of complacency which simply is not justified by the
facts." Whether measured by the "security situation, by the discussions
held between senior officials of our two governments . . . or by considerations of equitable burden sharing," it fell "seriously short."[18]

When Ronald Reagan became president in January 1981, he pledged to
enhance U.S. military power and prod American allies into sharing the
defense burden more equitably. Pentagon planners were especially eager
for Japan to increase its naval strength and adopt a policy of protecting sea
lanes out to a distance of 1,000 miles. In December 1982, the Senate Foreign

Relations Committee called on Japan to build up its defense, in part by purchasing more American weapons. The military appropriations bill passed by Congress in September 1983 specifically referred to Japan's responsibility to expand its naval defense perimeter.

While earlier pressure for rearmament provoked friction between the countries, Prime Minister Nakasone Yasuhiro, an outspoken nationalist who took office in November 1982, embraced Reagan's tough approach toward the Soviet Union. Nakasone described Japan as an "unsinkable aircraft carrier" and a bulwark against Soviet expansion. During his five years in office, Tokyo cooperated closely with Washington on defense planning, naval maneuvers, and intelligence gathering. Nakasone eventually pledged to defend sea lanes out to 1,000 miles and in January 1987 approved a defense buildup that exceeded the 1 percent of GNP ceiling on annual military expenditures imposed a decade before.

Despite these efforts, many Americans remained skeptical about Japan's commitment to real military burden sharing. In July 1985, Congress adopted a resolution calling on Japan to expand its defense perimeter or face trade sanctions. Two years later, the House of Representatives demanded that the secretary of state negotiate an agreement with Tokyo to raise Japanese defense spending to 3 percent of GNP or require that Tokyo pay an equivalent amount of money to Washington.

These strident complaints reflected both the ballooning trade gap with Japan—approaching $60 billion by 1987—and anger over recent revelations that for some years the Toshiba Corporation had violated COCOM rules and sold computer software and machine tools to the Soviet Union useful in building quieter submarines. In July 1987, Congress responded to Toshiba's belated admission of "unforgivable criminal acts" by imposing sanctions on selected Japanese electronic imports. The Senate voted to ban the import of certain Toshiba products for up to five years. Several outraged members of Congress set up a scaffold on the steps of the Capitol to hang the Toshiba Corporation in effigy. As cameras whirred, they bludgeoned a Toshiba portable radio with a sledgehammer. This action mimicked a group of automobile workers in Detroit who, to protest Japan's nearly 20 percent share of the American car market, staged a mock "execution" and burial of an imported Toyota.

Not even Nakasone's good personal relations with Reagan could obscure the continuing trade hemorrhage suffered by the United States. In 1981, Reagan's first year in office, the merchandise trade deficit with Japan stood at about $16 billion. By 1985, it topped $46 billion and climbed to between $50 and $60 billion for the remainder of the 1980s. The figures would have been even worse had not Tokyo agreed in 1981 to limit car exports to the United States to about 1.7 million units per year (rising to 2.3 million after 1985) and to restrain semiconductor and steel sales.

The Japanese used part of this dollar bonanza to buy large quantities of U.S. Treasury notes and dollar-denominated securities. Between 1981 and 1985, Japanese government and private investors bought something like 35 percent of the debt sold by the U.S. Treasury. In effect, Tokyo's "loans" helped finance the Reagan administration's immense deficit-spending scheme ("Reaganomics") that combined tax cuts with steep increases in defense expenditures. The national debt, which stood at $900 million in January 1981, climbed to $2.7 trillion by the time Reagan left office in 1989. In a single decade, the United States had gone from the world's biggest creditor to its largest debtor. Its cumulative foreign trade deficit during the 1980s totaled $1 trillion, about half with Japan. In the same period, Japan became the world's largest creditor, holding as much as 20 percent of the American government's debt.

By 1985, the trade deficit became a political as well as economic problem. Secretary of Commerce Malcolm Baldridge complained that Japanese export policy "had as its objective not participation in, but dominance of, world markets." Veteran journalist Theodore H. White expanded on this theme in an article in the *New York Times Magazine*. Forty years after the allied victory in World War II, White warned, the Japanese were "on the move again in one of history's most brilliant commercial offensives, as they go about dismantling American industry." Unlike the 1930s, this time the "whole world" had become Japan's "Greater Co-Prosperity Sphere." According to White, the Ministry of Finance provided the launching pad from which "MITI directed the guided missiles of the trade offensive." It would soon become clear "who finally won the war fifty years before."[19]

In an effort to reduce the trade deficit, Secretary of the Treasury James Baker III pursued a strategy pioneered by Richard Nixon and John Connally in 1971—forcing an upward valuation of the yen to raise the price of Japanese imports and lower that of American exports. The Plaza Accord of September 1985 and the follow-up Louvre agreement of February 1987 substantially raised the value of the yen against the dollar. Before the Plaza Accord, $1 yielded 254 yen. During the next year, the dollar bought only 200 yen. By early 1987, the dollar declined to 154 yen and following the Louvre agreement fell to 127 yen.

This nearly 50 percent depreciation of the dollar's value in yen had only a small effect on trade since Japanese manufacturers cut profit margins to retain market share. But Japanese investors holding dollar-denominated securities were badly battered. After 1985, they shifted away from securities and Treasury notes to purchase what now (given the strong yen) appeared as bargain-priced real estate and corporate assets in the United States. These included suburban shopping malls, Hawaiian resort hotels, entertainment companies such as MCA, CBS Records, Columbia Pictures, Universal Studios, and Rockefeller Center in New York City.

Although Dutch and British investors owned more American real estate than the Japanese, the sale of high-profile properties exacerbated popular resentment toward Japan. *Newsweek* headlined Sony's purchase of Columbia Pictures as "Japan Invades Hollywood." Andy Rooney, commentator on the popular CBS TV show *60 Minutes*, speculated derisively about Japan following up its purchase of "Lockefeller Center" by acquiring "the Gland Canyon, and Mount Lushmore." In New York, a Pontiac dealership exploited resentment over the sale of Rockefeller Center to Mitsubishi Real Estate by running an advertisement that proclaimed: "It's December, and the whole family's going to see the big Christmas Tree at Hirohito Center. . . . Go on, keep buying Japanese cars." Perhaps Americans worried that a miniature bonsai would replace the giant evergreen.[20]

In this new atmosphere, citing the Japanese threat helped shake money loose from Washington. In March 1989, for example, B. Stanley Pons, a professor of chemistry at the University of Utah, and his British collaborator, Martin Fleischmann, called a news conference to announce a remarkable phenomenon—the production of energy from fusion at room temperature with equipment available in an ordinary laboratory. The scientists claimed that with enough funding they could in a few years build an operational fusion reactor producing electricity too cheap to meter. The president of the university compared the event to the discovery of fire. Mankind faced a future free from the vagaries of Middle East oil and from the dangers of conventional nuclear reactors and acid rain. During the next year, scientists spent $100 million trying to confirm the discovery.

Before other researchers unmasked cold fusion as a sham, its proponents used the specter of Japan harnessing this force of nature as a reason why the U.S. government must fund the work of Pons and Fleischmann. As one observer noted, "the Japanese quickly became to cold fusion what the Soviets has been to the defense community, which is to say the Evil Empire." Lobbyists hired by the University of Utah urged members of Congress to finance a Cold Fusion Institute to be based on the campus. Enthusiastic state and federal representatives hastened to authorize a special $5 million fund for cold fusion research and considered providing $25 or even $100 million more.

Members of the House Space, Science and Technology Committee were riveted by testimony given by business consultant and lobbyist Ira Magaziner at an April 26, 1989 hearing. Magaziner told the committee that over the past decades Japan had appropriated American innovations such as color TV, computer chips, and the VCR. Now "cold fusion fever" gripped Japanese researchers and MITI bureaucrats who stayed up nights "working on the plan" to dominate this new technology. Magaziner pleaded for funding a crash cold fusion project and implored Congress not to "dawdle . . . until the science is proven." It must act, he urged, "for the sake of my children and all of America's next generation." Journalists quickly produced stories warning of Japan's nefarious plan to monopolize cold fusion in order to control the world. Within a year, however, reputable scientists disproved all of these claims and Pons and Fleischmann dropped from sight.[21]

Polemics appeared on both sides of the Pacific in which Japanese and American authors exchanged accusations of conspiracy. In 1989, an English translation surfaced of a recent book by Japanese politician Ishihara Shintaro (with a contribution by Sony Corporation founder Morita Akio) entitled

The Japan That Can Say No: Why Japan Will Be First Among Equals. Among other criticisms, Ishihara accused the United States of using the atomic bomb against Japan because its people "belong to the Yellow race." He boasted that the era of Tokyo meekly following Washington's lead was finally over.

American authors responded in kind. In 1992, Michael Crichton published *Rising Sun,* a bestselling "docu-novel" which included a scholarly bibliography. Crichton's thriller evoked turn-of-the-century images of the "yellow peril." He linked a kinky murder with a conspiracy by Japanese corporations to take over American high technology companies. Japan's strategic planners, Crichton warned, suborned U.S. politicians and made whores out of white women in their drive for world domination. Pat Choate's *Agents of Influence* proved only slightly less breathless in alleging that American trade officials routinely betrayed the national interest in exchange for payoffs from Japan. The genre of "Japan-bashing" books occupied growing shelf space in bookstores.[22]

Despite anxiety that the Japanese might do to real estate, science, and Hollywood what they had done to the automobile industry, the bubble burst in the early 1990s. Rockefeller Center proved such a financial sink hole that in 1995 Mitsubishi sold its stake in the Manhattan office complex for pennies on the dollar to a group headed by David Rockefeller, one of the original owners. Hollywood movie studios and Hawaiian hotels also proved disastrous for Japanese investors. Those eager to write the obituary of the U.S. automotive industry had to wait. Spurred by Japanese competition to greater efficiency, GM, Chrysler, and Ford reorganized and by the mid-1990s earned record profits.

The dramatic improvement in Soviet-American relations in the late 1980s, culminating in the end of the cold war and dissolution of the Soviet Union in December 1991, highlighted tensions between the United States and Japan. President George Bush, like his recent predecessors, sought ways to stanch the gaping trade deficit with Japan. In June 1990, he and Prime Minister Kaifu Toshiki negotiated a Strategic Impediments Initiative in which Japan undertook to remove structural trade barriers and boost expenditures on public works while Bush promised to lower the federal deficit and boost savings. The program resulted in only modest gains for American sales to Japan but had an important, if unintended, political impact within the United States. To hold up his end of the agreement to put the American economy back on track, Bush broke his celebrated "no new taxes" pledge of the 1988 campaign and made a budget deal with congressional Democrats in the fall of 1990 that provided for modest revenue increases. This outraged Republican conservatives and allowed Democrats to portray Bush as a waffler during the 1992 election campaign.

The Iraqi invasion of oil-rich Kuwait in August 1990 brought other questions to the fore. When President Bush organized an international coalition to fight Iraq, liberate Kuwait, and protect Saudi Arabia, Japan begged off from direct participation. It could not, however, resist pressure from the Western powers to contribute financially to the effort to defend oil supplies. Ultimately, Tokyo contributed about $11 billion toward the cost of the American-led war effort, leading some Japanese critics to describe U.S. forces as mercenaries. Meanwhile, public opinion surveys taken during 1991 revealed that a majority of Americans considered Japan's economic strength a major threat to national security.

In January 1992, President Bush, who almost fifty years before as the youngest carrier pilot in the navy had been shot down by the Japanese in the Pacific (photographs of a youthful, grinning Bush being plucked from the water were used with devastating effect in the election campaign of 1988), led a twenty-one-member delegation to Tokyo. The president and his entourage of executives from automobile and high technology companies intended to press Prime Minister Miyazawa Kiichi to increase the purchase of American goods by $10 billion over two years. To celebrate United States entrepreneurship, Bush presided over the opening of a Toys 'R' Us store near Tokyo.

This turned out to be the high point of the visit. At a state dinner, a fatigued president succumbed to an acute stomach flu. Without warning he slumped over Miyazawa, vomited into his host's lap, and fainted. Television cameras caught the gruesome scene of the shocked prime minister cradling Bush's head on the floor while the president slowly regained consciousness. Although he quickly recovered, the incident tainted Bush's visit which yielded few tangible results. Shortly afterward, Miyazawa— one of the LDP leaders closest to the United States since the Occupation, told the Diet that Americans "lacked a work ethic," produced shoddy goods, and had no one but themselves to blame for economic decline.[23]

References by Miyazawa and other Japanese officials to "lazy" and "illiterate" American workers prompted South Carolina's Democratic Senator Ernest F. Hollings to respond in kind. Hollings told a group of factory workers they should "draw a mushroom cloud and put underneath it: 'Made in America by lazy and illiterate Americans and tested in Japan.'"

Although his failure to win trade concessions from Japan comprised only one of Bush's mounting problems, it heightened the growing sense of economic failure dogging his administration. Early in 1992, one of Bush's potential Democratic challengers, former Massachusetts Senator Paul Tsongas paraphrased Japan scholar Chalmers Johnson to the effect that while the good news for America was that the cold war had ended, the bad news was that Germany and Japan had won. However much this caricatured reality, it resonated enough to grab popular attention.

Forty years after the Occupation ended, the international roles of Japan and the United States appeared to have reversed. Japan now provided capital and credits to both the United States and much of the developing world. Its technology and industry set global standards. Although it remained a military midget, the lapsing of the cold war rendered its status as an economic superpower all the more important.

Nevertheless, the end of the cold war affected domestic politics in both countries in oddly similar ways. In 1992 American voters turned out

President Bush in favor of Bill Clinton, the first president since Franklin D. Roosevelt with no personal memory of the Pacific War. Worried about economic decline and job losses, the electorate spurned Bush's foreign policy credentials, dismissed the relevance of his World War II heroism, ignored charges that Clinton had "dodged" the Vietnam-era draft, and embraced the challenger's campaign theme, "It's the economy, stupid."

Despite the many pundits who proclaimed that "Japan, Inc." had become the dominant world force, Japan also experienced economic and political distress in the wake of the Soviet collapse. In 1992, the economy began a slide that lasted into 1997. An aging work force demanding more benefits, escalating production costs, competition from Southeast Asia, a real estate investment bubble whose burst threatened the entire banking system, and American economic resurgence forced prognosticators to reconsider predictions that Japan was destined to dominate the twenty-first century.

Without such unifying elements such as an implacable Communist enemy and an assured American market, Japanese voters grew disgusted with the seemingly endless series of corruption scandals involving Liberal Democratic stalwarts and business interests seeking political favor. In 1993, the LDP fell apart, replaced in power for three years by a coalition of conservatives fronted, in 1994–95, by a Socialist prime minister. This seemingly incongruous grouping actually continued a pattern begun in the Yoshida era and played out during the subsequent half-century. As former LDP prime minister Takeshita Noboru noted about the pre-1993 period, "Liberal Democrats had used the possibility of criticism by the Socialists to avoid unpleasant demands by the United States to take a more active role internationally." This "burden sharing" and "cunning diplomacy," as Takeshita called it, continued in an amended form after the demise of the LDP. Each element of the coalition pointed to its partner as a reason for not yielding to American calls to liberalize trade or assume greater regional defense capability.

Still, absent cold war certainties, Americans and Japanese confronted a range of security questions and self-doubts. With the end of a Soviet threat, what stake did the United States have in Asian regional security? What purpose did the United States–Japan Security Treaty serve in the post-cold war era? Who, exactly, did it provide security for and against? With China's reemergence as an assertive regional power whose trade surplus with the United States approached that of Japan, how should Washington balance its interests between Beijing and Tokyo? How much harder should the United States press Japan to export less and import more? As the world's second largest economy, how should Japan contribute to the cost of "policing" the Middle East and defending world trade routes? In various forms, these questions had resonated for decades.

Although few Americans initially noticed, new tension simmered around the security treaty. Since the end of the Vietnam War and relaxation of U.S.–China relations, the U.S. military had redeployed a large proportion of American troops, planes, and ships from the Japanese home islands to Okinawa. Although this transfer pleased most Japanese, it made something of a mockery of the end of the American Occupation of Okinawa in 1972. The massive military presence dominated life on the small island as much as ever.

A brutal crime, which echoed the Girard case of 1957, brought home this point. In 1995, two marines and a navy enlisted man abducted and raped a thirteen-year-old Okinawan girl. Unlike their evasiveness in 1957, American civilian and military officials denounced the crime and assisted efforts at swift justice. No members of Congress or newspaper editorialists rose to defend the assault or protest the trial and conviction of the Americans in a Japanese court. Nevertheless, the crime highlighted the deep resentment felt by many Japanese and nearly all Okinawans over the fact that a foreign military establishment—with Tokyo's blessing—continued to dominate that part of their country. When, in the wake of the crime, Okinawa's governor refused to renew leases on farmland used for military airfields, Tokyo interceded to give the needed approval.

President Clinton and a new de facto LDP prime minister, Hashimoto Ryutaro, finessed contentious security and trade issues during the president's visit to Tokyo in the spring of 1996. Clinton offered to reduce forces on Okinawa over a ten-year period. The two leaders also announced progress on trade disputes. Although Japan still enjoyed a large trade surplus with the United States, its purchases of American goods had reached target levels set in negotiations the year before. No one, however, imagined they had heard the last of tensions over Okinawa or trade.

As the two nations approached the twenty-first century, the Japanese-American relationship stood poised to enter a new phase. Japan no longer depended solely on the United States either for security or economic growth. The two nations had become both competitors and consumers of each other's surplus, in effect, normal nations in a multipolar world. By most measures, this should be counted as a spectacular achievement of U.S. foreign policy since 1945.

Having cooperated to assure Japan's recovery from wartime ruin and then gone on to "win" the cold war, the Pacific allies discovered that success altered their relations in unpredictable ways. Since the Occupation they had progressed along a common road. Now, a half-century later, they faced a future whose destination neither could foresee.

NOTES

NOTES FOR CHAPTER 1

1. Diary entries of Aug. 18 and 26, 1945, Harold L. Ickes papers, Library of Congress; Robert H. Ferrell, *Off the Record: The Private Papers of Harry S. Truman* (New York, 1980), 61; Ickes hated MacArthur for several reasons, including his acceptance of illegal payments from Philippine President Manuel Quezon in 1942, association with neo-fascists in Manila during the 1930s, and manipulation of politics in the liberated Philippines. See Michael Schaller, *Douglas MacArthur: The Far Eastern General* (New York, 1989).

2. For a revealing collection of letters by American language officers sent to Japan, see Otis Cary, ed., *War Wasted Asia: Letters, 1945–46* (Tokyo, 1975), 48; for moving testimony by Japanese civilians, see Haruko Taya Cook and Theodore F. Cook, *Japan at War: An Oral History* (New York, 1992).

3. Theodore Cohen, *Remaking Japan: The American Occupation as New Deal*, ed. by Herbert Passin (New York, 1987). This posthumous memoir contains keen insights and anecdotes by its author, a labor specialist with SCAP; some 55,000 women worked in brothels run by the Recreation and Amusement Association, a government front. Occupation authorities never learned of the group's official status but closed the association's brothels in March 1946. Private prostitution thrived thereafter. See the *New York Times*, Oct. 27, 1995.

4. Cohen, *Remaking Japan*, 54, 63.

5. Faubion Bowers (a personal aide to MacArthur), Oral History and Charles Kades (Government Section), Oral History, Occupied Japan Oral History Project, Columbia University; diary entry of Dec. 9, 1948, O'Brien journal(excerpt supplied to author by Bowen Dees); MacArthur's testimony in U.S. Senate, Committee on Armed Services and Committee on Foreign Relations, 82nd Congress, 1st session, *Hearings to Conduct an Inquiry into the Military Situation in the Far East and the Facts Surrounding the Relief of General of the Army Douglas MacArthur from His Assignments in that Area*, 1951, pt. 1: 312–13 (hereafter cited as MSFE).

6. Among the standard works on the Occupation era are: John W. Dower, *Empire and Aftermath: Yoshida Shigeru and the Japanese Experience, 1878–1954* (Cambridge, Mass., 1979); Howard Schonberger, *Aftermath of War: Americans and the Re-Making of Japan, 1945–52* (Kent, Ohio, 1989); Richard Finn, *Winners in Peace: MacArthur, Yoshida, and Postwar Japan* (Berkeley, Ca., 1992); Cohen, *Remaking Japan*; Michael Schaller, *The American Occupation of Japan: The Origins of the Cold War in Asia* (New York, 1985); Schaller, *Douglas MacArthur*.

7. On MacArthur's defense of his reforms, see his letter of Jan. 12, 1948, to Robert E. Wood, MacArthur correspondence, Robert E. Wood papers, Herbert Hoover Presidential Library; Cohen, *Remaking Japan*, 64, 69; Perry Miller quoted in John C. Perry, *Beneath the Eagle's Wing* (Boston, 1981), 167; For a discussion of how MacArthur's character and personality influenced the occupation, see Schaller, *Douglas MacArthur*, chs. 9 and 10.

8. For a discussion of the origins and implementation of the SCAP reform program, see Dower, *Empire and Aftermath*; Schaller, *The American Occupation of Japan*; Schaller, *Douglas MacArthur*; Cohen, *Remaking Japan*; See Col. Charles Kades of Government Section reflections on the origins of land reform in his Oral History, Cineworld Transcript, MacArthur Memorial; Jiang's lament is reported by Gen. Edward M. Almond, Oral History, U.S. Military History Institute, Carlisle Barracks; For MacArthur's view that moderate reform would deter revolution, see his letter to Robert E. Wood, Jan. 12, 1948, MacArthur file, Wood papers.

9. I. F. Stone, "Behind the MacArthur Row," *Nation* 161 (Sept. 29, 1945), 297–99; John Maki, "Japan's Political Reconstruction," *Far Eastern Survey* (Apr. 9, 1947), 73–77.

10. Diary entries of Mar. 3 and 13, Apr. 16 and 18, 1947, James Forrestal papers, Princeton University; minutes of the meetings of the secretaries of State, War and Navy, Apr. 16, 1947, ibid.; Acheson to Patterson, Apr. 14, 1947, filed with 740.00119 control (Japan) 9–1347, Records of the Department of State (DOS), RG 59, National Archives; Patterson to Acheson, Apr. 21, 1947, ibid.; note to E. A. Locke, attached to ibid. On the evolution of the Truman administration's security policy, see Melvyn P. Leffler, *A Preponderance of Power: National Security, The Truman Administration, and the Cold War* (Stanford, Ca., 1992).

11. For a typical example of MacArthur's assertion that Japan was ready for a peace treaty, see Record of conversation with MacArthur, Sir Alvary Gascoigne to Foreign Office, Mar. 4, 1947, FO 371/63766, Public Record Office, London; MacArthur press conference, Mar. 17, 1947, *The Political Reconstruction of Japan*, Vol. 2: 765–67.

12. Dean Acheson, "The Requirements of Reconstruction," speech of May 8, 1947, Department of State *Bulletin* 16 (May 18, 1947), 991–94.

13. Kennan to Lovett and Marshall, Oct. 14, 1947, FRUS 1947, 6: 536–43; memorandum by Carlisle Humelsine to Willard Thorp, et al., Oct. 29, 1947, Policy Planning Staff Records, FOIA; Humelsine to Gen. Marshall Carter, Oct.16, 1947, ibid; diary entries of Oct. 31 and Nov. 7, 1947, Forrestal papers; Kenneth C. Royal Oral History, Columbia University.

14. Memorandum of Dec. 12, 1947, William H. Draper to Gordon Gray, Dec. 14, 1947, Undersecretary of the Army, General Correspondence–Security Classified, August 1947–January 1949, SAOUS 004, Japan, Records of the Office of the Secretary of the Army, RG 335, National Archives; for discussion of MacArthur's political ambitions in 1948, see Schaller, *Douglas MacArthur*, 146–57.

15. MacArthur particularly disliked his former aide, Eisenhower, and in 1948 threatened to blackmail Ike to keep him from seeking the presidency. See Schaller, *Douglas MacArthur*, 147–52.

16. Minutes of discussion of draft treaty, Meeting 48, Aug. 25, 1947, box 32, Records of the Policy Planning Staff, RG 59; Meeting 54, Sept. 4, 1947, ibid.; Meeting 65, Sept. 22, 1947, ibid. While the Policy Planning Staff focused on security issues, economic specialists in the State and Army Departments developed an economic rescue plan resembling the European Recovery Program, or Marshall Plan, then under consideration by Congress. SWNCC 381, the State Department plan, and SWNCC 384, the Army plan, both proposed a multiyear aid program to provide Japan with raw materials and capital for the renewal of industry. The program would encourage Japanese trade with Southeast Asia to assure Tokyo a future market and source of raw materials outside the area of Northeast Asia under Communist control. These ideas formed the heart of the Economic Recovery in Occupied Areas (EROA) program passed by Congress in June 1948. See SWNCC 360, 381, 384 files, Records of the State, War, Navy Coordinating Committee, RG 353.

17. Report by Kennan, FRUS 1948, 6: 697–706; George F. Kennan, *Memoirs, 1925–50* (Boston, 1967), 381–84; Kennan to W. W. Butterworth, Mar. 9, 14, 16, 1948, box 19, PPS Records, FOIA.

18. PPS 28, Mar. 25, 1948, PPS Records, RG 59; William H. Draper Oral History, Truman Library; MacArthur, Draper, Kennan conversation transcript, Mar. 21, 1948, FRUS 1948, 6: 706–12; *Pacific Stars and Stripes*, Apr. 12, 1948; the *New York Times*, Apr. 20, 1948.

19. Percy Johnston, et al., "Report on the Economic Position and Prospects of Japan and Korea and the Measures Required to Improve Them," released Apr. 26, 1948, copy in Joseph Dodge papers, Detroit Public Library.

20. The Economic and Reconstruction in Occupied Areas Program (EROA) appropriated about $125 million for Japanese industry. It formed one part of the nearly $500 million Government and Relief in Occupied Areas (GARIOA) program. Congress permitted the army to shift some GARIOA funding to EROA. Draper convinced Congress to pass PL 820, creating a revolving fund for Japanese textile mills to purchase American cotton; memorandum for the record by Ralph W. E. Reid, Nov. 19, 1948, Undersecretary of the Army, General Correspondence, Security Classified, Aug. 1947–Jan. 1949, SAOUS 091 Japan, Records of the Office of the Secretary of the Army, RG 335; Reid memorandum for the record, Dec. 9, 1948, ibid.; "Informal memorandum of understanding between State and Army departments concerning implementation of NSC 13," Dec. 7, 1948, Undersecretary of the Army, Draper/Voorhees Project Decimal File, 1947–50, 091 Japan, Records of the Department of the Army, RG 335; Draper-Lovett exchange, Dec. 13, 1948, FRUS 1948, 6: 1060; statement on economic stabilization in Japan, Dec. 10, 1948, ibid., 1059–60; William Draper drafted the economic directive Truman issued. It resembled earlier initiatives Draper had applied in Germany. Joseph Dodge had also served in Germany where he supervised economic reforms in the western zones. See Schaller, *The American Occupation of Japan*, 130–40.

21. Kern to Draper, July 25, 1948, CAD Decimal File CAD 014, Japan, sec. 3, June 1, 1948–Aug. 31, 1948, RG 165; Kern to Dodge, Jan. 24, 1949, cover letter and report by the American Council on Japan, copy in Joseph Dodge papers, Detroit Public Library. Council members hosted a dinner for top Army and State Department officials during February 1949 in which speakers made recommendations for Dodge to follow. See R. W. Barnett to Paul Nitze, notes on "American Council on Japan Dinner for Mr. Royall's Mission," Feb. 23, 1949, 740.00119 Control (Japan) 2–2349, Department of State Records, RG 49. The best study of the ACJ appears in Howard Schonberger, *Aftermath of War: Americans and the Remaking of Japan, 1945–1952* (Kent, Ohio, 1989), 134–61.

22. Chalmers Johnson, *MITI and the Japanese Miracle: The Growth of Industrial Policy, 1925–75* (Stanford, Ca., 1982).

23. Joseph Dodge, "The Role of Japan in Our Relations with the Orient," July 7, 1949, Memorandum to the Division of Northeast Asian Affairs, Department of State, copy in Dodge papers; Statement by Dodge to the National Advisory Council, Jan. 12, 1950, ibid.; Dodge quoted in Jon Halliday, *A Political History of Japanese Capitalism* (New York, 1967), 197.

24. Robert W. Barnett to Edwin F. Martin, "Memorandum Regarding Cranking-Up," Sept. 8, 1947, box 222, Records of the Far Eastern Commission, RG 43; Barnett to Martin, "Your Comments on Expansion of Crank-Up," Sept. 10, 1947, ibid.

25. Col. R. W. Porter, Jr., to Chief, Civil Affairs Division, Oct. 13, 1948, CAD 014, Japan, sec. 4, Sept. 1948–Dec. 31., 1948, Civil Affairs Division Decimal File, RG 165; Ralph E. Reid to Draper and Dodge, Oct. 18, 1948, box 222, FEC Records, RG 43.

26. Memorandum for the Record by Reid, Nov. 19, 1948, Undersecretary of the Army, General Correspondence, Security Classified, Aug. 1947–Jan. 1949, SAOUS 091, Japan RG 335; Memorandum for the record by Reid, Dec. 9, 1948, 091.3 Japan, ibid; Program for a Self-Supporting Economy, ESS, Nov. 1948, box 8361, Records of the Supreme Commander for the Allied Powers, RG 331; Draper to Lovett, Dec. 14, 1948, FRUS 1948, VI, 1062–63; "Study of a U.S. Aid Program for the Far East," Feb. 14, 1948, SAOUS, 400.3591, Draper/Voorhees Project Decimal File, RG 335.

27. Memorandum by Davies, "U.S. Policy with Respect to the Far East," Dec. 6, 1948, box 222, FEC Records, RG 43.

28. PPS 51, Mar. 29, 1949, in NSC 51, "U.S. Policy Toward Southeast Asia," July 1, 1949, NSC Files, National Archives. An excerpt appears in FRUS 1949, VII, 1128–33; minutes of Undersecretaries Meeting, "To Define U.S. Policy towards Southeast Asia," Apr. 6, 1949,

Records of the Policy Planing Staff, FOIA; In part because the State Department's European specialists considered the PPS too hostile to British and French colonial policy, Acheson shied away from pushing for the formal adoption the Southeast Asia paper. Nevertheless, it influenced subsequent policy.

29. Remarks by Kennan and Taylor appear in "Department of State Conference on Problems of U.S. Policy in China," Oct. 6–8, 1949, box 174, PSF, Truman papers. The discussants, drawn from the business, academic, and journalistic communities favored a "moderate" approach toward China, including the prospects of trade and diplomatic recognition if Communist behavior warranted. For a discussion of American opinion and the recognition question, see Nancy Tucker, *Patterns in the Dust: Chinese American Relations and the Recognition Controversy, 1949–50* (New York, 1983).

30. Acheson to Franks, Dec. 24, 1949, FRUS 1949, VII, 927–28.

31. See articles by Stewart and Joseph Alsop, Aug. 22, 24, 29, Sept. 18, 1949, *Washington Post*.

32. Stewart Alsop, "We Are Losing Asia Fast," *Saturday Evening Post* (Vol. 222, no. 37, March 11, 1950), 29ff. Alsop's draft notes on his Asian trip and early version of the article provide an even more vivid version of the domino threat to Japan. See draft article notes in Alsop papers, Library of Congress.

33. Clubb to Acheson, Apr. 30, 1949, FRUS 1949, IX, 974–76; OIR Report no. 4867, Jan. 24, 1949, "The Effect of a Communist Dominated China on other Areas of the Far East," RG 59. Clubb favored the restoration of trade, suggesting it could be used by Washington to pressure the Communists.

34. Costello, "Could Japan Go Communist"; OIR Reports no. 4687, Jan. 24, 1949, and no. 5063, Oct. 14, 1949, DOS, RG 59; *New York Times*, Nov. 25, 1949.

35. OIR Report no. 4867, DOS, RG 59.

36. NSC 41, "U.S. Policy Regarding Trade with China," Feb. 28, 1949, approved by Truman on Mar. 3, 1949, NSC Files, National Archives. This permitted both U.S. and allied commerce with China, except for designated military and strategic items. It remained operative until China entered the Korean War. For a discussion of the evolution of trade policy toward China, see Nancy Bernkoph Tucker, "American Policy Toward Sino-Japanese Trade in the Postwar Years: Politics and Prosperity," *Diplomatic History* (Vol. 8, no.3, Summer 1984), 183–208.

37. Testimony by Dean Acheson, Jan. 10, 1950, in U.S. Senate, Committee on Foreign Relations, *Reviews of the World Situation: 1949–50: Hearings Held in Executive Session on the World Situation*, 81st Cong., 1st and 2nd sess. (Washington, D.C. 1974), 105–71.

38. Ibid. Acheson made similar points in a public speech at the National Press Club in Washington on Jan. 12, 1950. Although he stressed the need to avoid confrontation with China, help Southeast Asia, and assure Japan's well-being, the speech is usually remembered for Acheson's failure to include South Korea in the first tier of U.S. defense commitments. This slip, critics charged, provoked North Korea's attack the next June. See Department of State *Bulletin* (Vol. 22, Jan. 22, 1950), 114–15; Acheson remarks on Southeast Asia appear in testimony of Sept. 11, 1950, in Senate Foreign Relations Committee, *Reviews of the World Situation*, 357–58; Tracy Voorhees to NSC, Jan. 10, 1950, in NSC 61 file, NSC Records, National Archives. Voorhees and Defense Secretary Louis Johnson competed with Acheson to administer MDAP and other aid money in Asia. They hoped to use the bulk of the funds for military aid to Southeast Asia, leaving less for the economic development programs advocated by State. See Schaller, *The American Occupation of Japan*, 194–215. Still, civilian defense analysts saw the underlying situation much as Acheson did. For example, army economist Ralph Reid convinced Voorhees and Joseph Dodge that China and the Soviet Union sponsored Nationalist uprisings in Southeast Asia as a form of indirect aggression against Tokyo. They hoped to make Japan "dependent upon Russia and her satellites for the bulk of her market and raw materials" so it would "fall of its own weight once Communists controlled" Southeast Asia and American aid to Japan came "to an inevitable end." See Reid to Voorhees, "Aid Program for Southeast Asia," Feb. 27, 1950, Dodge papers.

39. For a detailed discussion of these missions, see Schaller, *The American Occupation of Japan*, 220–26.

40. Voorhees Memorandum to Executive Secretary, NSC, "Coordination of U.S. Aid Programs for Far Eastern Areas," Apr. 5, 1950, Dodge papers; Voorhees Report of May 27, 1950, "A Proposal to Correlate Economic Aid to Europe with Military Defense," Cold War Coordination Staff memoranda, 39.32, box 62, Bureau of the Budget Records, RG 51; numerous schemes to finance the exchange of Japanese manufactured exports for Southeast Asian raw materials were put forward by the State, Treasury, and Defense Departments during the spring of 1950. See Schaller, *The American Occupation of Japan*, 226-31.

41. NSC 64, "The Position of the U.S. with respect to Indochina," Feb. 17, 1950, approved April 18, NSC Files, National Archives.

42. Memorandum by Gen. Omar Bradley to Secretary of Defense, Mar. 1, 1949, in NSC 44, Mar. 11, 1949, NSC Records; NSC 13/3, May 6, 1949, FRUS 1949, VII, pt. 2, 730-36; Acheson to Certain Diplomatic Officials, May 8, 1949, ibid., 736-37; MacArthur to Acheson, June 16, 1949, ibid., 778-81; Acheson to MacArthur, Sept. 9, 1949, ibid., 850-52; Sebald memorandum of conversation with MacArthur, Sept. 21, 1949, ibid., 862-64.

43. Treaty draft of Oct. 13, 1949, in Feary to Allison, Oct. 14, 1949, 740.0011 PW (peace)10-1449, DOS, RG 59; Notes on discussion of Peace with Japan, Oct. 21, 1949, 740.0011PW (peace)10-2149, ibid.

44. Memorandum by Acheson of discussion with the president, Sept. 16, 1949, FRUS 1949, VII, pt. 2, 860; transcript of a meeting with Col. Babcock, Nov. 10, 1949, JSSC 388.1, Japan, sec. 1 (9-1-47), JCS Records, RG 218; Report by the JSSC to the JCS on "Impact of an Early Peace Treaty with Japan on U.S. Strategic Requirements," Nov. 30, 1949, JCS 1380/75, ibid.; Voorhees notes of summary of Gen. MacArthur's opinions on a Japanese Peace Treaty, Dec. 14, 1949, CJCS 092.2 Japanese Peace Treaty 1950, ibid.; Gen. Carter B. Magruder to JCS, Dec. 3, 1949, enclosed in JCS 1380/76, CCS 388.1, Japan, sec. 1 (9-1-47); JCS 1380/77, Dec. 10, 1949, ibid; Johnson to Acheson, Dec. 23, 1949, with enclosure of memorandum by the JCS to the Secretary of Defense, Dec. 22, 1949, FRUS 1949, VII, pt. 2, 922-23—circulated as NSC 60, Dec. 27, 1949. Both MacArthur and the Joint Chiefs favored a stronger U.S. military commitment to defend Taiwan. To a degree, their opposition to part or all the Japan treaty provisions represented an attempt to force Acheson to alter his stand against military involvement on behalf of the Chinese Nationalists.

45. For the discussion among Truman, Acheson, and the military establishment on treaty prospects in early 1950, see Truman quoted in memorandum by Rusk, Jan. 24, 1950, FRUS 1950, VI, 1131; memorandum by Butterworth for Acheson, "Outline for Meeting with Secretary on Japanese Peace Settlement," prepared by John B. Howard, Jan. 18, 1950, ibid., 117-19; memorandum by Butterworth of conversation with MacArthur, Feb. 5, 1950, ibid., 1133-35; memorandum by Howard for Bohlen, Mar. 31, 1950, ibid., 1157-59; memorandum and summary of discussion with Truman, in John Howard to Butterworth, "Japanese Peace and Security Settlement," Mar. 9, 1950, ibid., 1138-49; memorandum by Voorhees for Acheson, in Howard to Jessup, Mar. 24, 1950, ibid., 1150-53; memorandum by Howard for Bohlen, Mar. 31, 1950, ibid., 1157-60; memorandum by John Howard of conversation between Acheson and the Joint Chiefs, "Japanese Peace Treaty," Apr. 24, 1950, ibid., 1175-82.

46. Memorandum of conversation by John Howard, "Japanese Peace Settlement," April 7, 1950, FRUS 1950, VI, 1161-66.

47. Memorandum by Huston, "American Bases in Japan," April 8, 1950, FRUS 1950, VI, 1166-67;

48. Dr. Bowen Dees, a member of SCAP Scientific and Technical Division in 1950, related this story to me. He and his colleagues knew little about the political aspects of the trip but hoped the delegation would promote scientific and educational exchanges.

49. Ikeda statement of May 2, 1950, in Reid to Butterworth, May 10, 1950, FRUS 1950, VI, 1194-98; Memorandum by Green for Allison, August 2, 1950, ibid., 1262-63; Butterworth to Acheson, May 3, 1950, 694.0015/5-350, DOS, RG 59. Ikeda's proposal is reported in a Japanese recollection by Miyazawa, cited in John Welfield, *An Empire in Eclipse: Japan in the Postwar American Alliance System* (Atlantic Highlands, N.J., 1988), 46.

50. Memorandum by W. W. Butterworth to Acting Secretary Webb, May 12, 1950, FRUS 1950, VI, 1198. Butterworth, then in charge of drafting a treaty with Japan, considered Ikeda's

remarks a breakthrough and circulated them to Dean Rusk, John Foster Dulles, and Secretary of State Dean Acheson, then in Europe.

51. The impact of the Ikeda–Yoshida remarks is seen in: Memorandum by Dulles for Dean Rusk, Paul Nitze, and Undersecretary Webb, May 18, 1950, FRUS 1950, I, 314–16; Memorandum by Acheson's aides Fisher Howe to W. Park Armstrong, May 31, 1950, Ibid, 347–49; Report by Dean Rusk, May 31, 1950, with accompanying documents, box 18, Chinese Affairs Lot File, DOS, RG 59.

52. Reid to Butterworth, May 10, 1950, FRUS 1950, VI, 1194–98.

53. The elaborate efforts by Rusk and Dulles to link the Japan treaty to the defense of Taiwan are detailed in Schaller, *The American Occupation of Japan*, 261–69. Both men dabbled in plots to replace Jiang with a more popular leader around whom the United States could rally. Rusk urged Truman to protect Taiwan while expanding military aid to Southeast Asia and the Philippines. When the Korean War erupted a month later, the president closely paraphrased Rusk's draft statements of May 1950 in announcing the American decisions to intervene in Korea, the Taiwan Strait, and Southeast Asia.

54. Ibid., 266–68.

55. See briefing paper for Bradley and Johnson prepared by Maj. Gen Carter B. Magruder, June 5, 1950, CJCS 092.2, Japanese Peace Treaty—1950, JCS Records, RG 218.

56. Memorandum by Dulles for Acheson, June 6, 1950, FRUS 1950, VI, 1207–12; memorandum by Allison for Sebald, June 14, 1950, ibid., 1212–13; memorandum by Dulles, June 15, 1950, ibid., 1222–23.

57. William J. Sebald, *With MacArthur in Japan* (New York, 1965), 252–53.

58. MacArthur memorandum on Formosa, June 14, 1950, FRUS 1950, VII, 161–65; MacArthur memorandum on peace treaty problem, ibid., VI, 1213–21.

59. Summary report by Dulles, July 3, 1950, ibid., 1230–37; Sebald, *With MacArthur*, 254; Kern to Dulles, Aug. 19, 1950, box 53, Dulles papers.

60. Memorandum by Gen. Omar Bradley to the JCS, June 26, 1950, CJCS 092.2 Japanese Peace Treaty, 1950, JCS Records, RG 218; memorandum on the concept governing security in postwar Japan by MacArthur, June 23, 1950, FRUS 1950, VI, 1227–29; memorandum by Dulles for Acheson, June 30, 1950, ibid., 1229–30, 1232–33; Michael Yoshitsu, *Japan and the San Francisco Peace Settlement* (New York, 1983), 41; Yoshida Shigeru Interview, Dulles Oral History Project, Princeton University.

NOTES FOR CHAPTER 2

1. Memorandum by Dulles, July 6, 1950, Dulles papers; FRUS 1950, VI, 1243–44; statement by Dulles in report to Council on Foreign Relations on "Japanese Peace Treaty Problems," Oct. 23, 1950, box 48, Dulles papers.

2. For the record of State–Defense negotiations, see FRUS 1950, VI, 1259–1304.

3. Kennan to Acheson, Aug. 21, 1950, FOIA.

4. For Dulles' contact with foreign nations regarding the treaty, see FRUS 1950, VI, 1332–54.

5. Allison, *Ambassador From the Prairie*, 151–52; FRUS 1950, VI, 1393–94.

6. Dulles to Acheson, Jan. 4, 1951, FRUS, 1951, VI, 781–83; Acheson to Marshall, Jan. 9, 1951, ibid., 787–89.

7. Yoshida's daughter quoted by John Welfield, *An Empire in Eclipse: Japan in the Postwar American Alliance System* (London and Atlantic Highlands, N.J., 1988), 52; Yoshida's views are partially reconstructed from interviews with officials who worked under his direction. See Michael Yoshitsu, *Japan and the San Francisco Peace Settlement* (New York, 1982), 43–53.

8. Kern to Dulles, Jan. 15 and Jan. 19, 1951, box 53, Dulles papers.

9. "Yoshida: Late Enemy into Latest Ally?," *Newsweek*, Jan. 22, 1951 (Vol. 37, no. 4), 32–35.

10. Memorandum by Feary, Jan. 26, 1951, FRUS 1951, VI, 811–15.

11. Memorandum by Allison, Jan. 29, 1951, FRUS 1951, VI, 827–30; diary entry of Jan. 29, 1951, Sebald papers.

12. Yoshida at times used intermediaries to inform Americans of what he would accept, despite his public opposition to rearmament. See, for example, the message conveyed by Shirasu Jiro in memorandum by Feary, Jan. 25, 1951, FRUS, 1951, VI, 810–11; memorandum by Allison, Jan. 29, 1951, ibid., 827–30; undated memorandum by Yoshida, ibid., 833–34; Weinstein, *Japan's Postwar Defense Policy*, 81; Dower, *Empire and Aftermath*, 389–93; Igarashi Takeshi, "Peace-Making and Party Politics: The Formation of the Domestic Foreign Policy System in Postwar Japan," *Journal of Japanese Studies*, 11,2 (Summer 1985), 323–56; Richard Finn, *Winners in Peace: MacArthur, Yoshida and Postwar Japan* (Berkeley, Ca., 1992), 276–77. Finn relies heavily on later accounts by Yoshida and his aides about their informal understandings with Dulles; on Yoshida's claim of a secret agreement with MacArthur, see his oral history in Dulles Oral History Project, Princeton University.

13. See, for example, Yoshida's undated memo handed to the Americans on Jan. 31, 1951, FRUS 1951, VI, 833–34.

14. See editorial note regarding Feb. 3, 1951, memorandum, FRUS 1951, VI, 849; Finn, *Winners in Peace*, 278.

15. Memorandum by Dulles Mission, Feb. 3, 1951 (delivered on Feb. 5), FRUS 1951, VI, 849–55.

16. FRUS 1951, VI, 856–66.

17. Dulles to Acheson, Feb. 10, 1951, FRUS 1951, VI, 874–80; Yoshitsu, *Japan and the San Francisco Peace Settlement*, 57–66; Finn, *Winners in Peace*, 281–283.

18. Memorandum by Allison, Feb. 12, 1951, FRUS 1951, VI, 880–83, memorandum by Feary, Feb. 17, 1951, ibid., 885–87; Dulles to MacArthur, Mar. 2, 1951, ibid., 900–03; memorandum by Feary, April 17, 1951, ibid., 979–82.

19. FRUS 1951, VI, 169–79, 885–87; Schonberger, *Aftermath of War*, 261–62.

20. The background of the decision to relieve MacArthur, including its nuclear dimension, is discussed in Schaller, *Douglas MacArthur: The Far Eastern General* (New York, 1989), 230–40.

21. Miyazawa to Ralph Reid, April 14, 1951, Japan 1951, Reid Correspondence file, box 3, Dodge papers.

22. Finn, *Winners in Peace*, 293–94.

23. Ibid., 296.

24. Memorandum on the Substance of Discussions at a Department of State-Joint Chiefs of Staff Meeting, April 11, 1951, FRUS 1951, VI, 969–71; Memorandum by Dulles, April 12, 1951, ibid., 972–76; notes of conference between Smith and Dulles, May 6, 1951, box 103, H. Alexander Smith papers, Princeton University.

25. Memorandum by Feary of Dulles Mission Staff Meeting, April 17, 1951, FRUS 1951, VI 979–82; memorandum by Feary of Dulles Mission Staff Meeting, April 18, 1951, 982–85; memorandum by Feary of conversation with Dulles and Japanese leaders, Apr. 18, 1951, ibid., 985–89.

26. Memorandum of Dulles conversation with Sir Oliver Franks, Mar. 30, 1951, ibid., 953–54; memorandum of Dulles conversation with Sir Oliver Franks, Apr. 12, 1951, ibid., 977–78; Dulles interview of May 15, 1951, quoted in Ronald Pruessen, *John Foster Dulles: The Road to Power* (New York, 1982), 486–87.

27. Summary of negotiations in London, by Feary, June 14 (?), 1951, ibid., 118–19; draft statement of the United Kingdom and United States Government, June 19, 1951, FRUS 1951, VI, 1134; memorandum by Dulles to Acheson, Dec. 26, 1951, ibid., 1467–70.

28. Dulles to Sebald, July 27, 1951, FRUS 1951, VI, 1226–27.

29. FRUS 1951, VI, 1289, 1344–45; Schonberger, *Aftermath of War*, 265–66.

30. Sebald oral history, Dulles Oral History Project.

31. Memorandum by Dulles of conversation with Truman, Oct. 3, 1951, FRUS 1951, VI, 1372–73; memorandum by Dulles of conversation with Acheson, Oct. 22, 1951, ibid., 1378–79; memorandum from Dulles to Rusk, Oct. 22, 1951, ibid., 1380–81.

32. Rusk's negotiations during February 1952 are described in FRUS 1951, XIV, 1102–1206; Yoshitsu, *Japan and the San Francisco Settlement*, 86–96.

33. On the domestic Japanese debate over the treaties, see Welfield, *An Empire in Eclipse*, 55–58.

34. FRUS 1951, VI, 1389; *New York Times*, Sept. 14, 1951.

35. Diary entry of Sept. 4, 1951, H. Alexander Smith papers.

36. Dulles to Allison, Dec. 13, 1951, FRUS 1951, VI, 1437–39; Dulles to Allison, Dec. 14, 1951, ibid., 1438–39; memorandum by Smith, ibid., 1447–48; Sebald oral history, Dulles Oral History Project; "Notes of a conversation between Mr. John Foster Dulles and Amb. Wellington Koo," Nov. 19, 1952, box 187, Wellington Koo papers, Columbia University.

37. Memorandum of conversation by Sebald, and draft letter, FRUS 1951, VI, 1443–46; Yoshida letters to Dulles, Dec. 22, 24, 1951, ibid., 1465–67.

38. Acheson to Dulles, Dec. 18, 1951, FRUS 1951, VI, 1448–50; Dulles to Acheson, Dec. 26, 1951, ibid., 1467–70; Dulles to Acheson, Dec. 28, 1951, ibid., 1477; for the complaints of Churchill and Eden, see FRUS 1952–54, XIV, 1069–70, 1075–80.

39. U.S. delegation minutes, Jan. 8, 1952, FRUS 1952–54, VI, 783; Bradley's remarks of Jan. 22, 1952, appear in Bradley to Ridgway, Mar. 26, 1952, CJCS 092.2 Japanese Peace Treaty (22 Jan 52), JCS Records, RG 218.

40. FRUS 1952–54, XIV, 1092–93; Dulles to Churchill, Jan. 17, 1952, FO 371/99404, PRO; L. H. Lamb, British Embassy in Beijing, to Foreign Office, Jan. 29, 1952, FO 371/99435, PRO.

41. Dulles statement to Senate Foreign Relations Committee, Jan. 21, 1952, box 61, Dulles papers; Report of the Committee on Foreign Relations, 82nd Congress, 2nd session, *Japanese Peace Treaty and Other Treaties Relating to Security in the Pacific* (Washington, 1952); Senate Committee on Foreign Relations, *Hearings Before the Committee on Japanese Peace Treaty and Other Treaties Relating to Security in the Pacific, Jan. 21–25, 1952* (Washington, D.C., 1952).

42. Memorandum by Dulles, Oct. 8, 1951, FRUS 1951, VI, 1372; Robert Murphy, *Diplomat Among Warriors* (New York, 1964), 339.

43. Murphy, *Diplomat Among Warriors*, 341, 344, 345; Staff of Asahi Shimbun, *The Pacific Rivals* (New York, 1972), 214.

44. Kowalski, later a member of Congress, published a memoir in Japanese about his role in organizing the NPR. That book, *Ninon Saigumbi* (Tokyo, 1969), was based on an English language manuscript entitled "The Rearmament of Japan." Kowalski's notes from the 1950s, which he used as the basis for his later book, are located in box 8, Frank Kowalski papers, Library of Congress.

45. Collins to Ridgway, Dec. 17, 1951, FRUS 1951, VI, 1141–43; Ridgway to Dept. of the Army, Dec. 20, 1951, ibid., 1451–53; Lovett to Truman, Apr. 22, 1952, FRUS 1952–52, XIV, 1243–44; memorandum of conversation by Young, ibid., 1309–10; Leffler, *Preponderance of Power*, 466.

46. Notes in box 8, Frank Kowalski papers, Library of Congress; Welfield, *An Empire in Eclipse*, 79.

47. The role of Japanese minesweepers in the Korean War is discussed in James E. Auer, *The Postwar Rearmament of Japanese Maritime Forces, 1945–71* (New York, 1973), 53–68; Murphy, *Diplomat Among Warriors*, 348.

48. Kern to Dulles, Dec. 9, 1951, box 43, Dulles papers.

NOTES FOR CHAPTER 3

1. "Japan's economic problems and prospects," report of May 15, 1952, box 13, Japan 1950–52, PSA Lot File, RG 59.

2. Schonberger, *Aftermath of War*, 226; William Borden, *The Pacific Alliance: United States Foreign Economic Policy and Japanese Trade Recovery, 1947–1955* (Madison, Wi., 1984), 98–102.

3. The impact of war orders on Japanese companies is recounted by the staff of *Asahi Shimbun* in the anthology, *Pacific Rivals: A Japanese View of the Japanese–American Relationship* (New York, 1972), 193–95; on Toyota management's use of war orders to restructure the company, see Fujita Kuniko, "Corporatism and the Corporate Welfare Program: The Impact of the Korean War on the Toyota Motor Corporation," in William F. Nimmo, ed., *The Occupation of Japan: The Impact of the Korean War* (Norfolk, Va., 1990), 111–26.

4. "Divine aid" played on the phrase *kamikaze*, the divine wind, or typhoon, that wrecked a Mongol invasion fleet centuries earlier. During World War II, the term referred to suicide

pilots who attacked American ships in the final battles of the Pacific War. Yoshida's two remarks are cited in "draft history of Japanese rearmament," box 8, Kowalski Papers, Library of Congress and Kozo Yamamura, *Economic Policy in Postwar Japan: Growth Versus Economic Democracy* (Berkeley, Ca., 1967), 53; economic data on the period 1951–53 is contained in Schonberger, *Aftermath of War*, 228–34; for comments on the Tokyo stock market, see William Diehl to Dodge, July 20, 1950, "Japan: Missions-Dodge," OASIA File, Department of the Treasury, FOIA; Robert Murphy, *Diplomat Among Warriors* (New York, 1964), 347. While acknowledging the economic significance of the Korean War, Roger Dingman argues that it affected the pace, not the nature or direction, of Japan's recovery. See Roger Dingman, "The Dagger and the Gift: The Impact of the Korean War on Japan," *Journal of American-East Asian Relations* (Spring 1993, Vol. 2, no. 1), 29–58.

5. Undersecretary of the Army Tracy Voorhees best articulated this idea. Before leaving office in May 1950 to work on mobilizing public opinion behind rearmament, Voorhees issued a call to "coordinate" containment and economic development programs by "modernizing" the Marshall Plan. He proposed using idle industrial capacity in Western Europe and Japan to contribute to the "production of defensive weapons." Dollars given to Germany and Japan could be targeted to resume weapons production. Money earned by the sale of weapons to other allies would then be used to "purchase our wheat, cotton and tobacco," allowing each aid dollar to do the work of two. Henceforth, he predicted, the Japanese should be expected to "earn their dollars by agreeing to provide most of the economic assistance required for Southeast Asia." By supplying low-cost military equipment to the region, Japan would assist containment, earn money, and require less American aid. See Voorhees to NSC, Jan. 10, 1950, in NSC 61 file, Jan. 27, 1950, NSC Record Group, National Archives; Voorhees report of May 27, 1950, "A Proposal to Correlate Economic Aid to Europe with Military Defense," Cold War Coordination Staff memoranda, 39 32, box 62, Bureau of the Budget Records, RG 51, NA; Borden, *Pacific Alliance*, 47–49. Similarly, Joseph Dodge described Japan as an economic and military "springboard" for American efforts to defend Southeast Asia. See Halliday, *A Political History of Japanese Capitalism*, 197; Dodge testimony to ECA Advisory Committee on Fiscal and Monetary Problems, Apr. 28, 1950, Dodge papers.

6. Statement by Dodge in Yokohama, Oct. 7, 1950, "Japan: Missions—Dodge," OASIA File, Department of Treasury Records, FOIA; Schonberger, *Aftermath of War*, 227; Borden, *Pacific Alliance*, 148.

7. Dulles remarks on "Japanese Peace Treaty Problems," Oct. 23, 1950, box 48, Dulles papers; memorandum by Allison, Jan. 11–12, 1951, FRUS 1951, VI, 790–92; memorandum by Allison, Jan. 18, 1951, ibid., 804–5.

8. "Notes on Conversation between Dulles and Gen. Marquat," Feb. 5, 1951, box 1, Japan Peace Treaty File, Lot 78D173, RG 59. Kenneth Morrow, head of the ESS Program and Statistics Division, prepared a report detailing ways in which Japan could produce military equipment for American and friendly Asian forces. The report, which circulated in the Army, Treasury, and State Departments, called for expanding procurement orders beyond the Korean context to permit Japanese industry to provide military items to the "non-communist . . . countries in the Far East area, such as French Indochina, Thailand, Formosa, the Philippines, Malaya, and Burma." Japan was "particularly well suited" to "fulfill supply functions as a Zone of the Interior for the U.S. and the Western Powers in the Asiatic region." Enhanced military production, the ESS report predicted, would predispose Japanese to accept rearmament and make Japan's "armed participation" as a cold war ally "more assured." See "Mobilization of Japanese Industrial Potential for U.S. Military Procurement," Feb. 7, 1951, copy in W. W. Diehl to Arthur Stuart, Mar. 20, 1951, box 13, OASIA File, Department of the Treasury, FOIA.

9. Borden, *Pacific Alliance*, 152–53. *Japan's Industrial Potential*, ESS reports of Feb. 1951, Oct. 1951, Feb. 1952, ibid.

10. Marshall to Secretaries of the Army, Navy, Air Force and Chairman of the Munitions Board, March 28, 1951, box 317, CD092 Japan, Office of the Secretary of Defense, RG 330.

11. Marquat to Department of the Army, Apr. 28, 1951, box 13, OASIA File, Department of the Treasury, FOIA.

12. NSC 48/5, "United States Objectives, Policies and Courses of Action in Asia," May 17, 1951, FRUS 1951, VI, 33–63.

13. Statement by Gen. Marquat, May 10, 1951, copy in Dodge papers; Statement released by Gen. Ridgway on May 16, 1951, *New York Times*, May 17, 1951, and the *Washington Post*, May 17, 1951.

14. *Nippon Times*, July 29, 1951; Tokyo press release of Aug. 2, 1951, "The First Step in Mr. Wilson's Plan," copies in Dodge papers.

15. Summary of Interdepartmental Committee on Far East Mobilization, Meeting #1, Aug. 24, 1951, box 6799, SCAP Records, RG 331.

16. SCAP announcement of "SCAP-Japanese Mission to Visit Southeast Asia for Raw Materials Study," July 4, 1951, copy in Dodge papers; British embassy in Tokyo to Foreign Office, dispatches of July 6, 10, 1951, FO 371/92642, PRO.

17. FRUS 1952–54, Vol. XIV, 1210–11; "SCAP/ESS Staff Study re Continuation of Current Activity for Integration of Japanese Potential in Overall U.S. Industrial Mobilization in Post Treaty Period," attached to memorandum of Jan. 7, 1952, CD092(Japan), box 317, Records of the Office of Secretary of Defense, RG 330; Borden, *Pacific Alliance*, 156, 192–93.

18. FRUS 1952–54, Vol. 14, 1295–1300, 1332–33; "The Probable Future Orientation of Japan," May 22, 1952, NIE –52, Truman Library; Yoko Yasuhara, "Japan, Communist China, and Export Controls in Asia, 1948–52," *Diplomatic History* (Vol. 10, no. 1, Winter 1986), 75–89; Dower, *Empire and Aftermath*, 410–14.

19. Joseph M. Dodge, "United States–Japan Economic Cooperation in the Post-Treaty Era," Feb. 1, 1952, box 1, "Office of Far East Operations—Japan Subject," RG 469; see also Carl Burness (Mutual Security Agency) to Edwin G. Arnold, "Meeting on Japan," Feb. 6, 1952, ibid.

20. Suto Hideo to Gen. Marquat, Feb. 12, 1952, "Establishment of a Viable Economy and Promotion of Economic Cooperation," copies in box 7, Japan–1951 Economic Cooperation, Dodge papers and box 1, Office of Far East Operations, Japan Subject Files, RG 469.

21. Marquat to Dodge, cover letter attached to ibid; SCAP report on "Japanese Industrial Potential, February 1952, quoted in Schonberger, *Aftermath of War*, 233.

22. Borden, *Pacific Alliance*, 158.

23. Chitoshi Yanaga, *Big Business in Japanese Politics* (New Haven, 1968), 240.

24. Ibid., 248–56.

25. Alan G. Robinson, Dean M. Schroeder, and Nalini Dayanand, "The U.S. Training Within Industries Program and Their Role in the Development of the Japanese Management Style," unpublished paper.

26. FRUS 1952–54, XIV, 1159–65.

27. Sebald to John Emmerson, Sept. 30, 1951, FRUS 1951, VI, 1363–1369.

28. "Japan's economic problems and prospects," report of May 15, 1952, box 13, Japan, 1950–52, PSA Lot File, RG 59.

29. U.S. Post-Treaty Policy Toward Japan, April 23, 1952, box 13, PSA Lot File, RG 59; FRUS 1952–54, XIV, 1298–1300.

30. FRUS 1952–52, XIV, 1295–1300.

31. Bendetsen to Secretary of Defense, "NSC 125/1, United States Objectives and Courses of Action with Respect to Japan and Annex Thereto," Aug. 1, 1952, box 317, CD 092 Japan, Office of Secretary of Defense, RG 330.

32. MacDonald to Foreign Office, Oct. 3, 1951, FO 371/92642, PRO.

33. MacDonald report to Foreign Office, July 1952, and Foreign Office Minutes attached to report, FO 371/99506, PRO; Report by MacDonald of talks with Foreign Minister Okazaki, July 8, 1952, FO 371/99506, PRO.

34. NSC 125/2 "United States Objectives and courses of Action with Respect to Japan," Aug. 7, 1952, FRUS 1952–54, XIV, 1300–8.

35. Omar Bradley to Secretary of Defense, July 28, 1952, FRUS 1952–54, XIV, 1289–90.

36. NSC 124/2, "United States Objectives and Courses of Action with Respect to Southeast Asia," June 25, 1952, President's Secretaries Files, Harry S. Truman papers, Truman Library.

37. Address by Dulles on "Far Eastern Problems," May 5, 1952, Dulles papers.

NOTES FOR CHAPTER 4

1. Sakaki Eisuke and Noguchi Yukio, quoted in Kenneth B. Pyle, *The Japanese Question: Power and Purpose in a New Era* (Washington, D.C., 1992), 42. For an elaboration of the argument that Japanese economic and trade policy since the early 1950s was part of a strategic foreign policy, see the perceptive essays by Chalmers Johnson, *Japan: Who Governs? The Rise of the Developmental State* (New York, 1995).

2. Ikeda's aide, Miyazawa Kiichi, recounted this discussion in a 1957 article. See Welfield, *Empire in Eclipse*, 98.

3. Memorandum of conversation by Dulles, Dec. 4, 1952, FRUS, 1952–54, XIV, 1364–65; John Allison, *Ambassador from the Prairie, or Allison in Wonderland* (Boston, 1973), 216; Welfield, *Empire in Eclipse*, 98.

4. Britain's ambassador in Tokyo, Sir Esler Dening, stressed this point to Foreign Minister Eden, Dec. 31, 1952, FO 371/105391, PRO.

5. Report by Naval Attache in Tokyo to Foreign Office, Mar. 17, 1953, FO 371/105391, PRO; Borden, *Pacific Alliance*, 172; Yanaga, *Big Business in Japanese Politics*, 260–61.

6. Allison, *Ambassador from the Prairie*, 230–35; Welfield, *Empire in Eclipse*, 99.

7. FRUS 1952–54, XIV, 1445–47; Allison, *Ambassador from the Prairie*, 235–36.

8. FRUS 1952–54, XIV, 1459–61; Allison, *Ambassador from the Prairie*, 239.

9. Allison, *Ambassador from the Prairie*, 240–43; Memorandum of Discussion at the 151st Meeting of NSC, June 25, 1953, FRUS 1952–54, XIV, 1438–44; ibid., 1471–72; Dulles press conference remarks of Sept. 3, 1953, ibid., 1496–97; Robertson to Allison, Oct. 1, 1953, ibid., 1521.

10. FRUS 1952–54, XIV, 1515.

11. FRUS 1952–54, XIV, 1513, 1529; Allison, *Ambassador from the Prairie*, 257–58.

12. FRUS 1952–54, XIV, 1489–90; Johnson, *The Right Hand of Power*, 161; Welfield, *Empire in Eclipse*, 101; Miyazawa quoted Yoshida's instruction in his 1956 memoir, *Tokyo-Washington no mistsudan* (Secret Talks between Tokyo and Washington) (Tokyo, 1956), cited in Kataoka Tetsuya, *The Price of a Constitution: The Origins of Japan's Postwar Politics* (New York, 1991), 118.

13. Eisenhower diary entry of Oct. 8, 1953, FRUS 1952–54, XIV, 1523.

14. Yoshida assured the United States that Japan would fulfill its "samurai" honor and repay the $2 billion GARIOA debt, but needed more time. Washington offered to "consult" Tokyo on the question of easing trade with China. Japanese and American position papers during the Ikeda–Robertson talks are contained in the Records of the Department of the Treasury, OASIA File, FOIA; State Department summaries of the talks appear in FRUS, 1952–54, XIV, 1523–39, 1549–51; see also Welfield, *Empire in Eclipse*, 101–2; Kataoka, *Price of a Constitution*, 117–20; Dower, *Empire and Aftermath*, 449–63; Borden, *Pacific Alliance*, 173–76.

15. Handwritten notes by Nixon for delivery in Tokyo, "Trip to Far East 1953," box 1, Nixon Series 378, Pacific Southwest Region, National Archives; Dower, *Empire and Aftermath*, 464–65; Kataoka, *Price of a Constitution*, 120–21; Allison, *Ambassador from the Prairie*, 252–55.

16. Department of State *Bulletin* 30, no. 771 (Apr. 5, 1954), 519; Embassy report on Japanese reaction to MSA Pact, March 22, 1954, box 1, Japan Subject File, Office of Far Eastern Operations, RG 469.

17. FRUS 1952–54, XIV, 1640–42, 1648–50, 1658–59; 1667–70; 1704–6.

18. FRUS 1952–54, XIV, 1714–15; 1720–23.

19. FRUS 1952–54, XIV, 1731–32.

20. FRUS 1952–54, XIV, 1714–15; on reflection, Allison told Dulles that since the United States neither could nor should abandon Japan, future economic and military assistance should concentrate on the gradual development of self-defense capacity, ibid., 1717–19; the ambassador and his staff submitted a lengthy "reappraisal" of policy in October arguing that for the short run no Japanese government would promote the kind of rapid rearmament Washington favored. See dispatch 611.94/10–2554, RG 59.

21. For a thoughtful discussion of the incident, see Roger Dingman, "Alliance in Crisis: The Lucky Dragon Incident and Japanese-American Relations," in Warren Cohen and Akira Iriye, eds., *The Great Powers in East Asia, 1953–1960* (New York, 1990), 187–214; for an excellent

contemporary account, see Robert Sherrod, "The Grim Facts of the H–Bomb Accident," *The Saturday Evening Post*, July 17, 1954, 20ff.

22. Dingman, "Lucky Dragon," 191–92.

23. FRUS 1952–54, XIV, 1622.

24. Sherrod, "The Grim Facts of the H–Bomb Accident."

25. Dingman, "Lucky Dragon," 194–95.

26. FRUS 1952–54, XIV, 1632–33, 1636–37, 1643–48, 1648–50, 1651–52.

27. FRUS 1952–54, XIV, 1665–70.

28. Dingman, "Lucky Dragon," 200–203; FRUS 1952–54, XIV, 1733–34.

29. FRUS 1952–54, XIV, 1746–52, 1758–60.

30. FRUS 1952–54, XIV, 1815–16.

31. Sato Kenji, *Godzillian Democracy: The Ideological Subtexts of Japanese Popular Culture* (Tokoyo, 1992); Merrill Goozner, "Godzilla's 40th Birthday a Boon to Filmmakers," *Chicago Tribune*, Sept. 8, 1994. During its initial run, over ten million Japanese viewed *Godzilla*. Aside from its anti-nuclear message, the film touched on such varied issues as arranged marriage, the reconciliation between an American journalist and his Japanese colleague who had been divided by World War II, and the morality of individual sacrifice to save one's country. Twenty sequels were released over the next forty years, with the star occasionally metamorphosing from villain to hero. Although many of the remakes had no social content, several reflected developments in Japanese-American relations. See also *New York Times*, Apr. 4, 1997, for Tanaka's obituary.

32. Yoshida address to National Press Club, *New York Times*, Nov. 9, 1954; Aichi's briefing papers are cited in Dower, *Empire and Aftermath*, 473–75.

33. FRUS 1952–54, XIV, 1175–86; Dower, *Empire and Aftermath*, 486–87. The Japanese desired to change the procedures related to the food aid program begun under MSA and continued under Public Law 480, the so-called Food for Peace program. For the United States, the program saved dollars and disposed of a costly surplus. The Japanese valued the commodity grants but wanted more of the yen proceeds earned from food sales to be applied toward non-military development projects. During 1955, Washington altered some of the procedures and allowed Japan greater flexibility.

34. Statement by President Eisenhower and Prime Minister Yoshida, Nov. 10, 1954, Department of State *Bulletin*, Nov. 22, 1954, 765.

35. Allison, *Ambassador from the Prairie*, 271–72.

36. Text of speech by Murphy to World Affairs Council of Northern California, Mar. 8, 1954, in FO 371/110182, PRO.

NOTES FOR CHAPTER 5

1. See dispatch by Frank Waring (with concurrence of Allison) to Department of State, Aug. 18, 1953, Japan Subject Files, Office of Far Eastern Operations, box 13, RG 469; for estimates of the impact of trade liberalization, see FRUS 1952–54, XIV, 1479–80.

2. FRUS 1952–54, XIV, 1488; 169th Meeting of NSC, Nov. 5, 1953, ibid., 265–77; 211th Meeting of NSC, Aug. 18, 1954, ibid., 526–40; 226th Meeting of NSC, Dec. 1, 1954, ibid., 968–78; discussion at the 191st Meeting of the NSC, Apr. 1, 1954, Whitman File, NSC Series, box 5, Eisenhower papers. Radford depicted the Soviet-Chinese "tie-up" as "religious in nature." He questioned the ability to fracture the alliance through economic pressure. Dulles felt more hopeful, arguing that "over a period of perhaps 25 years China and Russia would split apart because of the pressure of basic historical forces and because the religious fervor of Communism would have died down."

3. For an account of how the private trade program operated during the 1950s, see Soeya Yoshihide, "Japan's Postwar Economic Diplomacy with China: Three Decades of Non-Governmental Experience" (Ph.D. Dissertation, University of Michigan, 1987); and Sayuri Shimizu, "Perennial Anxiety: Japan–U.S. Controversy over Recognition of the PRC, 1952–1958," *Journal of American-East Asian Relations* (Fall, 1995, Vol. 4, no. 3), 223–48.

4. Shimizu, "Perennial Anxiety."

5. Memorandum of Discussion at 139th Meeting of NSC, Apr. 8, 1953, FRUS 1952–54, XIV, 180–82. For a discussion of Eisenhower's priorities regarding China, see Nancy B. Tucker, "A House Divided: The United States, the Department of State, and China," in Warren Cohen and Akira Iriye, eds., *The Great Powers in East Asia, 1953–60* (New York, 1990), 35–62. Tucker argues that Eisenhower and eventually Dulles marginalized the China "hardliners" and sought a middle ground of accommodation toward the PRC.

6. NSC 148, Apr. 6, 1953, FRUS 1952–54, XII, 285–98.

7. Memorandum of Discussion at Special Meeting of the NSC, Mar. 31, 1953, FRUS 1952–54, II, 264–66.

8. Memorandum of Discussion at the 139th Meeting of the NSC, April 8, 1953, FRUS, 1952–54, XIV, 1406–8. The background data generated by the NSC staff for policy papers 125/5 and 125/6 reported that Japan's "basic, long run economic problem" was "how, without undesirable trade with Communist areas, Japan can increase its trade sufficiently to become self-supporting." Although Japan's "economic viability" was of "critical importance to the security of the United States," the NSC staff cautioned that "viability will be extremely difficult to achieve." It noted Japanese pressure to boost trade with China and agreed that such trade, while politically dangerous, would certainly improve Japan's large trade imbalance with the United States. As an alternative, the NSC recommended measures to expand Japan's two-way trade with Southeast Asia and exports to the United States. Relatively little emphasis was laid on rearmament. The president formally approved these recommendations on June 26, 1953. See, ibid., 1411–15, 1448–52;

9. Memorandum of Discussion at the 151st Meeting of the NSC, June 25, 1953, FRUS 1952–54, XIV, 1438–44.

10. FRUS 1952–54, XIV, 1488–91.

11. Extract from Note on MacDonald's Talk with Vice President Nixon, October 1953, FO 371/105221, PRO.

12. Memorandum of Discussion at the 169th Meeting of the NSC, Nov. 5, 1953, FRUS 1952–54, XIV, 265–77. Several cabinet members described pressure from American business interests to be allowed to export to China if the Europeans and Japanese did. Most agreed on the need to liberalize trade at some point, but preferred to wait for a political settlement in Korea. Eisenhower warned that "demagogues" such as Senator Joe McCarthy "would raise a hue and cry" about any change in trade policy. But without a substantial revival of Sino-Japanese trade, Undersecretary of State Walter B. Smith observed, the Treasury Department would have to "pay the bill for the support of Japan's economy and for the maintenance of her military defense."

13. Discussion at the 188th Meeting of the NSC, Mar. 11, 1954, Whitman File, NSC Series, box 5, Eisenhower papers.

14. Churchill to Eisenhower, Mar. 24, 1954, and Eisenhower to Churchill, Mar. 27, 1954, Whitman File, DDE Diary Series, box 6, Eisenhower papers.

15. FRUS 1952–54, XIV, 1614–16, 1627–28, 1630–31, 1634–35.

16. Supplementary Notes on Legislative Leadership Meeting, June 21, 1954, FRUS 1952–54, XIV, 1662.

17. FRUS 1952–54, XIV, 1662–63.

18. Discussion at the 205th Meeting of the NSC, July 1, 1954, Whitman File, NSC Series, box 5, Eisenhower papers.

19. Cabinet discussion of Aug. 6, 1954, FRUS 1952–54, XIV, 1693–95, and diary entry of Aug. 6, 1954, box 1, James Hagerty papers, Eisenhower Library. Eisenhower complained that Congress failed to see the need to lower tariffs and import more Japanese products. Shutting Japan out of Western markets would drive it toward the Communist bloc, which would "really build up the war potential of the communist powers." See Memorandum of discussion at the 226th meeting of the NSC, Dec. 1, 1954, FRUS 1952–54, XII, 1002–14.

20. Memorandum of discussion at the 228th meeting of the NSC, Dec. 9, 1954, FRUS 1952–54, XIV, 1796–1799. As Eisenhower requested, the CIA prepared a report showing that if controls on Japanese exports to China were reduced to the level applied to the Soviet Union,

by 1957 Sino-Japanese trade would total between $100 and $150 million per year in each direction. China would exchange iron ore, coal, soybeans, and rice for Japanese manufactured goods. This would amount to only 7 percent of Japan's anticipated foreign trade for 1957. The study predicted that eliminating the China differential would not enhance the strategic threat posed by the PRC. See ibid., 1808–11; FRUS 1955–57, XXIII, 5–6.

21. Allison to Dulles, Jan. 29, 1955, 493.9431/1–2855, RG 59; Kerr to Department of State, Mar. 15, 1955, 493.944/3–1555, ibid; Allison to Dulles, Mar. 17, 1955, 493.9441/3–1755, ibid.; Kerr to Department of State, Mar. 22, 1955, 493.9441/3–2255, ibid.

22. Allison to Dulles, May 4, 1955, 493.9441/5–455, RG 59; Allison to Dulles, May 5, 1955, 493.9441/5–555, ibid.; Allison to Dulles, May 12, 1955, 493.9441/5–1255, ibid.; Allison to Dulles, May 16, 1955, 493.9441/5–1655, ibid; Dulles to Tokyo embassy, May 23, 1956, 493.9441/5–2356, ibid.; Shima-Parsons conversation, May 25, 1956, 493.9441/5–2556, ibid.

23. Memorandum of Discussion at the 244th Meeting of the NSC, Apr. 7, 1955, FRUS 1955–57, XXIII, 40–49; "U.S. Policy Toward Japan," NSC 5516/1, Apr. 9, 1955, FRUS 1955–57, XXIII, 52–62. Among senior advisers, Admiral Radford warned that elimination of the China differential "would cause the gravest probablity that the Pacific offshore island chain will fall under Communist domination." The Commerce Department worried that China planned to swamp free economies by dumping cheap products—such as pig bristles—on the open market. Joseph Dodge, named by Eisenhower to chair the council on Foreign Economic Policy, also defended the China differential as an essential economic weapon. See, Radford to Gen. Twinging re U.K. Proposals for Relaxation of Trade Controls with Communist China, June 24, 1955, Records of the JCS, RG 218, Chairman's File, Adm. Radford, 091 China (1956), N.A., and Sinclair Weeks to Dulles, Aug. 12, 1955, cited in Qing, "Changes in Western Embargo Policy Against China." A CFEP study of East-West trade, released on Oct. 17, 1955, urged further restricting trade with all Communist nations, the opposite of what Eisenhower hoped. For the evolution of this proposal, see Shimizu, "Creating People of Plenty," 108–14; Memorandum of conversation, Aug. 31, 1955, FRUS 1955–57, XXIII, 111–16. Dulles told Shigemitsu that Japan should request case-by-case exemptions for items it proposed to sell to China. Although Washington thought in terms of granting a few waivers, in October the Japanese presented a list of over 100 items for decontrol. FRUS 1955–57, X, 268.

24. FRUS 1955–57, X, 273–75.

25. Discussion at the 269th meeting of the NSC, Dec. 8, 1955, Whitman File, box 7, NSC series, Eisenhower papers; FRUS 1955–57, X, 275–76, 277.

26. Radford to Wilson, Dec. 12, 1955, FRUS 1955–57, X, 280–82; Dodge to Hoover, Jan. 13, 1956, ibid, 288–89; memorandum of discussion at meeting of the NSC, Dec. 22, 1955, FRUS 1955–57, III, 225–29; memorandum of discussion at meeting of NSC, Jan. 26, 1956, FRUS 1955–57, X, 301–04. On Jan. 31, the CIA and CFEP responded to the president's demand for a "one-page" trade study. It concluded that if *all* trade controls against the Soviet bloc, save for those on weapons and atomic materials, were eliminated, annual free world exports would grow by up to $350 million. China would account for $150 million of this new trade. If the United States maintained its total ban on exports to China, free world sales to Beijing would rise by only $60 million. Elimination of controls would boost exports to the Soviet bloc by only 15 percent, a small proportion of total free world trade. Only Japan, the CIA/CFEP report concluded, would significantly benefit from the lifting of controls. See, FRUS 1955–57, X, 313–15.

27. Memorandum of Eisenhower-Eden conversation, Jan. 31, 1956, FRUS 1955–57, X, 308–12; joint statement of Feb. 1, 1956, Department of State *Bulletin*, Feb. 13, 1956, 232–34.

28. For examples of CFEP, Defense, Treasury, and Economic Defense Advisory Council opposition to eliminating the China differential, see Minutes of the 40th Meeting of the CFEP, Apr. 3, 1956, FRUS 1955–57, X, 326–30.

29. Memorandum of discussion at the 281st meeting of the NSC, Apr. 5, 1956, FRUS 1955–57, X, 330–35.

30. FRUS 1955–57, X 317–19, 324–25, 338–39, 345–55.

31. Memorandum of Dulles-Makins conversation, Apr. 13, 1956, FRUS 1955–57, X, 339–41.

32. Memorandum of discussion at the 282nd meeting of the NSC, Apr. 26, 1956, FRUS 1955–57, X, 345–55.

33. Kalijarvi to Murphy, July 18, 1956, FRUS 1955–57, X, 380–81; Dulles to Randall, Aug. 7, 1956, ibid., 386–89; conversation with Amb. Shima, Sept. 13, 1956, ibid., 397–98.

34. Journal entries of Oct. 16, 1956, and Feb. 6, 1957, Clarence B. Randall papers, Princeton University. Randall complained that Walter Robertson, Admiral Radford, and Herbert Hoover, Jr., sabotaged the president's efforts to revise trade policy.

35. Journal entries of Oct. 17, Nov. 14, 1956, Randall papers.

36. Report on Foreign Economic Policy Discussions Between United States Officials in the Far East and Clarence B. Randall and Associates, Dec. 1956, box 2, Records of the Council on Foreign Economic Policy, Office of Chairman, Randall Series, Trips Subseries, Eisenhower Library.

37. Memorandum of conversation between Ishibashi and Robertson, Dec. 19, 1956, FRUS 1955–57, XXIII, 235–40.

38. Randall to DeLany, Jan. 4, 1957, box 9, CFEP/PPS; Minutes of the 53d Meeting of the CFEP, Feb. 5, 1957, FRUS 1955–57, X, 414–18; journal entry, February 6, 1957, Randall papers. Randall overruled the recommendation of the Economic Defense Advisory Council (EDAC), a CFEP task force chaired by Admiral Walter DeLany. In January 1957, a revised EDAC report recommended revising controls on exports to China because of the "problems [they] posed for our allies." Randall continued to accuse Walter Robertson of carrying out a "one-man campaign against liberalization."

39. Memorandum of discussion at the 315th meeting of the NSC, Mar. 6, 1957, FRUS 1955–57, X, 421–28; NSC 5704/1, Mar. 8, 1957, ibid., 428–29.

40. On March 13, the Japanese ambassador informed the Department of State that unless the United States took the lead in lowering controls on China, Tokyo would adopt whatever lower standard the Europeans put forward. FRUS 1955–57, X, 432–37.

41. FRUS 1955–57, X, 440–42; journal entry of Apr. 11, 1957, Randall papers.

42. FRUS 1955–57, X, 449–50.

43. For the British and Japanese positions, see FRUS 1955–57, X, 451–54.

44. FRUS 1955–57, X, 454.

45. FRUS 1955–57, X, 455–62.

46. Macmillan letters of May 21, 1957 to Eisenhower and Dulles, FRUS 1955–57, X, 460–61; FRUS 1955–57, X, 467.

47. Journal entry of May 29, 1957, Randall papers; FRUS 1955–57, X, 467.

48. Memorandum of conversation between Eisenhower and Asakai, June 4, 1957, FRUS 1955–57, XXIII, 338–39.

49. Eisenhower News Conference, June 5, 1957, PPDDE: 1957, 441–43; FRUS 1955–57, X, 474–75.

50. Eisenhower-Kishi talk, June 19, 1957, FRUS 1955–57, XXIII, 369–75.

51. Conversations of June 21, 1957, FRUS 1955–57, XXIII, 404–13; "Report on Follow Up of Kishi Visit," Aug. 16, 1957, ibid., 444–48. At a meeting of September 12, the NSC agreed to consider Randall's proposal to "take a bold new look at the future trade relationship" with China. Dulles, Secretary of Defense Wilson, and others distinguished between Japan's need to trade with China and the situation of the United States. Wilson simply declared his objection to "trade with the dirty S.O.B.s," while Dulles feared that non-Communist Asia would interpret Sino-American trade as a political defeat for the free world. See journal entries of June 22, 29, Aug. 19, Randall papers; FRUS 1955–57, X, 490; Memorandum of discussion at the 336th meeting of the NSC, Sept. 12, 1957, FRUS 1955–57, X, 491–97. Despite its refusal to lift the American trade embargo, the Eisenhower administration allowed foreign subsidiaries of U.S. corporations more leeway to export products to China after 1957. See Qing, "Changes in Western Embargo Policy Against China," 134–35.

52. Memorandum of discussion at the 356th meeting of the NSC, Feb. 27, 1958, Whitman File, NSC Series, box 9, Eisenhower papers.

53. "Fairless Mission's Meeting with Acting Prime Minister Kishi," Feb. 15, 1957, OASIA File, FOIA.

54. MacArthur to Dulles, Sept. 2, 1957, 493.9441/–247, RG 59, and memorandum of Dulles–Fujiyama conversations, Sept. 2, 3, 1957, State Department Lot File, Bureau of Far Eastern/Asian Affairs, 55D480, ibid.

55. Shimizu, "Perennial Anxiety," 243–46.

56. Yoshihide, "Japan's Postwar Economic Diplomacy with China," 54–55; Shimizu, "Perennial Anxiety," 246–48.

57. "Fairless Mission's Meeting with Acting Prime Minister Kishi," Feb. 15, 1957, OASIA File, Department of Treasury Records, FOIA; Department of State Study on "Chinese Communist Economic Warfare against Japan," July 7, 1958, with cover memorandum of Aug. 9, 1958 by Dulles, in OASIA File, ibid.

58. Ibid.; Chinese Communist Economic Warfare Against Japan, Position Paper for Fujiyama Visit, Sept. 4, 1958, OASIA, ibid.; Undersecretary of State Douglas Dillon to Treasury Secretary Robert B. Anderson, Aug. 9, 1958, and Anderson to Dillon, Aug. 22, 1958, OASIA, ibid.; Dillon to Secretary of State, Oct. 11, 1958, ibid.

NOTES FOR CHAPTER 6

1. Address by John Foster Dulles, Jan. 27, 1953, FRUS 1952–54, XIII, 360.

2. "Substance of Discussions of State-DMS-JCS Meeting at the Pentagon Building," Jan. 28, 1953, ibid., 361–63; Dulles told a Canadian diplomat that a Western defeat in Korea would be a major "setback" but the "consequences of a collapse of Indochina . . . would be incalculable." See F. S. Tomlinson to Robert Scott, Feb. 19, 1953, FO 371/105180, PRO.

3. FRUS 1952–54, XIII, 648–52, 714–17.

4. For the classic account of the battle at Dien Bien Phu, see Bernard Fall, *Hell in a Very Small Place*; on Chinese assistance to the Vietminh, see Chen Jian, "China and the First Indo-China War, 1950–54," *The China Quarterly*, 133 (March 1993), 85–110.

5. Memorandum by the JCS to Dulles, Mar. 12, 1954, FRUS 1952–54, XVI, 472–75.

6. Allison to Department of State, Apr. 10, 1954, FRUS 1952–54, XVI, 510–12.

7. Speech by Dulles to Overseas Press Club of America, Mar. 29, 1954, FO 371/110182, PRO; diary entries of Feb. 8, Mar. 27, 1954, in *The Diary of James C. Hagerty*, ed. by Robert H. Ferrell (Bloomington, Ind., 1983), 15, 35.

8. Entry of Apr. 1, 1954, *Diary of James C. Hagerty*, 39.

9. Efforts by the Eisenhower administration to develop a united front are discussed in David Anderson, *Trapped by Success: The Eisenhower Administration and Vietnam, 1953–61* (New York, 1991); Melanie Billings-Yun, *Decision Against War: Eisenhower and Dien Bien Phu, 1954* (New York., 1988); Lloyd Gardner, *Approaching Vietnam: From World War II Through Dienbienphu* (New York., 1988); George C. Herring and Richard H. Immerman, "The Day We Didn't Go to War, Revisited," *Journal of American History*, 71, 2 (Sept. 1984), 343–63.

10. Dulles conversation with the ambassadors of Australia and New Zealand, Apr. 4, 1954, FRUS 1952–54, XIII, 1231–36; Eisenhower to Churchill, Apr. 4, 1954, ibid., 1238–41.

11. Billings-Yun, *Decision Against War*, 100.

12. *Dwight D. Eisenhower, Public Papers, 1954* (Washington, D.C., 1955), 381–90; FRUS 1952–54, XIII, 1280–81.

13. For example, see discussion at NSC meeting of Apr. 6, 1954, FRUS 1952–54, XIII, 1250–65.

14. Dulles to U.S. delegation, May 8, 1954, FRUS 1952–54, XVI, 728–29; meeting of the NSC, May 13, 1954, ibid., XIII, 1548–49; Dulles conversation with president, May 19, 1954, ibid., XIV, 1583; meeting of NSC, May 20, 1954, ibid., XII, 498–99; Dillon to Dulles, June 20, 1954, ibid., XVI, 1188; Churchill to Eisenhower, June 21, 1954, ibid., XIII, 1728–29; Outline of Gen. Smith's remarks to president and Bipartisan Congressional Group, June 23, 1954, Special Assistant for National Security Affairs, NSC Briefing Notes, box 11, Eisenhower Library.

15. Supplementary Notes on Legislative Leadership Meeting, June 21, 1954, FRUS 1952–54, XIV, 1662; entry of June 21, 1954, *Diary of James C. Hagerty*, 70.

16. Eisenhower's remarks before the National Editorial Assoc., June 22, 1954, FRUS 1952–54, XIV, 1663.

17. Meeting of the NSC, July 22, 1954, FRUS 1952–54, XIII, 1869; entry of July 15, 1954, *Diary of James C. Hagerty*, 91.

18. FRUS 1952–54, XVI, 1698–1702.

19. For two versions of this Aug. 6, 1954, cabinet discussion, see FRUS 1952–54, XIV, 1693–95, and *Diary of James C. Hagerty*, Aug. 6, 1954, box 1, Hagerty papers, Eisenhower Library.

20. NSC 5429, "Draft Statement of Policy Proposed by the National Security Council on Review of U.S. Policy in the Far East," Aug. 4, 1954, FRUS 1952–54, XII, 697–703, and 769–76. The initial draft of the report posed alternative methods of dealing with China, ranging from normalization of relations to initiating a war. Memorandum of discussion at the 210th Meeting of the NSC, Aug. 12, 1954, ibid., 724–33.

21. FRUS 1952–54, XII, 735, 739–40.

22. FRUS 1952–54, XII, 723–34, 783–84, 789–90, 793–94, 800–802, 808–20. For documentation on the drafting of the SEATO treaty, see ibid., 823–901.

23. FRUS 1955–57, IX, Dec. 8, 1955, 167; memorandum of discussion at the 214th meeting of the NSC, Sept. 12, 1954, FRUS 1952–54, XII, 903–908; memorandum of discussion at the 216th meeting of the NSC, Oct. 6, 1954, ibid., 689–701; minutes of Dulles–Yoshida discussion, Nov. 9, 1954, ibid., 1779–83; Ambassador John Allison recalled the shirt incident in his oral history, Dulles papers.

24. "On The Promotion of Economic Cooperation with Southeast Asian Countries," May 20, 1953, quoted in Watanabe Akio, "Southeast Asia in U.S.–Japanese Relations," in Warren Cohen and Akira Iriye, eds., *The United States and Japan in the Postwar World*, (Lexington, Ky., 1989), 81.

25. *New York Times*, Nov. 9, 1954; Yoshida quoted in Lawrence Olson, *Japan in Postwar Asia*, 38.

26. Minutes of Dulles–Yoshida Meeting and Dulles press conference, Nov. 9, 1954, FRUS 1952–54, XIV, 1779–83; Kaufman, *Trade and Aid*, 52–53; Shimizu, "Creating a People of Plenty," 288.

27. Memorandum of discussion at 226th meeting of the NSC, Dec. 1, 1954, FRUS 1952–54, XIV, 968–76.

28. Memorandum of discussion at the 228th meeting of the NSC, Dec. 9, 1954, FRUS 1952–54, XIV, 1796–99.

29. Joseph Alsop, "Tokyo Depends on Saigon," *Washington Post*, May 4, 1955. CBS correspondent Eric Sevareid could not help poking fun at his friend's invocation of the "leaping domino theory" involving "communist labor unions in Singapore to the fall of Southeast Asia to the fall of the middle east to chaos in Britain to the collapse of the western alliance, etc." The whole business, Sevareid wrote Alsop, reminded him of the story of a man who "asked his doctor to give him a dose of clap." Although often asked to cure it, the startled physician replied, "This is the first time I've been asked to give it to anybody." The man explained that once infected, "I'll give it to the old lady; I know she'll give it to Jacobson, the butcher; he'll give it to Mrs. Jacobson; she's bound to give it to that Baptist preacher on the corner, and *that's* the son of a bitch I'm after." Alsop was not amused. If the calculations of the man in the story were correct, he informed Sevareid, "the joke would not be very funny to the Baptist preacher." Alsop criticized those who ignored the "mass of communist literature" that confirmed the accuracy of the "back door attack on the west." Lenin himself had reportedly remarked that "the shortest way to Paris is through Peking," and the same held true for Tokyo and Saigon. See Eric Sevareid to Joseph Alsop, Nov. 14, 1955, pt. 1, box 12, General Correspondence—Joseph Alsop, Joseph and Stewart Alsop Collection, Library of Congress; Alsop to Sevareid, Nov. 17, 1955, ibid.

30. "Japan's Long-term Economic Prospects," W. Park Armstrong to Dulles, June 27, 1955, 894.00/6–2755, RG 59, DOS.

31. Memorandum with attached note to Randall, Jan. 31, 1957, Records of the Committee on Foreign Economic Policy, box 12, Eisenhower Library.

32. Memorandum of conversation, Oct. 5, 1955, Department of State, 611.94/10–555, RG 59; for a similar exchange between Dulles and Japanese cabinet members, see FRUS 1955–57, XXIII, Mar. 18, 1956, 156–63.

33. Testimony of Adm. Felix B. Stump, Commander in Chief, Pacific, May 17, 1956, Hearings on Mutual Security Program (Far East), 84th Congress, 2nd Sess., in *Executive Sessions of*

the Senate Foreign Relations Committee (Historical Series), Vol. VII (Washington, D. C., 1978), 267–87.

34. Burton Kaufman, "Eisenhower's Foreign Economic Policy with Respect to Asia, in Warren Cohen and Akira Iriye, eds., *The Great Powers in East Asia, 1953–60* (New York, 1990) 104–20.

35. Shimizu, "Creating a People of Plenty," 292–330.

36. "Fairless Mission's Meeting with Acting Prime Minister Kishi," Feb. 11, 1957, OASIA file, Department of the Treasury, FOIA.

37. Memorandum of conversation between MacArthur and Kono, March 28, 1957, Department of State, 611.94/3–2857, RG 59.

38. MacArthur to Dulles, Apr. 17, 1957, Department of State, 611.94/4–1757, RG 59.

39. Eisenhower–Kishi talk, June 19, 1957, FRUS 1955–57, XXIII, 369–75; Kishi meeting with Dulles, Humphrey, Weeks, June 20, 1957, ibid., 397–403; Memorandum to Randall, June 18, 1957, Chronological File, box 3, CFEP, Eisenhower papers.

40. Dulles–Fujiyama meeting, Sept. 23, 1957, FRUS 1955–57, XXIII, 488–504; Robertson to Dulles, Oct. 21, 1957, Records of the Bureau of Far Eastern Affairs, 1956–58, box 3, RG 59; Dulles–Kono conversation, Oct. 21, 1957, 611.94/10–2197, RG 59.

41. See, for example, MacArthur to Dulles, Aug. 14, 1958, 611.94/8–1458, RG 59 and MacArthur to Dulles, Aug. 21, 1958, 611.94/8–2158, RG 59.

42. On ICA programs, see "Outline of ICA Activities in Japan—For use in connection with the visit of Clarence Randall, Dec. 9–12, 1956," Mission to Japan, Office of Director of ICA, Subject Files 1952–59, box 5, RG 469; Warren S. Hunsberger, *Japan and the United States in World Trade* (New York, 1964), 34–53, 186.

43. On industry and congressional demands for quotas, see memorandum on "Japanese Cotton Textile Imports," Dec. 12, 1955, Office of Northeast Asian Affairs, Japan Subject Files, 1947–56, box 7, RG 59; "Discriminatory State Legislation in Conflict with FCN Treaties," Apr. 19, 1956, ibid. During 1956, textile lobbyists met frequently with State Department officials to press for quotas. The department, like the CFEP, opposed this, noting that Japanese textile imports constituted barely 1 percent of American production; *Textile World*, 105 (Feb. 1955), 65; The most thorough discussion of textile restrictions during the 1950s appears in William M. McClenahan, "Orderly Restraint: American Government, Business and the Role of Voluntary Export Restraints in United States–Japan Trade, 1934–1972" (Ph.D. Thesis, Georgetown University, 1993), 137–40.

44. Yanaga, *Big Business in Japanese Politics*, 267; Tanzan Ishibashi, "Trading With China," *Oriental Economist* (Aug. 1956), 397; *Washington Post*, Dec. 7, 1956.

45. Dulles to Gov. Timmerman, Apr. 17, 1956, FRUS 1955–57, IX, 177–78; minutes of Cabinet meeting, Apr. 20, 1956, ibid., XXIII, 173.

46. CFEP Report on Import Restrictions and Export Subsidies on Cotton, Apr. 20, 1956, FRUS 1955–57, IX, 179–82; Deputy Undersecretary of State Kalijarvi to the Chairman of the Senate Finance Committee, June 26, 1956, ibid., 192–96.

47. Department of State press release, no. 509, Sept. 27, 1956; Hunsberger, *Japan and the United States in World Trade*, 319.

48. Memorandum of conversation between Ishibashi and Robertson, Dec. 19, 1956, FRUS 1955–57, XXIII, 235–40.

49. Minutes of Cabinet meeting, Jan. 18, 1957, FRUS 1955–57, XXIII, 247–48; Memorandum of conversation between MacArthur and Randall, Jan. 7, 1957, 894.00/1–757, RG 59.

50. Dulles to U.S. Embassies in Asia, Aug. 9, 1958, "Chinese Communist Economic Warfare Against Japan," copy in OASIA File, Department of the Treasury, FOIA.

51. Memorandum of conversation on U.S.—Japan trade with Japanese ambassador, June 5, 1958, FRUS 1958–60, IV, 162–65; Howard L. Parsons to Outerbridge Horsey, Aug. 14, 1958, Office of Northeast Asian Affairs, Japan Subject Files 1947–56, box 6, RG 59; Asst Secretary of State for Economic Affairs Thomas Mann to Asst. Secretary of State for Commerce Kearns, Dec. 31, 1958, 411.949/12–3158, box 1803, RG 59 and Robertson to Mann, "Japanese Textile Quotas to the United States," Apr. 2, 1959, 411.949/4–259, box 1804, RG 59, both quoted in McClenahan, "Orderly Restraint," 227–29.

52. "Address at the Gettysburg College Convocation: The Importance of Understanding," Apr. 4, 1959, *Public Papers of the Presidents of the United States, Dwight D. Eisenhower, 1959* (Washington D.C., 1959), 309–17; memorandum of conversation between Fujiyama and MacArthur, J. Graham Parsons, Marshall Green, and Stanley Carpenter, May 7, 1959, Despatch #1268, Department of State Records, Microfilm of 1955–59.

53. Between 1955 and 1960, the NSC and its Operations Coordination Board periodically reviewed the status of Japanese–American relations. Japan's willingness to remain a loyal ally, the NSC observed, was largely a function of economic dependence. If Japan prospered—or suffered economic setbacks—it would inevitably assert greater independence. Any loss of Western markets would prompt a shift toward reliance on trade with the Communist bloc. See NSC 5516/1 series, beginning Mar. 29, 1955, WHO/OSA, NSC/PPS, box 15, Eisenhower Library.

NOTES FOR CHAPTER 7

1. Dulles to Allison, Jan. 10, 1955, FRUS 1952–54, XIV, 5–6.

2. Notes of meeting #54, September 4, 1947, box 32, Records of the Policy Planning Staff, RG 59.

3. Memorandum of discussion at NSC, Sept. 12, 1954, FRUS 1952–54, XIV, 1724–26; memorandum by Dulles for Eisenhower, Dec. 1, 1954, ibid., 1793; memorandum by Murphy for Cutler, Dec. 30, 1954, ibid., 1817–18.

4. Allison to Dulles, Apr. 2, 1954, FRUS 1952–54, XIV, 34–35; Dulles to Allison, Apr. 2, 1954, ibid., 36–37.

5. Notes of NSC meeting of Mar. 10, 1955, FRUS 1955–57, XXIII, 28–29; memorandum of discussion at 244th meeting of NSC, Apr. 7, 1955, ibid., 40–48; NSC 5516/1, "U.S. Policy Towards Japan," Apr. 9, 1955, ibid., 52–62.

6. Memorandum from Sebald to Murphy, Apr. 20, 1955, FRUS 1955–57, XXIII, 65–68; for Allison's communication to Tokyo, see Mark Gallicchio, "The Kuriles Controversy: U.S. Diplomacy in the Soviet-Japanese Border Dispute, 1941–56," *Pacific Historical Review*, 60 (Feb. 1991, no. 1), 69–101.

7. Japanese factional disputes, based on memoir accounts by participants, are discussed in Kataoka, *Price of a Constitution*, 143–47.

8. Allison to Department of State, August 12, 1955, FRUS 1955–57, XXIII, 85; memorandum by Richard H. Lamb of discussion with Kishi, July 9, 1955, box 2, Office of Northeast Asian Affairs, Japan Subject File, DOS, RG 59.

9. Memorandum of Conversation, Aug. 25, 1955, FRUS 1955–57, XXIII, 84–88; Department of State position papers for Foreign Minister Shigemitsu's Visit to Washington, Aug. 23, 1955, Office of the Chairman, Dodge Series/Subject Subseries, box 3, Records of the Committee on Foreign Economic Policy, Eisenhower Library.

10. Memoranda of Conversations with Shigemitsu, et al., Aug. 29–Sept. 1, 1955, FRUS 1955–57, XXIII, 96–118; after his return to Japan, Kishi told embassy officials that Shigemitsu played up the Communist threat to prod Dulles to revise the security treaty. Kishi agreed with Dulles that it was "premature" to consider treaty revision. See Allison to Department of State, Sept. 13, 1955, ibid., 121.

11. FRUS 1955–57, XXIII, 119–20; Kataoka, *Price of a Constitution*, 144–45.

12. Dulles to Eisenhower, Sept. 1, 1955, FRUS 1955–57, XXIII, 118.

13. Nathaniel Thayer, *How the Conservatives Rule Japan* (Princeton, N.J., 1969), 317.

14. Takeshita quoted in *New York Times*, Oct. 14, 1994. Yoshida had articulated a similar view during the negotiation of the peace treaty (when he encouraged Socialist demonstrations at the time Dulles visited Tokyo) and in 1954 when he answered demands that Japan rearm faster to receive U.S. aid by pointing to Article IX of the constitution and the threat of a left-wing backlash.

15. Robertson to Dulles, with attachments, Sept. 18, 1955, FRUS 1955–57, XXIII, 122–23. Dulles insisted that the security treaty gave the U.S. Navy full transit rights in the waters around Japan. He also argued that because the Soviet Union was a nonsignatory of the San

Francisco peace treaty, Japan could not transfer territorial rights to the USSR without the consent of other signatories.

16. Kataoka, *Price of a Constitution*, 146–47.

17. Memorandum of conversation, Tokyo, March 18, 1956, FRUS 1955–57, XXIII, 156–63.

18. Memorandum of conversation by Dulles, May 19, 1956, FRUS 1955–57, XXIII, 175–78; Allison to Department of State, May 24, 1956 and Hoover to Embassy in Japan, May 26, 1956, ibid., 179; Kataoka, *Price of a Constitution*, 148–49; Dulles to Eisenhower, May 11, 1956, "Report on Public Opinion on International Issues" (Japan), folder #2, box 30, International Series, Ann Whitman Files, Eisenhower Library; "Japanese Public Opinion, Mid-1956," box 38, ibid.

19. Kataoka, *Price of a Constitution*, 151–54.

20. Memorandum of conversation between Dulles and Shigemitsu, Aug. 19, 1956, FRUS 1955–57, XXIII, 202–4; Dulles to Department of State, Aug. 22, 1956, ibid., 204–5; memorandum of conversation between Dulles and Shigemitsu, Aug. 24, 1955, ibid., 207–9; notes prepared in the Office of Northeast Asian Affairs, Aug. 24, 1956, ibid., 210–11; transcript of Dulles press conference, Aug. 28, 1956, ibid., 211.

21. FRUS 1955–57, XXIII, 222–32. The State Department, in a formal response to a Japanese query on the legal status of the northern territories, stated that "after a careful examination of the historical facts," the United States concludes that all four disputed islands had always been "part of Japan proper and should in justice be acknowledged as under Japanese sovereignty." See Department of State *Bulletin*, 35 (1956), 484.

22. Kataoka, *Price of a Constitution*, 155–56; FRUS 1955–57, XXIII, 234–35.

23. Allison to Secretary of State, Sept. 21, 1956, copy in U.S. Council on Foreign Economic Policy, Office of the Chairman, Records 1954–61, Randall Series, Trips Subseries, box 2, Eisenhower Library.

24. A. J. de la Mare to Peter Dalton, Dec. 31, 1956, FO 371/127538, PRO.

25. Ibid; A.J. de la Mare to O. C. Morland, Jan. 10, 1957, FO 371/127239, PRO.

26. "Outline Plan of Operations with Respect to Japan," January 15, 1957, Operations Coordination Board, MR 93–322, #2, Eisenhower Library.

27. Memorandum by Richard A. Lamb of conversation with Kishi, July 9, 1955, Office of Northeast Asian Affairs, Japan Subject Files 1947–56, box 2, RG 59.

NOTES FOR CHAPTER 8

1. *Sayonara* appeared first in serialized form in *McCall's* magazine in 1953 and as a book the next year. Michener touched on Japanese events in his nonfiction *The Voice of Asia* (1951) and a short novel, *The Bridges at Toko-Ri* (1953). Both had strong anti-Communist themes. The novel and film treatment of *Sayonara* extol the virtue of racial equality even as they celebrate the "superiority" of submissive Japanese women to their brash, assertive American counterparts. While generally faithful to the novel, the film alters the story in one critical aspect. As written, Gruver and his Japanese lover, Hana-ogi, bow to American pressure against mixed marriage. He says "Sayonara" (farewell) to Hana-ogi and returns to a career in the air force while she continues her life in the theater. On screen, Gruver says "Sayonara" to the air force as he and Hana-ogi go off to marry and start a family. This satisfied Hollywood's demand for a happy ending. It also reflected the passage of time since the fighting ended in Korea and, possibly, a more favorable view of Japan among Americans.

2. Dwight D. Eisenhower, *Waging Peace, 1956–1961* (New York, 1965), 140–44; MacArthur to Dulles, May 24, 1957, FRUS 1955–57, XXIII, 315–16; Dulles to MacArthur, June 5, 1957, ibid., 342–43; on the Bow bill, see ibid., 422; During May, the State Department prepared two summaries of the case for use by Dulles and Eisenhower. See ibid., 293–96, 323–25; Congress deferred action on the Bow bill in 1954. An effort was made to append it to a foreign military aid bill the following year, but that failed.

3. George R. Packard III, *Protest in Tokyo: The Security Treaty Crisis of 1960* (Princeton, N.J., 1966), 55. As an inducement to Japan, Mao offered to sign a nonaggression pact with Tokyo even before abrogation of the Japan–U.S. treaty.

4. Progress Report on U.S. Policy Toward Japan (NSC 5516/1) Feb. 6, 1957, Operations Coordinating Board, box 15, Office of the Special Assistant for National Security Affairs, NSC Series, Policy Papers Subseries, Eisenhower Library.

5. Transcript of a Recorded Interview with Douglas MacArthur, II, December 16, 1966, The John Foster Dulles Oral History Project, Princeton University Library.

6. See MacArthur to Department of State, Feb. 25, Feb. 26, March 14, Apr. 17, 1957, FRUS 1955–57, XXIII, 270–79.

7. Dulles to MacArthur, Apr. 18, 1957, FRUS 1955–57, XXIII, 280; see also Dulles to MacArthur, May 14, 1957, ibid., 286.

8. The extensive debate within the administration and with members of Congress is detailed in FRUS 1955–57, XXIII, 298–343, 368–69; British embassy officials took special note of the Girard affair and summarized many newspapers reports. See A. J. de la Mare to P.G.F. Dalton, Far Eastern Department, Foreign Office, May 24, 1957, FO 371/127577, PRO; *Minneapolis Sunday Tribune*, July 21, 1957.

9. Supplementary Notes on the Legislative Leadership Meeting, June 4, 1957, FRUS 1955–57, XXIII, 337; *Public Papers of the Presidents of the United States: Dwight D. Eisenhower, 1957*, 436–37.

10. Memorandum of conversation between the president and the Japanese ambassador, June 4, 1957, FRUS 1955–57, XXIII, 338–39.

11. Memorandum of a meeting between Dulles and Nash, June 5, 1957, FRUS 1955–57, XXIII, 339–42; for Eisenhower's determination to reduce force levels in Japan, see ibid., 343, 345; memorandum of conversation with the president, June 18, 1957, ibid., 357–60.

12. Memorandum from Dulles to Eisenhower, June 12, 1957, FRUS 1955–57, XXIII, 346–49; memorandum of conference with the president, June 18, 1957, ibid., 357–60; the Joint Chiefs of Staff, Adm. Radford informed Eisenhower, had doubts about force reductions in Japan and adamantly opposed any concessions over the status of the Bonin and Ryukyu Islands. See memorandum from the JCS to the Secretary of Defense, June 13, 1957, ibid., 349–51; JSC memorandum for Goodpaster, June 19, 1957, ibid., 376.

13. Memorandum of conversation, June 19, 1957, FRUS 1955–57, XXIII, 369–75; memorandum of conversation, June 20, 1957, ibid., 377–86; Kishi had submitted a list of topics for discussion. It included: (1) security and defense relationships between the United States and Japan; (2) territorial questions relating to the Ryukyu and Bonin Islands; (3) testing of large nuclear weapons and disarmament; (4) Japanese war criminals [numbering about 66] still detained by the United States; (5) U.S.–Japanese trade relations, including the laws designed to discriminate against Japanese textiles in Alabama and South Carolina; (6) U.S.–Japanese cooperation in fostering economic development in South and Southeast Asia; (7) trade with Communist China. See ibid., 347.

14. Memorandum of conversation between Dulles and Kishi, June 20, 1957, FRUS 1955–57, XXIII, 387–97.

15. Ibid.

16. Ibid.

17. FRUS 1955–57, XXIII, 404–10; war criminals posed another problem. Dulles agreed to have a commission look into the disposition of 66 cases once the Girard affair had been settled.

18. Memorandum of conversation at the White House, June 21, 1957, FRUS 1955–57, XXIII, 410–12; the final wording of the communiqué was agreed to after speaking with Eisenhower. See ibid., 413–15. The text of the joint statement appears in Department of State *Bulletin*, July 8, 1957, 51.

19. MacArthur to J. Graham Parsons, July 29, 1958, Department of State records, 794.00/7–2958, RG 59.

20. MacArthur to Dulles, Oct. 18, 1957, FRUS 1955–57, XXIII, 517–23.

21. FRUS 1958–60, XVIII, 1–3, 16–17.

22. Reference to secret funding for the LDP during the 1958 election appears in an internal CIA study. See Wayne G. Jackson, "Allen Welsh Dulles As Director of Central Intelligence, 26 February 1953–29 November 1961, Vol. III, Covert Activities," 97. For accounts by retired

intelligence personnel active in Japan, see "C.I.A. Spent Millions to Support Japanese Right in 50s and 60s," by Tim Weiner, *New York Times*, Oct. 9, 1994; Hillsman's detailed description of the secret payments appears in interviews of Oct. 9 and Nov. 1, 1994, with Masui Shigeo, New York Bureau Chief of *The Yomiuri Shimbun*, copies in my possession.

23. Robertson to Dulles, March 22, 1958, FRUS 1958-60, XVIII, 10-14; MacArthur to Dulles and Robertson, Apr. 18, 1958, ibid., 22-29. As called for during the Dulles-Kishi talks, a "Japanese-American Committee on Security" began meeting in July 1958. The well-publicized gatherings communicated a sense of greater mutuality. The participants (Ambassador MacArthur, the U.S. military commander in Japan, the Japanese foreign minister, and the head of the Defense Agency) discussed issues relating to the departure of American ground forces and consequent base closings. The withdrawal of nearly all American combat troops, and the resulting loss of some 20,000 to 30,000 jobs held by Japanese civilians, took some of the steam out of demands for a complete pullout of forces. The number of naval and air force personnel stationed in Japan remained steady. See FRUS 1955-57, XXIII, 449-75.

24. MacArthur to Dulles, June 5, 1958, FRUS 1958-60, XVIII, 34-36.

25. Steeves to Robertson, July 18, 1958, FRUS 1958-60, XVIII, 38-42; see also, Adm. Harry Felt to JCS, Aug. 19, 1958, ibid., 52-57.

26. MacArthur to Department of State, July 31 and Aug. 1, 1958, FRUS 1958-60, XVIII, 43-49; memorandum of conversation, Sept. 8, 1958, ibid., 58-63.

27. Memorandum of conversation, Sept. 9, 1958, FRUS 1958-60, XVIII, 64-73.

28. Memorandum of conversation, Sept. 11, 1958, FRUS 1958-60, XVIII, 73-84. Fujiyama won a promise that MacArthur would be empowered to discuss with Japanese authorities changes in Okinawa, compensation to Bonin Islanders, and the release of war criminals. An agreement to pay $6 million in property compensation to the Bonin Islanders was reached in January 1960. In December 1958, the United States expedited parole of the small number of class B and C war criminal still imprisoned.

29. Department of State to Embassy in Japan, Sept. 29, 30, and Oct. 2, 1958, FRUS 1958-60, XVIII, 88-92; the draft treaty of mutual cooperation and security that served as the basis of discussion with Japan bore little resemblance to the 1951 document. It eliminated virtually all the "unequal" clauses of the original treaty and included a ten-year time limit after which either side could terminate. See ibid., 85-88, 92-105.

30. MacArthur to Department of State, Nov. 28, 1958, FRUS 1958-60, XVIII, 100-104; MacArthur to Department of State, Dec. 7, 1958, ibid., 108-10; MacArthur to Department of State, Dec. 17, 1958, ibid., 111-13; MacArthur to Department of State, Dec. 24, 1958, ibid., 116-19; Dulles to MacArthur, Jan. 24, 1959, ibid., 119-21; MacArthur Oral History, 33; P.G.F. Dalton to A. J. de la Mare, Feb. 13, 1959, FO 371/141216, PRO.

31. MacArthur to Department of State, Mar. 7, 14, Apr. 29, 1959, FRUS 1958-60, XVIII, 121-26, 131-39; for a detailed discussion of LDP factionalism, see Packard, *Protest in Tokyo*, 33-80.

32. Packard, *Protest in Tokyo*, 75-80.

33. A partial record of treaty negotiations, omitting reference to nuclear issues, appears in FRUS 1958-60, XVIII, 181-258. As the preface to the volume indicates, documentation related to certain "modern weapons"—a euphemism for nuclear weapons—was deleted from the published record; Memorandum from Steeves to Herter, Dec. 26, 1959, ibid., 256-58; Reischauer, *My Life*, 250; "Nuclear Agreement on Japan Reported," *New York Times*, May 19, 1981; Daniel Ellsberg oral history on nuclear weapons in Japan, National Security Archive, Washington, D.C.

34. Packard, *Protest in Tokyo*, 131-34.

35. Packard, *Protest in Tokyo*, 156-66.

36. Fujiyama quoted in *Japan Times*, Jan. 1, 1960.

37. Packard, *Protest in Tokyo*, 173-78.

NOTES FOR CHAPTER 9

1. *Time*, January 25, 1960; *Newsweek*, January 25, 1960.

2. Summary of Press Opinion, Jan. 19, 26, 1960, Bureau of Public Affairs, Department of State, RG 59.

3. "Joint Communiqué, January 19," Department of State Bulletin, Feb. 8, 1960, 179-81; Security Treaty Between the United States of America and Japan [and related documents], Vol. 11, *United States Treaties and Other International Agreements, TIAS 4509*, (Washington, G.P.O., 1961) 1633-35; Kishi's discussions with Eisenhower, Herter, et al., as reflected in State Department minutes, appear extraordinarily bland. He raised only two substantive points: expanding U.S.-Japan trade was as important as assuring military security, and Japan needed to trade with China, although it would still refuse to recognize the PRC. See FRUS 1958-60, XVIII, 259-82; more revealing information is contained in the still heavily censored briefing book prepared for Eisenhower in advance of his meeting Kishi. See "Briefing Papers on U.S.-Japan Relations," White House Central Files (confidential), 1953-61, Subject Series, box 79, Eisenhower Library.

4. A. J. de la Mare to Peter Dalton, Feb. 9, 1960, FO 371/105574, PRO.

5. FRUS 1958-60, XVIII, 283; Kataoka, *Price of a Constitution*, 203; Packard, *Protest in Tokyo*, 184-86.

6. "Memorandum for the Record," Jan. 11, 1960, 611.947/1-1160, DOS, RG 59.

7. MacArthur to Department of State, Apr. 6, 1960, FRUS 1958-60, XVIII, 290-91. Memorandum for Eisenhower on visit of Yoshida, May 5, 1960, Eisenhower papers, Whitman File, International Series, box 31, Eisenhower Library; FRUS 1958-60, XVIII, 284-91; Packard, *Protest in Tokyo*, 187-92.

8. Packard, *Protest in Tokyo*, 125-30; for details about secret U.S. payments to disrupt the Socialists, see "CIA Spent Millions to Support Japanese Right in '50s and '60s," by Tim Weiner, *The New York Times*, Oct. 9, 1994; transcripts of interviews with Roger Hillsman, Oct. 9, Nov. 1, 1994, provided by Shigeo Masui; Ikeda's confirmation of payments to Nishio appears in MacArthur to Parsons, June 21, 1960, FRUS 1958-60, XVIII, 376-77.

9. Yanaga, *Big Business in Japanese Politics*, 278.

10. For a thoughtful discussion of the anti-treaty coalition, see Packard, *Protest in Tokyo*, 82-100, 134-41.

11. *Japan Times*, Feb. 10-21, 1960.

12. *Asahi Shimbun*, editorials, Jan. 14, May 13, 1960, quoted in Packard, *Protest in Tokyo*, 215.

13. On the U-2 incident, see Michael Beschloss, *Mayday: Eisenhower, Khrushchev, and the U-2 Affair* (New York, 1986).

14. *Japan Times*, May 11-13, 29, 1960; Packard, *Protest in Tokyo*, 229-33.

15. FRUS 1958-60, XVIII, 292-93; Department of State *Bulletin*, May 23, 1960, 818-19; Packard, *Protest in Tokyo*, 231-33.

16. MacArthur to Department of State, May 11, 1960, FRUS 1958-60, XVIII, 299; Packard, *Protest in Tokyo*, 237-42.

17. *Asahi Shimbun*, May 20, 21, 1960; Packard, *Protest in Tokyo*, 242-44.

18. MacArthur to Herter, May 24, 1960, 795.00/5-2460, DOS, RG 59; efforts by Kishi and MacArthur to pressure "anti-mainstream" LDP factions are discussed in Masumi Junnosuke (Trans. by Lonny E. Carlile), *Contemporary Politics in Japan* (Berkeley, Ca., 1995), 41-44.

19. MacArthur to Department of State, May 21 and May 23, 1959, FRUS 1958-60, XVIII, 297-300.

20. Ibid., 301; memorandum for president, May 5, 1960, White House Office of Staff Secretary, International Series, box 9, Eisenhower papers, Eisenhower Library; Herter to MacArthur, May 23, 1960, 794.00/5-2360, DOS, RG 59 and Herter to MacArthur, May 26, 1960, 794.00/5-2660, ibid.

21. Packard, *Protest in Tokyo*, 247.

22. Segmaier to Department of State, "Memorandum of conversation between Ambassador MacArthur and Kawashima Shojiro," May 23, 1960, 794.00/5-2760, DOS, RG 59.

23. MacArthur to Herter, May 25, 1960, FRUS 1958-60, XVIII, 303-4; MacArthur to Herter, May 25, 1960, ibid., 304-5; Herter to MacArthur, May 25, 1960, ibid. (microfiche supplement); MacArthur to Herter, May 26, 1960, ibid., 306-9; MacArthur to Herter, May 27, 1960, ibid., 309; Herter to MacArthur (forwarding confirmation from Eisenhower), May 26, 1950, Whitman File, International Series, box 32, Eisenhower papers; Eisenhower's position

was described by a high State Department official to a British diplomat. See A. J. de la Mare to Peter Dalton, June 7, 1960, FO 371/150575, PRO.

24. Public Opinion Study of June 7, 1960, Bureau of Public Affairs, Department of State, RG 59.

25. Memorandum of discussion at the 446th meeting of the NSC, May 31, 1960, FRUS 1958–60, XVIII, 314–24. At this meeting the Defense Department and JCS suggested pressuring Japan to provide greater military cooperation in the Pacific. Eisenhower observed that in light of the situation in Tokyo, this was hardly the time to scold Japan about its military role.

26. Memorandum of telephone conversation between Eisenhower and Herter, June 7, 1960, ibid., 327–28; Fulbright's statement in the *New York Times*, June 7, 1960.

27. Transcript of hearings of June 7, 14, 1960, *Executive Sessions of the Senate Foreign Relations Committee (Historical Series)* (Washington, D.C., 1982), 405–14, 423–31; Herter to MacArthur, June 7, 1960, White House Office of Staff Secretary, International Series, box 9, Eisenhower papers.

28. MacArthur to Parsons, June 8, 1960, FRUS 1958–60, XVIII, 329–31; MacArthur to Herter, June 7, 1960, ibid. (microfiche supplement); Koji Nakamura, "The Samurai Spirit," *Far Eastern Economic Review*, Oct. 16, 1971, 22–25; Masumi, *Contemporary Politics in Japan*, 43–44.

29. Memorandum of discussion at 447th meeting of the NSC, June 8, 1960, Whitman File, NSC Series, Eisenhower papers.

30. Notes on Legislative Meeting, June 9, 1960, Whitman File, Legislative Meeting Series, box 3, Eisenhower papers; Public Opinion Studies of June 7, 14, 1960, Bureau of Public Affairs, Department of State, RG 59.

31. MacArthur to Herter, June 10, 1960, FRUS 1958–60, XVIII, 331–32; Packard, *Protest in Tokyo*, 285–91; Merrimen Smith, *A President's Odyssey* (New York, 1961), 211.

32. Herter to MacArthur, June 10, 1960, FRUS 1958–60, XVIII, 333–35.

33. Communications between Tokyo and Washington in the aftermath of the Hagerty incident are found in FRUS 1958–60, XVIII, 349–56; MacArthur to Herter, June 12, 1960, FRUS 1958–60 (microfiche supplement); MacArthur to Herter, June 13, 1960, ibid.

34. MacArthur to Herter, June 15, 1960, FRUS 1958–60, XVIII, (microfiche supplement); MacArthur to Herter, June 7, 1960, ibid.

35. David E. Kaplan and Alec Dubro, *Yakuza* (Reading, Mass., 1986), 84–86; Nakamura, "The Samurai Spirit."

36. MacArthur to Herter, June 15, 1960, FRUS 1958–60, XVIII, 386–62; MacArthur to Herter, June 20, 1960, ibid. (microfiche supplement).

37. Packard, *Protest in Tokyo*, 293–97.

38. See, FRUS 1958–60, XVIII, 362–71.

39. Masumi, *Contemporary Politics in Japan*, 45–47.

40. Public Opinion Study, June 21, 1960, Bureau of Public Affairs, Department of State, RG 59; R. T. D. Ledward to Nigel Trench, June 23, 1950, FO 371/150576, PRO.

41. Author's interview with confidential informant.

42. MacArthur to Parsons, June 21, 1960, FRUS 1958–60, XVIII, 376–77.

43. MacArthur to Department of State, June 24, 1960, FRUS 1958–60, XVIII, 377–84.

44. FRUS 1958–60, XVIII, 385–88; Memorandum of conversation with Kosaka, Sept. 12, 1960, ibid., 398–401; Packard, *Protest in Tokyo*, 303–5.

45. *The Mainichi Shimbun*, July 4, 1960.

46. Yutaka Kosai, *The Era of High-Speed Growth: Notes on the Post–War Japanese Economy* (Tokyo, 1986), 130.

47. Packard, *Protest in Tokyo*, 308–26.

48. NSC 6008/1, "United States Policy Toward Japan," June 11, 1960, FRUS 1958–60, XVIII, 335–49; NSC meeting of July 1, 1960, Whitman File, NSC Series, box 11, Eisenhower papers.

49. MacArthur to Department of State, Dec. 16, 1960, FRUS 1958–60, XVIII, 413–23.

NOTES FOR CHAPTER 10

1. Edwin O. Reischauer, "The Broken Dialogue with Japan," *Foreign Affairs*, Vol. 39 (Oct. 1960), 13.

2. Kennedy to Lem Billings, May 6, 1943, quoted in Nigel Hamilton, *JFK: Reckless Youth* (New York, 1992), 531.

3. Donald M. Wilson to Pierre Salinger, Mar. 6, 1961, WHCF, CO 141 Japan, box 62, John F. Kennedy Library; Lawrence F. O'Brien to John F. Baldwin, March 8, 1961, ibid; Lawrence F. O'Brien to Rep. Leo W. O'Brien, May 4, 1961, ibid.

4. Interviews with Roger Hillsman, Oct. 9, and Nov. 1, 1994, conducted by Shigeo Masui, correspondent of *Yomiuri Shimbun*. Copies in possession of author; Ambassador Reischauer, Army Secretary Stanley Resor, and others discussed subsidies to LDP candidates in a discussion on July 16, 1965. See "U.S. Policy in the Ryukyus," Memorandum of Discussion among Amb. Reischauer, Secretary of the Army Stanley R. Resor, et al., Department of State Records, Central Foreign Policy File, 1964–67, box 2383, RG 59, National Archives.

5. Memorandum for Ralph A. Dungan, Mar. 24, 1961, NSF–Japan, box 123, Kennedy Library; memorandum of conversation between Kennedy and MacArthur, Apr. 8, 1961, 794.00/4–861, DOS, RG 59.

6. Memorandum of discussion, Apr. 21, 1961, FRUS 1961–63, IX, 461–62; Kennedy statement of May 2, 1961, *Public Papers of the Presidents of the United States: John F. Kennedy, 1961* (Washington, 1962), 345–46.

7. See "Policy Toward Communist China," June 14, 1951, Briefing Book for Prime Minister Ikeda's Visit to Washington, NLK 92–135, Kennedy Library.

8. A. L. Mayall, British Embassy, Tokyo, to Foreign Office, Apr. 27, 1961, FO 371/158484, PRO; Mayall to Foreign Office, June 2, 1961, ibid.; British Embassy dispatch to Earl of Home, June 8, 1961, ibid.; Rostow memorandums of conversation with Mr. Wakaizuma, April 25, 1961, and Kosaka Tokusaburo, April 25, 1961, NSF Japan, box 123, Kennedy Library.

9. Edwin O. Reischauer, *My Life Between Japan and America* (New York, 1986), 169.

10. Reischauer, *My Life*, 164–65; Edwin O. Reischauer Oral History, Kennedy Library.

11. For a description of the criticism he faced from Japanese and American conservatives, see John K. Emmerson, *The Japanese Thread: A Life in the U.S. Foreign Service* (New York, 1978).

12. Reischauer, Oral History, Kennedy Library.

13. Reischauer, *My Life*, 201–2.

14. Robert H. Johnson to Rostow, "Prime Minister Ikeda's Visit," June 19, 1961, President's Official File, Japan, box 120; Rostow to Kennedy, June 19, 1961, ibid.

15. Sneider, "The Japanese Political Situation," June 13, 1961, Background Paper for President, NLK–92–135, Kennedy Library; Reischauer, *My Life*, 202.

16. *Time*, June 30, 1961; *Newsweek*, June 26, 1961.

17. Memorandum of conversation, June 21, 1961, FRUS 1961–63, IX, 468–69.

18. Joint Communiqué Issued by the President and Prime Minister Ikeda, June 22, 1961, President's Official File, box 120, Kennedy Library; Sneider to McGeorge Bundy, "Visit of Prime Minister Ikeda," June 23, 1961, White House Central File, box 62, ibid.; U.S. Department of State *Bulletin*, 45, no. 1150 (July 10, 1961), 57–58; Chihiro Hosoya, "From the Yoshida Letter to the Nixon Shock," in Warren Cohen and Akira Iriye, eds., *The United States and Japan in the Postwar World* (Lexington, Ky., 1989), 21–35.

19. Ball, *Past Has Another Pattern*, 196.

20. Reischauer, *My Life*, 204; for Caraway's view of Reischauer, see his Oral History, Vol. II, section 8, part 2, Military History Institute, Carlisle Barracks, Pa. U.S. policy on Okinawa is treated more fully in Nicholas Sanantakes, "Keystone: The American Occupation of Okinawa and U.S.–Japan Relations, 1945–1972" (Ph.D. dissertation, University of Southern California, 1996).

21. Caraway quoted in Welfield, *Empire in Eclipse*, 223.

22. Reischauer, *My Life*, 205.

23. "Report and Recommendations of the Task Force Ryukyus," Dec. 1961, POF, box 123b, Kennedy Library.

24. "Notes on China policy," undated, early 1964, box 18, James C. Thomson papers, Kennedy Library.

25. Gordon H. Chang, "JFK, China, and the Bomb," *Journal of American History* 75 (March 1988), 1287–1310; Nancy B. Tucker, *Taiwan, Hong Kong, and the United States, 1945–92* (New York, 1994), 65, 101.

26. Soeya, "Japan's Postwar Economic Diplomacy with China," 74–75; Hosoya, "Yoshida Letter to the Nixon Shock."

27. Soeya, "Japan's Postwar Economic Diplomacy with China," 72.

28. Ibid., 75–76.

29. Ibid., 159–60; Warren Cohen, "China in Japanese–American Relations," in Cohen and Iriye, eds., *United States and Japan in the Postwar World*, 37–60.

30. Memorandum of Harriman–Shiga conversation, Nov. 14, 1962, 794.5/11–1462, DOS, RG 59.

31. Emmerson to Rusk, Dec. 5, 1962, 611.94/12–562, DOS, RG 59; Luncheon Meeting between Rusk and Ohira, et al., Dec. 4, 1962, 794.5/12–462, ibid.

32. Welfield, *Empire in Eclipse*, 179–80; Reischauer, *My Life*, 250–54.

33. Welfield, *Empire in Eclipse*, 181; Hosoya, "Yoshida Letter to the Nixon Shock"; Cohen, "China in Japanese–American Relations."

34. Barnett to Rostow, "Japan and Credit to Communist China," Aug. 7, 1963, NLK–94–57, Kennedy Library.

35. Hosoya, "Yoshida Letter to the Nixon Shock"; Cohen, "China in Japanese–American Relations."

36. George Ball, *The Past Has Another Pattern* (New York, 1982), 188–89.

37. Embassy in Japan to Department of State, May 4, 1961, FRUS 1961–63, IX, 464–65; letter from members of Congress to President Kennedy, June 22, 1961, ibid., 469–70.

38. Memorandum, Peterson to Christopher, approved by Ball, Aug. 18, 1961, 611.94/8–1661, DOS, RG 59.

39. Ball, *The Past Has Another Pattern*, 188–92.

40. Ball to Feldman (copied to Kennedy), Sept. 25, 1961, FRUS Japan, 1961–63, IX, 479–84.

41. Ball to Kennedy, Oct. 23, 1961, POF, box 50, Kennedy Library, and FRUS, 1961–63, IX, 493–95; Department of State to Embassy in Japan, Nov. 1, 1961, ibid., 496–97; Ball, *Past Has Another Pattern*, 197–200.

42. Reischauer to Department of State, Nov. 13, 1961, FRUS 1961–63, IX, 497–501; Reischauer, *My Life*, 213–14.

43. Reischauer to Department of State, Dec. 5, 1961, FRUS 1961–63, IX, 504–5; Reischauer to Department of State, Dec. 12, 1961, ibid., 509–10; memorandum of discussion among George Ball, Ambassador Asakai, et al., Dec. 21, 1961, ibid., 510–12; Ball to Rusk, Feb. 9, 1962, ibid., 517–19; White House press release concerning long-term cotton textile arrangement, Feb. 16, 1962, ibid., 520; Ball to Kennedy, Aug. 21, 1962, ibid., 532–36.

44. For a discussion of industrial planning and trade promotion in Japan, see Chalmers Johnson, *MITI and the Japanese Miracle: The Growth of Industrial Policy, 1925–75* (Stanford, Ca., 1975); for an account of Japanese automotive success, see David Halberstam, *The Reckoning*.

45. Reischauer, *My Life*, 236; Reischauer, Oral History, Kennedy Library.

46. Embassy in Tokyo to Department of State, "Communist Reaction to the Reischauer Offensive," Nov. 1, 1962, 794.00/11–162, DOS, RG 59; Tokyo Embassy to Department of State, Nov. 8, 1963, box 3958, Central Foreign Policy File, 1963, ibid.

47. Hillsman to Rusk, Oct. 31, 1963, "A Presidential Trip to the Far East in Early 1964," box 5, Presidential Far Eastern Trip Plans, Roger Hillsman papers, Kennedy Library.

NOTES FOR CHAPTER 11

1. Department of State Policy on the Future of Japan, June 26, 1964, NLJ 91–12, Lyndon B. Johnson Library.

2. Rostow to Johnson, Oct. 12, 1966, Memos to the President, Walt Rostow, box 10, Folder: Vol. 14, Oct. 1–31, 1966, Johnson Library.Rostow believed that Johnson's escalation in Vietnam had stymied Communist expansion elsewhere in Asia. For example, early in 1965, Indonesian President Sukarno proclaimed "the Year of Living Dangerously." He quit the United Nations, threatened to invade Malaysia, and flirted with Communist China. In September, a botched coup by the Indonesian Communist Party (PKI) provoked Muslim generals to seize power, crush the PKI, and depose Sukarno. Rostow believed that Washington's defense of South Vietnam had inspired the Indonesian generals to act boldly and save their country. When Rostow requested intelligence data to support his theory, CIA Director Richard Helms responded that he had "searched in vain for evidence that the U.S. display of determination in Vietnam directly influenced the outcome of the Indonesian crisis in any significant way." Sukarno's fall "evolved purely from a complex and long-standing domestic political situation," Helms replied, not from a display of American muscle in Saigon. See Helms to Rostow, May 13, 1966, NSC Files, Country files, box 248, Johnson Library.

3. Johnson to Kennedy, memorandum on "Mission to Southeast Asia, India, and Pakistan," May 23, 1961, *The Pentagon Papers (New York Times Edition)* (New York, 1971), 127–30.

4. Taylor to Robert S. McNamara, Jan. 22, 1964, *Pentagon Papers (N.Y. Times Edition)*, 274–77.

5. Memorandum of conversation, Rusk, Ohira, et al., Jan. 26, 1964, National Security File, Country File, Japan, box 250, Johnson Library.

6. Memorandum of conversation between Rusk and Ohira, Jan. 28, 1964, National Security File, Country File, Japan, box 250, Johnson Library; memorandum for the president, Jan. 28, 1964, ibid.

7. Memorandum of conversation between Rusk and Ikeda, Jan. 29, 1964, National Security File, Country File, Japan, box 250, Johnson Library.

8. Reischauer, *My Life*, 230.

9. Reischauer to Rusk, March 25, 1964, National Security File, Country File, Japan, box 250, Johnson Library; Reischauer, *My Life*, 264.

10. Memorandum of conversation between Fukuda and McNamara, June 30, 1964, McNamara Records, folder: Mem Cons, Non-NATO, Vol. II, Sec. 3, R 73028, RG 200 (copy in National Security Archive).

11. Memorandum of conversation between Takeuchi and Rusk, Dec. 23, 1964, National Security File, Country File, Japan, box 250, Johnson Library; Reischauer to Rusk, Dec. 29, 1964, ibid., box 253; Aide Memoire (undated), National Security File, "Japan, Sato's Visit Memos & Cables," ibid.

12. Bundy to Johnson, Jan. 11, 1965, National Security File, Country file, Japan, Sato Visit Briefing Book, 1/65, box 253, Johnson Library; Thomson to Johnson, Jan. 11, 1965, ibid.

13. Memorandum of Johnson–Sato conversation, Jan. 12, 1965, National Security File, Country File, Japan, box 253, Johnson Library.

14. Memorandum of Rusk–Sato conversation, Jan. 12, 1965, National Security File, Country File, Japan, box 253, Johnson Library; for a summary of negotiations on trade questions during the Johnson years, see U.S. Department of State, Japan, Administrative History, Johnson Library.

15. Memorandum of Miki–Humphrey conversation, July 13, 1965, National Security File, Country File, Japan, box 250 Johnson Library.

16. U.S. Department of State, Department of State *Bulletin*, 52, no. 1336 (Feb. 1, 1965), 135.

17. Joint State-Defense Message to Embassy in Tokyo, Jan. 30, 1965, National Security File, Country File, Japan, box 250, Johnson Library.

18. National Security File, Meeting Notes File, box 2, F: November 4, 1967, Meeting with Foreign Policy Advisors, Johnson Library.

19. Reischauer, *My Life*, 257.

20. Reischauer to Rusk, Feb. 10, 1965, National Security File, Country File, Japan, box 250, Johnson Library; Emmerson to Rusk, July 30, 1965, ibid.

21. James C. Thomson Oral History, Johnson Library.

22. Meeting Notes, July 21, 1965, National Security File, Meeting Notes File, box 1, Johnson Library; Kahin, *Intervention*, 366–401.

23. Thomas Havens, *Fire Across the Sea: The Vietnam War and Japan, 1965–1975* (Princeton, N.J., 1987), 28, 84, 88–89.

24. Reischauer, *My Life*, 286–87; Havens, *Fire Across the Sea*, 41–42.

25. Havens, *Fire Across the Sea, 42–43*.

26. Havens, *Fire Across the Sea*, 44–50; Welfield, *Empire in Eclipse*, 211–13.

27. Havens, *Fire Across the Sea*, 78.

28. Reischauer, *My Life*, 285–90.

29. *New York Times*, Dec. 22, 1965; *Foreign Affairs*, Jan. 1966.

30. Humphrey to Johnson, Jan. 5, 1966, "Japan," National Security File, Name File, box 4, Johnson Library; "Record of Meeting between Humphrey and Sato," Jan. 3, 1966, National Security File, Country File, Japan, box 251, ibid; Havens, *Fire Across the Sea*, 107.

31. Havens, *Fire Across the Sea*, 110.

32. American Consul General in Hong Kong Edward Rice to Secretary of State, Feb. 3, 1966, NSF, China, box 239, "cables, vol.5," Johnson Library.

33. Havens, *Fire Across the Sea*, 71; Reischauer, *My Life*, 285.

34. "U.S. Policy in the Ryukyu Islands," memorandum of discussion among Ambassador Reischauer, State Department Director of East Asian Affairs Robert Feary, Secretary of the Army Stanley R. Resor, Deputy Undersecretary of the Army John M. Steadman, et al., July 16, 1965, in Department of State Records, Central Foreign Policy File, 1964–67, box 2383, RG 59, National Archives. Havens, *Fire Across the Sea*, 52; Welfield, *Empire in Eclipse*, 196–99; "Growing Severity of Japanese Press on U.S.–Related Issues," Nov. 9, 1967, National Security File, Country File, Japan, box 252, Johnson Library; United States Information Agency, "Some Recent Japanese Public Opinion Indications on Issues Affecting Japanese–American Relations," Nov. 9, 1967, ibid.

35. Havens, *Fire Across the Sea*, 85–88.

36. "The Future of Japan," Department of State, June 26, 1964, NLJ 91–12, Johnson Library; Havens, *Fire Across the Sea*, 87.

37. Daniel Ellsberg, "Nuclear Weapons in Japan," Oral History, National Security Archive, Washington, D.C.

38. Ellsberg Oral History, National Security Archive.

39. Reischauer, *My Life*, 299.

40. Ibid., 300–301.

41. Ibid., 303.

42. For MITI data, see "Vietnam: Japan's Major Role," *Far Eastern Economic Review*, March 12, 1973, 33–45; "Economic Benefits to Japan Traceable to the Vietnam Conflict," Nov. 9, 1967, National Security File, Country File, Japan, box 252, Johnson Library; "Vietnam Special Procurement and the Economy," *Japan Quarterly*, 14, no. 1, (Jun.–Mar. 1967), 13–16; Havens, *Fire Across the Sea*, 92–102.

43. "Vietnam Special Procurement and the Economy," *Japan Quarterly*; U.S. Treasury Report on "Economic Benefits to Japan Traceable to the Vietnam Conflict," Nov. 9, 1967, National Security File, Country File, Japan, box 252, Johnson Library; Havens, *Fire Across the Sea*, 91–102.

44. Havens, *Fire Across the Sea*, 101.

45. "Vietnam: Japan's Major Role," *Far Eastern Economic Review*; "Economic Benefits to Japan Traceable to the Vietnam Conflict," Nov. 9, 1967, National Security File, Country File, Japan, box 252, Johnson Library; "Vietnam Special Procurement and the Economy," *Japan Quarterly*; Havens, *Fire Across the Sea*, 92–102; Bunker quoted in Armin H. Meyer, *Assignment Tokyo: An Ambassador's Journal* (Indianapolis, Ind., 1974), 183.

46. Humphrey to Johnson, Jan. 5, 1966, "The Philippines," National Security File, Name File, box 4, Johnson Library; Kahin, *Intervention*, 334–36.

47. Kahin, *Intervention*, 334–36.

48. Ibid.

49. U. Alexis Johnson, *The Right Hand of Power* (Englewood Cliffs, N.J., 1984), 444–45.

50. Ibid.

51. Ibid.

52. Bundy to Lyndon Johnson, May 23, 1966, National Security File, Subject File, U.S. Trust Territories, box 51, Johnson Library.

53. Johnson, *Right Hand of Power*, 472; Joint Chiefs of Staff, Memorandum for the Secretary of Defense, undated, Fall 1967, National Security File, Country File, Japan, box 251, Johnson Library.

54. McNamara memorandum for the President, Aug. 30, 1967, Confidential File, CO 141, ST 51–3, box 10, Johnson Library; Rostow to Johnson, Sept. 11, 1967, box 76, President's Appointment File, ibid.

55. Memorandum for the Record of NSC Meeting on Reversion to Japan of the Ryukyus, Bonins, and other Western Pacific Islands, Aug. 31, 1967, National Security File, NSC Meetings File, box 2, Johnson Library; Treasury Secretary Henry Fowler, Memorandum for the President, "Talking Points for Use with Japanese Officials," Aug. 31, 1967, Confidential File, CO 140, C0 141 Japan, box 10, ibid.; Rusk to Johnson, "United States–Japan Cabinet-Level Talks," Sept. 4, 1967, ibid.; Joint State/Treasury/Defense Memorandum, "U.S. Financial and Military Expenditures Relationships with Japan," Aug. 22, 1967, NLF 93–1,40, ibid.

56. "Statement by Secretary Fowler for Meeting with Minister Mizuta," Sept. 14, 1967, National Security File, Country File, Japan, box 252, Johnson Library; Rusk to Johnson, Nov. 10, 1967, ibid., box 253; "Talking Points for Sato Visit," no date, ibid.; Johnson, *Right Hand of Power*, 476.

57. For a discussion of Japanese and American positions on Okinawa and related issues on the eve of Sato's visit, see "Japan, Sato Visit, Briefing Book, 11/67," National Security File, Country file, Japan, box 253, Johnson Library.

58. Memorandum of conversation of Nov. 14, 1967, McNamara, Sato, et al., Nov. 28, 1967, Mandatory Review Case #NLF 92–159, Johnson Library.

59. Sato File, "Japan, Sato Visit, Briefing Book, 11/67," National Security File, Country file, Japan, box 253, Johnson Library; Johnson, *Right Hand of Power*, 482.

60. Johnson, *Right Hand of Power*, 485–86.

61. Chester L. Cooper to Averell Harriman, Sept. 26, 1967, box 499, Averell Harriman Papers, Library of Congress.

62. Johnson, *Right Hand of Power*, 499–501.

63. Ibid.

64. Richard Sneider to William Bundy, Apr. 26, 1968, National Security File, Country File, Japan, box 252, Johnson Library; Bundy to Rusk, with copies to Clifford, Nitze, Rostow, Warnke, May 7, 1968, ibid.; David Osborn, U.S. Embassy in Tokyo to Department of State, June 5, 1968, ibid., box 251; for evidence that the president read the June 5 telegram, see Memorandum for Mr. Rostow by Alfred Jenkins, June 14, 1968, ibid., box 252.

65. Ibid.

66. Memorandum of conversation, Rusk and Ushiba, June 6, 1968, National Security File, Country File, Japan, box 251, Johnson Library.

67. Rostow memorandum for the President, June 12, 1968, National Security File, Country File, Japan, box 252, Johnson Library; memorandum for Rostow, "Amb. Johnson's call on the President," June 14, 1968, ibid.

68. Johnson, *Right Hand of Power*, 504–7.

NOTES FOR CHAPTER 12

1. *Asahi Shimbun*, Jan. 22, 1971.

2. *Time*, May 10, 1971; Connally quoted in Haldeman Daily Notes, Aug. 13, 1971, H. R. Haldeman papers, White House Special Files, Nixon Project, National Archives. Hereafter, "Haldeman notes." This valuable collection consists of the written notes kept by Haldeman of his conversations with Nixon and of talks between the president and visitors. They are distinct from his "diary," which he dictated at night; Nixon's boast about "sticking it to Japan" is cited in Joan Hoff, *Nixon Reconsidered* (New York, 1994), 140.

3. Johnson, *Right Hand of Power*, 520.

4. Nixon biographer Stephen Ambrose discovered that in Nixon's initial draft of this article, he urged Japan to expand its "non-nuclear" armed forces. When Dwight D. Eisenhower read the draft he remarked that Japan required its own nuclear capacity. Nixon removed the qualifier "non-nuclear" from the published version. See Stephen Ambrose, *Nixon: The Triumph of a Politician* (New York, 1989), 115.

5. Tad Szulc, *The Illusion of Power: Foreign Policy in the Nixon Years* (New York, 1978), 168.

6. Szulc, *Illusion of Power*, 169–69; Johnson, *Right Hand of Power*, 521.

7. Henry A. Kissinger, *The White House Years* (Boston, 1979), 321–25, 950; Henry A. Kissinger, *Years of Upheaval* (Boston, 1982), 735–46. In his memoir, Kissinger pled a lack of expertise on Japan—and then offers readers a lengthy if superficial description of Japanese political culture and history. Kissinger attributed most of the problems he encountered to the complexities of consensus decision-making in the Japanese government. This affected some issues, but had little to do with the "China shock" of July 1971 or the economic shock of August. The Nixon administration's efforts to negotiate textile quotas were mismanaged, quite apart from alleged cultural quirks of the Japanese.

8. Roger Morris, *Uncertain Greatness: Henry Kissinger and American Foreign Policy* (New York, 1977), 102–03; Paul A. Volcker and Toyoo Gyohten, *Changing Fortunes: The World's Money and the Threat to American Leadership* (New York, 1992), 64–65; I. M. Destler, Haruhiro Fukui, Hideo Sato, *The Textile Wrangle: Conflict in Japanese–American Relations, 1969–71* (Ithaca, N.Y., 1979), 79–80.

9. Kissinger, *White House Years*, 326–27; Morton Halperin to author, March 11, 1996. Under the secret protocol of the 1960 security treaty, U.S. ships and planes had the right to "transit" nuclear weapons through American bases in Japan. This "home level" of control would apply to Okinawa after reversion.

10. Seymour M. Hersh, *The Price of Power: Kissinger in the Nixon White House* (New York, 1983), 148, 381; Kissinger, *White House Years*, 327. Morton Halperin to author, March 11, 1996; in their memoirs, neither Nixon nor Kissinger mention any interest in helping Japan acquire nuclear weapons.

11. Kissinger, *White House Years*, 329; Hersh, *Price of Power*, 93–94; Johnson, *Right Hand of Power*, 540–41; NSDM 13 quoted in memorandum from Winthrop and Brown to U. A. Johnson, Oct. 28, 1969, FOIA; Morton Halperin to author, March 11, 1996.

12. A message from the Japanese diplomat was intercepted by American intelligence agencies. Nixon, Kissinger, and Alexander Haig condemned both Halperin and Hedrick Smith for undermining the national interest by giving away the U.S. "fallback position" before negotiations began. In fact, both Smith and Halperin hoped to assure success in the Okinawa negotiations that the administration had endangered by coyly refusing to discuss the one issue that Japan had to secure. Anyone familiar with the talks realized that the United States had no real option but to compromise on nuclear weapons storage. Nevertheless, Nixon used the alleged "leaks" to justify additional FBI wiretaps on journalists and members of his own administration. Kissinger, *White House Years*, 329; Hersh, *Price of Power*, 94, 101–2; Morton Halperin to author, March 11, 1996.

13. Armin H. Meyer, *Assignment Tokyo: An Ambassador's Journal* (Indianapolis, Ind., 1974), 36–37; Johnson, *Right Hand of Power*, 542–44.

14. Johnson, *Right Hand of Power*, 544–46; Meyer, *Assignment Tokyo*, 37–43.

15. Kissinger, *White House Years*, 223–25; Szulc, *Illusion of Power*, 125–27; memorandum from Kissinger for Nixon, "The President's Private Meeting With Prime Minister Edward Heath," Dec. 20, 1971, Nixon Project, FOIA.

16. Kissinger, *White House Years*, 329–30.

17. Destler, et al., *Textile Wrangle*, 66–68.

18. Ibid.

19. Ibid.

20. Ibid.

21. Ibid.

22. Kissinger, *White House Years*, 330–31.

23. Kissinger, *White House Years*, 332–33; Destler, et al., *Textile Wrangle*, 112.

24. Agreements reached prior to the Nixon–Sato summit on the issues of nuclear storage, Japan's support for the defense of South Korea and Taiwan, and use of Okinawa bases for Vietnam operations are discussed in the following documents: "Okinawa—Preparations for Sato Visit," Withrop and Brown to Undersecretary for Political Affairs, Oct. 28, 1969, Department of State, FOIA; William Rogers to Nixon, "Sato Visit—with Talking Points," ca. Nov. 1969, Department of State, FOIA; memorandum for President from Secretary of State Rogers, ca. Nov. 1969, "Meeting with Congressional Leaders on Okinawa," Department of State, FOIA; Meyer to Secretary of State, Nov. 10, 1969, Department of State, FOIA; Johnson to Rogers, Nov. 13, 1969, "Okinawa Talking Points," Department of State, FOIA; Kissinger, *White House Years*, 335.

25. Hersh, *Price of Power*, 381; Welfield, *Empire in Eclipse*, 142. In his memoirs and public statements in Japan, Wakaizumi confirms his role as Sato's go-between with Kissinger and the prime minister's pledge on nuclear weapons. Japan signed the Non-Proliferation Treaty early in 1970, but delayed ratification until 1976. This reflected concern in Tokyo that the treaty might inhibit efforts to develop a "breeder" nuclear reactor. This technology would make Japan less dependent on imported uranium, but would produce weapons-grade reactor fuel that might cause a problem under the treaty. After technical issues were resolved, the Diet ratified the pact.

26. Morris, *Uncertain Greatness*, 104–5; Szulc, *Illusion of Power*, 170–71; Kissinger, *White House Years*, 336–37; Johnson, *Right Hand of Power*, 448–50; Destler, et al., *Textile Wrangle*, 134–35.

27. Kissinger, *White House Years*, 334–36; Meyer, *Assignment Tokyo*, 44; Johnson, *Right Hand of Power*, 546; Destler, et al., *Textile Wrangle*, 139; Welfield, *Empire In Eclipse*, 246–50. Welfield notes that Japanese government spokesmen modified Sato's pledge of prior approval for using the bases to defend Korea and Taiwan. According to statements made by Foreign Minister Aiichi, requests to use the bases would be studied sympathetically, but approval was not automatic. For China's criticism, see *Renmin Ribao* (People's Daily), Nov. 28, 1969, and *Peking Review*, Nov. 28, 1969, 28–30.

28. Kissinger, *White House Years*, 336; entry of Nov. 25, 1969, Diary of H. R. Haldeman (CD-ROM version), National Archives; Patrick Buchanan to Nixon, "Notes from Legislative Leadership Meeting," Feb. 17, 1970, Nixon Presidential Project, National Archives, FOIA.

29. Memorandum from C. Fred Bergsten to Kissinger, March 30, 1970, White House Special Files, Peter Flanigan Files, box 11, Textiles, Nixon Project, National Archives.

30. Kissinger to Nixon, "Your Meeting with Don Kendall," Apr. 13, 1970, WHSF, Flanigan Files, box 11, Textiles, Nixon Project; memorandum of conversation, Prime Minister Sato and Treasury Secretary Kennedy, Apr. 13, 1970, Department of State, FOIA; Destler, et al., *Textile Wrangle*, 160–76.

31. Entry of Apr. 27, 1970, Diary of H. R. Haldeman (CD-ROM version), National Archives.

32. Stans to Nixon, "Long Term Implications for the United States of Japan's Economic Growth and Potential and Policy Consequences," Apr. 1970, with attachments by Kissinger, Flanigan, Bergsten, et al. Filed under cover memorandum by Flanigan for Nixon, June 19, 1970, WHSF, Flanigan file, box 11, Nixon Project; Destler, et al., *Textile Wrangle*, 170–76.

33. Destler, et al., *Textile Wrangle*, 185–200.

34. Ibid., 200–205

35. Ibid., 206.

36. Ibid., 209–13

37. Ehrlichman to Kissinger or Gen. Haig, Sept. 21, 1970, White House Special Files, Peter Flanigan Files, box 11, Nixon Project; Shultz memorandum for the files, Sept. 21, 1970, ibid; Kissinger to Secretary of State, Commerce, et al., Sept. 25, 1970, ibid; "The Dispensable Ally," *Far Eastern Economic Review*, Aug. 28, 1971, 21–22.

38. Kissinger, *White House Years*, 338–39; Destler, et al., *Textile Wrangle*, 208–18.

39. U. A. Johnson for Nixon, "Meeting with Prime Minister Sato," Oct. 21, 1970, Flanigan Files, box 11, Nixon Project; Kissinger for Nixon, "Meeting with Prime Minister Sato," Oct. 23, 1970, ibid.; Kissinger, *White House Years*, 339; Destler, et al., *Textile Wrangle*, 220–22.

40. Destler, et al., *Textile Wrangle*, 223–30.

41. Ibid., 230–50.

42. "Memorandum for the Files," Jan. 26, 1971, Peter Flanigan, WHSF, Flanigan papers, box 11, "Textiles," Nixon Project; Flanigan for Nixon, March 9, 1971, "Meeting With Ad Hoc Textile Group, ibid; Flanigan for Nixon, Mar. 11, 1971, ibid.; Memorandum for the Files, Mar. 12, 1971, ibid; Meyer to Secretary of State, Mar. 12, 1971, Cable #2238, Department of State, FOIA; Destler, et al., *Textile Wrangle*, 251–74. During May and June, Kennedy negotiated export restraint agreements with Taiwan, Hong Kong, and South Korea. Implementation depended on Japanese cooperation.

43. Bergsten to Kissinger, Mar. 18, 1971, CO 75, Japan, WHSF, Nixon Project; Flanigan to Kissinger, Mar. 31, 1971, CO 75 Japan, ibid; Destler, et al., *Textile Wrangle*, 283–84.

44. Nixon to Kissinger, Sept. 29, 1969, WHSF, CF, box 6, CO 34, China, 1969–70, Nixon Project. The evolution of the Nixon-Kissinger China policy is discussed in several sources. Among the best are Robert D. Schulzinger, *Henry Kissinger: Doctor of Diplomacy* (New York, 1989), 75–101; Walter Isaacson, *Kissinger: A Biography* (New York, 1992), 333–54; Raymond L. Garthoff, *Detente and Confrontation: American–Soviet Relations from Nixon to Reagan* (Washington, D.C., 1985), 199–247; Richard Nixon, *RN: The Memoirs of Richard Nixon* (New York, 1978); Robert S. Ross, *Negotiating Cooperation: The United States and China, 1969–89* (Stanford, Ca., 1995); Hersh, *Price of Power*, 374–82; Welfield, *Empire in Eclipse*, 275–324; Kissinger, *White House Years*, 163–94, 684–787, 1049–96. Nixon's account of the opening to China adds little to the public record. Kissinger's lengthy discussion of his China diplomacy is rich in dramatic tone but thin on details. Both men went to great lengths to prevent others from examining the original diplomatic record.

45. Kissinger, *White House Years*, 687.

46. Nixon comments to cabinet members, June 13, 1971, Haldeman notes, WHSF, Haldeman papers, Nixon Project; Kissinger, *White House Years*, 687.

47. Kissinger, *White House Years*, 685, 745–50; Isaacson, *Kissinger*, 435; Hersh, *Price of Power*, 376.

48. Haldeman notes, July 13, 14, 15, 19, 1971, WHSF, box 44, Nixon Project; Haldeman Diary, CD ROM version, entries of July 13–19; Kissinger, *White House Years*, 762.

49. Kusuda recounted these events in a presentation at conference on March 11, 1996, at the Wilson Center; Laird's assurance to Sato is contained in Meyer to Secretary of State, "Secretary of Defense Laird Visit to Japan, 4–11 July, cable #6522, July 6, 1971, Department of State, FOIA; Johnson, *Right Hand of Power*, 553–55; Meyer, *Assignment Tokyo*, 111–12; Quansheng Zhao, *Japanese Policymaking: The Politics Behind Politics, Informal Mechanisms and the Making of China Policy* (Westport, Conn., 1993), 70; Henry Brandon, *The Retreat of American Power* (New York, 1973), 169.

50. Kusuda's remarks of March 11, 1996, Wilson Center; Sato's reply to Nixon's belated message is contained in Meyer to Secretary of State, cable #6979, July 17, 1971, Department of State, FOIA; Haldeman notes, July 23, 1971, WHSF, box 44, Nixon Project; Whitlam's account quoted in Welfield, *Empire in Eclipse*, 295.

51. *Peking Review*, Nov. 28 and Dec. 15, 1969; Apr. 10, 1970; *Renmin Ribao*, Nov. 28, 1969; Welfield, *Empire in Eclipse*, 289–91.

52. Welfield, *Empire in Eclipse*, 294.

53. Isaacson, *Kissinger*, 348; on Radford's activities, see Stanley I. Kutler, *The Wars of Watergate* (New York, 1990), 116–19; Ambrose, *Nixon*, II, 486–90. The Joint Chiefs and Kissinger deeply mistrusted each other. JCS chairman Admiral Thomas Moorer encouraged Yeoman Charles Radford, a naval aide to Kissinger, to copy material relating to subjects such as SALT, detente, and the secret China negotiations.

54. Meyer to Secretary of State, "Secretary of Defense Laird Meeting With Sato," Cable #6522, July 6, 1971, Department of State, FOIA; Meyer to Secretary of State, "Secretary of Defense Laird Visit to Japan," Cable #6718, July 11, 1971, ibid; *Japan Times*, July 10, 1971; "Old Pillars Fallen," *Far Eastern Economic Review*, Aug. 7, 1971, 49–51; Kissinger, *White House Years*, 740; Welfield, *Empire in Eclipse*, 295.

55. Hersh, *Price of Power*, 380–81. The Watergate task force's interest in Radford centered on the White House response to his pilfering, not the foreign policy implications. The prose-

cutor who heard Nixon's testimony told Hersh he recalled the exchange because of Nixon's intense response. Radford's only direct involvement with China occurred during Kissinger's July 1971 trip, but he probably had access to documents relating to earlier and later contacts. Radford's activities were exposed at the end of 1971. In a complex power play between Nixon, Kissinger, and the Joint Chiefs of Staff, Radford was reassigned rather than prosecuted.

56. Terrill quoted in Hersh, *Price of Power*, 382; Zhou's statements to Reston quoted in "The Dispensable Ally," *Far Eastern Economic Review*, Aug. 28, 1971, 21–22.

57. Jonathan Unger, "Japan: The Economic Threat," *Far Eastern Economic Review*, Oct. 16, 1971, 49–52.

58. *Japan Times*, Aug. 15, 1971.

59. Robert C. Angel, *Explaining Economic Policy Failure: Japan in the 1969–71 International Monetary Crisis* (New York, 1991), 87–107.

60. *Time*, May 10, 1971; *Newsweek*, May 3, 1971; Welfield, *Empire in Eclipse*, 286–87; Angel, *Explaining Economic Policy Failure*, 107; *New York Times*, July 30, 1971.

61. Lyrics cited in Welfield, *Empire in Eclipse*, 287–88.

62. Dent to Peterson, July 13, 1971, WHSF, Peterson papers, box 1, Nixon Project; Haldeman notes, July 12, 1971, WHSF, Nixon Project; memorandum for president from Kennedy, July 16, 1971, Nixon Project, FOIA; Nixon to Sato, July 16, 1971, Nixon Project, FOIA; Peterson to President and Cabinet, Aug. 6, 1971, WHSF, Flanigan papers, box 11, Nixon Project; Flanigan to Peterson, Aug. 7, 1971, WHSF, ibid.

63. Angel, *Explaining Economic Policy Failure*, 117.

64. Kissinger, *White House Years*, 951; Ambrose, *Nixon*, II, 457; Hersh, *Price of Power*, 462.

65. Haldeman notes, Aug. 12, 13, 14, 1971, WHSF, Nixon Project; Haldeman Diary entries of August 12, 13, 14, 15, 16, CD ROM version; William Safire, Notes on Camp David Weekend, box k 31, Name-Correspondence Files, Arthur Burns Papers, Gerald Ford Presidential Library; Kissinger, *White House Years*, 954–55; Szulc, *Illusion of Power*, 454–56; Ambrose, *Nixon*, II, 458–59.

66. Haldeman notes, Aug. 14, 1971, WHSF, Nixon Project; Haldeman Diary entry of Aug. 14, 1971, CD ROM version.

67. Haldeman Diary entry of Aug. 16, 1971, CD ROM version; Nixon later spoke of his desire to "stick it to the Japanese." See Hoff, *Nixon Reconsidered*, 140.

68. Haldeman notes, Aug. 14, 1971, WHSF, Nixon Project; Haldeman Diary entry, Aug. 14, 1971, CD ROM version; Destler, et al., *Textile Wrangle*, 292–93.

69. Meyer, *Assignment Tokyo*, 169–70; Nixon remarks to Veterans of Foreign Wars, Aug. 19, 1971, *Weekly Compilation of Presidential Documents* (Washington, D.C., 1971), 1198–1204.

70. Kissinger, *White House Years*, 957–58; Paul A. Volcker and Toyoo Gyohten, *Changing Fortunes: The World's Money and the Threat to American Leadership* (New York, 1992), 81–82, 93–96; Angel, *Explaining Economic Policy Failure*, 120–34.

71. Angel, *Explaining Economic Policy Failure*, 165–67; Destler, et al., *Textile Wrangle*, 296–97.

72. Destler, et al., *Textile Wrangle*, 294–97.

73. Memoranda for the President's File, "RE: Nixon-Fukuda discussions on China, internal politics, and textiles," Sept. 10, 1971, Nixon Project, FOIA; Destler, et. al., *Textile Wrangle*, 298–99.

74. Destler, et al., *Textile Wrangle*, 300–301.

75. Haldeman notes, Oct. 1, 2, 1971, WHSF, Nixon Project.

76. Destler, et al., *Textile Wrangle*, 302–11.

77. Ibid., 312, 352–57.

78. Exchange of toasts between the President and Prime Minister of Japan, July 31, 1973, cited in *Weekly Compilation of Presidential Documents, 1973* (Washington, D.C., 1973), 942–43.

79. Patrick J. Buchanan, "Memorandum for the President's File—Leadership Meeting held Nov. 16, 1971," Nixon Project, FOIA.

80. Volcker and Gyohten, *Changing Fortunes*, 80–90, 95–100; Kissinger, *White House Years*, 957–62; Szulc, *Illusion of Power*, 461–64; Angel, *Explaining Economic Policy Failure*, 220–41, 259–60.

81. Volcker and Gyohten, *Changing Fortunes*, 90.

82. Ibid., 96; Memorandum from Kissinger for Nixon, "The President's Private Meeting with British Prime Minister Edward Heath," Dec. 20, 1971, Nixon Project, FOIA. Nixon spoke in similar terms about Germany and Japan. In the changing framework of the cold war, both needed a "home." The "biggest reason for staying on in Vietnam is Japan. . . . We have to reassure the Asians that the Nixon Doctrine is not a way for us to get out of Asia but a way for us to stay in."

83. Hori's December 1971 article is cited in Welfield, *Empire In Eclipse*, 297.

84. On Sato's abortive effort to strike a deal with China, see Welfield, *Empire in Eclipse*, 304–5; and, Kusano Atsushi, *Two Nixon Shocks and Japan–U.S. Relations* (Princeton, N.J., 1987), 30–31.

85. Meyer, *Assignment Tokyo*, 161–62; Anderson column in *Yomiuri Shimbun*, Jan. 7, 1972.

86. Memoranda for the President's File from James J. Wickel, "Meetings with Eisaku Sato, Jan. 6–7, 1972," Jan. 7, 1972, Nixon Project, FOIA; Welfield, *Empire in Eclipse*, 308; Kusano, *Two Nixon Shocks*, 34–35, 37–38. In news coverage and an editorial on the San Clemente meeting probably inspired by a presidential leak, the *New York Times* (Jan. 6, 11, 1972) criticized Sato for giving into "Peking's pressure for change" by not standing firm enough behind Taiwan and South Korea. The *Times* also chastised Tokyo for encouraging a "kind of yen block in Asia that faintly recalls the World War II Greater East Asia Co-Prosperity Sphere" and for contemplating a self-reliant "nuclear defense." This was especially odd given Nixon's hectoring of Sato on military issues.

87. Nixon, *RN: Memoirs*, 560–67; Kissinger, *White House Years*, 1061–63.

88. Kissinger, *White House Years*, 1062–63; for a reference to Nixon's pledge, see Zbigniew Brzezinski, *Power and Principle: Memoirs of the National Security Adviser, 1977–81* (New York, 1983), 198.

89. Kissinger, *White House Years*, 1053, 1072; Nixon, *RN*, 560–67; Szulc, *Illusion of Power*, 521–24.

90. For the text of the Shanghai Communiqué and a discussion of its preparation, see Kissinger, *White House Years*, 1490–92.

91. Information on the meetings with Green and Kissinger was published in the Japanese press and is cited in Welfield, *Empire in Eclipse*, 310.

NOTES FOR EPILOGUE

1. Welfield, *Empire in Eclipse*, 315–17.

2. Memorandum of conversation, Tanaka, Nixon, et al., Aug. 31, 1972. Released by U.S. Department of State, FOIA. This bland synopsis of the Nixon–Tanaka talks omits any mention of the Lockheed deal.

3. David E. Kaplan and Alec Dubro, *Yakuza: The Explosive Account of Japan's Criminal Underworld* (Reading, Mass., 1986), 101–15; Chalmers Johnson, *Japan: Who Governs?* (New York, 1995), 183–203. Some of the Lockheed money may have been connected to the CIA's long-standing program of channeling funds to favored LDP leaders. Several Japanese and American participants had links to both Lockheed and the CIA. On the other hand, payments by Japanese companies seeking business to politicians was fairly routine.

4. Welfield, *Empire in Eclipse*, 319.

5. Memorandum of Foreign Minister Ohira's call on the President, Oct. 18, 1972, National Security Files, Nixon Project, FOIA. Nixon took credit for China's change of heart, telling Ohira that he had hammered home the point during his February 1972 visit to China that the "security treaty serves the interests of the PRC as well as the United States in maintaining peace in the Pacific." He did not report his other point—that the treaty helped contain Japan; Kissinger to Nixon, Meeting with Chairman Mao, Feb. 24, 1973, copy in National Security Archive and reports of Feb. 24 and 27, Presidents Personal File, box 6, Nixon Project; Kissinger, *White House Years*, 1061–62, 1072, 1089, 1490–92; Henry A. Kissinger, *Years of Upheaval* (Boston, 1982), 47–60.

6. Welfield, *Empire in Eclipse*, 336–37.

7. Ibid., 346–47.

8. Poll data cited in ibid., 299

9. Volcker and Gyohten, *Changing Fortunes*, 128–29.

10. Kissinger, *Years of Upheaval*, 708–09.

11. Ibid., 693.

12. Ibid., 741.

13. Kissinger, *Years of Upheaval*, 744–45; William Horsley and Roger Buckley, *Nippon: The New Superpower* (London, 1990), 109, 112–13.

14. Welfield, *Empire in Eclipse*, 344–45; Horsley and Buckley, *Nippon: New Superpower*, 109, 112–13.

15. Horsley and Buckley, *Nippon: New Superpower*, 112–13, 123; Kissinger, *Years of Upheaval*, 745.

16. Kissinger briefing of March 1974, quoted in Hersh, *Price of Power*, 382.

17. Gerald Ford, *A Time to Heal* (New York, 1979), 204–5.

18. U.S. Department of State, *American Foreign Policy: Basic Documents, 1977–80* (Washington, D.C., 1983), document 548; Brzezinski, *Power and Principle*, 469.

19. Theodore H. White, "The Danger from Japan," *New York Times Magazine*, July 28, 1985.

20. The Pontiac advertisement is quoted in Horsley and Buckley, *Nippon: New Superpower*, 240.

21. Gary Taubes, *Bad Science: The Short Life and Weird Times of Cold Fusion* (New York, 1993), 233–34, 259–60. For a sample of his views about Japan, see Ira C. Magaziner, *Japanese Industrial Policy* (Berkeley, Ca., 1980). Magaziner later played a major role drafting the Clinton administration's abortive health care plan.

22. Michael Crichton, *Rising Sun* (New York, 1992); Pat Choate, *Agents of Influence* (New York, 1990); George Friedman, *The Coming War with Japan* (New York, 1991); Clyde Prestowitz, *Changing Places: How America Allowed Japan to Take the Lead* (New York, 1988); Robert L. Kearns, *Zaibatsu America: How Japanese Firms are Colonizing Vital U.S. Industries* (New York, 1992); for more measured criticism of Japan, see James Fallows, *More Like Us: Putting America's Native Strengths and Traditional Values to Work to Overcome the Asian Challenge* (Boston, 1989); Martin and Susan Tolchin, *Buying Into America: How Foreign Money is Changing the Face of Our Nation* (New York, 1988).

23. *New York Times*, Jan. 2, 8, 9, and Feb. 4, 1992. For an overview of Bush's policy toward Japan, see the memoir by Ambassador Michael H. Armacost, *Friends or Rivals? The Insider's Account of U.S.–Japan Relations* (New York, 1996).

BIBLIOGRAPHY

The following primary and secondary materials were most useful in this study. For a detailed description of these and other sources, see the chapter notes.

GOVERNMENT DOCUMENTS

Allied Council for Japan, RG 43, National Archives
British Foreign Office Records, FO 371, Public Record Office
Committee on Foreign Economic Policy Records, Dwight D. Eisenhower Library
Department of the Army Records, RG 335, National Archives
Far Eastern Commission Records, RG 43, National Archives
Joint Chiefs of Staff Records, RG 218, National Archives
National Security Council File, Dwight D. Eisenhower Library
National Security Council File, Lyndon B. Johnson Library
National Security Council File, John F. Kennedy Library
Office of the Secretary of Defense Records, RG 330, National Archives
Secretary of the Army Records, RG 335, National Archives
State, War, Navy Coordinating Committee Records, RG 353, National Archives
Supreme Commander for the Allied Powers Records, RG 331, Washington National Records Center
United States Agency for International Development Records, RG 469, Washington National Records Center
United States Department of State Records, RG 59, National Archives
United States Department of State, *Foreign Relations of the United States*, annual published volumes for the period 1945–65
United States Senate, *Executive Sessions of the Senate Foreign Relations Committee (Historical Series)*
United States Department of the Treasury Records, Office of the Assistant Secretary for International Affairs
White House Special Files: Staff Member and Office Files, Nixon Presidential Materials Project, National Archives

MANUSCRIPT COLLECTIONS

Joseph and Stewart Alsop Papers, Library of Congress
Arthur Burns Papers, Gerald Ford Presidential Library
Joseph Dodge Papers, Detroit Public Library
John Foster Dulles Papers, Princeton University
Dwight D. Eisenhower Papers, Dwight D. Eisenhower Library
Gerald Ford Papers, Gerald Ford Presidential Library
James C. Forrestal Papers, Princeton University
James C. Hagerty Papers, Dwight D. Eisenhower Library
Roger Hillsman Papers, John F. Kennedy Library
H. R. Haldeman Daily Notes and Diary
Harold L. Ickes Papers, Library of Congress
Lyndon B. Johnson Papers, Lyndon B. Johnson Library
George F. Kennan Papers, Princeton University
John F. Kennedy Papers, John F. Kennedy Presidential Library
Wellington Koo Papers, Columbia University
Frank Kowalski Papers, Library of Congress
Douglas MacArthur Papers, MacArthur Memorial Archives
Richard M. Nixon Presidential Materials Project, National Archives
Clarence B. Randall Papers, Princeton University
H. Alexander Smith Papers, Princeton University
James Thomson Papers, John F. Kennedy Presidential Library
Harry S. Truman Papers, Harry S. Truman Presidential Library
Robert E. Wood Papers, Herbert C. Hoover Library

BOOKS, ARTICLES, DISSERTATIONS

Allison, John. *Ambassador from the Prairie, or Allison in Wonderland*. Boston, 1973.
Ambrose, Stephen E. *Nixon: The Triumph of a Politician*. N.Y., 1987.
Angel, Robert C. *Explaining Economic Policy Failure: Japan in the 1969-71 International Economic Crisis*. N.Y., 1991.
Asahi Shimbun Staff. *The Pacific Rivals: A Japanese View of the Japanese-American Relationship*. N.Y., 1972.
Atsushi, Kusano. *Two Nixon Shocks and U.S.–Japan Relations*. Princeton, N.J., 1987.
Ball, George. *The Past Has Another Pattern*. N.Y., 1982.
Borden, William. *The Pacific Alliance: United States Foreign Economic Policy and Japanese Trade Recovery, 1947–55*. Madison, Wisc., 1984.
Brzezinski, Zbigniew. *Power and Principle: Memoirs of the National Security Adviser, 1977–81*. N.Y., 1983.
Buckley, Roger. *U.S.–Japan Alliance Diplomacy 1945–90*. N.Y., 1992.
Burkman, Thomas W. *The Occupation of Japan: The International Context*. Norfolk, Va., 1984.
Cary, Otis, ed. *War Wasted Asia: Letters 1945–46*. Tokyo, 1975.
Chapman, William. *Inventing Japan: The Making of a Postwar Civilization*. N.Y., 1991.
Cohen, Theodore. *Remaking Japan: The American Occupation as New Deal*. ed. by Herbert Passin. N.Y., 1987.
Cohen, Warren, ed. *Pacific Passage: The Study of American–East Asian Relations on the Eve of the Twenty-First Century*. N.Y., 1996.
Cohen, Warren and Akira Iriye, eds. *The Great Powers in East Asia, 1953–60*. N.Y., 1990.
Cohen, Warren and Akira Iriye, eds. *The United States and Japan in the Postwar World*. Lexington, Ky., 1989.
Cook, Haruko Taya and Theodore F. Cook, *Japan at War: An Oral History*. N.Y., 1992.
Destler, I. M., Haruhiro Fukui and Hideo Sato. *The Textile Wrangle: Conflict in Japanese-American Relations, 1969–71*. Ithaca, N.Y., 1979.

Dingman, Roger. "The Dagger and the Gift: The Impact of the Korean War on Japan," *Journal of American-East Asian Relations* (Spring 1993, Vol. 2, no. 1), 29–58.

Dingman, Roger. "Alliance in Crisis: The Lucky Dragon Incident and Japanese-American Relations," in Warren Cohen and Akira Iriye, eds., *The Great Powers in East Asia*. N.Y., 1990.

Dower, John W. *Japan in War and Peace*. N.Y., 1993.

Dower, John W. *Empire and Aftermath: Yoshida Shigeru and the Japanese Experience, 1878–1954*. Cambridge, Mass., 1979.

Emmerson, John K. *The Japanese Thread: A Life in the U.S. Foreign Service*. N.Y., 1978.

Fallows, James. *More Like Us*. N.Y., 1989.

Ferrell, Robert H. *Off the Record: The Private Papers of Harry S. Truman*. N.Y., 1980.

Ferrell, Robert H., ed. *The Diary of James C. Hagerty*. Bloomington, Ind., 1983.

Finn, Richard. *Winners in Peace: MacArthur, Yoshida, and Postwar Japan*. Berkeley, Ca., 1992.

Foot, Rosemary. *The Practice of Power: U.S. Relations with China Since 1949*. Oxford, U.K., 1995.

Gordon, Andrew, ed., *Postwar Japan as History*. Berkeley, Ca., 1993.

Haldeman, H. R., *The Haldeman Diaries: Inside the Nixon White House*. N.Y., 1994.

Halliday, John. *A Political History of Japanese Capitalism*. N.Y., 1967

Hamilton, Nigel. *JFK: Reckless Youth*. N.Y., 1992.

Havens, Thomas. *Fire Across the Sea: The Vietnam War and Japan, 1965–75*. Princeton, N.J., 1987.

Hersh, Seymour M. *The Price of Power: Kissinger in the Nixon White House*. N.Y., 1983.

Hoff, Joan. *Nixon Reconsidered*. N.Y., 1994.

Horsley, William and Roger Buckley. *Nippon: The New Superpower*. London, 1990.

Hunsberger, Warren S. *Japan and the United States in World Trade*. N.Y., 1964.

Isaacson, Walter. *Kissinger: A Biography*. N.Y., 1992.

Johnson, U. Alexis. *The Right Hand of Power*. Englewood Cliffs, N.J., 1984.

Johnson, Chalmers. *MITI and the Japanese Miracle: The Growth of Industrial Policy, 1925–75*. Stanford, Ca., 1982.

Johnson, Chalmers. *Japan: Who Governs?* N.Y., 1995.

Johnson, Sheila K. *The Japanese Through American Eyes*. Stanford, Ca., 1988.

Kaplan, David E. and Alec Dubro. *Yakuza: The Explosive Account of Japan's Criminal Underworld*. Reading, Mass., 1986.

Kataoka, Tetsuya. *The Price of a Constitution: The Origins of Japan's Postwar Politics*. N.Y., 1991.

Kennan, George F. *Memoirs, 1925–50*. Boston, 1967.

Kissinger, Henry A. *Years of Upheaval*. Boston, 1982.

Kissinger, Henry A. *The White House Years*. Boston, 1979.

Kurzman, Dan. *Kishi and Japan: The Search for the Sun*. N.Y., 1960.

Kutler, Stanley I. *The Wars of Watergate*. N.Y., 1990.

Langdon, F.C. *Japan's Foreign Policy*. Vancouver, 1973.

Leffler, Melvyn P. *A Preponderance of Power: National Security, the Truman Administration, and the Cold War*. Stanford, Ca., 1992.

Maga, Timothy. *John F. Kennedy and the New Pacific Community, 1961–63*. N.Y., 1990.

Masumi, Junnosuke (Trans. by Lonny E. Carlile). *Contemporary Politics in Japan*. Berkeley, Ca., 1995.

McClenahan, William M. "Orderly Restraint: American Government, Business and the Role of Voluntary Export Restraints in United States–Japan Trade, 1934–72." Ph.D. dissertation, Georgetown University, 1993.

Meyer, Armin H. *Assignment Tokyo: An Ambassador's Journal*. Indianapolis, Ind., 1974.

Morris, Roger. *Uncertain Greatness: Henry Kissinger and American Foreign Policy*. N.Y., 1977.

Murphy, Robert. *Diplomat Among Warriors*. N.Y., 1964.

Nimmo, William F., ed. *The Occupation of Japan: The Impact of the Korean War*. Norfolk, Va., 1990.

Nixon, Richard. *RN: The Memoirs of Richard Nixon*. N.Y., 1978.

Packard, George R. III. *Protest in Tokyo: The Security Treaty Crisis of 1960*. Princeton, N.J., 1966.

Perry, John C. *Beneath the Eagle's Wing*. Boston, 1981.

Prestowitz, Clyde. *Trading Places: How America Allowed Japan to Take the Lead*. N.Y., 1988.

Pruessen, Ronald. *John Foster Dulles: The Road to Power*. N.Y., 1982.

Pyle, Kenneth B. *The Japanese Question: Power and Purpose in a New Era*. Washington, 1994.

Reischauer, Edwin O. *My Life Between Japan and America*. N.Y., 1986.

Ross, Robert S. *Negotiating Cooperation: The United States and China, 1969–89*. Stanford, Ca., 1995.

Sanantakes, Nicholas. "Keystone: The American Occupation of Okinawa and U.S.–Japan Relations, 1945–1972." Ph.D. Dissertation, University of Southern California, 1996.

Schaller, Michael. *The American Occupation of Japan: The Origins of the Cold War in Asia*. N.Y., 1985.

Schaller, Michael. *Douglas MacArthur: The Far Eastern General*. N.Y., 1989.

Schonberger, Howard. *Aftermath of War: Americans and the Re-Making of Japan, 1945–52*. Kent, Oh., 1989.

Schulzinger, Robert D. *Henry Kissinger: Doctor of Diplomacy*. N.Y., 1989.

Sebald, William J. *With MacArthur in Japan*. N.Y., 1965.

Shimizu, Sayuri. "Perennial Anxiety: Japan–U.S. Controversy over Recognition of the PRC, 1952–58," *Journal of American–East Asian Relations* (Fall 1995, vol. 4, no.3), 223–48.

Shimizu, Sayuri. "Creating a People of Plenty: The United States and Japan's Economic Alternatives, 1953–58." Ph.D. Dissertation, Cornell University, 1991.

Soeya, Yoshihide, "Japan's Postwar Economic Diplomacy with China: Three Decades of Non-Governmental Experience." Ph.D. Dissertation, University of Michigan, 1987.

Szulc, Tad. *The Illusion of Power: Foreign Policy in the Nixon Years*. N.Y., 1978.

Thayer, Nathaniel. *How the Conservatives Rule Japan*. Princeton, N.J., 1969.

Tucker, Nancy. *Patterns in the Dust: Chinese–American Relations and the Recognition Controversy, 1949–50*. N.Y., 1983.

van Wolferen, Karel. *The Enigma of Japanese Power*. N.Y., 1989.

Volcker, Paul A. and Toyoo Gyohten. *Changing Fortunes: The World's Money and the Threat to American Leadership*. N.Y., 1992.

Weinstein, Martin E. *Japan's Postwar Defense Policy, 1947–68*. N.Y., 1971.

Welfield, John. *An Empire in Eclipse: Japan in the Postwar American Alliance System*. Atlantic Highlands, N.J., 1988.

Yanaga, Chitoshi. *Big Business in Japanese Politics*. New Haven, 1968.

Yoshitsu, Michael. *Japan and the San Francisco Peace Settlement*. N.Y., 1983.